T0235087

# Lecture Notes in Computer Science 9856

Commenced Publication in 1973
Founding and Former Series Editors:
Gerhard Goos, Juris Hartmanis, and Jan van Leeuwen

## Editorial Board

David Hutchison
  *Lancaster University, Lancaster, UK*
Takeo Kanade
  *Carnegie Mellon University, Pittsburgh, PA, USA*
Josef Kittler
  *University of Surrey, Guildford, UK*
Jon M. Kleinberg
  *Cornell University, Ithaca, NY, USA*
Friedemann Mattern
  *ETH Zurich, Zürich, Switzerland*
John C. Mitchell
  *Stanford University, Stanford, CA, USA*
Moni Naor
  *Weizmann Institute of Science, Rehovot, Israel*
C. Pandu Rangan
  *Indian Institute of Technology, Madras, India*
Bernhard Steffen
  *TU Dortmund University, Dortmund, Germany*
Demetri Terzopoulos
  *University of California, Los Angeles, CA, USA*
Doug Tygar
  *University of California, Berkeley, CA, USA*
Gerhard Weikum
  *Max Planck Institute for Informatics, Saarbrücken, Germany*

More information about this series at http://www.springer.com/series/7408

Cristian Bogdan · Jan Gulliksen
Stefan Sauer · Peter Forbrig
Marco Winckler · Chris Johnson
Philippe Palanque · Regina Bernhaupt
Filip Kis (Eds.)

# Human-Centered and Error-Resilient Systems Development

IFIP WG 13.2/13.5 Joint Working Conference
6th International Conference on Human-Centered Software Engineering, HCSE 2016
and 8th International Conference on Human Error, Safety,
and System Development, HESSD 2016
Stockholm, Sweden, August 29–31, 2016
Proceedings

Springer

*Editors*

Cristian Bogdan
KTH Royal Institute of Technology
Stockholm
Sweden

Jan Gulliksen
KTH Royal Institute of Technology
Stockholm
Sweden

Stefan Sauer
Universität Paderborn
Paderborn
Germany

Peter Forbrig
Universität Rostock
Rostock
Germany

Marco Winckler
University Paul Sabatier
Toulouse
France

Chris Johnson
University of Glasgow
Glasgow
UK

Philippe Palanque
University Paul Sabatier
Toulouse
France

Regina Bernhaupt
Ruwido Austria GmbH
Neumarkt
Austria

Filip Kis
KTH Royal Institute of Technology
Stockholm
Sweden

ISSN 0302-9743          ISSN 1611-3349   (electronic)
Lecture Notes in Computer Science
ISBN 978-3-319-44901-2          ISBN 978-3-319-44902-9   (eBook)
DOI 10.1007/978-3-319-44902-9

Library of Congress Control Number: 2016948596

LNCS Sublibrary: SL2 – Programming and Software Engineering

© IFIP International Federation for Information Processing 2016
This work is subject to copyright. All rights are reserved by the Publisher, whether the whole or part of the material is concerned, specifically the rights of translation, reprinting, reuse of illustrations, recitation, broadcasting, reproduction on microfilms or in any other physical way, and transmission or information storage and retrieval, electronic adaptation, computer software, or by similar or dissimilar methodology now known or hereafter developed.
The use of general descriptive names, registered names, trademarks, service marks, etc. in this publication does not imply, even in the absence of a specific statement, that such names are exempt from the relevant protective laws and regulations and therefore free for general use.
The publisher, the authors and the editors are safe to assume that the advice and information in this book are believed to be true and accurate at the date of publication. Neither the publisher nor the authors or the editors give a warranty, express or implied, with respect to the material contained herein or for any errors or omissions that may have been made.

Printed on acid-free paper

This Springer imprint is published by Springer Nature
The registered company is Springer International Publishing AG Switzerland

# Preface

With this IFIP working conference, we premiered joining the International Conference on Human-Centered Software Engineering (HCSE) and the International Conference on Human Error, Safety, and System Development (HESSD). Together they became HCSE+HESSD 2016.

In the tradition of both conference series, HCSE+HESSD 2016 was a single track working conference which aimed at bringing together researchers and practitioners interested in different areas of human-centered software engineering and in the development of systems, in particular safety-critical systems, that are resilient to human error. HCSE's focus is on strengthening the scientific foundations of user interface design, examining the relationship between software engineering and human-computer interaction, and on establishing user-centered design as an essential part of software engineering processes. HESSD emphasizes the design, management, and control of safety-critical systems, the role of human error both in the development and in the operation of complex processes, and leading-edge techniques for mitigating the impact of human error on safety-critical systems, especially techniques that can be easily integrated into existing systems engineering practices.

HCSE 2016 was the sixth in a series of conferences promoted by the International Federation for Information Processing (IFIP) Working Group WG 13.2 on Methodologies for User-Centered Systems Design. Previous events were held in Salamanca, Spain (2007); Pisa, Italy (2008); Reykjavik, Iceland (2010); Toulouse, France (2012); and Paderborn, Germany (2014). While HCSE had initially been organized in conjunction with other conferences, it has grown over the years and was held as a biennial standalone conference in 2012 and 2014. HESSD 2016 was the eighth event in a series of conferences promoted by the IFIP Working Group WG 13.5 on Resilience, Reliability, Safety, and Human Error in System Development. This conference series has been running for more than a decade. Since then its scope has grown with new concerns – especially in autonomous systems and cyber security. Other problems – in task analysis and situation awareness – continue to provide motivation for research today just as they did back in 2004. The generation of new challenges illustrates the vitality of the work being done in this area, the sustained focus on core problems illustrates the generic importance of this area of research. In 2016 we joined HCSE and HESSD together since there is a substantial overlap of topics, interests, and participants.

HCSE+HESSD 2016 took place in Stockholm, Sweden, on August 29–31, 2016. It was hosted and locally organized by the Media Technology and Interaction Design Group of the KTH Royal Institute of Technology, Stockholm. The conference venue was KTH's OpenLab center.

HCSE+HESSD 2016 welcomed eleven full research papers, describing substantial novel contributions and advanced results, and ten short papers, presenting late breaking results, practice and experience reports, and practical evaluations. The program was complemented by tool demonstrations and research poster presentations. Four of them had their own paper contributions. All these papers are featured in this collection. We received 32 complete submissions for peer review. All qualified submissions were independently reviewed in a joint single-blind process by, in general, three reviewers, who were selected members of the HCSE+HESSD 2016 Program Committee. In addition, the papers and reviews were extensively discussed by the Program, Technical Paper, and Demo and Poster Chairs to make the decisions. The Program Committee made use of the possibility to recommend accepting submissions in other categories than they were originally submitted for in some cases. The final decision on acceptance was based on an additional meta-review after the authors had improved their contributions according to the first-round review results. Our sincere gratitude goes to the members of our Program Committee, who devoted countless hours to providing valuable feedback to authors and ensuring the high quality of the shared HCSE +HESSD 2016 technical program.

We thank Danica Kragic and Ivar Jacobson, our keynote speakers, who accepted to give inspiring and insightful speeches at HCSE+HESSD 2016. Abstracts of their talks are also presented in this proceedings volume. In addition, we express special appreciation to the local organizer team in Stockholm. We are indebted to our sponsors for their generous support in helping to make our conference special and successful. Finally our thanks go to all the authors who actually did the research work and especially to the presenters who sparked inspiring discussions with all the participants at HCSE+HESSD 2016 in Stockholm.

July 2016

Cristian Bogdan
Jan Gulliksen
Stefan Sauer
Peter Forbrig
Chris Johnson
Philippe Palanque
Marco Winckler
Regina Bernhaupt
Filip Kis

# HCSE+HESSD 2016 Technical and Organizing Committee

## General Conference Chairs

Cristian Bogdan      KTH Royal Institute of Technology, Sweden
Jan Gulliksen      KTH Royal Institute of Technology, Sweden

## Technical Program Chair

Stefan Sauer      SICP, Paderborn University, Germany

## HCSE Technical Paper Chairs

Peter Forbrig      University of Rostock, Germany
Marco Winckler      ICS-IRIT, University Paul Sabatier, France

## HESSD Technical Paper Chairs

Chris Johnson      University of Glasgow, UK
Philippe Palanque      ICS-IRIT, University Paul Sabatier, France

## Demo and Poster Chairs

Regina Bernhaupt      ruwido, Austria
Filip Kis      KTH Royal Institute of Technology, Sweden

## Proceedings Chair

Stefan Sauer      SICP, Paderborn University, Germany

## Publicity Chair

Filip Kis      KTH Royal Institute of Technology, Sweden

## Program Committee

Carmelo Ardito      University of Bari Aldo Moro, Italy
Regina Bernhaupt      ruwido, Austria
Cristian Bogdan      KTH Royal Institute of Technology, Sweden
Birgit Bomsdorf      Fulda University of Applied Science, Germany

| Anders Bruun | Aalborg University, Denmark |
| Luca Chittaro | University of Udine, Italy |
| Bertrand David | École Centrale de Lyon, France |
| Jonathan Day | City University London, UK |
| Simone D.J. Barbosa | Pontifical Catholic University (PUC) of Rio de Janeiro, Brazil |
| Anke Dittmar | University of Rostock, Germany |
| Camille Fayollas | ICS-IRIT, University Paul Sabatier, France |
| Xavier Ferré | Universidad Politecnica de Madrid, Spain |
| Holger Fischer | SICP, Paderborn University, Germany |
| Peter Forbrig | University of Rostock, Germany |
| Jan Gulliksen | KTH Royal Institute of Technology, Sweden |
| Chris Johnson | University of Glasgow, UK |
| Anirudha Joshi | Indian Institute of Technology, India |
| Hermann Kaindl | Vienna University of Technology, Austria |
| Filip Kis | KTH Royal Institute of Technology, Sweden |
| Kati Kuusinen | University of Central Lancashire, UK |
| Rosa Lanziolotti | University of Bari Aldo Moro, Italy |
| Célia Martinie | ICS-IRIT, University Paul Sabatier, France |
| Francisco Montero | University of Castilla-La Mancha, Spain |
| Randall Mumaw | NASA Ames Research Center, USA |
| Philippe Palanque | ICS-IRIT, University Paul Sabatier, France |
| Fabio Paterno | CNR-ISTI, Italy |
| Regina Peldszus | Leuphana University of Lüneburg, Germany |
| Michael Pirker | ruwido, Austria |
| Amy Pritchet | Georgia Institute of Technology, USA |
| Stefan Sauer | SICP, Paderborn University, Germany |
| Ahmed Seffah | Lappeenranta University of Technology, Finland |
| Alistair Sutcliffe | University of Manchester Business School, UK |
| Ricardo Tesoriero | University of Castilla-La Mancha, Spain |
| Jan Van Den Bergh | Hasselt University, Belgium |
| Åke Walldius | KTH Royal Institute of Technology, Sweden |
| Janet Wesson | Nelson Mandela Metropolitan University, South Africa |
| Marco Winckler | ICS-IRIT, University Paul Sabatier, France |

## Institutional Sponsors

KTH Royal Institute of Technology
and
School of Computer Science and Communication

OpenLab

## Scientific Sponsors

International Federation for Information Processing (IFIP)
Technical Committee TC 13 Human-Computer Interaction
Working Group WG 13.2 on Methodologies for User-Centered Systems Design
Working Group WG 13.5 on Resilience, Reliability, Safety and Human Error in
System Development

# Keynote Abstracts

# Industrial Scale Agile – From Craft to Engineering

Ivar Jacobson

Ivar Jacobson International
ivar@ivarjacobson.com

**Abstract.** The move towards agility has led to many benefits for the software industry. It has broken the tyranny of the prescriptive waterfall approach to software engineering, an approach that was causing more and more large project failures, and it has allowed software developers to keep up with the ever increasing demand for more and more innovative IT solutions. It has enabled many companies to do great things, but in many cases has led to a culture of entitlement, heroic programming and short-term thinking that threatens the sustainability of the parent companies and the IT solutions that they depend on. Little or no thought is put into maintainability, the heroes become potential single points of failure, and the costs of keeping the lights on just keep growing and growing. What is needed is a way to maintain the values of agility whilst making software development more an engineering discipline than a craft; a human-centered form of agile software engineering fit for the Internet Age.

# Robotics and Automation: Challenges and Potential

Danica Kragic Jensfelt

KTH Royal Institute of Technology
dani@kth.se

**Abstract.** Physical autonomous systems, also known as robots, are a result of a long-term integration of mathematical modeling, software and hardware advances in several fields of technology as well as social sciences. Robots are equipped with various sensors and actuators that enable autonomous interaction with the environment. Similarly to biological systems, the environment provides context for interactions, tools for executing tasks and means for grounding semantics. Central to achieving this is representation and parameterization of multimodal sensory data that enables safe, robust and scalable action generation. But deploying these systems in human-populated environments is still an open problem and there are many scientific challenges that need to be addressed. For humans and robots alike, objects in the environment provide context for interactions, tools for executing tasks and means for grounding semantics. In robotics, an important open problem is to detect, recognize and categorize objects given sensory data, both prior to and during interaction with objects. Central to solving this problem is to represent and parameterize sensory data so to provide fast, robust and scalable solutions. This talk summarizes the current state of the art and provides an insight in why robots are still not an integral part of our daily lives.

# Contents

## Human Error and Safety-Critical Systems

## User and Developer Experience

## Models and Methods

## Using and Adopting Tools

## Demos and Posters

# Agile and Human-Centered Software Engineering

# Responsibilities and Challenges of Product Owners at Spotify - An Exploratory Case Study

Sigurhanna Kristinsdottir[1], Marta Larusdottir[2], and Åsa Cajander[3(✉)]

[1] Kolibri, Reykjavik, Iceland
sigurhanna@gmail.com
[2] Reykjavik University, Reykjavik, Iceland
marta@ru.is
[3] Uppsala University, Uppsala, Sweden
asa.cajander@it.uu.se

**Abstract.** In Scrum, the Product Owner (PO) role is crucial for the team to be successful in developing useful and usable software. The PO has many responsibilities and challenges, including being the link between customers, other stakeholders and their development teams. This exploratory case study conducted at the software development company Spotify focuses on POs three responsibilities: (a) Identification of customers, (b) Estimation of value of their teams' work and c) Forming a vision for the product. Additionally, challenges perceived by the POs are studied. Data was gathered through five interviews and on site observations. Results show that the POs activities are divided between daily work, such as making sure that their teams are functional and long-term activities such as making a vision for the product. The main challenge of the POs is to inspire and encourage team members to collaborate and communicate within the team and with stakeholders.

**Keywords:** Project management · Product management · Agile · Agile methods · Scrum · Product Owner (PO) · Software development

## 1 Introduction

Traditional project management approaches for software development, like the waterfall approach, have been challenged by Agile approaches in recent years [2]. Agile is an umbrella term for project management approaches such as Scrum, XP, and Kanban [21], where Scrum is the most widely adopted Agile approach [25].

Scrum is an approach with a few ceremonies, roles and artefacts. The roles are called: Product Owner (PO), Scrum Master (SM) and Team Member (TM) [20]. Management responsibilities are divided among these three roles [19]. Pichler describes the PO role as a new, multi-faced role that unites authority and responsibility that traditionally, in the traditional processes was scattered across separate roles such as customer, product manager and project manager [15]. Hence, when using Agile approaches the PO role in some aspects replaces the role of various stakeholders. The PO has the authority to set goals and shape the vision of a product and therefore the PO has other responsibilities

© IFIP International Federation for Information Processing 2016
Published by Springer International Publishing Switzerland 2016. All Rights Reserved
C. Bogdan et al. (Eds.): HCSE 2016/HESSD 2016, LNCS 9856, pp. 3–16, 2016.
DOI: 10.1007/978-3-319-44902-9_1

than the project manager that mainly writes requirements and does prioritization for the team [15]. For example, the POs in Scrum projects in Iceland had various responsibilities [23]. The proportion of the POs time collaborating with the team varied from 5 % to 70 % of their total working time. Furthermore, the POs used from 10 % to 50 % of their working time collaborating with customers, users and other stakeholders [23].

The Product Owner role has not had much focus in academic research; the main focus has been on productivity, teamwork and collaborative decision-making in Agile teams rather than studying specific Agile roles. Additionally, more attention has been on examining factors that drive organizations to initially adopt Agile approaches than on those that affect their continued usage [16]. Still, the use of Agile approaches is constantly increasing in software development [3, 25], thus the Product Owner role is interesting and important since this role is often the link between business and development departments of an organization. One of the fundamental principles of Agile approaches is to aim at satisfying the customers by producing valuable pieces of the final product early in the development lifecycle [14].

This paper is an exploratory case study conducted at the software development company Spotify at the end of February 2014. It is a description of the PO role at this point in time and the main focus of the research is to study how POs identify customers for their teams, how they measure value of their teams' work, how they form vision and communicate that to their teams, what their challenges are and how they deal with those.

**The research questions in this study are:**

1. What are the main responsibilities of the Product Owners? Particularly:
   (a)  How do Product Owners identify customers for their teams?
   (b)  How do they measure the value of their teams' work?
   (c)  How do they form the product vision for their teams?
2. What are the challenges of a Product Owner, and how does he or she cope with them?

The structure of the paper is that first we describe some of the background literature on Agile approaches and Scrum. We particularly describe the definitions of the POs role. Then we describe the data gathering methods used in the study, followed by a section describing the results. Finally we discuss the findings and give concluding remarks.

## 2   Background

This section describes Agile approaches and Scrum, the teamwork of Agile teams and the PO role.

### 2.1   Agile Approaches and Scrum

The origin of Agile project management (Agile) was first described in a paper by Takeuchi and Nonaka in 1986 [24], but Agile as a methodology gained attraction when Sutherland and Schwaber [22] discussed the first Agile process (also called Agile approach) for software development in the 1995 OOPSLA conference. They had analysed common software development processes and found that traditional development approaches were not suitable for empirical, unpredictable and non-repeatable processes such as development of software. The fundamental values and principles behind Agile are described in the Agile manifesto [1].

Six obstacles in decision making in Agile have been analysed, which are: (a) unwillingness to commit to decisions; (b) conflicting priorities; (c) unstable resource availability; and lack of: (d) implementation; (e) ownership; (f) empowerment [6]. The effect of these obstacles is a lack of longer term, strategic focus for decisions, an ever-growing list of delayed work from previous iterations, and a lack of team engagement.

In Scrum, the most common Agile process [25], the projects should be split up into two to four week long iterations called sprints, each aiming to end up with a potentially shippable product. In Scrum, self-organizing and strongly united teams are heavily emphasized, typically with six to eight interdisciplinary team members. One of the benefits of using Agile was claimed to be that customers' needs are taken more into account than when developing software using sequential processes [18]. The Scrum team is self-organising and works independently during the sprints. Daily Scrum meetings are prescribed where the Scrum team meets and plans the work during the day, and where the tasks are distributed in the group. The work in the Scrum team should be guided by collaboration and communication. Demos of the outcome are made at the end of every sprint. Agile teams should have a common focus, mutual trust and the ability to reorganize repeatedly to meet new challenges. IT professionals appreciate the inherent values in Scrum, which are speed and communication internal to the Scrum team. Also, working in teams and focusing on a small number of tasks at a time is valued. The main challenges are that including specialists in the teams is hard and Scrum does not always match with external requirements for the organizations [13].

Being self-organised does not mean leaderless, uncontrolled teams but that the leadership is meant to be light-touch and adaptive, providing feedback and subtle direction. Leaders of Agile teams are responsible for setting direction, aligning people, obtaining resources and motivating the team [9]. The leader can be anyone with influence or authority over the team and can include managers, POs and the SM [4]. In the next subsection, definitions of the responsibilities of POs are described.

## 2.2 Definitions of the POs Role

Schwaber [19; pp. 6–7] defines the PO role as follows:

> *"The Product Owner is responsible for representing the interests of everyone with a stake in the project and its resulting system. The Product Owner achieves initial and ongoing funding for the project by creating the project's initial overall requirements, return on investment (ROI) objectives, and release plans. The list of requirements is called the Product Backlog. The Product Owner is responsible for using the Product Backlog to ensure the most valuable functionality is produced first and built upon; this is achieved by frequently prioritizing the Product Backlog to queue up the most valuable requirements for the next iteration."*

Both the developing team and the people driving the business need to collaborate to develop the final required product [14]. The PO is the link between the customer and the user side of an organization and the development team. The team and the PO should constantly collaborate and plan together how to produce the most value for the business [19]. The primary duties of the POs are making sure that all team members are pursuing a common vision for the project, establishing priorities so that the highest-valued functionality is always being worked on and making decisions that lead to a good return on the investment in the project or for the product [5, 11]. The responsibility of the PO is to prioritize the work to be done by the team, but he or she should not be involved with how the team does their work [10]. In commercial software development, the PO is often someone from the marketing or production management side of an organization [5].

Picher describes that the PO should lead the development team to create a product that generates the desired benefits for the customer and the user [15]. This includes creating the product vision, prioritizing the product backlog, planning the releases, involving stakeholders, managing the budget, preparing the product launch, attending meetings, collaborating with the team and many other tasks.

Cohn [5] states that the PO role is challenging because the PO needs to address both inward and outward facing needs simultaneously. The inward facing responsibilities being participating in daily stand-up meetings, reviews, retrospectives as well as management meetings, managing the product backlog, answering questions from the team and being available to the team as much as possible. Outward facing responsibilities are to attend to user's needs, manage stakeholder expectations, prioritize the product backlog and develop a product strategy and vision. Furthermore Cohn [5] states that the PO should provide just enough boundaries for the project so that the team is motivated to solve the difficult problems but not providing so many boundaries that solving the problems becomes impossible. In that way the role is more of an art than science.

Galen [8] states that the PO role is the most difficult one within the Agile or Scrum team. A PO needs to be a highly skilled individual who understands the nuances of the role and is enabled by the organization to take the time necessary to fully engage the teams in value-based delivery. A skilled PO is a member of his team and should consider the team as his or her primary customer. PO is a distinct member of the team in which overall success or failure is a joint endeavour. The PO needs to give the team the right things to do and make sure they do everything possible to qualify the work [8]. The PO role can be difficult to staff with a single individual because the competences are so broad and intimidating that it is hard to find an individual having all these skills [8].

In summary, Cohn, Galen and Pichler describe four aspects of the PO role, which are: involving customers, focusing on value, creating a vision and that it is a challenging role. Schwaber has a bit more focused definition, emphasising customer involvement and value of the product as the main aspects. We therefore analyse the results according to four themes in the paper: (1) customer involvement, (2) focusing on value, (3) making a vision and (4) challenges of the PO role.

## 3    Method

Little research exists on the Product Owner role, and this study is exploratory in nature and examines the role of Product Owners. The research is a qualitative case study conducted at Spotify at the end of February 2014. This study was first presented as a master thesis study and has been rewritten for the purpose of this publication.

### 3.1 Context of the Study and Participants

Spotify was founded in 2006 in Sweden and in 2008 they released their core product, a music player named Spotify that can be used online or downloaded as an app on desktop or mobile. Its users have access to one of the fastest growing catalogues of licensed music in the world [17]. It has grown tremendously since it was founded, has a good track record of product delivery and its products are loved by users and artists [12] Active users are growing fast, they were over 20 million at the beginning of 2013 and paying subscribers around 5 million [12]. At the time of this case study Spotify's employees were around 1.000 with software development taking place in three locations: Stockholm, Gothenburg and New York.

Spotify has used Agile approaches in one form or another since it was founded in 2006. Their teams, which are called squads, used Scrum in the past but when they started delivering all tasks ahead of the end of each three-week sprint they decided that each team could be completely autonomous in the way they work. Some teams use Scrum today but that is a minority of all the development teams. Most of the teams use Kanban or some form of that. But each team still has a Product Owner and a Scrum Master. At the time of the study, the product that was being developed was quite mature. The Agile teams had been working on the product for years, and their way of working had matured a lot, since the company was established.

As this is a case study the participants were selected in consultation with a professional from Spotify. The participants were spread across the organization to insure that they did not have the same background and were working in different projects and with different parts of the product.

Five interviews were conducted. Three Product Owners were interviewed, one director of Product Development, that was previously a Product Owner and one Scrum Master, called Agile Coach at Spotify, to receive a better view on the Product Owner role and his challenges. One of the Product Owners also had the role of an Agile Coach at the time of the interview. The participants had various backgrounds; most of them started as developers but had changed roles, two participants said it was because they like to speak their opinion on the way things are done so they were asked to take the Product Owner role on a team. The participants all had a good understanding of agile processes and the business of Spotify.

The others happened to take on this role when the teams were set up according to Scrum. The Product Owners work in different parts of the organization, which might explain differences in their opinions.

### 3.2 Research Method

Case studies are the preferred method when how or why questions are being posed, when the investigator has little control over events and the focus is on a contemporary phenomenon within a real-life context [26]. The case study method allows the investigator to retain the holistic and meaningful characteristics of real-live events, such as organizational and managerial processes.

As one of the researchers had the chance of conducting a research of the Product Owner role at Spotify's headquarters in Stockholm this research method was chosen. Knowledge gained from this study is transferable to other settings through the interpretations of the reader.

In this exploratory case study we have used a mixed methods approach. The primary data collection method was in-depth, face-to-face semi-structured interviews with five employees at Spotify. The first step in data gathering was to prepare the interview protocol and pilot test it prior to the study. After the pilot test there were minor changes to the protocol. The protocol had: 7 questions on the background and experience of the participants, 2 questions on the stakeholder focus, 2 questions focusing on value, 3 questions on the vision, 5 questions on teamwork, 4 questions on the challenges for POs and 9 questions on the PO role in general.

The interviews were audio-recorded with the permission of the participants and then transcribed verbatim. Their length was between 50–65 min. The quotations in the results chapter are not always verbatim but slightly rephrased to be more readable.

Observation on site were also made through shadowing a Product Owner for a day to observe his daily role. The shadowing included being present in all meetings the Product Owner had that day: stand-up meetings with his teams, one-on-one meetings with his team members and managerial meetings. Additionally informal conversation was performed people in various roles around the organization.

Source data hence included field notes from the observations, transcripts from the interviews, documents and photographs taken at site. The researcher spent three days at Spotify finishing each day by documenting the observations as field notes and then used the next day to seek clarification and gather more data.

### 3.3 Analysis of the Data

In the analysis we identified and coded the results into the four themes: (1) customer involvement, (2) focusing on value, (3) making a vision and (4) challenges of the PO role. When analysing customer involvement, both statements about the customers (the person paying) and end users (the person using the software) are analysed, since the users for the Spotify service are also customers.

The source documents were grouped by each participant and then analysed by the use of the themes according the theme analysis [7]. Conclusions were finally drawn from the data collected. Emphasis was put on understanding the participants' lived experiences in the Product Owner role and their different views. In order to answer the research questions, the transcripts and field notes were read several times to obtain insight into each case.

# 4  Results

In this section the research results are divided into two sections, the first subsection presents results from the interviews when it comes to the POs experience of the three responsibilities. The second subsection presents the challenges the POs described that they have had in practice.

## 4.1  Responsibilities of the Product Owners

In this subsection the Product Owners experiences regarding the three responsibilities that are connected to their role in literature are described: (1) customer involvement, (2) focusing on value and (3) making a vision.

### 4.1.1  Customer Involvement

The Product Owners that participated in the research worked with different kinds of teams, those that develop new features and those that work on infrastructure or measurements that other teams then use to build their features on. The Product Owners did agree that the teams should know who their customer is but they did not all find it their responsibility to identify those customers and their needs and communicate those needs to their team so that the teams are working on the most valuable tasks for the customer at any given time. Some felt strongly about it being their responsibility while others found it to be a team effort and not even something they should think about in their role. Some said that the PO should make sure that discussing the customer needs should take place within their team. Some of the Product Owners also tried to bring end user focus to their teams by pointing out that even though their team was working on a platform for an internal customer the team members still have to think of the end users as their customers.

As one participant said: *"We [Product Owners] should represent the customers' interest, we are here to deliver something that users want to use and will love. Our success should ultimately be customers who love the product."* But another one said: *"I would say that both the Product Owner and the team have an input on what the users want, it might not be only the Product Owners responsibility to communicate that to the team but he should be the one seeing to that we know what are the customers' needs."* One participant said that in a very broad sense this was his responsibility and in his daily work he talked to many people in the organization to find out where there are needs for his team to come in and work for other teams.

Some of the Product Owners mentioned customer services as being their main connection to the end user. They felt that if the users are not happy with the software or the changes the teams are doing to it they should see that in the number of complaints from users and ultimately the number of users and take action if they were going down. Spotify's success should therefore be judged by numbers of users, if the numbers are going up the users are satisfied and vice versa: *"Internally I play the devil's advocate; I try to empathize with the users and make clear to the team that everyone depends on us by asking questions like: If we brake something who will that affect?"*

One Product Owner mentioned that his team tried to write user stories to understand their user's situation and figure out what their needs are. He believed that it is his responsibility to make the team focus on why the program or system is working on this specific task rather than another one but he said it can be a challenges as there are developers who are happy to continue writing software and not ship anything to the end user. He would like his developers to think of the end user and launch the software out to them as soon as possible: *"For me the heart of agility is getting software to users and learning from them, listening to them and getting feedback fast and that's all there is to it."*

### 4.1.2 Focusing on Value

Most of the Product Owners found it difficult to measure the value of the work their team was doing because often there was no transaction of money taking place. They tried to use measurements but the teams themselves did not always control those as they are mostly working for internal customers so it was hard to figure out what of the actual end value is generated from each team. As one Product Owner put it: *"We see very little money here as Product Owners, it is strange but I don't concern myself with money at all actually."*

Spotify tracks global user satisfaction usage for changes of the software but as the iterative changes to the software are so incremental it is difficult for the user to see them or know about them. So the Product Owners use the number of users as their main parameter of success. Then they try to build a dependency chain on metrics and work with hypothesis, for example if Spotify has more music they have more users, if users collect more music they will play more music, if users are able to find music easily they will collect more music and so on.

One participant said that it should be up to the team to deliver return on investment, not the Product Owner. He or she should just be the contact point for other parts of the organization to make it a bit easier for the team to work uninterrupted but in the best of teams the Product Owner is just another team member and the team as a whole sets the goals that then bring value to the organization. If the Product Owner tries to do it by himself chances are that the team will not buy into the goals: *"You can usually see when the team has set the goals as a whole rather than the goals being delivered from someone else."*

One participant said that his team did not measure return on investment in any way but verbal feedback from his internal customer was what he focuses on. His gut feeling was therefore his main form of measurement.

### 4.1.3 Making a Vision

When the participants were asked if they lead the vision of the product development for their teams most of them agreed that it was a difficult responsibility that they struggled with. One participant said: *"I think it's important that the Product Owners sees to that the team has a vision, that they know what it is, but I don't think it is solely the Product Owner who creates that vision, I think that the team does that together but the Product Owner is responsible for that they have it".*

The Product Owners do not always know what that vision is as the organization has been growing fast and the vision of a team tends to change relatively quickly: *"Speaking completely openly it is something we are struggling with, this question of the vision and sharing it with the other teams because we are big and distributed. So how do you share that vision? I think we overcomplicate it at the moment and I think we just need an objective and should focus less on measurements."*

Each team is encouraged to come up with five measureable goals each quarter, but one of the participants said that he does not like that because he thinks that often metrics are gamed, especially if they come from the top down. He would rather have a vision set at the top and then trust the teams and let them prove to the organization that what they are doing is moving the whole organization in the right direction. Another participant agreed on this, the Product Owner should provide a vision but said that somebody had to provide them with the organizational vision so that he is able to do that, the Product Owner cannot come up with the vision on his own.

One participant said that he would like to think that he facilitates the visionary activities for his team. But he said that his team has a much better insight into the needs of the customers as the team is working much closer with them than he is. He does trust his team to have much input on the vision of the development: *"I get a very fluffy high level overview but the team has very concrete details so I facilitate the vision but they provide most of it."*

Another participant said he had a clear vision of how his product should be developed but the organization as a whole did not have a shared vision for the end product. He said his team starts to converge of this unspoken vision every two or three months so they sit down and take a conversation about it but they never write it down, their world is changing so fast that they do not want to put it in a document that is obsolete in a few weeks. Another participant involves others in the visioning activities but then he communicates the vision: *"High-level vision for the company takes place in broad hall meetings. That's for the entire company and then I translate that into the reasons why we are doing the things we are doing now."*

One participant said that his team works a bit with story mapping to try to figure out what the big items for the future could be but as their goals changes so quickly it is extremely hard to work on a long-term basis: *"The longest project I've seen so far has been about a year. And the business landscaped has typically changed so much over time that at the end the product might not be quite right, good examples are the download store and the iPod integration which were a good idea at the time but when they were finally released it wasn't anymore. Over all we change the goals, what we prioritize, so often that it's hard to have a longer term vision."*

## 4.2 Challenges of the PO Role

Part of this study was to gather information on the challenges a Product Owner faces at Spotify.

One participant described the role as a combination of a diplomat adviser and juggler because there are a lot of voices with different needs and the Product Owner needs to communicate with all of them. The best way to do this was to be transparent so people see for themselves why things are done this way and not the other: *"Be transparent because you are not going to please everyone all the time. As long as you are transparent about how you are doing things, how you make decisions and why certain things need to be prioritized over other things you will succeed."*

It is the most challenging role on the team, said one participant, because there is ultimately more responsibility in the Product Owner role than in other roles in the team: *"You have all those people wanting things from your team and for everyone what they want is very important and that is the diplomat part of the role. The team should be exposed to this pressure to an extent but the Product Owner should also protect the team from that. The developers need to know that they are not working in a vacuum, there are people who really care about what they are delivering but the Product Owner is also protecting them which makes it a more challenging role."*

One participant said that the Product Owner role is challenging because even though the team is responsible for their delivery the Product Owner is in the forefront of that, the one seeing to that the delivery happens and it is compatible to what was initially planned: *"I think that is a tough thing to have on your shoulders."*

Being a Product Owner also means to align other people so that everyone has the information they need to do the right job at every given moment: *"It's all about alignment and knowing what others are doing, you should not be working in isolation, it's very hard to do the right thing if you don't know what others are doing so the Product Owners are the ones who just make sure that we don't deviate on our own into what we think it is we should be doing."*

Every Product Owner found it extremely important to spend time with the team every day, as much as they physically could to but some struggled with that as they worked with more than one team and had to attend to various meetings. Teamwork and collaborative decision making seem to play a crucial role in the work the Product Owner does with their team. The Product Owner is often guided by the team in what is technically right, so he has to listen to the team and take their advice on how things should best be done: *"I'm there to represent the teams interest, fight their corner and to make their case. Just this week we said we're not going to make a release because the quality is not there yet. That message comes from me to the stakeholders but it is informed and guided by the voices of the team."*

The challenge is also that the Product Owner has to be an indirect leader of the team, he has some authority to make decisions for the team but he very rarely wants to act on that authority and be the only one making decisions that affect the whole team and their work: *"Product Owners are indirect leaders and many of them are totally inexperienced when it comes to leading someone. Especially if it's a junior team, so that is a big challenge for a lot of the Product Owners."* The Product Owner has to get people excited and aligned so that they know what is expected of them without actually telling them: *"The Product Owner is supposed to lead the team, engage and inspire it, make sure that things are moving forward but it is very artificial to have just one person that does that, the team itself needs to be interested in these kind of topics and discussions."* And the challenge is also to see what is missing and add that to the mix: *"I think the Product Owner role involves picking up the slack, so if something isn't working then it's clearly your Product Owners fault. Anything that is missing you'll have to pitch in."*

Most of the Product Owners talked about the stakeholder side as being one of the most challenging parts of their role. It is difficult to motivate a team that does not know for whom it is working and lacks a purpose: "*I think the special challenge is that we are not very often doing particularly exciting or glamorous parts of the development, we're providing a platform and keeping developers motivated around that is a particular challenge here. And focusing on the user value and remembering that we've not just got internal customers, we've got users as well.*" One participant said that his biggest challenge was to sell his vision of the development to the developers on his team: "*The challenge is not only to sell the product to the end users but to sell the work that the team needs to do to the team. Both are important but if I have to order them it's selling the work to the engineers that is more important.*" Part of the role is to trust the team to do their job and leave them to do just that: "*Part of our role is actually to back off, let people try things and trust them to do something interesting.*"

Communication was also mentioned as being one of the Product Owners' main challenge: "*When the Product Owner is good at communication I see the teams do a really good job and when the Product Owner isn't good at communication the teams seem to struggle with what they should be working on.*" And it's not enough that the Product Owner is a communicative person but he also has to make other people speak to each other and see the big picture instead of focusing on their own task: "*The more people talk to each other the more they realize that teamwork is important and they get more humble as they know what others are doing instead of getting stuck in their own corner of the universe.*"

All participants mentioned that they have come a long way and now find the role a bit easier than when taking the role. The challenges were often the same but in different situations and they feel they can use previous experience to handle them.

## 5 Discussion

The results show that all the participants are well aware of the responsibilities that are described in literature [5, 8, 15, 19] and all of them attend those in some way or another, although they have different approaches in their daily work to fulfil them. As described by both Cohn [5] and Pichler [15] the role is multi-faced, inward and outward facing and challenging. The results in this study show this quite clearly. Some respondents commented that they needed to have one foot in the daily work and one foot in the future and lead people to work on the right things at any given moment. Since Spotify has been growing during the past years it might be that the POs have had to focus more on their inward facing responsibilities as Cohn [5] describes them, dealing with their own team on daily basis to make sure they are functional. The results indicate that when these challenges have been met the POs can look ahead to the future and start to focus on customer involvement, the vision of the product and the value their team is delivering as these are among the outward facing needs [5].

At Spotify the role of the PO varies from one person to another. One aspect is that the POs have a very communicative role and the individuals in the PO role have different communication competences. An additional aspect is that the responsibilities of the POs are not necessarily the same in one part of the organization compared to another part of it.

The participants agreed that the PO role is often complicated and diverse and in some ways it can be hard to describe what the actual daily work is and should be. There are many tasks to juggle each day and the POs often felt that they were not delivering any visible work to the team or the organization.

The biggest risk for Spotify is building the wrong product, meaning that the product does not delight users or does not improve success metrics such as user acquisition or user retention [12]. This is what is called "product risk" at Spotify. To compensate for this, the POs make sure that the customers (end users) are represented when the teams plan their work. Within the teams that build infrastructure or internal tools, there seems to be a lack of understanding of whether the concept customer includes the end user or not, that is if the teams should be focusing on the system from the users point of view or focusing on the customer, which ofter are internal managers at Spotify or other teams they are developing for. The end user is not always in the developers' mind when they are developing for infrastructure or measurement, we could say that the end user is somewhat invisible. There were examples of teams not knowing who their primary customer is. Helping the POs to identify their teams' customers would give the teams a better vision for the reason for why they are doing what they are doing and hopefully empower team members and make them more involved in defining the vision for the product. As the organization has different teams working for each other and a few are developing directly for the end user, the visionary activities are blurred. There are indications that strategic work is strong for the organization as a whole but that does not seem to help the POs with their vision for their specific product development and the communication of that to their teams.

As Cohn [5] states the PO should establish priorities so that the highest-valued functionality is always being worked on to maximise return on investment. The POs did not think about the value of the tasks their teams are working on and did not prioritize them according to return on investment, mainly because they don't have the right tools to measure the value of every task. It is also difficult to put a price on something you don't know how much effort is needed to finish.

Leading visioning activities for the product and communicate that to the team like both Cohn [5] and Pichler [15] describe as one of the main responsibilities of the POs is what the POs all struggle with. It is difficult for the teams to focus on the big picture when they work on a limited amount of tasks each time.

This case study has contributed to the software development and project management literature by examining the PO role at Spotify. This is a complex role with both inward and outward facing responsibilities. Studying POs for three days might not give a generalizable picture of their duties, but the study gives an understanding of the POs responsibilities and challenges. The findings are interesting in regards to how the POs describe the complexity of the role, how it is much more of a leadership role than a manager role and how communication and people skills are crucial to the competences of a PO. The PO has to work closely with the team and as soon as the team feels that they don't have a clear vision of where they are going they start to drift of and become dysfunctional.

# 6  Conclusion

It seems that the PO role is as diverse in practice as the literature describes it and the challenges a PO faces each day are many as the results indicate. The POs need to have one foot in the daily work and one foot in the future and lead people to work on the right things at any given moment. The POs do not want to use their authority to make decisions for the team but they want everyone to be involved in the work and in that way the team should be able more productive and develop valuable products.

The PO is not a person who knows it all, as one participant put it: *"I don't think the Product Owner is a magical person who has all the answers. You can give a steer on priority, you can help make sure we are focusing on customer value but you don't have all the answers."*

In practice, the PO role seems to be much more of a leadership role than literature has indicated so far and it would be interesting to research the role in relation to the academic literature on leadership. The main challenge of the PO might therefore be to inspire and encourage team members communicate openly. If the team members are empowered and interested in their work the challenges seem to become much easier.

**Acknowledgement.**   The authors would like to thank the participants and people at Spotify for the opportunity to do this research at their offices in Stockholm. Special thanks to Anders Ivarson who helped with arrangements and gave valuable comments on a draft of a thesis that this paper is based on.

# References

1. Beck, K., et al.: The Agile Manifesto (2001). http://www.Agilealliance.org/the-alliance/the-Agile-manifesto/. Accessed 13 Jan 2014
2. Cervone, H.F.: Understanding Agile Project Management Methods using Scrum. Managing Digital Libraries: the view from 30,000 feet. OCLC Syst. Serv. **27**(1), 18–22 (2010)
3. Cooper, R.G.: What's next? Res. Technol. Manage. **57**, 20–31 (2014)
4. Cohn, M.: Agile Estimating and Planning. Prentice Hall, Upper Saddle River (2010)
5. Cohn, M.: Succeeding with Agile: Software development using Scrum. Addison-Wesley Signature Series. Addison-Wesley, Pearson Education Inc., Upper Saddle River, NJ (2010)
6. Drury, M., Conboy, K., Power, K.: Obstacles to decision making in Agile Software development teams. J. Syst. Softw. **85**, 1239–1254 (2012)
7. Ezzy, D.: Qualitative Analysis: Practice and Innovation. Psychology Press, UK (2002)
8. Galen, R.: SCRUM Product Ownership: Balancing Value from the Inside Out, 2nd edn. RGCG, LLC, Cary, NC (2013)
9. Hoda, R., Noble, J., Marshall, S.: The impact of inadequate customer collaboration on self-organizing Agile teams. Inf. Softw. Technol. **53**, 521–534 (2011)
10. Ivarsson, A., Kniberg, H.: Scaling Agile @ Spotify with Tribes, Squads, Chapters and Guilds (2012). https://dl.dropboxusercontent.com/u/1018963/Articles/SpotifyScaling.pdf. Accessed 13 Jan 2014
11. Kniberg, H.: Scrum and XP from the Trenches: How we do scrum (2007). http://infoq.com/minibooks/scrum-xp-from-the-trenches. Accessed 7 Jan 2014

12. Kniberg, H.: How Spotify Builds Products (2013). http://dl.dropboxusercontent.com/u/1018963/Articles/HowSpotifyBuildsProducts.pdf. Accessed 13 Jan 2014
13. Larusdottir, M.K., Cajander, A., Erlingsdottir, G., Lind, T., Gulliksen, J.: Challenges from integrating usability activities in scrum - why is scrum so fashionable? In: Cockton, G., Larusdottir, M.K., Gregory, P., Cajander, A. (eds.) Integrating User Centred Design in Agile Development. Springer, London (2016)
14. Misra, S.: Agile software development practices: evaluation, principles, and criticism. Int. J. Qual. Reliab. Manage. **29**(9), 972–980 (2011)
15. Pichler, R.: Agile Product Management with Scrum: Creating Products that Customers Love. Addison-Wesley Signature Series. Addison-Wesley, Pearson Education Inc., Upper Saddle River, NJ (2010)
16. Senapathi, M., Srinivasan, A.: Understanding post-adoptive Agile usage: an exploratory cross-case analysis. J. Syst. Softw. **85**, 1255–1268 (2012)
17. Spotify (n.d.) Labels and artists. https://www.spotify.com/se/about-us/labels/. Accessed 15 Jan 2014
18. Schwaber, K.: Scrum development process. In: Business Object Design and Implementation, pp. 117–134. Springer, London (1995)
19. Schwaber, K.: Agile Project Management with Scrum. Microsoft Press, Redmond (2004)
20. Schwaber, K., Beedle, M.: Software Development with Scrum (2002)
21. Strode, D.E., Hope, B., Huff, S.L., Link, S.: Coordination in clocated Agile software development projects. J. Syst. Softw. **85**, 1222–1238 (2012)
22. Sutherland, J.V., Schwaber, K.: The SCRUM methodology. In: Business Object Design and Implementation: OOPSLA Workshop (1995)
23. Sverrisdottir, H.S., Ingason, H.T., Jonasson, H.I.: The role of the product owner in Scrum – comparison between theory and practices. Proceidia – Soc. Behav. Sci. **119**, 257–267 (2014)
24. Takeuchi, H., og Nonaka, I.: The new product development game. Harvard Bus. Rev. **64**(1), 137–146 (1986)
25. VersionOne: The 10th State of Agile Survey (2015). https://versionone.com/pdf/VersionOne-10th-Annual-State-of-Agile-Report.pdf
26. Yin, R.K.: Case Study Research: Design and Methods, 4th edn. SAGE Publications, Thousand Oaks (2009)

# Supporting the HCI Aspect of Agile Software Development by Tool Support for UI-Pattern Transformations

Peter Forbrig[✉] and Marc Saurin

University of Rostock, Albert-Einstein-Str. 22, 18051 Rostock, Germany
`peter.forbrig@uni-rostock.de`

**Abstract.** Continuous changing requirements of software are the result of continuously changing reality. This reality can be considered as the context of the software. Agile development methods allow quick adaptations to changing requirements. Initially, agile development methods were focused on the development of the application core only. Recently, process models were discussed that integrate HCI aspects. This paper will discuss ideas to integrate user evaluations into the development process. User interfaces are structured as UI-pattern instances. Tool support is provided that allows the specification of pattern instances as XAML specifications. Additionally, the tool allows the replacement of one pattern instance by another one. In this way, different versions of the same user interface can be generated rapidly without much effort. These different versions can be evaluated with the help of users. Based on these usability tests final decisions for the software design can be made. New requirements can be captured additionally. This will be based on feedback of the users.

**Keywords:** UI-Patterns · Pattern instance transformation · Agile software development · Human-Centered Design

## 1 Introduction

Our society changes continuously. Therefore, software solutions have to be adapted during usage. However, even during the development requirements are not stable. Developers have to react on dynamical changes. This is the reason for the need of agile approaches. Classical development methods often fail.

Unfortunately, software engineers often focus on the development of the application core only. Aspects of user interface design and HCI methods are not in the focus of their work. That is the reason why process models of agile methods like SCRUM do not contain HCI activities. Recently, there are several approaches like [2, 5–8, 15].

Agile development methods very much support the communication between developers and customers. However, users should be involved as well.

The Human-Centered approach is accompanied with a phase where design decisions are evaluated. To support design decisions tool support would be helpful that generated different alternatives. Based on the user evaluation the best design can be selected and further developed. We will present a tool that allows developers the development of

© IFIP International Federation for Information Processing 2016
Published by Springer International Publishing Switzerland 2016. All Rights Reserved
C. Bogdan et al. (Eds.): HCSE 2016/HESSD 2016, LNCS 9856, pp. 17–29, 2016.
DOI: 10.1007/978-3-319-44902-9_2

different user interfaces based on pattern transformations. Additionally, we will discuss how this tool fits into agile development methods. We will discuss this aspect on a specific process model for SCRUM.

The rest of the paper will be structured in the following way. First, we will discuss the idea of UI patterns and the corresponding tool support. Afterwards, the integration of the Human-Centered Design into SCRUM will be discussed. Additionally, it will be shown how the developed tool can be used within the development process. Finally, there will be a summary and an outlook.

## 2    UI-Patterns and Tool Support

### 2.1    UI-Patterns

The success story of patterns in computer science started with the well-known book by the "Gang of Four" [3]. Later, this idea was adapted to different subdomains. In the meantime, there exist patterns about workflows, tasks, ontologies, and a lot of other aspects.

UI-Patterns have been proven to be very useful for designing interactive software systems. Resource for that are e.g. [11, 16, 17], to mention only a few of them. Most of existing libraries are for human browsing only. The application has to be performed manually. However, there exist tools that allow the application of UI patterns.

The term pattern is sometimes used a little bit vague. In the final user interface, one cannot see neither any pattern nor any pattern instance. One can only see the result of the application of a pattern instance. Let us assume the following application process of UI patterns:

1. **Identification:** A subset S' of user interface elements S is identified that can be transformed by a pattern. $S' \subseteq S$
2. **Selection:** A pattern P is selected that can be applied to S'.
3. **Adaptation:** The pattern P is adapted to the current context of use M'.
   As a result, a pattern instance I is delivered. $A(P,S') = I$
4. **Integration:** The instance I is integrated. It replaces M' in M.
   $I(S', S) = S*$ (Pattern instance I is applied to subset S' of S and delivers a new set of user elements $S*$ – a new user interface)

Using this terminology a user interface presents the result of the application of pattern instances. Pattern instances are the result of adaptations of patterns to the current context of use. They are applied to existing elements and deliver new user interface elements. However, to be short sometimes the structure of user interfaces is presented by the names of the corresponding patterns only.

It was already mentioned that there exist tools supporting the application of UI patterns. However, about the transformation of user interfaces by pattern is yet not much reported even there exist papers about such transformations for a relatively long time. Already in 2004 in [4] it was reported about the opportunity to transform user interfaces that were constructed based on patterns. The paper discusses ideas, which pattern applications should be replaced by other ones in case the application should run on mobile devices. They call it pattern mapping. We will recall only three mapping rules of their Table 12.4. The enumeration comes from their pattern catalog.

P.1   Bread crumbs is replaced by

   P.1 s – Shorter bread crumb trail; and
   P.15 – Drop-down 'History' menu
P.2   Temporary horizontal menus replaced by

   P.2 s – Shorter menu; and
   P.3 – Link to full-page display of menu options ordered vertically.

We adapt this idea for mapping or transformations of pattern applications on the same platform. It can be considered as refactoring like in [10]. With tool support, different versions of a user interface can be generated quickly. A horizontal menu could e.g. be transformed to a vertical one. Such kind of tool support is discussed in the next section.

## 2.2   Tool Support of UI-Patterns Using XAML

Within a Master Thesis [12] a tool was developed for constructing and transforming user interfaces based on UI-patterns. The tool is based on Visual Studio using the technology of VSIX extensions and XAML specifications of user interfaces. Figure 1 shows the XAML representation of the Split Pane Pattern in its horizontal version.

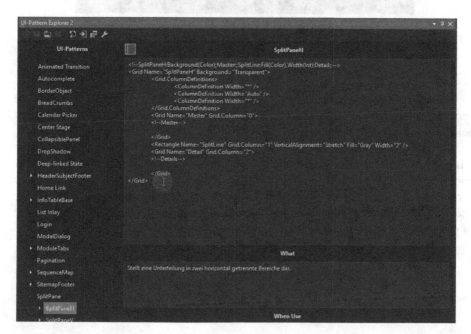

**Fig. 1.** Pattern specification in UI-Explorer 2.

The UI-Explorer 2 tool uses representation files for patterns. Currently XAML is used. It fits well to the provided features of WPF (Windows Presentation Foundation). However, any other XML-based specification language like HTML or ASPX could be used as well. The Grid-tag was used to represent patterns. Some attribute can be set initially- They can be changed later. In the example above the master and detail part are still empty. They can be filled later. Figure 2 demonstrates the application of the pattern.

**Fig. 2.** Application of the horizontal Split Pane Pattern.

Let us have a look at replacing the application SplitPaneH by SplitPaneV (split pane vertical). UI Explorer 2 supports this kind of transformation and delivers the result below.

Currently pattern applications can be transformed at one location only. For the future it is planned to allow the replacement of all instances of a pattern application by another one. It will also be possible to allow to replace a sequence of pattern applications by another sequence of pattern application. This would include the replacement of one pattern application by a sequence of applications as well as the replacement of a sequence of pattern applications by one pattern application (Fig. 3).

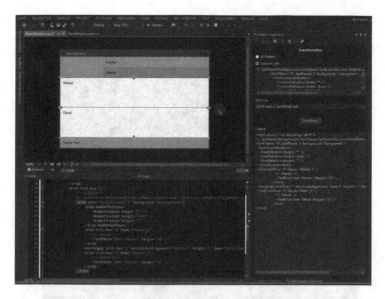

**Fig. 3.** Replacement of the application of the SplitPaneH by SplitPaneV.

Formally, this can be described by the following notation:

| | | |
|---|---|---|
| P1(X) | => P2(X) | Pattern P1 is replaced by P2 |
| P1(X, P2(Y)) | => P3(X, Y) | Patterns P1 and P2 are replaced by P3 |
| P3(X, Y) | => P1(X, P2(Y)) | Pattern P3 is replaced by P1 and P2 |
| P1(X, P2(Y)) | => P3(X, P4(Y)) | Patterns P1 and P2 are replaced by P3 and P4 |

### 2.3 Case Study

To get an impression of the applicability of the tool, a case study was performed. The websites of Lufthansa, Eurowings, and Norwegian were analyzed und their structure according to UI-Patterns applications were analyzed. The resulting structure is shown in Fig. 4.

An already refined and transformed version of the user interface is presented as Fig. 5. The horizontal version of Master and Detail was replaced by a vertical one.

A further transformation yields to the result of Fig. 6. The navigation in the calendar is replaced by a new pattern application. This structure corresponds to the structure of the webpage of Norwegian (Fig. 7).

The case study had shown that the approach worked for examples of real applications. The tool was able to handle transformations of different levels of abstractions (Fig. 8).

**Fig. 4.** Structure of the web-page of Eurowings.

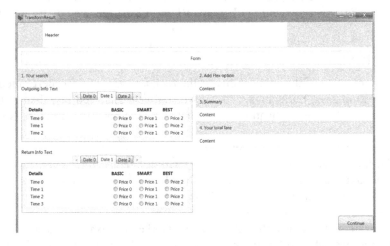

**Fig. 5.** Refined and transformed part of the user interface of the web page of Eurowings.

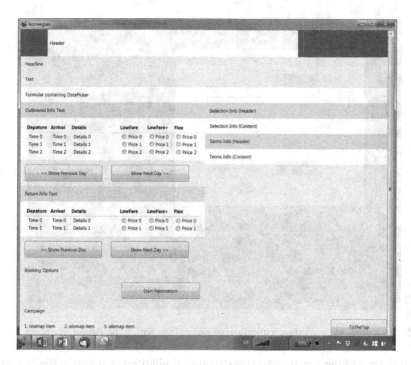

**Fig. 6.** Further transformed page that corresponds to the structure of that of Norwegian.

**Fig. 7.** Part of the detailed user interface of Eurowings.

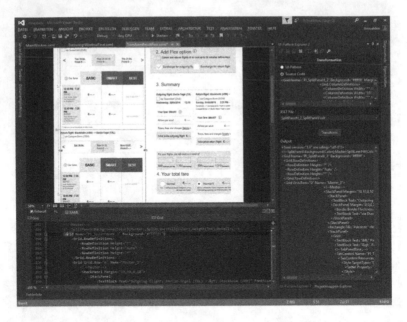

**Fig. 8.** Transformed detailed user interface of Eurowings within the Pattern Explorer 2 tool.

It is not astonishing, that based on the structure similarities even the detailed webpage of Norwegian could be generated (Fig. 9).

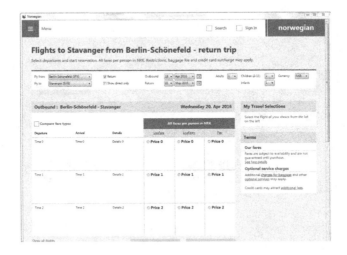

**Fig. 9.** Detailed webpage that is very similar to that of Norwegian.

Currently, the structure of the user interface has to be modeled by hand. That means that the creation of the result of the pattern instance applications has to be done by hand.

However, in the future it is planned to integrate the approach into a model-based tool chain that allows the generation of user interfaces. Parts of this tool chain can even be model-driven. A combination with the approach of Yigitbas et al. [18] seems to be promising.

## 3    Agile Development and Continuous Human-Centered Design

After introducing the developed tool a little bit, we will focus on the development process and in which way the tool could be used. Additionally, we are interested to combine the better of two worlds - the best of Human-Centered Design and Agile Development. The first principle of the Agile Manifesto [1] is: "Our highest priority is to satisfy the customer through early and continuous delivery of valuable software". According to this principle, customers are most important. This might be perfect from the business perspective because the customer has to pay the bill. However, from the quality aspect it is important to get the users involved as well.

User-Centered Design and nowadays Human-Centered Design are in the same way popular within the community of usability and user experience experts as agile methods for software engineers that focus on the application core. HCD focusses especially on the context of use and the evaluation of design decisions. That seems to be the major reasons for its popularity. In this context, user requirements are considered to be more important than functional requirements coming from the customer. Finally, the users will really get what they need to get their working tasks supported. ISO 9241-210 is a standard for the HCD process that consists of a planning phase and four phases that are performed in an iterative way.

In the first phase, stakeholders and their context of use are identified by analysts. Typical application scenarios are specified. Additionally, tasks that have to be supported are analyzed. Users and their roles are identified. The roles are related to tasks. However, tasks are also related to objects that are changed by performing the task or that are used as tools. Additionally, the context of use of the software under development is specified. This can be the location, the surrounding persons or objects and in some cases available services.

User requirements are specified based on this analysis. They contain besides functional and non-functional requirements additionally the goals of the users and their profiles.

First design solutions are produced afterwards. They have to fulfill the identified requirements. Such design solutions focus mainly on first ideas of user interfaces. This can be mock-ups or running prototypes.

In the last phase of the HCD process, developed design solutions are evaluated. Very often, the design solutions do not meet the requirements. They are not the wanted result. Therefore, new considerations have to be made. In the worst case, one has to start with the first phase again. The context of use has to be analyzed again. However, if the general analysis of the context of use seems to be correct but some requirements were specified in the wrong way, one has only to rewrite some requirements or has to identify some new ones. If only some design solutions did not meet the requirements, one has to look for an alternative design. The optimal case is of course if the requirements of the users are met immediately. In this case, the development process comes to an end and the implementation of the application core can be performed.

Most of the time there will be several cycles until the design fulfills the analyzed user requirements. A visual impression of the HCD process model is given by Fig. 10.

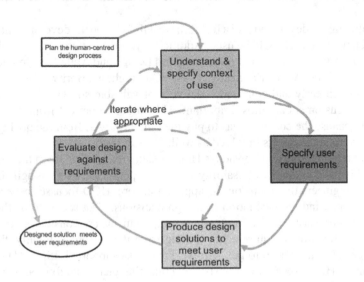

**Fig. 10.** The design process from ISO 9241-210–Human-centered design process (from https://thestandardinteractiondesignprocess.wordpress.com/).

Even that Fig. 10 provides a good overview of the main ideas of the HCD process, it does not provide hints how the idea of HCD can be integrated into the agile development process. However, the agile development process neglects the problems of HCD as well. Indeed, it would be perfect to have an integrated process model considering both aspects, the development of the application core and the development of the user interface. Additionally, a common understanding of the role of the users would be perfect.

A joined process model of both approaches was published by Paelke et al. [7]. They called it Agile UCD-Process. (User-Centered Design was the predecessor of HCD.). The process model suggests to have a common initial phase for developers and HCI specialists. Afterwards there are activities of both groups. Unfortunately, it is not quite clear in which order these activities are performed. Additionally, the requirements elicitation is a little bit too much uncoupled from the software development process. A stronger coupling was suggested by Paul et al. [9]. It additionally provides the names of models that have to be specified in the corresponding phase of the software development like user or task model.

Two interleaving processes for developers and HCI specialists are suggested by Sy [15]. She suggests that at the beginning, there has to be a common plan and some user data have to be gathered. Afterwards, developers start in the first development cycle with implementations that are not much related to the user interface. This could be e.g. certain services of the application that are not related to user interface aspects. In parallel HCI specialists provide certain design solutions for cycle two and gather customer data for cycle three.

In cycle two developers implement the design solutions from cycle one and in parallel their code from cycle one is tested by HCI specialists. Additionally, they design for the next cycle and analyze for the cycle after the next cycle. This is the general development pattern. In some way, interaction designers work two cycles ahead to developers in analyzing customer data and one cycle ahead in developing design solutions.

A similar approach by separating the activities of analysts and developers was presented in [2] for the SCRUM approach. The development cycle of analysts is executed in parallel to the cycle of the developers. It runs at least one cycle ahead.

The suggested process model starts with an initial phase of all project members to get a common understanding. Later it is intended that the HCD process is executed in parallel to the development of the software. The HCD process should always be executed on cycle ahead of the development process. This can be reached by in such a way that developers start with configuration of the software development tools and with some features not related to the user interface.

Following Sy [15], both cycles have always the same length. This is also the way, companies we interviewed, work at the moment. However, this number of observed companies is very small and the companies are not representative. We also recognized, that they most of the time do not evaluate alternative designs. Most of the time there is one design solution only and this solution goes into the final software system.

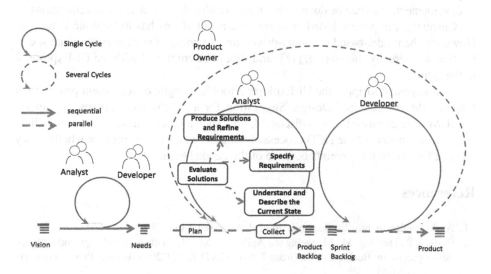

**Fig. 11.** Human-Centered Design Process for SCRUM.

Indeed, applying HCD methods is sometimes long lasting. The usage of question-naires and interviews could sometimes not be possible within one sprint. In this way, the HCD process could last two, three, or more sprints. A synchronization of these activities might be the challenge for the future. A precise analysis of the requirements and an intelligent planning would be necessary for these cases. It has to be observed in the future, how companies behave, whether they pick up this idea or have activities of the same length.

There is also the question, when to stop with the development. The distinction between development and maintenance might not be useful anymore. Maintenance, should also be done in an agile way and fits to the process of Fig. 11. Continuous Software Engineering might be a solution for that. It can be characterized as combination of Software Engineering, Human-Centered Design, and Business Administration. An overview of integrating SE and UE can be found in [14].

## 4    Summary and Outlook

In this paper, we discussed the advantages of following a pattern-based approach in designing user interfaces. It allows the transformation of existing user interfaces based on the exchange of one pattern instance by another one. In a case study based on the websites Eurowings, Lufthansa, and Norwegian it was shown that pattern-based repre-sentations and transformations on different level of abstraction were possible.

It was shown that the structure of the website from Norwegian differs to the structure of the website of Eurowings by some pattern transformations only. The results of the transformations on an abstract and on a detailed refined level were presented. In this way, different version of a user interface can be generated easily without many efforts. Partici-patory design can be supported is supported very well by the application of the UI-Explorer 2 tool. Evaluations of different alternatives can be performed in an early stage of development. This can be done with abstract or already very detailed specifications.

Currently, the pattern-based creation of user interfaces has to be done manually. However, the model-based or model-driven development of such user interface speci-fication was already shown (e.g. [18]) and should be combined with the UI-Explorer 2 in the future.

It is suggested to apply the UI-Explorer 2 tool in an agile development process that respects Human-Centered Design. Suggestion for a development process model for SRCUM were discussed. It was discussed, how such a process model could looks like, and whether sprints of the HCD process should last exactly one sprint or whether they can last for two or three sprints because of the needed time.

## References

1. Agile Manifesto. http://agilemanifesto.org/. Accessed 4 June 2015
2. Forbrig, P., Herczeg, M.: Managing the Agile process of human-centred design and software development. In: Beckmann, C., Gross T. (eds.) INTERACT 2015 Adjunct Proceedings, pp. 223–232 (2015)

3. Gamma, E., Helm, R., Johnson, R., Vlissides, J.: Design Patterns: Elements of Reusable Object-Oriented Software. Addison-Wesley Professional, Reading (1994)
4. Javahery, H., Seffah, A., Engelberg, D. and Sinnig, D.: Migrating user interfaces across platforms using HCI patterns. In: [13], pp. 241–259 (2004)
5. Kuusinen, K.: Task allocation between UX specialists and developers in agile software development projects. In: Abascal, J., Barbosa, S., Fetter, M., Gross, T., Palanque, P., Winckler, M. (eds.) INTERACT 2015. LNCS, vol. 9298, pp. 27–44. Springer, Heidelberg (2015)
6. Memmel, T., Gundelsweiler, F., Reiterer, H.: Agile human-centered software engineering. In: Proceedings of the 21st British HCI Group Annual Conference on People and Computers: HCI…but not as we know it (BCS-HCI 2007), vol. 1, pp. 167–175. British Computer Society, Swinton (2007)
7. Paelke, V., Nebe, K.: Integrating agile methods for mixed reality design space exploration. In: Proceedings of the 7th ACM Conference on Designing Interactive Systems (DIS 2008), pp. 240–249. ACM, New York. http://doi.acm.org/10.1145/1394445.1394471
8. Paul, M., Roenspieß, A., Mentler, T., Herczeg, M.: The usability engineering repository (UsER). In: Hasselbring, W., Ehmke, N.C. (eds.) Software Engineering 2014 - Fachtagung des GI-Fachbereichs Softwaretechnik, 25.-28. Februar 2014, Kiel. Gesellschaft für Informatik e.V. (GI), pp. 113–118 (2014)
9. Paul, M.: Systemgestützte Integration des Usability-Engineerings in den Software-Entwicklungsprozess, Ph.D. thesis, University of Lübeck (2015)
10. David Ricardo Do Vale Pereira, Uirá Kulesza: Refactoring a web academic information system using design patterns. SugarLoafPLoP 2010, pp. 17:1–17:14 (2010)
11. Richard, J., Robert, J.-M., Malo, S., Migneault, J.: Giving UI developers the power of UI design patterns. In: Smith, M.J., Salvendy, G. (eds.) HCII 2011, Part I. LNCS, vol. 6771, pp. 40–47. Springer, Heidelberg (2011)
12. Saurin, M: Integration der Werkzeugunterstützung für die Anwendung von UI-Patterns in der agilen Softwareentwicklung. Master Thesis, University of Rostock 2016 (2016)
13. Seffah, A., Javahery, H.: Multiple User Interfaces - Cross-Platform Applications and Context-Aware Interfaces. John Wiley & Sons, Ltd. (2004). ISBN: 0-470-85444-8
14. Sohaib, O., Khan, K.: Integrating usability engineering and agile software development: a literature review. In: Proceedings of the International Conference on Computer design and Applications (ICCDA), vol. 2, pp. 32–38 (2010)
15. Sy, D.: Adapting usability investigations for agile user-centered design. J. Usability Stud. 2(3), 112–132 (2007)
16. Tidwell, J.: Designing Interfaces. http://designinginterfaces.com/patterns/
17. Welie, M.: Patterns in interactive design. http://www.welie.com/patterns
18. Yigitbas, E., Mohrmann, B., Sauer, S.: Model-driven UI Development Integrating HCI Patterns. LMIS@EICS 2015, pp. 42–46 (2015)

# Human-Centered Software Engineering as a Chance to Ensure Software Quality Within the Digitization of Human Workflows

Holger Fischer[(✉)] and Björn Senft

SICP, Paderborn University, Zukunftsmeile 1, 33102 Paderborn, Germany
{hfischer,bsenft}@s-lab.upb.de

**Abstract.** Nowadays, a technological development boost can be observed within information technology and its application possibilities. This development results in a digitization of economic processes and human workflows, e.g. within the manufacturing industry. Furthermore, the discussion between digital assistance of employees vs. automation of processes leads to an ongoing change of work tasks or employees' responsibilities. Decision-makers will have to focus on organizational, human as well as on technological aspects to ensure organizational and employee's acceptance of digital solutions likewise. Despite all efforts, today's software products still lack of quality with regards to missing or unused functionality and bad usability. Thus, current software engineering methods seem to be insufficient. Therefore, this paper describes an iterative approach combining software engineering paradigms like human-centered design and agility to enable decision-makers within manufacturing industry to build digital tools that are accepted by their employees and are of value for the company itself.

**Keywords:** Digital transformation · Change · Acceptance · Workflows · Human-centered design · Agile · Software engineering · Work 4.0

## 1 Introduction

Having a look on today's occupations, there are lots of reasons why people work. The primary objective as well as the most important one is earning a living for themselves and their families [1]. Further objectives include to be part of the society, to create an own identity and to keep one's own dignity. Work is vital for everyone and for the society at all. It allows the people to participate, to use their talents, to find contact, recognition and validation within a community. Nowadays, we can perceive an evolution of the working environment due to the digitization of manual workflows, work places or tools. Digitization within the context of manufacturing industry describes the transformation process from traditional handmade activities towards computer-supported activities, e.g. operate

© IFIP International Federation for Information Processing 2016
Published by Springer International Publishing Switzerland 2016. All Rights Reserved
C. Bogdan et al. (Eds.): HCSE 2016/HESSD 2016, LNCS 9856, pp. 30–41, 2016.
DOI: 10.1007/978-3-319-44902-9_3

a robot or maintain a machine getting assistance through digital glasses. This ongoing change and its impacts on the employees is also known as a part of "Work 4.0" [2].

The overall term of Work 4.0 addresses multiple topics. Besides a cultural shift (e.g. work-life balance, demographic change), changes in the standard employment relationship or the globalized knowledge society, the main driver for all these topics is the digitization and automation of human workflows. Software solutions are increasing within the professional work context [3], e.g. enterprise resource planning (ERP) solutions in the administration, cooperative robots in the production or augmented reality glasses in the commissioning. The possibilities are versatile, but they also encourage further discussions about the impacts on the human working life. For example, thinking about the degree of automation within manufacturing industry, there are advantages and disadvantages for digital assistance systems as well as for the complete automation [4]. Shall the people or the system be in charge of control and decision within a process? Shall we store the organization's knowledge within the system or shall it be the knowledge of the employee to react on sudden anomalies?

Bainbridge [4] describes some ironies of automation in her previous work, which are still up to date. For example, developers of systems designate the human to be the main source of error and build an automated substitute. At the same time, these developers are also humans. Thus, operational errors are often development failures based on insufficient assumptions. In addition, employees are replaced with a system because these systems should be more efficient. Simultaneously, the employees shall monitor and maintain the system and manually take over if necessary using all their knowledge that was replaced by the system before. Hence, an adequate human-system interaction has to focus on the supply with status information as well as to ensure situational awareness at any time.

In summary, human working environments, workflows and areas of responsibilities are continuously changing. In addition, the concerns from outside the organization are rising, too. Planning a digitization within an organization challenge the persons in charge to take multiple perspectives into account (see Fig. 1) and deal with possible impacts of used technologies in advance, e.g. ensuring jobs, prevent the loss of knowledge, prevent a temporal condensation of work, increase the product quality. Therefore, modern software and system development will have to increase their focus on the employees using the systems. Project managers or IT departments cannot cope with the challenges on their own. Especially employees respectively end users have to participate in the change process due to the fact that they have to work with the systems at last. Thus, the individual and organizational acceptance as well as the usability and user experience of the system are crucial quality aspects. According to the World Quality Report [5], CIOs and IT executives nominate "Ensure end-user satisfaction" along with "Protect the corporate image" and "Increase quality awareness among all disciplines" for the main three top quality objectives in the quality assurance of software products. "Customer [or user] experience" is also one of the five top influences on today's IT strategies. Despite all efforts, today's software

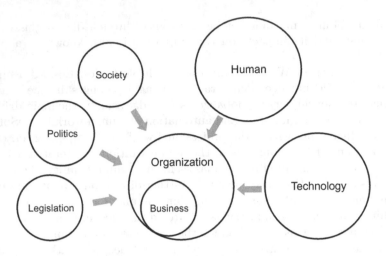

**Fig. 1.** Concerns from outside the organization

products still lack of quality with regard to functionality and usability. According to the CHAOS manifesto [6], approximately 45 % of the analyzed software projects have challenges within missing functionalities. In addition, business software in the European medium-sized enterprises lack on unused functionalities (36 %) as well as on unusable software (21 %) [7]. Thus, current software engineering (SE) methods seems to be insufficient, because they don't consider end users in terms of active involvement during the development process.

The challenge addressed in this design paper is to establish a participatory and iterative software engineering method combining paradigms like human-centered design (HCD) and agility. Thus, decision-makers within industrial manufacturing companies should be enabled to interdisciplinary build digital tools instead of monolithic systems that are accepted by their employees, by the work councils and are of value for the company itself.

The paper is structured as following: First, the authors discuss existing approaches of SE methods with a focus on users and iterations regarding their potentials for the use in the digitization within manufacturing industry. Then, the authors present some contexts from industry project and elicit requirements for an agile SE method. Finally, the concept is outlined and future work is described.

## 2   Related Work

Several different software development approaches exist that focus on user participation and iterative development. Therefore, an introduction to human-centered design and agile development is given. Furthermore, a brief overview of combined approaches is presented.

## 2.1  Human-Centered Design

Human-Centered Design (HCD) is an established methodology within software development with a focus on the users of a prospective system [8]. HCD intends to create interactive solutions that match the users' needs and expectations as well as to support their tasks towards their specific goals. The advantages are far-reaching and include increased productivity, improved quality of work, and increased user satisfaction [9]. One of the central quality attributes for interactive systems is their usability [10]. Especially tasks that are either time-sensitive or security-critical benefit from user interfaces (UI), which are suitable, easily to understand as well as controllable.

HCD includes lots of techniques to foster user participation (e.g. interviews, observation, prototyping, etc.), but it is still a discussion how to select appropriate techniques and how to integrate them on an operational level within existing software development processes. Thus, outcomes are mostly not directly convertible to software development, e.g. due to their narrative textual representation. Furthermore, HCD is living the prototyping and experimentation concept. Using paper-based or high-fidelity mockups, users' needs will be validated or even discovered during the ongoing development. Current software development methods mostly focus on evolutionary high-fidelity prototypes close to final user interface. However, low-fidelity paper-based prototype will encourage users to provide more feedback because they hold the status of incompleteness and enable people to think about their needs [11]. Hence, it will be necessary to "encourage" the organizations in order to ensure software quality using throw-away prototypes.

## 2.2  Agile Software Development

Agile development (e.g. Scrum [12]) enables an incremental development of software having a continuously runnable part of the software ready for reviews with the customer. Therefore, transparency and inspection are two key factors to create a common understanding within a project. However, agile development is not targeted on modeling user requirements and human behavior in a comprehensive way. Having inspections with the customer does not fulfill the expectations of having a broad analysis and evaluation with multiple users who are currently working with a system. Additionally, a systematic and documented way of decisions concerning the interaction or the UI as well as a systematic treatment of user feedback is missing. Talking about users within agile development often means customer feedback or user stories. Unfortunately, customers are not necessary real users of a system and may have a different idea about how a system should work. While the customers' focus is on the business values, the users are more related to their workflow and tasks. In addition, user stories that are only based on assumptions about users instead of empirical data might misdirect to unutilized functionalities.

Agile model-driven development (AMDD) is an approach to specify models and implement solutions in an agile manner. Hence, it foster iterations of specifications as well as on solutions. Ambler [13] propose a method to work on models, "which are just barely good enough that drive your overall development efforts". This is done in contrast to model-driven software development approaches, where extensive models are created before starting to write source code. Therefore, the AMDD lifecycle begins with an envisioning stage to specify initial requirements and to sketch an initial architecture. After that, the actual iterations start using model storming, modeling iteration and test-driven development stages completed by an optional review of the developed increment. The iterations are repeated until a software product result meets the requirements.

## 2.3    Agile HCD

Despite different positions towards requirements elicitation or upfront design, agile development and HCD have some similarities. Both focus on quality assurance while iterating with representative persons – business customers (agile development) or users (HCD) – to request continuous feedback. Thus, the main aspects are "quality", "iterations" and "active involvement".

Over the last years, several approaches have arisen that addresses the combination of agile methodologies and HCD. For example, Silva et al. [14] presented a systematic literature review identifying 58 relevant papers as well as defining eleven "agile usability patterns" [15] for the early stages of HCD [8]: Plan the HCD activities, describe the context of use, specify user requirements. Belchev and Baker [16] describe the pattern of having a "sprint zero", conducting one-to-one interviews in the users' workplace to better understand the overall view of a system before starting to develop. Sy and Miller [17] formulate the "one sprint ahead" pattern to enable and synchronize the communication between the development and UX team at defined times. Gothelf and Seiden [18] describes his experience being a "UX specialist as product owner" to take real user needs as well as customers' interests into account for the prioritization of the product backlog.

In summary, several approaches on user participation and iterative development exist. Software engineering methods based on the Agile Manifesto [19] (e.g. Scrum, XP, Kanban) help us to get more agile but focus on the development itself. Taking the findings of Adolph [20], agile itself is a relative concept, a time based strategy for operational success. It is about reacting to changing environments, respectively the model we have of an environment. This in an utterly important finding as it shifts the focus from a building perspective to a holistic view. Not only speeding up the development process is important, but also improving the decision process. This means that the whole organization have to be open-minded for agility instead of just the development itself. Existing agile methods focus on single detached solutions or monolithic systems, which become deployed at the end of the project. Addressing industrial manufacturing, it will become necessary to digitize the process step-by-step with multiple digital assistance services supporting human workflows. Deploying one digital service might lead to impacts within the organization (e.g. temporal condensation of work or changing tasks) and it will need an overall agility to react on these changing work environments. Thus, digitization will be an ongoing process without any real end and the feedback during the everyday runtime of digital services have to be taken into account.

# 3 Human-Centered Software Engineering Method

In order to develop a human-centered software engineering method for the manufacturing industry, the different contexts within three industrial projects have been analyzed using semi-structured one-to-one interviews as well as observations and visits of production facilities. Key questions of this procedure were: How does the workflows look like? Is digital assistance a topic and for which tasks? Are employees involved in the digitization process and how? Insights and statements by the participants have been transcribed. Afterwards, requirements for a software engineering method have been derived within a team workshop based on these information. Then, an engineering method has been sketched to discuss and evaluate its validity and applicability within the three industrial projects.

## 3.1 Digitization Within Manufacturing Industry

Having a look at the digitization of human workflows within manufacturing industry it is difficult to choose the suitable degree between digital assistance and complete automation (see Fig. 2). Taking the example of order picking, the first kind of digitization is the (1) "digital copy" of an actual workflow. Thus, a clipboard can be switch to a mobile device with a digital checklist. The overall workflow remains the same as before. A more automated digitization is the (2) "digital assistance". Using augmented reality (AR) and smart glasses the worker can be supported with a pick-by vision system. Thus, the workflow will change because the system undertakes human tasks and will make some automated decisions. Now, the first impacts of the system within the workplace environment might occur, because the person using the smart glasses might be distracted by the system and might not observe its surrounding carefully, e.g. a forklift truck that pass by. The third kind of digitization is the (3) "complete automation". A self-driving industrial truck might collect all parts from a warehouse by its own. The worker in charge will become unnecessary. Thus, all the knowledge about the process is implemented within the system. In a kind of system breakdown, the remaining worker might not be familiar with the previous picking process and the organization might struggle with the situation. Hence, the digitization of human workflows within manufacturing industry depends on the decision with multiple perspectives: business (e.g. reducing costs), human (e.g. changing tasks or responsibilities), society (e.g. work-life balance), politics (e.g. saving jobs) or legislation (e.g. work safety). Decision makers might not be able to predict every impacts before starting to work on a digital system. An agile and human-centered method will provide industrial organizations with an approach to deal with the challenge.

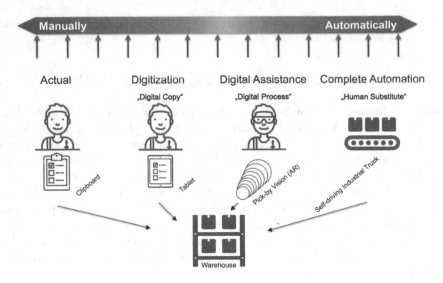

**Fig. 2.** Example: decision about the degree of automation within order picking

## 3.2   Industrial Contexts

**Case 1: Facade Engineering.** The organization of this case is active within the context of building construction and supports their customers (e.g. architects, engineers, constructors) with free of charge services in order to convince them to buy their building elements later on. Some stand-alone solutions exist that supports the involved people with some assistance. With the aim to improve the overall construction planning and coordination process and to connect existing solutions, a project has been set up to analyze the context of use within the company (sales, engineering, consulting) as well as with the users of their services.

**Case 2: Door and Window Fittings Production.** The organization of this case is specialized in the production of individual door and window fittings. The employees in the assembly line perform different task and have to pick the parts of an order from the warehouse or have to adjust their machines or tools according to the order specification. Every information is written on a printed paper sheet that accompany the product through the assembly line. Maintenance information are based on the experience of the employees. For example, information about the quality of drill heads from the ones of Brazil vs. the ones of France is individual knowledge and unknown by the sales department. A project has been set up to analyze possibilities for assistance services and to ensure the individual acceptance by the workers.

**Case 3: ATM Assembly.** The organization of this case produce all different kinds of self-service systems, e.g. automated teller machines (ATM). The automated production of the parts needed is followed by a manual assembly line. Multiply quality gates within this assembly line ensure the quality of the products. As the number of produced machines is low within each order due to individualization by the customer, quality problems are reported at a time when they cannot be fixed anymore. A project has been set up to identify possibilities for digitalization of paper-based documentation and quality assistance for the worker.

## 3.3 Requirements

Based on the analysis of the industrial contexts, some requirements were elicited to develop a software engineering method for the digitization within industrial manufacturing.

**Decision support:** The decision-makers within an organization have to decide which workflows they would like to digitize and in which way they would like to do this. They have to balance different perspectives with different objectives for a digitization. To take all perspectives into account, to foresee possible impacts and to formulate a strategy, a matrix of key performance indicators (KPI) have to be developed in order to ensure *organizational acceptance*.

**Employee participation:** All stakeholders (employee directly interacting with the system; employee that are affected by the system; employee that perceive itself to be affected by a decision, activity, or outcome) have to be involved in the software development lifecycle. They have to participate in every development stage starting with requirements elicitation in order to ensure an appropriate workplace design and *individual acceptance*.

**Big picture:** Dependencies of human workflows and organizational processes have to be identified in advance to achieve a broader view of the organization and to enable an appropriate interaction and user experience of digitized assistance services.

**Task suitability:** Users' tasks have to be elicited properly as the system represents a tool to support the users in fulfillment of their tasks and goals.

**Iterations:** User requirements have to be elicited over iterations to evoke implicit knowledge and user needs. The amount of iterations has to depend on the quality of a functionality.

**Agility:** The organizational culture have to allow agile management of workflows and assistance services during runtime in order to immediately react on impacts within the work environment.

**Interdisciplinary nature:** Interdisciplinary decision-maker teams have to be introduced comprising manager as well as workers, technology scientists, psychologists, sociologists and designer to deploy an appropriate digitization and to enable innovations through the employee. It will support the organizational change within the software-using organization and will create a feeling of participation and decision on the employee level.

**Architecture:** The systems' architecture has to be as flexible as possible to react on changed as well as on new added requirements for the digitization.

## 3.4   HCSE Method

An agile SE method has been developed in accordance with the defined requirements and the given context of manufacturing industry (see Fig. 3). It is divided into four major iterations: Envisioning, modelling, development, operation.

**Envisioning:** The approach starts with an envisioning stage to build an abstract "big picture" of participating roles, their responsibilities and interactions within the work environment. Thus, dependencies of human workflows and organizational processes as well as later impacts can be identified. Performing contextual inquiries with interviews and observations all stakeholders are analyzed and their context of use is described on an upper level using the concept of flow models (addressed earlier in [21]). Based on this abstract model of the organization a KPI matrix of acceptance criteria for organizational as well as individual acceptance of digital transformation is built. Thereby, a first architectural envisioning of a possible systems' architecture is conducted and quality metrics are defined. Digitization of complex human workflows is step-by-step project. Therefore, the system's architecture should be designed as flexible as possible using e.g. modularization concepts as well as service-oriented architectures (SOA). Hence, a kind of "service toolbox" with multiple assistance services for the workers may arise.

**Modelling:** To develop each assistance service the concrete human workflow that shall be digitized is analyzed using a deeper contextual inquiry. One focus is also on the workplace to identify restrictions, e.g. no space for installing a touch display or touch isn't an option due to safety gloves the worker wears. All analyzed information about the current workflow are described using task models, e.g. HAMSTER notation [22]. Then, the modeled tasks are allocated between the human or the system based on the acceptance criteria the team decided on before. Using these information, prescriptive task models are developed and the needed functionality is derivated. A first validation of the new concept can be achieved using evaluation techniques, e.g. focus groups. Preparing the development of the modeled assistance service a model-to-model (M2M) transformation is used. Thus, the task model is transformed into a dialog model respectively an abstract user interface (AUI) model using interaction description languages, e.g. IFML [23].

**Development:** The development of the user interface (UI) and the software functionality may be done according to model-driven user interface development paradigms, e.g. the CAMELEON reference framework [24]. Using model-to-model transformations, the AUI model is than transformed in a concrete user interface (CUI) model specified for the target platform. Based on the CUI model the initial code for the final user interface (FUI) can be generated with a model-to-code (M2C) transformation taking appropriate guidelines and style guides into account. Performing usability test with usability experts as well as with employees will ensure the quality of the interaction with the UI.

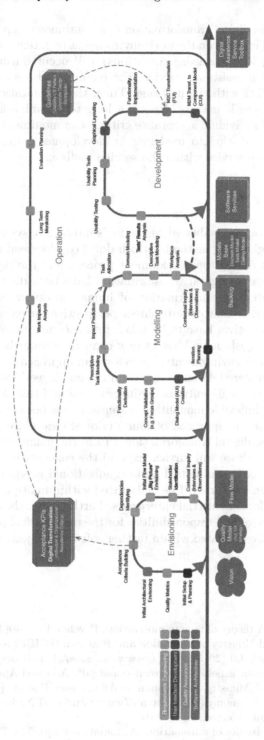

**Fig. 3.** Design & development method for employee-centered assistance systems

**Operation:** As the digital transformation is a continuous step-by-step project, lots of changes and impacts on the work environment (e.g. temporal condensation of work, changing job knowledge conditions) will occur during runtime after the deployment of a assistance service. For example, also an earlier deployed service might conflict with the new one. Thus, the organization should be set up according to an agile manner. Hence, a long term evaluation based on the organizational and individual acceptance criteria can monitor these changes and reflect the feedback back into modeling or development stage to improve or replace an assistance service within the service toolbox.

## 4 Conclusion

In this paper, the lack of quality within today's interactive systems due to insufficient software engineering methods, which don't consider end users in terms of active involvement during the development process, and the rigidity of requirements in the context of digital transformation have been discussed. The focus has been on the digital transformation of human workflows within the manufacturing industry. Next to the business perspective on reducing production costs, further perspectives have to be taken into account. Employees as well as society, politics or legislation addresses new challenges towards work structures, working time or work environments. Therefore, an approach has been presented that uses human-centered design to focus on the employees' workflow as well as iterations to set up an agile software engineering method that develop assistance services instead of inflexible monolithic systems. It has been shown, but not yet fully validated that the approach of four major stages addresses the specified requirements of the digital transformation within the manufacturing industry.

In our future work we will further expand the concepts in more detail. In a next step the matrix for individual and organizational acceptance criteria as a concept for decision support will be elaborated within multiple workshops with representatives of local industrial enterprises. Furthermore, the approach will be enriched defining roles and responsibilities for the most critical parts. All steps of the approach will be evaluated within further software projects as well as within teaching activities.

## References

1. Maslow, A.H.: A theory of human motivation. Psychol. Rev. **50**(4), 370–396 (1943)
2. German Federal Ministry of Education and Research (BMBF) re-imagining work - green paper work 4.0 (2015). http://www.bmas.de/SharedDocs/Downloads/DE/PDF-Publikationen/arbeiten-4-0-green-paper.pdf. Accessed April 2016
3. German Federal Ministry for Economic Affairs and Energy (BMWi) monitoring report digital economy (2014). http://www.bmwi.de/EN/Service/publications, did=686950.html. Accessed April 2016
4. Bainbridge, L.: Ironies of automation. Automatica **19**(6), 775–779 (1983)

5. Buenen, M., Walgude, A.: World quality report 2015–16, 7th edn. (2015). https://www.capgemini.com/thought-leadership/world-quality-report-2015-16. Accessed April 2016
6. Johnson, J.: CHAOS 2014. The Standish Group (2014)
7. Sage software GmbH: independent study on IT investments (2014). http://goo.gl/qy0eM0. Accessed April 2016
8. ISO 9241–210: Ergonomics of human-system interaction - Part 210: Human-centred design for interactive systems (2010)
9. Jokela, T.: An assessment approach for user-centred design processes. In: Proceedings of EuroSPI 2001. Limerick Institute of Technology Press, Limerick (2001)
10. Bevan, N.: Quality in use - meeting user needs for quality. J. Syst. Softw. **49**, 89–96 (1999). Elsevier Science Inc., New York
11. Walker, M., Takayama, L., Landay, J.A.: High-fidelity or low-fidelity, paper or computer? Choosing attributes when testing web prototypes. In: Proceedings of the Human Factors and Ergonomics Society Annual Meeting, vol. 46, no. 5, pp. 661–665 (2002)
12. Schwaber, K., Sutherland, J.: The Scrum Guide (2013). http://www.scrumguides.org. Accessed April 2016
13. Ambler, S.W.: Agile model driven development (AMDD): the key to scaling agile software development. http://agilemodeling.com/essays/amdd.htm. Accessed April 2016
14. da Silva, T.S., Martin, A., Maurer, F., Silveira, M.: User-centered design and agile methods: a systematic review. In: Proceedings of the AGILE Conference, pp. 77–86. IEEE Computer Society, Washington (2011)
15. Bertholdo, A.P.O., da Silva, T.S., de O. Melo, C., Kon, F., Silveira, M.S.: Agile usability patterns for UCD early stages. In: Marcus, A. (ed.) DUXU 2014, Part I. LNCS, vol. 8517, pp. 33–44. Springer, Heidelberg (2014)
16. Belchev, B., Baker, P.: Improving Obama campaign software: learning from users. In: Proceedings of the AGILE Conference, pp. 395–399. IEEE Computer Society, Washington (2009)
17. Sy, D., Miller, L.: Optimizing agile user-centred design. In: Proceedings of CHI Extended Abstracts on Human Factors in Computing Systems, pp. 3897–3900. ACM, New York (2008)
18. Gothelf, J., Seiden, J.: Lean UX: Applying Lean Principles to Improve User Experience. O'Reilly, Sebastopol (2012)
19. Manifesto for agile software development (2001). http://www.agilemanifesto.org. Accessed June 2016
20. Adolph, S.: What lessons can the agile community learn from a maverick fighter pilot. In: Proceedings of the AGILE Conference, pp. 1–6. IEEE Computer Society, Washington (2006)
21. Fischer, H., Rose, M., Yigitbas, E.: Towards a task driven approach enabling continuous user requirements engineering. In: 2nd Workshop on Continuous Requirements Engineering (CRE) (REFSQ-JP 2016), CEUR-WS.org, vol. 1564 (2016)
22. Martinie, C., Navarre, D., Palanque, P.: A multi-formalism approach for model-based dynamic distribution of user interfaces of critical interactive systems. Int. J. Hum. Comput. Stud. **72**(1), 77–99 (2014). Academic Press, Duluth
23. Interaction flow modeling language (IFML). http://www.ifml.org
24. Calvary, G., Coutaz, J., Thevenin, D., Limbourg, Q., Bouillon, L., Vanderdonckt, J.: A unifying reference framework for multi-target user interfaces. Interact. Comput. **15**, 289–308 (2003). Elsevier

# Usability Evaluation and Testing

# Usability Problems Experienced by Different Groups of Skilled Internet Users: Gender, Age, and Background

Jane Billestrup[⊠], Anders Bruun, and Jan Stage

Department of Computer Science, Aalborg University,
9220 Aalborg East, Denmark
{jane,bruun,jans}@cs.aau.dk

**Abstract.** Finding the right test persons to represent the target user group, when conducting a usability evaluation is considered essential by the HCI research community. This paper explores data from a usability evaluation with 41 participants with high IT skills, to examine if age, gender, and job function or educational background, has an impact on the amount and types of usability problems experienced by the users. All usability problems were analysed and categorised through closed coding, to group the test persons differently in relation to gender, age, and job function or educational background. The study found that the usability problems experienced across gender, age group and job function or educational background, are approximately the same. This indicates that the usual characteristics of test persons, might not be as important, and opens up for further research in regards to, if users with different skill levels, in regards to internet usage, might be more applicable.

**Keywords:** Usability evaluation · Test persons · Demography

## 1 Introduction

Usability evaluation is a strong tool for identifying areas of an interactive system that need improvement. In practice, one of the key challenges for usability evaluators is to find users that can participate as tests subjects. Recruitment of test subjects is challenging, and the time required for test sessions and the subsequent data analysis is usually dependent on the number of the number of test subjects. Therefore, there have been attempts to determine the minimal number of test users required for a usability evaluation [4, 7, 11].

Combining Other researchers have criticised these attempts to define the minimal number. One of the arguments is that different users experience different usability problems [6, 9]. In these discussions, there has been little evidence as to the actual differences between the usability problems experienced by different groups of users.

For specialised systems that are used by a homogeneous group of users, this issue is not particularly relevant. However, for systems that are aimed at diverse and heterogeneous groups of users, it is highly relevant.

© IFIP International Federation for Information Processing 2016
Published by Springer International Publishing Switzerland 2016. All Rights Reserved
C. Bogdan et al. (Eds.): HCSE 2016/HESSD 2016, LNCS 9856, pp. 45–55, 2016.
DOI: 10.1007/978-3-319-44902-9_4

This paper presents results from an exploratory study of the usability problems experienced by different users. The focus of this study was to what extent different test persons, who are all experienced internet users, experience different types of usability problems, across gender, age, and educational background or job function.

The system we evaluated was a government data dissemination website aimed at a very broad user population. In the following section, the related work is presented, followed by a description of the method used for data collection and analysis. Then the results are presented, and finally, the results are discussed and concluded upon.

## 2 Related Work

The question about the number of test subjects needed in a usability evaluation has been discussed for many years. Virzi [11] focused on the need exists to reduce the cost of applying good design practices, such as user testing, to the development of user interfaces. He was one of the first to experiment with the number of test subjects needed. Over a series of 3 experiments, he found that 80 % of the usability problems were detected with four or five subjects, additional subjects were less and less likely to reveal new information, and the most severe usability problems were likely to be detected with the first few subjects. In the experiments, he used test subjects who were from the surrounding community or undergraduate students. There is no further description of their demography.

Lewis [7] emphasices that the aim of a usability evaluation is to have representative participants. He reports from an experiment with fifteen employees of a temporary help agency who all had at least three months' experience with a computer system but had no programming training or experience. Five were clerks or secretaries and ten were business professionals. In this study, using five participants uncovered only 55 % of the problems. To uncover 80 % of the problems would require 10 participants. The results show that additional participants discover fewer and fewer problems. The most important result was that problem discovery rates were the same regardless of the problem severity. Again, there is no concern for the demography of the test subjects.

Caulton [2] argues that the results obtained in these early experiments were based on the assumption that all types of users have the same probability of encountering all usability problems, and he denotes this as the homogeneity assumption. If that is violated, more subjects are needed. He argues that with heterogeneous user groups, problem detection with a given number of subjects is reduced. The more subgroups, the lower the proportion of problems expected. If ten unknown user subgroups exist, 50 randomly sampled subjects should yield 80 % of the problems.

Law and Hvannberg [6] have worked more on the influence of subgroups on problem detection through an experiment with usability tests conducted in four different European countries. They conclude that the heterogeneity of subgroups in a test will dilute the problem detection rate. Not only for severe problems but also for moderate and minor ones, the diluting effect implied a reduction. The problem detection rate for the severe problems is significantly higher than for the less severe, but the absolute value for the severe problems is not particularly high. Between nine and ten participants were required to uncover 80 % of the severe problems, whereas

15 participants were required to uncover 80 % of the minor problems. In addition, they found no significant correlation between problem detection rate and problem severity level. Based on their results, they reject that so-called "magic five" assumption as 11 participants were required to obtain 80 % of the usability problems.

More recently, there has been another attempt to define a specific "magic" number [4]. This new attempt has been criticised for being flawed [9]. A detailed analysis has been made of the use of the "magic five" assumption. None of these or the previous references in this area have explored in more detail how heterogeneous different subgroups are and how different user groups experience different usability problems.

## 3 Method

We have conducted an exploratory study of usability problems experienced by different user groups. This section describes how the data was collected and analysed.

### 3.1 Data Collection

The data was gathered through a usability evaluation of a data dissemination website (dst.dk). This site provides publicly available statistics about the population (e.g. educational level or IT skills), the economy, employment situation, etc.

**Test Persons.** All test persons were invited through emails distributed across the university. For this study data from 41 usability evaluations were included. The test persons consist of 12 faculty members from Ph.D students to professors, from different departments, 15 students in technical or non-technical educations, and 14 participants from technical and administrative staff from different departments. All participants received a gift with a value of approximately 20 USD for their participation. An overview of the participants can be seen in Table 1 on the following page.

All test persons were placed in one of six groups in regards to gender and age. The test persons varied in age between 21 and 66 years and consisted of 19 males and 22 females. All test persons were asked to assess their own skill level in regards to Internet usage on a scale from 1 to 5, where 1 was the lowest and 5 the highest score. The average for each group is shown in the table, none of the 41 test persons assessed themselves lower than 4. Originally 43 usability evaluations were conducted, but the data from two usability evaluations were excluded from this study, due to these test persons assessed themselves at skill level 3 in regards to Internet usage. All test persons were asked if they were familiar with, and used this website. 19 people answered that they had never used the website, 20 answered that they were familiar with the site and used it approximately once a year, and, two people answered that they use the website approximately once a month.

**Usability Evaluations.** All tests were conducted as think-aloud evaluations in a usability laboratory. The test monitor and test person were placed in different rooms and communicated through microphone and speakers in order to avoid the possibility of the test moderator's body language or other visible expressions, influencing each test person. All test persons were asked to fill out a short questionnaire after the test in regards to their participation.

**Tasks.** Each user solved eight tasks all varying in difficulty. Examples of this were that the first task was to find the total number of people living in Denmark while a more difficult task was to find the number hotels and restaurants with one single employee in a particular area of Denmark.

**Data Handling.** All usability evaluations were recorded and the collected recordings were analysed by conducting video analysis. All recordings were analysed by two evaluators. Both evaluators had extensive previous experience in analysing video data. The videos were analysed in different random order, to reduce possible bias from learning.

**Table 1.** Demography for the 41 test persons.

| Number of people in each category | Age | Age average | Gender | Backgrounds | Average Internet experience |
|---|---|---|---|---|---|
| 6 | < 27 | 24 | M | 5 Computer Science students 1 Computer Science faculty member | 5 |
| 8 | < 27 | 22 | F | 5 Computer science students 2 humanities students 1 office trainee | 4.6 |
| 8 | 27–44 | 36 | M | 4 computer science faculty members 1 social science faculty member 1 technical staff 1 administrative staff 1 engineering student | 4.8 |
| 8 | 27–44 | 38 | F | 6 administrative staff 1 social science faculty member 1 information science student | 4.3 |
| 5 | 44 < | 55 | M | 3 computer science faculty members 1 faculty member medicine 1 technical staff | 4.8 |
| 6 | 44 < | 50 | F | 4 administrative staff 1 faculty member computer science 1 faculty member medicine | 4.5 |

The following characteristics were used to determine a usability problem;

(A)  Slowed down relative to their normal work speed
(B)  Inadequate understanding e.g. does not understand how a specific functionality operates or is activated
(C)  Frustration (expressing aggravation)
(D)  Test moderator intervention
(E)  Error compared to correct approach.

The data handling resulted in a list of 147 usability problems after duplicates had been removed. To determine similarities between problems from each list, the usability problems found by each evaluator were discussed. Across the analysis, the evaluators had an any-two agreement of 0.44 (SD = 0.11), which is relatively high compared to other studies [3]. Further information about the data collection can be found in [1].

**Data Analysis.** We also uncovered which types of usability problems that were experienced by the different groups of participants. We did this through closed coding [10] where each problem was categorised according to the 12 types listed in Nielsen et al. [8]. Two of the authors conducted this coding and did so independently of each other. It was decided in advance that the raters would code all and only use the data from the codings where the authors agreed on the category independently of each other. An interrater reliability analysis using the Fleiss Kappa statistic was performed to validate the result. This determines the level of consistency among the two raters. The result of was a moderate level of agreement (Kappa = 0.44, p < 0.001, 95 % CI =0.37, 0.52) [5]. The 12 categorised used for this study are described next.

**Affordance** relates to issues on the user's perception versus the actual properties of an object or interface.
**Cognitive load** regards the cognitive efforts necessary to use the system.
**Consistency** concerns the consistency in labels, icons, layout, wording, commands etc. on the different screens.
**Ergonomics** covers issues related to the physical properties of interaction.
**Feedback** regards the manner in which the interface relays information back to the user on an action that has been done and notifications about system events.
**Information** covers the understandability and amount of information presented by the interface at a given moment.
**Interaction styles** concern the design strategy and determine the structure of interactive resources in the interface.
**Mapping** is about the way in which controls and displays correlate to natural mappings and should ideally mimic physical analogies and cultural standards.
**Navigation** regards the way in which the users navigate from screen to screen in the interface.
**Task flow** relates to the order of steps in which tasks ought to be conducted.
**User's mental model** covers problems where the interactive model, developed by the user during system use, does not correlate with the actual model applied to the interface.
**Visibility** regards the ease with which users are able to perceive the available interactive resources at a given time.

The coding and analysis by two raters resolved in a list of 83 coded usability problems, out of originally 147 usability problems. This reduction happened as all usability problems where the raters did not agree on the category was removed from the study.

These categorisations were used to distinguish if test persons experienced the same type of usability problems, or if there were deviations across gender, age, job function or educational background. The results of this analysis are presented in the following section.

## 4  Results

In this section, we present the results from conducting this study. The results are presented from four different perspectives. First, the test persons are divided into males and females, then into the three age groups without taking the gender into perspective, then, the test persons are divided into groups both in regards to age and gender, and finally, the test persons are divided into groups in regards to education or work function. This was conducted to show if gender, age or background plays a role in regards to differences in the perceiving of usability problems. The numbers shown in the tables in the result section represent an average number of usability problems found per test person in each category. This was conducted to be able to compare groups containing different numbers of test persons, and still make the numbers comparable.

The results show that problems were found in regards to five of the twelve closed codings. Affordance, Cognitive Load, Feedback, Information, and Visibility, respectively. As problems were not found relating to Consistency, Ergonomics, Interaction Styles, Mapping, Navigation, User's Mental Model, and Task Flow, these categorisations will not be mentioned further.

Note that all results are based on the number of problems to which the two raters agreed on the categorisations, e.g. if the two raters did not agree on the code of a particular problem, this was excluded from the result. Out of the total 147 problems the raters agreed on 83.

### 4.1  Gender

We analysed whether males and females with similar skills in regards to internet usage experienced the same amount and type of usability problems. The results are presented in Table 2.

An independent samples t-test revealed no significant differences in the total number of experienced between the genders ($t = -0.9$, $df = 39$, $p > 0.2$). We did, however find significant differences when considering the problem types related to feedback ($t = -1.2$, $df = 10$, $p < 0.01$) and information ($t = -1.8$, $df = 39$, $p < 0.01$).

**Table 2.** The average number of usability problems experienced when dividing the test persons by gender.

| Group statistics | | | | | |
|---|---|---|---|---|---|
| Gender | | N | Mean | Std. deviation | Std. error mean |
| Affordance | M | 10 | 1,40 | 0,516 | 0,163 |
| | F | 11 | 1,36 | 0,674 | 0,203 |
| Cognitive load | M | 19 | 2,32 | 2,126 | 0,490 |
| | F | 22 | 3,77 | 2,159 | 0,460 |
| Feedback | M | 7 | 1,00 | 0,000 | 0,000 |
| | F | 5 | 1,20 | 0,447 | 0,200 |
| Information | M | 19 | 3,58 | 1,610 | 0,369 |
| | F | 22 | 4,95 | 2,952 | 0,629 |
| Visibility | M | 17 | 2,00 | 1,225 | 0,297 |
| | F | 19 | 1,58 | 0,769 | 0,176 |
| Total | M | 19 | 9,79 | 3,896 | 0,894 |
| | F | 22 | 11,05 | 4,904 | 1,045 |

## 4.2  Age

We also analysed if age had an impact on the experienced amount of usability problems. The results are presented in Table 3 on the following page.

A one-way ANOVA test revealed no significant differences in number of experienced problems between the three age groups ($F = 1.02$, df = 40, $p > 0.3$).

**Table 3.** Usability problems experienced by different age groups.

| | | N | Mean | Std. deviation |
|---|---|---|---|---|
| Affordance | <27 | 5 | 1,40 | 0,548 |
| | 27–44 | 9 | 1,56 | 0,726 |
| | >44 | 7 | 1,14 | 0,378 |
| | Total | 21 | 1,38 | 0,590 |
| Cognitive load | <27 | 14 | 3,79 | 2,326 |
| | 27–44 | 16 | 3,81 | 2,257 |
| | >44 | 11 | 2,91 | 1,700 |
| | Total | 41 | 3,56 | 2,134 |
| Feedback | <27 | 5 | 1,00 | 0,000 |
| | 27–44 | 6 | 1,17 | 0,408 |
| | >44 | 1 | 1,00 | |
| | Total | 12 | 1,08 | 0,289 |
| Information | <27 | 14 | 5,29 | 2,555 |
| | 27–44 | 16 | 4,19 | 2,562 |
| | >44 | 11 | 3,27 | 2,005 |
| | Total | 41 | 4,32 | 2,494 |

*(Continued)*

**Table 3.** (*Continued*)

|  |  | N | Mean | Std. deviation |
|---|---|---|---|---|
| Visibility | <27 | 13 | 1,62 | 0,961 |
|  | 27–44 | 13 | 1,69 | 0,855 |
|  | >44 | 10 | 2,10 | 1,287 |
|  | Total | 36 | 1,78 | 1,017 |
| Total | <27 | 14 | 11,43 | 4,767 |
|  | 27–44 | 16 | 10,69 | 4,771 |
|  | >44 | 11 | 8,91 | 3,419 |
|  | Total | 41 | 10,46 | 4,456 |

### 4.3 Job Function and Educational Background

Finally, we analysed if a large number of test persons with a background in computer science had an impact in regards to the amount of usability problems experienced. The results are presented in Table 4.

The table shows, that when dividing the test persons into job function or educational background, students which are not in computer science, experience more problems related to cognitive load and information. A one-way ANOVA test revealed no significant differences in the total number of problems experienced across job function or educational background ($F = 0.6$, $df = 40$, $p > 0.6$).

**Table 4.** The average amount of usability problems experienced when dividing the test persons in regards to job function or educational background.

|  |  | N | Mean | Std. deviation |
|---|---|---|---|---|
| Affordance | Other students | 2 | 1,00 | 0,000 |
|  | CS students | 3 | 1,67 | 0,577 |
|  | TAP | 10 | 1,50 | 0,707 |
|  | CS faculty | 3 | 1,00 | 0,000 |
|  | Other faculty | 3 | 1,33 | 0,577 |
|  | Total | 21 | 1,38 | 0,590 |
| Cognitive load | Other students | 4 | 5,75 | 0,500 |
|  | CS students | 11 | 3,27 | 2,195 |
|  | TAP | 15 | 3,47 | 1,846 |
|  | CS faculty | 7 | 4,00 | 2,887 |
|  | Other faculty | 4 | 1,75 | 0,500 |
|  | Total | 41 | 3,56 | 2,134 |
| Feedback | Other students | 0 |  |  |
|  | CS students | 3 | 1,00 | 0,000 |
|  | TAP | 3 | 1,00 | 0,000 |
|  | CS faculty | 4 | 1,00 | 0,000 |

(*Continued*)

**Table 4.** (*Continued*)

| | | N | Mean | Std. deviation |
|---|---|---|---|---|
| | Other faculty | 2 | 1,50 | 0,707 |
| | Total | 12 | 1,08 | 0,289 |
| Information | Other students | 4 | 5,00 | 3,559 |
| | CS students | 11 | 4,55 | 2,067 |
| | TAP | 15 | 4,87 | 3,021 |
| | CS faculty | 7 | 3,14 | 1,069 |
| | Other faculty | 4 | 3,00 | 1,826 |
| | Total | 41 | 4,32 | 2,494 |
| Visibility | Other students | 3 | 1,33 | 0,577 |
| | CS students | 10 | 1,60 | 1,075 |
| | TAP | 14 | 1,79 | 0,802 |
| | CS faculty | 6 | 2,33 | 1,506 |
| | Other faculty | 3 | 1,67 | 1,155 |
| | Total | 36 | 1,78 | 1,017 |
| Total | Other students | 4 | 12,25 | 4,031 |
| | CS students | 11 | 10,00 | 4,123 |
| | TAP | 15 | 11,20 | 5,003 |
| | CS faculty | 7 | 10,14 | 4,140 |
| | Other faculty | 4 | 7,75 | 4,787 |
| | Total | 41 | 10,46 | 4,456 |

# 5  Discussion

This study has focused on comparing the amount of usability problems found when grouping the test persons in regards to gender, age, and job function or educational background. This was conducted as all test persons assessed themselves as experienced internet users, as each rated themselves as either 4 or 5 on a scale from 1 to 5, where five was the highest score. This way, it could be explored if test persons of a high degree of internet skills experienced different types of usability problems, or if they could be considered a homogeneous group, where neither age, gender, and job function or educational background made a difference in regards to the average amount of usability problems.

## 5.1  Comparison with Related Work

Related work has shown that the amount of needed test persons varies [7, 11]. As demographical data was not included in these studies it is not possible for us to draw any conclusions in relation to the results from this study, though it raises the question of, if the test persons chosen by Virzi [11] were more homogeneous than the test persons chosen by Lewis [7] in regards to the skills of Internet usage or IT in general.

This study has found indications that a user group can be homogeneous though a variety in age and background. Our results indicated that the test persons from this study experience around the same amount of usability problems in regard to each categorization (Affordance, Cognitive Load, Feedback, Information, Visibility), across gender, age, and background. This corresponds with Caultons' conclusions about homogeneous user groups experiencing the same usability problems [2].

This study shows no greater difference in regards to the types of usability problems experienced by the test persons. This does not correspond with the findings of Law and Hvannberg who concluded that the heterogeneity of subgroups in a test will dilute the problem detection rate [6].

### 5.2   Implications for Usability Practitioners

Though further research is needed, this study indicates that recruiting test persons across gender, and age might not be necessary, as these findings show that users with approximately the same level of skills in regards to Internet usage, experience the same amount of usability problems. If, the indication that skill level is key, when recruiting test persons for usability evaluations, this means that the most important is to recruit test persons of all skill levels of the target user group for the website or application, and, that variety in age or gender is not important when recruiting test persons. The implications might especially be of interest, when developing websites or applications for large heterogeneous user groups e.g. public websites or self-service applications, as these types of sites are targeted for all citizens in a country. This will make it challenging to represent all types of users when conducting usability evaluations, as a lot of test persons would need to be recruited, and it would be costly to conduct this amount of usability evaluations. On the contrary, if test persons only need to be recruited in regards to their skill level of Internet usage and IT in general, this would reduce the cost considerably.

## 6   Conclusion

This paper presents a study of to what extent different test persons, who are all experienced internet users, experience different types of usability problems. This has been presented across age, gender, and educational background or job function. The results are interesting as it is indicated that the usability problems experienced by users with a high level of internet experience do not vary significantly, across gender, age or background. This means that finding test persons might not have to be balanced in regards to neither gender or age, but that is more important to find test persons on all levels of internet experience in the target user group. Our results also indicate that people with an education in Computer Science do not experience significantly fewer usability problems, than other experienced internet users.

## 6.1    Limitations

We do recognise that further studies need to be conducted to be able to actually draw conclusions across user groups at different levels of Internet experience and that these results do not provide enough evidence to definitively rejecting the previously mentioned criticism of the "homogeneity assumption" by Law and Hvannberg [6]. This means that further research should be conducted with more homogeneous user groups with different levels of internet skills, and not just one group of experienced users. As it needs to be investigated further if these results also are valid for other user groups with lower skill levels in regards to Internet usage.

We also recognise the limitations of our test persons having a higher educational background and a self-reported high expertise in internet usage. Also the fact that a lot of the found usability problems were discarded at the coding phase and therefore not included in the data analysis.

## References

1. Bruun, A., Stage, J.: An empirical study of the effects of three think-aloud protocols on identification of usability problems. In: Abascal, J., et al. (eds.) INTERACT 2015. LNCS, vol. 9297, pp. 159–176. Springer, Heidelberg (2015)
2. Caulton, D.A.: Relaxing the homogeneity assumption in usability testing. Behav. Inf. Technol. 20(1), 1–7 (2001)
3. Hertzum, M., Jacobsen, N.E.: The evaluator effect: a chilling fact about usability evaluation methods. Int. J. Hum. Comput. Interac. 15, 183–204 (2003)
4. Hwang, W., Salvendy, G.: Number of people required for usability evaluation: The 10 ± 2 rule. Commun. ACM 53(5), 130–133 (2010)
5. Landis, J.R., Koch, G.G.: The measurement of observer agreement for categorical data. Biometrics 33, 159–174 (1977)
6. Law, E.L.-C., Hvannberg, E.: Analysis of combinatorial user effect in international usability test. In: Proceedings of CHI (2004)
7. Lewis, J.R.: Sample sizes for usability studies: Additional considerations. Hum. Factors 36, 368–378 (1994)
8. Nielsen, C.M., Overgaard, M., Pedersen, M.B., Stage, J., Stenild, S.: It's worth the hassle! the added value of evaluating the usability of mobile systems in the field. In: Proceedings of NordiCHI. ACM Press (2006)
9. Schmettow, M.: Sample size in usability studies. Commun. ACM 55(4), 64–70 (2012)
10. Strauss, A., Corbin, J.: Grounded theory methodology. Handbook of qualitative research (1994)
11. Virzi, R.A.: Refining the test phase of usability evaluation: how many subjects is enough? Hum. Factors 34, 457–468 (1992)

# User-Test Results Injection into Task-Based Design Process for the Assessment and Improvement of Both Usability and User Experience

Regina Bernhaupt[1], Philippe Palanque[2], François Manciet[1], and Célia Martinie[2(✉)]

[1] ruwido austria gmbh, Köstendorfer Straße 8, 5202 Neumarkt a. W., Austria
{regina.bernhaupt,francois.manciet}@ruwido.com
[2] ICS-IRIT, University of Toulouse, 118, route de Narbonne, 31062 Toulouse, France
{palanque,martinie}@irit.fr

**Abstract.** User Centered Design processes argue for user testing in order to assess and improve the quality of the interactive systems developed. The underlying belief is that the findings from user testing related to usability and user experience will inform the design of the interactive system in a relevant manner. Unfortunately reports from the industrial practice indicate that this is not straightforward and a lot of data gathered during user tests is hard to understand and exploit. This paper claims that injecting results from user-tests in user-tasks descriptions support the exploitation of user test results for designing the n+1 prototype. In order to do so, the paper proposes a set of extensions to current task description techniques and a process for systematically populating task models with data and analysis gathered during user testing. Beyond the already known advantages of task models, these enriched task models provide additional benefits in different phases of the development process. For instance, it is possible to go beyond standard task-model based performance evaluation exploiting real performance data from usability evaluation. Additionally, it also supports task-model based comparisons of two alternative systems. It can also support performance prediction and overall supports identification of usability problems and identifies shortcomings for user experience. The application of such a process is demonstrated on a case study from the interactive television domain.

**Keywords:** Task models · Usability evaluation · User experience evaluation · Process

## 1 Introduction

User-Centered Design (UCD) processes argue for user testing in order to assess and improve the quality of the interactive systems developed. User-centered design and development is typically performed iteratively with four major phases: (1) Analysis, (2) Design, (3) Development/Implementation and (4) Evaluation [4]. In the analysis phase the main goal is to understand who is (or will be) using the system, in what kind of environment and for what kind of activities or tasks. Many notations, processes and

© IFIP International Federation for Information Processing 2016
Published by Springer International Publishing Switzerland 2016. All Rights Reserved
C. Bogdan et al. (Eds.): HCSE 2016/HESSD 2016, LNCS 9856, pp. 56–72, 2016.
DOI: 10.1007/978-3-319-44902-9_5

tools have been proposed for gathering information about the users either in formal (via formal requirements as in [27] or formal task models [37]) or informal ways (via brainstorming [11] or prototyping [43]). One of the main advantages put forward by notations is that they make it possible to handle real-size applications and, if provided with a formal semantics, make it possible to reason about the models built with the notations and assess the presence or absence of properties.

The design phase encompasses activities to create or construct the system according to the analysis results. In the development phase the system is implemented and builds the basis for the evaluation of the interactive system [33].

One of the most used methods to evaluate early versions of a system or a prototype is user testing. The term user testing is broadly used in the area of human-computer interaction but in general describes any form of evaluation of an interactive system that involves users. User testing is associated with evaluating usability and now also incorporates user experience evaluation [18]. Goal of user testing is to gather feedback from users to identify usability problems or to understand what type of experience users have when interacting with the product. User testing can be classified into user tests that are either performed in the laboratory or in the field [29], where a user is asked to perform a set of tasks during that study. Users performance is typically observed and recorded (by video and for example measuring bio-physiological data) and users are asked for verbal responses (interviews) or ratings (e.g. via standardized questionnaires like SUS [8] or AttrakDiff [2].).

One key limitation for the majority of such user testing is how the results are made available for the next iteration in the design and development process [18]. To help inform the next iteration of a prototype, product and system, this information would be ideally fed back to the analysis phase to inform or improve design.

To support usability and user experience (UX) as key software qualities in the design and development cycle there is a need to:

(1) find a way to *document* the results of evaluation studies,
(2) allow the *comparison* of alternative approaches or systems,
(3) enable *prediction* of user behaviour and performance,
(4) support analysis of *usability* problems (efficiency, effectiveness and satisfaction), and
(5) show how different functions or tasks of the user contribute to the various user experience dimensions like aesthetics, emotion, identification, meaning and value and in general to the overall *user experience*.

Goal of this paper is to show a solution for how to integrate results from user tests in task models to support documentation, comparison, prediction and analysis of usability problems and relation of tasks to the overall user experience.

The paper is structured as follows: section two presents a state of the art on usability evaluation with a focus on user testing and an overview on user experience evaluation followed by a short overview on task analysis and modelling.

Section three describes our proposed process model and section four shows how this process model was applied in a case study in the area of interactive TV. We conclude with a summary and a discussion of the paper in section five.

## 2 State of the Art

### 2.1 Usability Evaluation Methods

Usability Evaluation is a phase in iterative UCD processes with the goal to investigate if the system is efficient to be used, effective when used and if users are satisfied [19]. Another central goal is to understand how users learn to use the system and (for complex systems) how to train users. Methods for usability evaluation can be classified in methods that are performed by usability experts, automatic methods, and those involving real end-users.

Usability evaluation methods that are performed by experts rely on ergonomic knowledge provided by guideline recommendations, or on the experts' own experiences to identify usability problems while inspecting the user interface. Known methods belonging to this category include Cognitive Walkthrough [23, 42], formative evaluation and heuristic evaluation [32] and benchmarking approaches covering issues such as ISO 9241 usability recommendations or conformance to guidelines [3]. Inspection methods can be applied in the early phases of the development process through analysis of mock-ups and prototypes. The lack of ergonomic knowledge available might explain why inspection methods have been less frequently employed. Automatic methods include approaches that enable automatic checking of guidelines for various properties (e.g. user interface design, accessibility...).

Methods involving real users are commonly referred to as user testing. User tests can be performed either in a laboratory or in the field with the main goal to observe and record users' activity while performing predefined activities that are typically described as scenarios [29] representing parts of the tasks users can perform with the overall system.

User tests are performance measurements to determine whether usability goals have been achieved. These measurements if performed scientifically rigorous are then called experiments or experimental evaluations [22], while tests with low numbers of participants and the main goal to identify usability problems are referred to as usability studies or usability tests [16].

A typical user test consists of several steps starting for example to obtain demographic information (e.g. gender, age, competencies, experiences with systems, ...) and information on their preferences or habits. Participants provide that information typically by answering questionnaires or answering interview questions. A second step is then to ask users to perform a set of tasks. Their behaviour is observed and classified e.g. identifying if users performed the task successful, how long it took them to perform the task or how many errors were made. Users most often are video recorded (observation of certain behaviours, movements or reactions) and system interaction can be logged. Finally, users will provide feedback on the system e.g. filling out questionnaires or answering interview questions. Questionnaires have been extensively employed [40] to obtain quantitative and qualitative feedback from users (e.g. satisfaction, perceived utility of the system, user preferences for modality) [32] and cognitive workload (especially using the NASA-TLX method).

More recently, simulation and model-based checking of system specifications have been used to predict usability problems such as unreachable states of the systems or conflict detection of events required for fusion. [31] proposed to combine task models (based on Concur Task Tree (CTT) notation) with multiple data sources (e.g. eye-tracking data, video records) in order to better understand the user interaction.

## 2.2 User Experience and Its Evaluation

User Experience (UX) still misses a clear definition especially when it comes to the fact to try to measure the concept or related constructs or dimensions [21]. As of today the term user experience can be seen as an umbrella term used to stimulate research in HCI to focus on aspects which are beyond usability and its task-oriented instrumental values. UX is described as dynamic, time dependent [20] and beyond the instrumental [17]. From an HCI perspective the overall goal of UX is to understand the role of affect as an antecedent, a consequence and a mediator of technology. The concept of UX focuses rather on positive emotions and emotional outcomes such as joy, fun and pride [17].

There is a growing number of methods available to evaluate user experience in all stages of the development process. Surveys on these contributions are already available such as [5] who present an overview on UX and UX evaluation methods or HCI researchers who have summarized UX evaluation methods in a website [1]. Beyond that work on generic methods, contributions have been proposed for specific application domains, e.g. for interactive television [41]. User experience does include a look on all the (qualitative) experience a user is making while interacting with a product [28]. The current ISO definition on user experience focuses on a *"person's perception and the responses resulting from the use or anticipated use of a product, system, or service"* [19]. From a psychological perspective these responses are actively generated in a psychological evaluation process, and it has to be decided which concepts can best represent the psychological compartments to allow to measure the characteristics of user experience. It is necessary to under-stand, investigate and specify the dimensions or factors that are taken into account for the various application domains.

User experience evaluation is done in the majority of cases in combination with a usability study or test, applying additional UX questionnaires focusing on a selection of user experience dimensions. Examples are the AttrakDiff questionnaire [2] measuring hedonic and pragmatic quality and attractiveness, or Emo Cards [12] enabling the user to show their emotional state [1].

Data from user experience evaluation can be classified in qualitative (e.g. descriptions of feelings of a user when interacting with a system) or quantitative (e.g. rating scores). They can either reflect the user's experience for the whole system, or can be specifically associated to a task or sub-task (e.g. a physiological reaction like an increased heart-rate while doing a specific sub-task).

All these usability and user experience evaluation methods have a common limitation: they do not specify in detail how the evaluation results, for example reports of usability problems, task times, users' perception of difficulty for usability or appreciation levels, ratings or bio-physiological data for user experience can be used to inform the next design iteration.

## 2.3   Task Models: Benefits and Limitations

Introduced by [34, 37], tasks models for describing interactive systems are used during the early phases of the user-centered development cycle to gather information about users' activities. They bring several benefits when they are used throughout the development process and the operation time:

- They support the assessment of the effectiveness factor of usability as well as usability heuristic evaluation [10, 39];
- They support the assessment of task complexity [14, 33, 44];
- They support the construction of training material and training sessions [25];
- They support the construction of the documentation for users [15];
- They help to support the errors done by users as wells as their anticipations [13, 38];
- They help to identify the good candidates for migration [24, 45];
- They help to provide users contextual help [35, 36];
- They support the redesign of system [46].

Nonetheless, task models suffer from various limitations:

- They miss quantitative information about performance data (number of errors per task, ratings for each task…);
- They miss connection to user experience and other software quality attributes;
- Tool support and process support is limited when it comes to the integration of usability and user experience evaluation data to inform the next iteration of design.

In terms of tools there are only few available that allow to describe tasks not only representing activities but enabling the notion of error as well as the annotation of necessary knowledge and system used for the interaction [26]. We thus decided to extend the existing tool supported notation called HAMSTERS [13], as it is closest to what we would need for re-injecting results from user tests.

# 3   How to Enhance Task Models with Data: A Process Proposal

For any complex system that is developed following an iterative UCD process it has been reported that results from the usability evaluation phase of the system in stage (n) have not been incorporated in the next version of the prototype or system (n+1). We argue that task models can be beneficial in such an approach given that the tool support is able to represent an interactive system in detail.

A task modelling tool thus has to be able to store the information gathered during user-tests related to usability and UX. It must allow to connect task descriptions with user test results to support the understanding and analysis of collected data related to the task models. This way it is possible to identify limitations and how small activities of the user, like performing a sub-task like a log-in to a system, can influence the overall perception of the user experience of the system. We have been choosing HAMSTERS as a tool to show how task models can be enhanced to show data gathered in user tests.

We propose a **PR**ocess to **EN**hance **TA**sk **M**odels (PRENTAM) shown in Fig. 1, enabling the insertion of the data from the user tests in task models. Starting with (1) a task analysis that is based on a variety of artefacts and insights obtained with methods like focus groups, interviews or ethnographic methods, the tasks a user can perform when interacting with the system are described. Based on the task analysis the tasks are modelled (2). Task modelling is supported by a variety of different tools; in our case HAMSTERS[1] [13].

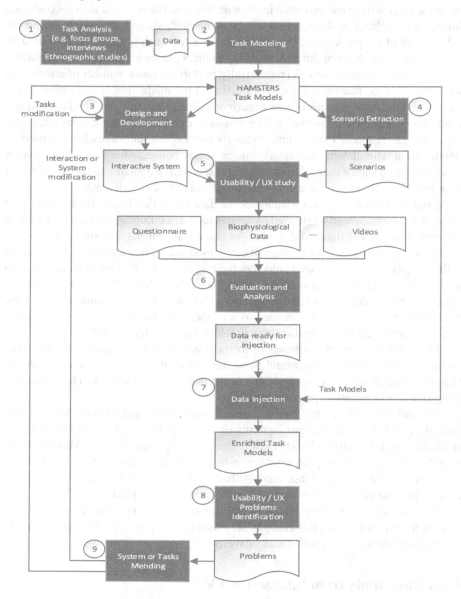

**Fig. 1.** Proposed process flow to enhance task models 'PRENTAM'

---

[1] https://www.irit.fr/recherches/ICS/softwares/hamsters/.

(3) Task models form the basis for the next step that is the design and development of the systems. We are aware that there is a variety of processes, methods and development stages included in this activity, but given that our contribution lies in how to re-inject user test results into task models, we just provide an abstract phase in the process model. Once a first prototype is available for evaluation the task models can be used to extract scenarios that shall be tested in the user test (4). The user test then is conducted through a Usability/UX study, following the same methods and procedures during the test for each of the participants (5). Within the user test each scenario is performed by a number of users. A set of different usability metrics can be measured which typically include metrics for effectiveness (successfully performed tasks, number of errors, task time in total, time measures for abstract tasks…) or satisfaction (users rating of the perceived difficulty). In terms of user experience dimensions are measured using questionnaires or interviews, observation like videos or eye-tracking, sometimes using bio-physiological feedback. Typical dimensions for user experience are aesthetics, emotion, identification, stimulation, meaning/value or social connectedness [7]. Data that is collected during such a user test thus can be (a) qualitative data like responses of a user in an interview, (b) quantitative data - ranging from ordeal to ratio data.

In (6), evaluation provides a multitude of data (sets) that has to be analysed, and where data is subsequently extracted. Analysis includes grouping of data (for example computing means and standard deviation) or statistical analysis (significance tests).

The analysed data then is injected in the task model (7). The important novelty aspect of this proposed process is that it enhances the task models used with the data gathered during the evaluation. Data is analysed and extracted from the evaluation and is injected inside the task models. Each task is enriched with data, for example minimal task time or maximal task time can be annotated as a property for the whole tasks or sub-tasks (see also later Fig. 3 for a depiction how this looks like in HAMSTERS).

Data is injected on several levels of the task model. For data that is related to the overall system evaluation this would be at the root of the task, while for data that is related to a small activity or an error this is at the nodes of a sub-task. The notation is using similar extensions as presented in [26].

The enriched task models can be used to understand and identify for example usability problems or limitations in terms of user experience (8). Depending on the problems found this will lead to changes in the system (System or Tasks Mending), e.g. by enhancing or improving an interaction technique or by re-ordering sub-tasks or activities (9). The enhanced task models then build the basis for the iteration of the system. In some cases, this can also lead back to the analysis phase.

This process ends when results from the user study are good enough to allow a release of the product. Given that changes are made to the system the new system has to be described starting again with a task analysis.

## 4 A Case Study from Interactive TV

Goal of this case study is to show how we followed the 'PRENTAM' during the development of an interactive TV system.

### 4.1   The Interactive TV Prototype

The prototypical system that we designed and developed enables the user to watch live television broadcast with associated functionalities including direct control like changing channels, regulating volume or muting the sound and additional functionality including Electronic Program Guide (EPG), a Video On Demand section (VOD), the support of personalization with individual user profiles, storage of personal data like photos and access to system settings (e.g. pin code registration to restrict access to content for children). The system also allows the user to control video content (forward, back, pause) and to time-shift programs. Figure 2 shows the main user interface and EPG. The system is based on a simple six button navigation (up, down, left, right, ok, back) with an overall good usability [40].

**Fig. 2.**  Main menu (left) and electronic program guide (right) of the User Interface prototype.

In this Case Study we focus on one aspect of the system which was the introduction of the ability to transfer content from the TV to other devices via selectable menu options on the TV user interface. For example, this function allows the user to take away the movie being watched on the TV to a mobile device (e.g. a tablet).

### 4.2   Following the "PRENTAM" Process Step by Step

**Task Analysis (Step 1).**  A task analysis was performed to understand activities and user goals that are related to using several devices while watching TV, including moving data or content (movies) between these devices. The task analysis involves approaches such as focus groups, interviews and ethnographic studies [41].

**Task Modelling (Step 2).**  Based on the task analysis of the interactive TV system we modelled the main system tasks using HAMSTERS. This modelling was based on previous descriptions from [30].

**Design and Development (Step 3).**  Based on the task models we have been designing and developing three additional functionalities: (1) enabling the user watching a TV show or program to access additional information related to that TV show on the tablet (2) allow users to take away the currently displayed TV show or program on the tablet and (3) to compare different movies in terms of user ratings before buying them.

**Scenario Extraction (Step 4).** One advantage of using task models is the ability to use them to extract scenarios for the evaluation of the proposed system. We chose four scenarios that covered the three additional functionalities:

0. *User Test Scenario 0: Trial task to discover the system (change channels and access video on demand section);*
1. *User Test Scenario 1: Get more information (number of episodes) about a TV show in the program guide;*
2. *User Test Scenario 2: Get extra information about a movie (number of Os-car/ ratings);*
3. *User Test Scenario 3: Store information (ratings) about movies before buy-ing them in order to compare them;*
4. *User Test Scenario 4: Continue to watch a movie on the second screen.*

**Usability and UX Study (Step 5).** Thirty-two students in computer science from the University of Toulouse took part in the study. Twenty-four were male and 8 were female. The age of participants ranged from eighteen to twenty-five, with an average of 21.7 (SD = 1.65).

The evaluation study took place in a room that was arranged with two sofas, one table and the desk where the TV screen and the audio system were placed. The TV screen used was in fact a 21.5" computer screen, full HD. The second screen used was a tablet Google Nexus 7 running android 4.4. Users were video-taped during the session and we had an eye-tracker installed to follow the eye-gaze.

The evaluation study was structured into four parts. During the first one, we asked users questions about their media consumption habits, as well as their knowledge about TV systems and second screen apps. The second part was dedicated to the use of the system. The experimenter gave the user basic information about how the sys-tem works. Each participant conducted four tasks with the system. For each task, a short introduction into the scenario was given, followed by an explicitly formulated task assignment. Hints were provided after a predefined time period. Additionally, each task had a time limit. If a participant needed more time the task was stopped, counted as not solved and the correct way to solve the task was explained to the user. After performing the four tasks, and answering questions about each tasks (difficulty, comfort, naturalness of the inter-action technique) the experimenter asked the user to fill out the AttrakDiff [2] and the SUS [8] questionnaire. The final part was an inter-view and the debriefing of the user.

During the evaluation study the following types of data have been gathered:

(a) data about demographics (age, gender, media consumption habits)
(b) data about the use of the system including time needed (measuring time in the system) to complete a task, errors (performing a user observation with a written protocol by the test leader), general user behaviour (video), eye-gaze (Eye-Tracking) and user's appreciation of the system including ratings on user experi-ence like naturalness or comfort
(c) data related to the user experience (e.g. AttrakDiff) and usability (e.g. SUS) of the system
(d) interview data from the final interview.

**Evaluation and Analysis (Step 6).** After a first step of cleaning up the data by identifying outliers and verifying the video material, data was analysed and prepared for injection in the task model. This included a video analysis and re-visiting of observation protocols reporting number of errors, task success and failures, preparation of average task completion time, averages of ratings etc. (see Table 1).

**Table 1.** Tasks results: Average Execution Times for Successful Tasks (N, time, Standard Deviation) and Rating of Difficulty of the Task and Standard Deviation (SD).

|    | Total | | | | |
|----|-----|-----|-----|-----------|-----------|
|    | S | H | F | Time (SD) | R (SD) |
| T1 | 20 | 7 | 5 | 122 (51,53) | 2,4 (1,21) |
| T2 | 25 | 6 | 1 | 111 (50,70) | 2,1 (1,09) |
| T3 | 22 | 9 | 1 | 193 (68,26) | 2,3 (1,02) |
| T4 | 39 | 2 | 1 | 67 (25,44) | 1,6 (0,81) |

For qualitative data like answers in interviews we summarized the number of positive and/or negative comments related to usability and identified comments related to six user experience dimensions including aesthetics, emotion, identification, stimulation, social connectedness and meaning/value [7].

**Data Injection into Task Model (Step 7).** Once the evaluation results are analysed and summarized the data related to the various usability and UX dimension is fed back into the task model. The tool HAMSTERS allows the users to describe properties of tasks and activities. Figure 3 shows screenshots of the tree tabs of the frame Properties associated to a task model in HAMSTERS tool. Second and third tabs of this frame are respectively presenting the Usability and the User Experience dimensions where data can be included.

For the different types of data there are various other ways to represent them in the task model. For data related to the overall system appreciation (AttrakDiff) or user ratings on the overall usability of the system (SUS) the data is stored at high levels nodes located at the top of the task tree. Data that is related to tasks or more specifically situations e.g. when the user was reporting difficulties with the interaction technique at a special instance while performing a task are stored directly at the relevant node (typically a leaf of the tree).

**Identification of Usability and User Experience Problems (Step 8).** After the measurement information about usability and user experience has been entered in task properties frame for each evaluated task in task models, usability and user experience issues can be analysed in an integrated way. The data can complement standard performance metrics like KLM [9]. Especially interesting in our case is an analysis of behaviours where performance times are rarely available like time to change a devices or time for speech and touch interaction for remote controls. In the presented case study, in terms of usability problem identification, the task models clearly showed that the tasks were rather long (see minimum and maximum execution time for sub-task "Transfer the displayed program to the tablet" in Fig. 3(a)), complicated (see field "Difficulty rating"

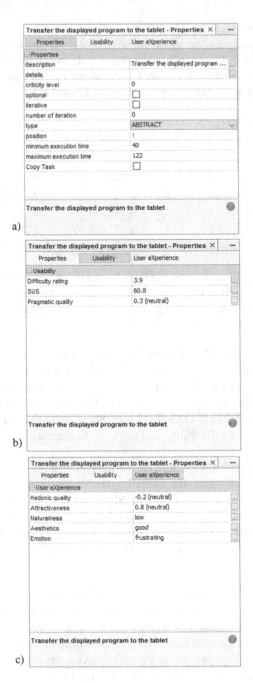

**Fig. 3.** In HAMSTERS tool, the Properties Frame Displaying Usability (b) and UX Data (c).

for the sub-task "Transfer the displayed program to the tablet" in Fig. 3(b)) and users were not much satisfied (see Fig. 3(b)), they would have preferred that the system performs these tasks automatically. In addition, in terms of user experience, the transfer if the viewed program from one device to another was perceived as less natural in terms of user experience and needed improvement.

Furthermore, when looking at user experience, the annotations in the task model allow the designer to revisit the task models and see what user experience dimensions are most important for the users for the different (sub-) tasks. They showed especially that users felt the tasks to be not natural (see field "Naturalness" for sub-task "Transfer the displayed program to the tablet" in Fig. 3(c)).

**System or Tasks Mending (Step 9).** To decrease the task difficulty for transferring the program to the second screen, as well as to improve the naturalness UX dimension of the interactive TV prototype, we decided to introduce an automation for these tasks were data is transferred between the devices. In order to enhance the usability and the user experience, the process of performing tasks including both a TV and a tablet have been simplified. By adding a remote control function on the tablet, the interactive TV prototype automatically communicates the current state/information from the TV to the tablet and supports the user accomplishing the task (e.g. take away of the movie). Figure 4 shows the new version of the task models for the task of content transfer including automation.

This new version of the task model is linked to a new version of the prototype. The insertion of results from user testing in task models was beneficial for the development of the system. Having task models for the iterations of the system allowed us to compare

**Table 2.** Differences between the two task models (Opt: number of optional tasks, Ite: number of iterative tasks, Nb: number of tasks)

| | | Automation | | | No automation | | |
|---|---|---|---|---|---|---|---|
| | | Opt | Ite | Nb | Opt | Ite | Nb |
| *User Tasks* | *Perceptive Tasks* | | | 1 | | | 1 |
| | *Motor Tasks* | 1 | 1 | 3 | | | 1 |
| *System Tasks* | *System Tasks* | 1 | 1 | 2 | | | 0 |
| *Interactive Tasks* | *Input tasks* | | 1 | 3 | | 2 | 7 |
| | *Output tasks* | | 1 | 2 | | 2 | 2 |
| | *I/O Tasks* | | | 0 | | 1 | 1 |
| *Cognitive Tasks* | *Cognitive Tasks* | | | 0 | | | 2 |
| | *Cognitive Analysis Tasks* | | | 0 | | | 1 |
| | *Cognitive Decision Tasks* | | 1 | 1 | | 1 | 1 |
| *Total* | *Total User Tasks* | *1* | *1* | *4* | *0* | *0* | *2* |
| | *Total System Tasks* | *1* | *1* | *2* | *0* | *0* | *0* |
| | *Total Interactive Tasks* | *0* | *2* | *5* | *0* | *5* | *10* |
| | *Total Cognitive Tasks* | *0* | *1* | *1* | *0* | *1* | *4* |
| | *Total* | *2* | *5* | *12* | *0* | *6* | *16* |

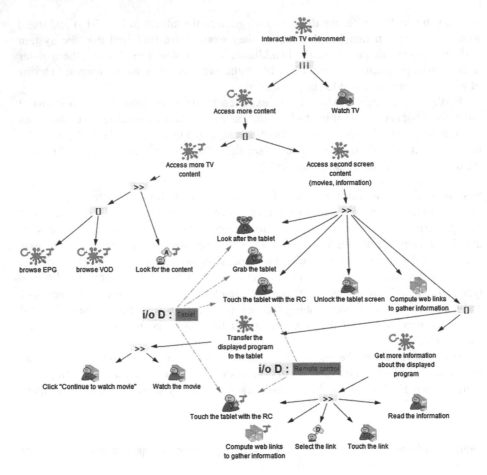

**Fig. 4.** Task model: Showing an automated task that allows to transfer content by simply touching the device with the remote control to indicate the transfer.

how different types of automation affect the usability and the user experience of the system, and what changes in the tasks and sub-tasks provoke a change in the perception of the usability or user experience. Table 2 shows such an analysis of how the two task models are different, in terms of number of tasks and tasks type involved (optional tasks, or iterative tasks, i.e. tasks the user have to repeat several times).

Based on the evaluation of the automated system we found that efficiency and effectiveness were improved. For example, Usability was investigated using the SUS questionnaire. A closer inspection of the SUS scores revealed that the type of the system did have an observable influence on the SUS score (System A – with automation: mean = 83.2, SD = 13.0; System B - without automation: mean = 68.2, SD = 15.5). The results of the evaluation study have been published in [6].

# 5   Discussion: Benefits and Limitations

The interplay between usability evaluation and user interaction design is not as perfect as we would wish for [18]. In lots of cases, evaluation results are simply not taken into account for a design iteration, or are reinterpreted. Using a formal description including task models can help to improve such a feedback of evaluation results to be better (re) presented for design iterations. The proposed Task Model Enhancement Process (PRENTAM) supports design and development with the following:

(1)   the selection of scenarios for usability and user experience studies (e.g. check of coverage)
(2)   representation of evaluation data in the task model covering dimensions like user satisfaction that were not represented until now in a task model
(3)   representation of user performance values in the task model to sup-port/complete predictive models like KLM
(4)   validity checks if reality matches the assumptions and predictions. E.g. if the post completion error is really a problem: how often does the error happen and is that really an issue in terms of overall usability (and UX) perception
(5)   the support for design and design decisions enabling to understand how to improve the design to overcome usability problems and user experience limitations, and to understand what parts of the current solution to keep (which avoids re-testing of these branches)
(6)   predict (forecast) for new designs if they have the same structure (which limits the scope of the next evaluations)
(7)   compare systems (e.g. different TV systems that support the same task can be compared) or compare interaction techniques (e.d. different types of interaction techniques for the same system).

In terms of user experience, the enhanced task model allows to understand how tasks do contribute to an overall UX judgement and the various dimensions of UX.

# 6   Summary and Conclusion

There is a fundamental belief when applying user-centered design and development processes that the findings from usability evaluations inform the user interaction design in a relevant manner. Unfortunately this is very often not the case [18]. To overcome this problem this article proposed the task model enhancement process (PRENTAM), that feeds back evaluation data into task models and enhances them. Applying this process to an (industrial) case study was a challenge but has shown that task modelling has its rightful place in a design and development cycle for large and complex interactive systems.

This is the first promising step toward systematic integration of usability and user experience evaluation data into artefacts used and produced in the design phases. The HAMSTERS tool currently only provides support to integrate quantitative values for usability and user experience.

Further contributions will be to integrate continuous data like observation data (videos, sound) or bio-physiological measurements (like eye-tracking, blood pressure...) which are currently simply connected via a link, but not integrated in the visual display of the task model.

We will continue to explore this Task Model Enhancement Process (PRENTAM) in the following iterations of the interactive TV prototype and at the same time start enhancing the HAMSTERS tool to support even more data visualization especially for the user experience dimensions.

# References

1. All About UX: All UX Evaluation Methods. http://www.allaboutux.org/all-methods
2. AttrakDiff. www.attrakdiff.de
3. Bach, C., Scapin, D.: Ergonomic criteria adapted to human virtual environment interaction. In: Proceedings of the 15th Conference on L'Interaction Homme-Machine, pp. 24–31. ACM, New York (2003)
4. Baecker, R.M.: Readings in Human-computer Interaction: Toward the Year 2000. Morgan Kaufmann Publishers, San Francisco (1995)
5. Bargas-Avila, J.A., Hornbæk, K.: Old wine in new bottles or novel challenges: a critical analysis of empirical studies of user experience. In: Proceedings of the SIGCHI Conference on Human Factors in Computing Systems, pp. 2689–2698. ACM, Vancouver (2011)
6. Bernhaupt, R., Manciet, F., Pirker, M.: User experience as a parameter to enhance automation acceptance: lessons from automating articulatory tasks. In: Proceedings of the 5th International Conference on Application and Theory of Automation in Command and Control Systems, pp. 140–150. ACM, New York (2015)
7. Bernhaupt, R., Pirker, M.: Evaluating user experience for interactive television: towards the development of a domain-specific user experience questionnaire. In: Kotzé, P., Marsden, G., Lindgaard, G., Wesson, J., Winckler, M. (eds.) INTERACT 2013, Part II. LNCS, vol. 8118, pp. 642–659. Springer, Heidelberg (2013)
8. Brooke, J.: SUS-A quick and dirty usability scale. In: Jordan, P.W., Thomas, B., Weerdmeester, B.A., McClelland, A.L. (eds.) Usability Evaluation in Industry, pp. 189–194. Taylor & Francis, London (1996)
9. Card, S.K., Moran, T.P., Newell, A.: The keystroke-level model for user performance time with interactive systems. Commun. ACM **23**, 396–410 (1980)
10. Cockton, G., Woolrych, A.: Understanding inspection methods: lessons from an assessment of heuristic evaluation. In: Blandford, A., Vanderdonckt, J., Gray, P. (eds.) People and Computers XV—Interaction without Frontiers, pp. 171–191. Springer, London (2001)
11. Dennis, J.S.V.A.R.: Computer brainstorms: more heads are better than one. J. Appl. Psychol. **78**, 531–537 (1993)
12. Desmet, P., Overbeeke, K., Tax, S.: Designing products with added emotional value: development and application of an approach for research through design. Design J. **4**, 32–47 (2001)
13. Fahssi, R., Martinie, C., Palanque, P.: Enhanced task modelling for systematic identification and explicit representation of human errors. In: Abascal, J., Barbosa, S., Fetter, M., Gross, T., Palanque, P., Winckler, M. (eds.) INTERACT 2015, Part IV. LNCS, vol. 9299, pp. 192–212. Springer, Heidelberg (2015)

14. Fayollas, C., Martinie, C., Palanque, P., Deleris, Y., Fabre, J.-C., Navarre, D.: An approach for assessing the impact of dependability on usability: application to interactive cockpits. In: 2014 Tenth European Dependable Computing Conference (EDCC), pp. 198–209 (2014)

15. Gong, R., Elkerton, J.: Designing minimal documentation using a GOMS model: a usability evaluation of an engineering approach. In: Proceedings of the SIGCHI Conference on Human Factors in Computing Systems, pp. 99–107. ACM, Seattle (1990)

16. Gram, C., Cockton, G. (eds.): Design Principles for Interactive Software. Springer, Boston (1996)

17. Hassenzahl, M.: The interplay of beauty, goodness, and usability in interactive products. Hum.-Comput. Interact. 19, 319–349 (2008)

18. Hornbaek, K., Stage, J.: The interplay between usability evaluation and user interaction design. Int. J. Hum.-Comput. Interact. 21, 117–123 (2006)

19. ISO 9241-210 Ergonomics of Human-System Interaction Ergonomics of human-system interaction – Part 210: Human-centred design for interactive systems (2010)

20. Karapanos, E., Zimmerman, J., Forlizzi, J., Martens, J.-B.: Measuring the dynamics of remembered experience over time. Interact. Comput. 22, 328–335 (2010)

21. Law, E.L.-C., Roto, V., Hassenzahl, M., Vermeeren, A.P.O.S., Kort, J.: Understanding, scoping and defining user experience: a survey approach. In: Proceedings of the SIGCHI Conference on Human Factors in Computing Systems, pp. 719–728. ACM, New York (2009)

22. Lazar, D.J., Feng, D.J.H., Hochheiser, D.H.: Research Methods in Human-Computer Interaction. Wiley, New York (2010)

23. Lewis, C., Polson, P.G., Wharton, C., Rieman, J.: Testing a walkthrough methodology for theory-based design of walk-up-and-use interfaces. In: Proceedings of the SIGCHI Conference on Human Factors in Computing Systems, pp. 235–242. ACM, New York (1990)

24. Martinie, C., Palanque, P., Barboni, E., Ragosta, M.: Task-model based assessment of automation levels: application to space ground segments. In: 2011 IEEE International Conference on Systems, Man, and Cybernetics (SMC), pp. 3267–3273 (2011)

25. Martinie, C., Palanque, P., Navarre, D., Winckler, M., Poupart, E.: Model-based training: an approach supporting operability of critical interactive systems. In: Proceedings of the 3rd ACM SIGCHI Symposium on Engineering Interactive Computing Systems, pp. 53–62. ACM, New York (2011)

26. Martinie, C., Palanque, P., Ragosta, M., Fahssi, R.: Extending procedural task models by systematic explicit integration of objects, knowledge and information. In: Proceedings of the 31st European Conference on Cognitive Ergonomics, pp. 23:1–23:10. ACM, New York (2013)

27. Mavin, A., Maiden, N.: Determining socio-technical systems requirements: experiences with generating and walking through scenarios. In: Proceedings of the 11th IEEE International Requirements Engineering Conference, pp. 213–222 (2003)

28. McCarthy, J., Wright, P.: Technology as experience. Interactions 11, 42–43 (2004)

29. McGrath, J.E.: Methodology matters: doing research in the behavioral and social sciences. In: Readings in Human–Computer Interaction, pp. 152–169. Elsevier (1995)

30. Mirlacher, T., Palanque, P., Bernhaupt, R.: Engineering animations in user interfaces. In: Proceedings of the 4th ACM SIGCHI Symposium on Engineering Interactive Computing Systems, pp. 111–120. ACM, New York (2012)

31. Mori, G., Paterno, F., Santoro, C.: CTTE: support for developing and analyzing task models for interactive system design. IEEE Trans. Softw. Eng. 28, 797–813 (2002)

32. Nielsen, J., Mack, R.L. (eds.): Usability Inspection Methods. Wiley, New York (1994)

33. Norman, D.A., Draper, S.W.: User Centered System Design; New Perspectives on Human-Computer Interaction. L. Erlbaum Associates Inc., Hillsdale (1986)

34. Palanque, P.A., Bastide, R., Sengès, V.: Validating interactive system design through the verification of formal task and system models. In: Proceedings of the IFIP TC2/WG2.7 Working Conference on Engineering for Human-Computer Interaction, pp. 189–212. Chapman & Hall, Ltd., London (1996)

35. Palanque, P., Martinie, C.: Contextual help for supporting critical systems' operators: application to space ground segments. In: AAAI, pp. 7–11 (2011)

36. Pangoli, S., Paternó, F.: Automatic generation of task-oriented help. In: Proceedings of the 8th Annual ACM Symposium on User Interface and Software Technology, pp. 181–187. ACM, New York (1995)

37. Paternó, F., Mancini, C., Meniconi, S.: ConcurTaskTrees: a diagrammatic notation for specifying task models. In: Howard, S., Hammond, J., Lindgaard, G. (eds.) Human-Computer Interaction, INTERACT 1997, pp. 362–369. Springer, US (1997)

38. Paternó, F., Santoro, C.: Preventing user errors by systematic analysis of deviations from the system task model. Int. J. Hum.-Comput. Stud. **56**, 225–245 (2002)

39. Pinelle, D., Gutwin, C., Greenberg, S.: Task analysis for groupware usability evaluation: modeling shared-workspace tasks with the mechanics of collaboration. ACM Trans. Comput.-Hum. Interact. **10**, 281–311 (2003)

40. Pirker, M., Bernhaupt, R., Mirlacher, T.: Investigating usability and user experience as possible entry barriers for touch interaction in the living room. In: Proceedings of the 8th International Interactive Conference on Interactive TV&Video, pp. 145–154. ACM, New York (2010)

41. Pirker, M.M., Bernhaupt, R.: Measuring user experience in the living room: results from an ethnographically oriented field study indicating major evaluation factors. In: Proceedings of the 9th International Interactive Conference on Interactive Television, pp. 79–82. ACM, New York (2011)

42. Polson, P.G., Lewis, C., Rieman, J., Wharton, C.: Cognitive walkthroughs: a method for theory-based evaluation of user interfaces. Int. J. Man Mach. Stud. **36**, 741–773 (1992)

43. Rettig, M.: Prototyping for tiny fingers. Commun. ACM **37**, 21–27 (1994)

44. Swearngin, A., Cohen, M.B., John, B.E., Bellamy, R.K.E.: Human performance regression testing. In: Proceedings of the 2013 International Conference on Software Engineering, pp. 152–161. IEEE Press, Piscataway (2013)

45. van Welie, M., van der Veer, G.C.: Groupware task analysis. In: Handbook of Cognitive Task Design, LEA, NJ, pp. 447–476 (2003)

46. Wilson, S., Johnson, P.: Bridging the generation gap: from work tasks to user interface designs. In: Computer-Aided Design of User Interfaces I, Proceedings of the Second International Workshop on Computer-Aided Design of User Interfaces, Namur, Belgium, 5–7 June, pp. 77–94 (1996)

# Framework for Relative Web Usability Evaluation on Usability Features in MDD

Shinpei Ogata$^{(\boxtimes)}$, Yugo Goto, and Kozo Okano

Shinshu University, 4-17-1, Wakasato, Nagano 380-8553, Japan
{ogata,okano}@cs.shinshu-u.ac.jp, 12t5033c@shinshu-u.ac.jp

**Abstract.** Web usability in business applications is crucial for enhancing productivity and preventing critical user errors. One of the effective methods to enhance the usability is employment of usability features such as auto-complete and input validation. Then, such employment should be designed so as to conform to actual end-users. However, its evaluation forces developers to expend a lot of effort to design an application, to create its Web prototypes, to observe user operations with the prototypes, and to assess the usability of the employed usability features. In this paper, a framework is proposed for evaluating the usability depending on the employment efficiently even if the developers are non-usability-specialists. Our framework has characteristics as follows so that the developers can easily determine the usability with low creation costs. (1) Support for creating Web prototypes, observing user operations, and assessing the usability are integrated centered on a model-driven approach. (2) The usability can be evaluated relatively and quantitatively by recording user operations and analyzing the resulting logs.

**Keywords:** Model driven development · Screen transition model · Usability evaluation · Business web application · Operability · User error protection

## 1 Introduction

Web usability in business applications is crucial for enhancing productivity and preventing critical user errors. Efficiency and the ability to avoid user errors belongs to "Operability" and "User error protection" respectively as sub-characteristics of "Usability" [1].

One of the effective methods to enhance the usability is employment of usability features [3–5] such as auto-complete and input validation. Developers should evaluate the effectiveness of such employment in the early steps of application development because failure of the employment often causes fundamental restructuring a radical modification of the design of the interaction between the users and the application.

© IFIP International Federation for Information Processing 2016
Published by Springer International Publishing Switzerland 2016. All Rights Reserved
C. Bogdan et al. (Eds.): HCSE 2016/HESSD 2016, LNCS 9856, pp. 73–85, 2016.
DOI: 10.1007/978-3-319-44902-9_6

However, the evaluation forces developers to expend a lot of effort to design an application, to create its Web prototypes, to observe user operations with the prototypes, and to assess the usability of the employed usability features. What is worse, such evaluation is often iterated many times to adjust the employment. In addition to the effort problem, the observation and assessment requires a high degree of special knowledge even though usability specialists do not often participate in the development.

In this paper, a framework to improve the effort and special knowledge problems is proposed focusing on an important but limited area in the operability and user error protection. Our framework helps developers to efficiently evaluate the usability of usability features employed with low creation costs even if the developers are non-usability-specialists. The evaluation process is supported by our framework as follows.

**Web prototype creation:** Several different Web prototypes employing usability features can be generated from a screen transition model by applying our previous work [7] in order to mitigate the effort problem.

**User operation observation:** User operation logs consisting of browser events and input values are recorded in order to assess the operability and user error protection with input time and user errors respectively.

**User operation assessment:** Many raw logs are processed in order to compare them relatively and quantitatively. This process also aims to help the developers to grasp the result of the observation easily.

The effectiveness of our framework is preliminarily evaluated by applying it to a part of a virtual e-commerce application. As a result of the evaluation, our framework quantitatively showed how the usability features affected the usability.

## 2   Usability in Ordinal Use of Business Web Applications

Usability generally covers various aspects of appropriateness recognizability, learnability, operability, user error protection, user interface aesthetics and accessibility according to ISO/IEC 25010 [1]. Enhancing usability can also enhance productivity of companies [2].

### 2.1   Scope Limitation

Our research aims to help skilled end-users to operate their Web application efficiently and correctly in normal use. In addition, our research also assumes that such end-users can be easily specified by a development project. Under this condition, the scope of usability is limited as follows.

- The priority of the appropriateness recognizability, learnability, user interface aesthetics, and accessibility is low in comparison with the operability, and user error protection because we target "skilled and specified" users.

– Each skilled office worker knows generally an important or laborious part of his/her work even if he/she has never operated any existing applications. This premise is advantageous in planning usability evaluation as follows.

1. Usage scenarios can be prepared concretely with hearing requirements for the actual users. For "unspecified" users, such preparation is difficult. Here, a usage scenario means concrete input/output values for achievement.
2. Although a skilled office worker often makes careless mistakes such as incorrect inputs, he/she does not make serious mistakes. Consequently, the evaluation does not need excessive coverage of user operation paths extended over irrelevant use cases.

These premises are important to make the iterative usability evaluation more realistic because the number of combinations of usability features is too numerous to evaluate the usability together with users.

### 2.2   Usability Measurement

Fundamental metrics, which form an essential guideline for improving the operability and user error protection, are defined as follows so that developers who are non-usability-specialists can easily understand effective usability feature employment.

**Input time.** Input time is directly related to not only the operability but also the productivity. In our research, input time is measured variously as the time between specific browser events, as explained in Sect. 3.4.

**User error.** Preventing user errors makes the productivity more reliable. In our research, user errors are defined as follows.

– One is a sequence of user operations that differ from the expected sequence of user operations. The expected sequence means the sequence of user operations that developers, customers or actual users can accept as correct and non-redundant.
– The other error is the input of incorrect values. The expected input value is a value that developers, customers or end-users can accept as correct.

## 3   Proposed Framework

### 3.1   Overview of Proposed Framework

A lot of usability evaluation methods have been proposed [6]. Also, methods focusing on metrics which are measured from user operation or access logs have been proposed [8–10]. As far as we know, there is no method of systematically evaluating the usability feature employment in order to take one step further.

Figure 1 shows the overview of our framework. This framework consists of three phases. The first one is the "preparation" in which several different Web

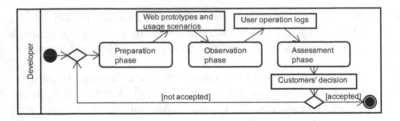

**Fig. 1.** The overview of our framework.

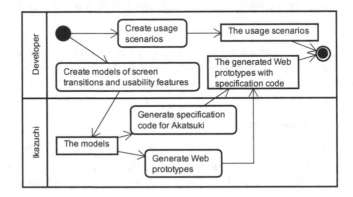

**Fig. 2.** The preparation phase of our framework.

prototypes and scenarios for evaluating the usability are created. The second one is the "observation" in which logs of user operations as browser events are recorded. The last one is the "assessment" in which the logs among different Web prototypes are analyzed and compared. Each of these processes is explained in detail from Sect. 3.2. Our framework provides three tools called Ikazuchi, Akatsuki, and Hibiki respectively, for the process support.

## 3.2 Preparation Phase

Figure 2 shows the preparation phase of our framework. Developers create Web prototypes and usage scenarios in this phase. Generally, absolute evaluation is difficult for developers who are non-usability-specialists because they may be not able to determine the usability from its evaluation result. Therefore, relative evaluation comparing user operation logs between different Web prototypes is supported in our framework. In the relative evaluation, the developers can easily understand which prototype is better for users. However, the cost for creating several different Web prototypes is not low. To mitigate this problem, our framework applies Ikazuchi [7] which is a Web prototype generation tool.

**Ikazuchi.** Ikazuchi is a tool for generating Web prototypes from a design model of screen transitions. This tool and model have been proposed in

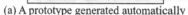

(a) A prototype generated automatically       (b) A prototype created manually

**Fig. 3.** Parts of prototypes to which specification code can be applied.

previous work [7]. A main characteristic of the method of the previous work [7] is separation of concerns between the usability features and screen transitions in this model. Then, different Web prototypes can be generated from this model. For example, a Web prototype employing the usability features can be generated by interpreting the whole model as it is. On the other hand, another Web prototype employing no usability features can be generated from the screen transition part without any usability features.

Thereby, Web prototypes that are compared in relative evaluation can be obtained at a low creation cost. Ikazuchi tentatively supports four usability features: auto-complete, auto-save, undo, and validator, which can be attached to input items without changing screen's structure. The screen transition model can represent screens, screen components, and the items that are categorized into three types as Input, Output, and Link. Figure 3(a) shows a part of a Web prototype generated with the Ikazuchi. Figure 3(b) shows a part of a Web prototype created by hand.

**Specification Code.** The specification code represents correspondence between HTML tag ids and the model. An example of code written in JSON format is shown as follows. The code consists of a page title, input items, and link items.

*Specification code*

```
{"title": "PaymentSettings",
  "inputs":
    {"name": ["input-977674685"],
     "cardType": ["input-836427078"],
     "cardNumber": ["input-1322642290"],
     "expirationYear": ["input-2121199924"],
     "expirationMonth": ["input-431570856"]},
  "links": {"next": ["link-520162288"] }
}
```

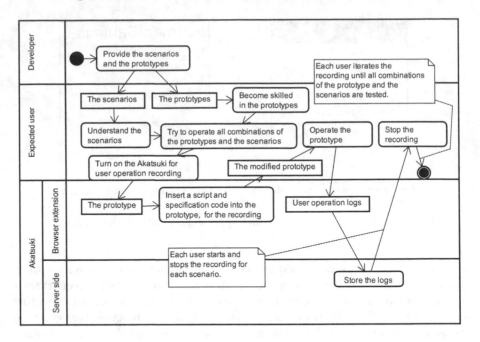

**Fig. 4.** The observation phase of our framework.

This specification code can be generated for the generated Web prototypes with the Ikazuchi but not for the product. That is, our framework requires the hard coded values in the specification code so as to conform to the scenarios. Such simplicity is useful for manually inserting the specification code into a Web prototype even if the prototype was created manually. For our framework, the Ikazuchi was extended so as to insert specification code into a generated prototype in order to record user operations corresponding to the model. Specification code can be manually inserted into Web prototype created manually.

### 3.3   Observation Phase

Figure 4 shows the observation phase of our framework. The precondition of this phase is preparation of both the scenarios and the Web prototypes containing the specification code. That is, developers do not always need the Web prototypes which can be generated with Ikazuchi but which are too simple. The following actions must be conducted by expected users before recording user operations.

– The users have to become skilled in each prototype because the focus is on operability and user error protection and not learnability. By excluding learnability evaluations, it's approximately valid to reuse the prepared scenarios between use of the different prototypes.
– The users have to understand and validate the prepared scenarios by using each prepared prototype because it's difficult to imagine that skilled office

**Table 1.** The kinds of user operations and recording timing by Akatsuki

| User operation | Recording timing |
| --- | --- |
| Change of window size | (1) A `window.onResize` event occurred, or (2) a script for the recording was inserted |
| Change of scroll position | (1) A `window.onScroll` event occurred, or (2) the script was inserted |
| Change of mouse position | (1) A `document.onMouseMove` event occurred |
| Operation of mouse buttons | (1) A `document.onMouseDown` event occurred, or (2) a `document.onMouseUp` event occurred |
| Input of keys | (1) A `document.onKeyDown` event occurred, or (2) a `document.onKeyUp` event occurred |
| Start of item input | (1) A `focus` event on the item occurred |
| End of item input | (1) A `blur` event on the item occurred |
| Screen transition | (1) A `click` event on a link occurred |

workers would misunderstand the scenarios even if they often make mistakes. The validity of normal flow can be ensured at least by the validation.

With the above assumption, the users operate Web prototypes in accordance with the scenarios. The Akatsuki tool is utilized to record the user operations.

**Akatsuki.** Akatsuki consists of a browser extension and a server side program for recording user operations as browser events. The extension inserts a logging script into a rendered Web page, while the server side program receives the user operations from the extension and stores them into a database. The extension is implemented as a Google chrome extension. The server side program and database are implemented with PHP and MySQL respectively.

Table 1 shows both the kinds of user operations recorded by Akatsuki and the timing of the recording. Table 2 shows the log contents for each kind of user operation. The page title and input, output, and link items are recorded together with their names represented in the screen transition model so that the developers can review the model on the basis of the analyzed logs. The specification code is used when an HTML tag as an event target is transformed into such names.

### 3.4 Assessment Phase

Figure 5 shows the assessment phase of our framework. In this phase, the developers relatively evaluate the usability feature employment of the prototypes on the basis of the user operation logs. The raw logs are numerous and difficult to understand. To mitigate this problem, our framework provides the Hibiki tool which analyzes the raw logs and transforms them into useful information.

**Table 2.** The user operations and corresponding log contents created by Akatsuki

| User operation | Log contents |
|---|---|
| Commons | The recorded timestamp, page title, and recording id of a log |
| Change of window size | The width and height of a window |
| Change of scroll position | The x axis of the horizontal scroll of a page and the y axis of the vertical scroll |
| Change of mouse position | The x and y axis of the cursor in a browser |
| Operation of mouse buttons | The state (`press` or `release`) of a button and the button type such as `left`, `right`, `middle`, `undefined` |
| Input of keys | The state (`press` or `release`) of an alphabet or number key, the key code, and the state (`press`) of specific keys such as Shift, Ctrl, Alt |
| Start of item input | The name of an input item when the item was focused |
| End of item input | The name of an input item and the value of the item when the item was focused |
| Screen transition | The name of a link when the link is clicked |

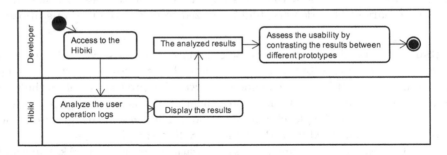

**Fig. 5.** The assessment phase of our framework.

**Hibiki.** Hibiki is a server side program in PHP that summarizes the recorded logs into user operation time and input values. The largest unit of the summarized information shows the user operations from the start of the recording to the end. The information in this unit shows the result when a certain user operated a certain prototype in accordance with a certain scenario. Table 3 shows the summarized information shown by Hibiki. Various differences can be analyzed by collecting this information. For example, differences in the users, in the prototypes, in the scenarios, and in combinations of them can be shown.

# 4  Preliminary Evaluation

## 4.1  Overview

This evaluation aims to determine whether the difference in the usability resulting from usability feature employment can be quantitatively recognized from the data shown by Hibiki. A part of a virtual e-commerce application is adopted as an application example because a partial prototype is often used to evaluate specifications in early stages of development.

For evaluating the potential effectiveness of the proposed method for observing user operations under conditions assuming actual development is important, weakly restricted prototypes and scenarios which are often create by actual developers are used. In this evaluation, we observed user operations with weakly

**Table 3.** The kinds of analyzed information by Hibiki

| Information type | Explanation |
|---|---|
| Scenario achievement time [millisecond] | Time from the start of user operation recording to the end. The individual time is measured per scenario |
| Page sojourn time [millisecond] | Time between screen transitions. Both the individual and cumulative times are measured per page |
| Input time [millisecond] | Time focusing on any input item on a page. The individual time is measured per page |
| Mouse input time [millisecond] | Time from a button press to the release on a page, except for focus change. The individual time is measured per release event |
| Click frequency [number of times] | The number of button clicks on a page. One click is countered per release event of the mouse button |
| Key input time [millisecond] | Time from a key press to the release on a page. This individual time is measured per release event of the key |
| Key type frequency [number of times] | The number of key types on a page. One key type is countered per release event of a key |
| Backspace key type frequency [number of times] | The number of backspace key types on a page. One key type is counted per release event of the key |
| Time interval to input next item [millisecond] | Blur time until focusing the next input item. The individual time is measured per focus event of the input item |
| Sequence of screen transitions | Sequence of displayed pages in chronological order |
| Sequence of input item focuooo | Sequence of focused input items in chronological order |
| Values of input item | The last value of an input item in a scenario |

restricted prototypes because such prototypes are similar to one obtained in an actual development process.

In this evaluation, there were two prototypes, six scenarios, and five users. In this paper, we call the two prototypes A and B. A was automatically generated and B was created manually as shown in Fig. 3. Each prototype represents screen transitions from the `CartView` screen to the `PurchaseComplete` screen. This structure simply consists of five screens and transitions between them without any branches. The scale of each of the six scenarios was categorized as large, middle or small resulting in two of each category. Combinations of the prototypes, scenarios, and users were determined so that no bias in learning resulted.

## 4.2   Result

From the evaluation, the total number of the logs obtained was 176,278. Of the 30 combinations that we tried, 26 of them resulted in valid data.

Table 4 shows the result of comparing the average input times (avg.) between A and B where the difference between the averages is three or more seconds. ID 1, 2, 3, 4, and 6 shows that the users were able to efficiently operate A than B, in average. All of these items of A employed an auto-complete as a usability feature although these items of B employed no usability features. On the other hand, all items of ID 5, 7, and 8 of B made the user operation more efficient. The items of ID 7 and 8 of B employed a spinner with a default value as "1" although the items of A employed no usability features. Regarding the item of

**Table 4.** The result for operability evaluation

| ID | Input item | Avg. of A [sec.] | Avg. of B [sec.] |
|----|-----------|------------------|------------------|
| 1 | PaymentSettings .name[0] | 7.993 | 13.508 |
| 2 | PaymentSettings .cardNumber[0] | 8.463 | 15.442 |
| 3 | BillingAddressSettings .billingAddress[0] .address[0] | 9.051 | 24.116 |
| 4 | BillingAddressSettings .billingAddress[0] .phoneNumber[0] | 10.906 | 14.551 |
| 5 | ShippingAddressSettings .shippingAddress[0] .address[0] | 26.404 | 21.995 |
| 6 | ShippingAddressSettings .shippingAddress[0] .assignedItems[0] .name[0] | 7.822 | 12.533 |
| 7 | ShippingAddressSettings .shippingAddress[0] .assignedItems[0] .quantity[0] | 5.299 | 1.774 |
| 8 | ShippingAddressSettings .shippingAddress[0] .assignedItems[1] .quantity[0] | 4.376 | 0.183 |

**Table 5.** The result for user error protection evaluation

| Kinds of the errors | Freq. | Example |
|---|---|---|
| [MI] Mis-input a 1-byte character instead of a 2-byte one | 11 | |
| [MU] Misunderstanding of the scenarios | 11 | "Kawakami" as a last name was inputted instead of "Kami kawa". |
| [O] Omission of a part of a string | 5 | "5300001" as postal code was inputted instead of "530-0001" |
| [T] Typo | 2 | "Satoru" as a first name was inputted instead of "Satoshi". Both of the "ru" and "shi" are one 2-byte characters in Japanese |
| [MC] Mis-capitalization | 1 | "noboru" as the name on a credit card was inputted instead of "NOBORU" |

ID 5, both of A and B however employed the same input method without any usability features.

As for user error protection evaluation, we analyzed input mistakes against 222 values expected in the total of all scenarios. A few of the expected values were excluded because some values that were inputted through a date picker written in Javascript were not collected. A total of 906 values were obtained for the 222 expected values. 30 of the actual values were different than the expected ones.

Table 5 shows user errors discovered in the evaluation. Usability features to decrease those errors were not employed in both A and B. The errors such as MI, MC, and a part of O can be automatically corrected employing functions for formatting characters. A part of the errors of MU, O, and T may be avoidable by employing auto-completes because the users inputted the correct value at least once in a scenario although he/she inputted the wrong value in another scenario. Meanwhile, auto-completes were useful to avoid most of these errors but it promoted the error a little. For instance, one of the users inputted the number of a credit card with blind acceptance of the auto-complete even though the completed value was different than the expected value.

### 4.3 Discussion

The effectiveness of usability feature employment was shown quantitatively by utilizing the information analyzed by Hibiki. Hibiki made the analysis of the preliminary evaluation result efficient even though there were numerous logs. However, it seems that the result shown as ID 5 of Table 4 did not depend on the usability features. Consequently, various aspects such as user characteristics and qualitative aspects should be considered for more precise evaluation. Tool support is also needed to make the usability evaluation practical.

In the preliminary evaluation, there were still various non-stable factors such as differences in scenario properties such as the amount of input/output data, rigorous user operation sequences, and exhaustiveness and differences in prototype properties such as layout and input methods. These factors may make the effectiveness of usability feature employment ambiguous. Therefore, a more rigorous evaluation process well supported by proper tools should be considered.

In addition, Ikazuchi can handle a few number of usability features yet. The strategies of attaching usability features, the combinations of usability features and the strategies of comparing the obtained logs should be considered for observing a complex combinations of usability features by improving the capability of Ikazuchi. We plan to extend Ikazuchi to support more existing usability features [3–5].

## 5    Conclusion

A framework for evaluating the operability and user error protection relatively and quantitatively was proposed in this paper. In our framework, Web prototype creation, user operation observation, and usability assessment are supported so as to obtain the prototypes, the user operation logs, and the summarized logs semi-automatically. Our framework strictly controls the evaluation conditions to clarify the effectiveness of usability feature employment. As a result of the preliminary evaluation, this paper quantitatively showed that the usability changed depending on usability feature employment.

As future work, we plan to extend Ikazuchi so as to deal with more usability features and their employment algorithms. We also attempt to extend Hibiki so as to more easily grasp differences between different employment methods by applying artificial intelligent algorithms. In addition, we consider how to obtain the exhaustive scenarios by applying a model-based testing approach. Finally, a large scale and rigorous evaluation applying experimental research approaches is planned to show more reliably the effectiveness of our framework and to evaluate the user error protection from the aspect of user mis-operation sequences.

**Acknowledgment.** This work was supported by JSPS KAKENHI Grant Number JP15K15972.

## References

1. ISO/IEC: systems and software engineering - systems and software quality requirements and evaluation (SQuaRE) - system and software quality models. ISO/IEC Std. 25010: 2011 (2011)
2. Nielsen, J.: Usability Engineering. Morgan Kaufmann Publishers Inc., San Francisco (1993)
3. Folmer, E., Gurp, J.V., Bosch, J.: A framework for capturing the relationship between usability and software. Softw. Process Improv. Pract. **8**(2), 67–87 (2003)
4. Juristo, N., Moreno, A.M., Sanchez-Segura, M.-I.: Guidelines for eliciting usability functionalities. IEEE Trans. Softw. Eng. **33**(11), 744–758 (2007)

5. Roder, H.: Specifying usability features with patterns and templates. In: First International Workshop on Usability and Accessibility Focused Requirements Engineering, pp. 6–11 (2012)
6. Insfran, E., Fernandez, A.: A systematic review of usability evaluation in web development. In: Hartmann, S., Zhou, X., Kirchberg, M. (eds.) WISE 2008. LNCS, vol. 5176, pp. 81–91. Springer, Heidelberg (2008)
7. Kamimori, S., Ogata, S., Kaijiri, K.: Automatic method of generating a Web prototype employing live interactive widget to validate functional usability requirements. In: 3rd International Conference on Applied Computing and Information Technology/2nd International Conference on Computational Science and Intelligence, pp. 9–14 (2015)
8. Atterer, R., Wnuk, M., Schmidt, A.: Knowing the user's every move: user activity tracking for website usability evaluation and implicit interaction. In: 15th International Conference on World Wide Web, pp. 203–212 (2006)
9. Nakamichi, N., Sakai, M., Shima, K., Matsumoto, K.: Detecting low usability web pages using quantitative data of users' behavior. In: 28th International Conference on Software Engineering, pp. 569–576 (2006)
10. Pansanato, L.T.E., Rivolli, A., Pereira, D.F.: An evaluation with web developers of capturing user interaction with rich internet applications for usability evaluation. Int. J. Comput. Sci. Appl. 4(2), 51–60 (2015)

# Testing Prototypes and Final User Interfaces Through an Ontological Perspective for Behavior-Driven Development

Thiago Rocha Silva[✉], Jean-Luc Hak, and Marco Winckler

ICS-IRIT, Université Paul Sabatier, Toulouse, France
{rocha,jean-luc.hak,winckler}@irit.fr

**Abstract.** In a user-centered development process, prototypes evolve in iterative cycles until they meet users' requirements and then become the final product. Every cycle gives the opportunity to revise the design and to introduce new requirements which might affect the specification of artifacts that have been set in former development phases. Testing the consistency of multiple artifacts used to develop interactive systems every time that a new requirement is introduced is a cumbersome activity, especially if it is done manually. This paper proposes an approach based on Behavior-Driven Development (BDD) to support the auto-mated assessment of artifacts along the development process of interactive systems. The paper uses an ontology for specifying tests that can run over multiple artifacts sharing similar concepts. A case study testing Prototypes and Final User Interfaces is presented to demonstrate the feasibility of this approach in early phases of the design process, providing a continuous quality assurance of require-ments, and helping clients and development teams to identify potential problems and inconsistencies before commitments with software implementation.

**Keywords:** Automated requirements checking · Behavior-Driven Development · Ontological modeling · Prototyping · Multi-artifact testing

## 1 Introduction

It is a common understanding that in user-centered design (UCD) processes, users' requirements and needs are not always identified at once but they are rather revised/ tuned and incrementally introduced along the multiple iterations through the use of Prototypes. When requirements are updated and/or new ones are introduced, the devel-opment team must cross-check their consistency with artifacts set in former development phases. Testing and tracing requirements during the development of interactive system is a daunting task specially because the development team has to deal with many cycles of iterations, multiple artifacts (such as Task Models, Prototypes, User Stories, Scenarios, etc.), and many design options for Prototypes that evolve until they reach the status of Final Product.

The traceability of artifacts can be said as vertical and horizontal [19]. Vertical traceability describes the relationship between artifacts that can be derived from each

© IFIP International Federation for Information Processing 2016
Published by Springer International Publishing Switzerland 2016. All Rights Reserved
C. Bogdan et al. (Eds.): HCSE 2016/HESSD 2016, LNCS 9856, pp. 86–107, 2016.
DOI: 10.1007/978-3-319-44902-9_7

other, for example from customer requirements to acceptance test cases. Horizontal traceability refers to the evolution of the same artifact. The artifacts traceability problem has been studied by several authors and a wide set of commercial tools have been developed to address this problem in various approaches [16]. Nonetheless, solutions to promote vertical traceability of artifacts are not allowing to effectively testing them against requirements specifications.

Testing the consistency of artifacts with respect to user requirements is crucial for the quality of the software under development. Moreover, the sooner the teams pay attention to test their software components and especially their requirements specifications, more effective will be the results towards a quality assurance of the product. As argued by Lindstrom [21], failing to trace tests to requirements is one of the five most effective ways to destroy a project. Nonetheless, according to Uusitalo et al. [17], traceability between requirements and tests used to assess the implementation are rarely maintained in practice not only because of stringent enforcement of schedules and budgets, but also because it is difficult to update traces when requirements change and due to the difficulties to conduct testing processes manually.

In this context, Behavior Driven Development (BDD) [10] has aroused interest from both academic and industrial community in the last years. Supported by a wide development philosophy that includes Acceptance Test-Driven Development (ATDD) [22] and Specification by Example [23], BDD drives development teams to a requirements specification based on User Stories [4] in a comprehensive natural language format. This format allows specifying executable requirements, conducting to a "live" documentation and making easier for clients to set their final acceptance tests. It guides the system development and brings the opportunity to test Scenarios directly in the User Interface with the aid of external frameworks for different platforms. However, this technique is currently limited to test requirements against a fully implemented user interface using specialized robots like Selenium WebDriver. Besides that, specifications using only Scenarios are not self-sufficient to provide a concrete perception of the system to the users and, at the same time, allow an overall description of the system in terms of tasks that may be accomplished. This is particularly true in early phases of the development process when the Prototypes are rudimental samples of interactive system.

In this paper we explore the use of BDD techniques for supporting automation of user requirements testing of artifacts produced throughout the development process of interactive systems. Our ultimate goal is to test multiple artifacts throughout the development process looking for vertical and bidirectional traceability of functional requirements. To achieve this goal, a formal ontology model is provided to describe concepts used by platforms, models and artifacts that compose the design of interactive systems, allowing a wide description of UI elements (and its behaviors) to support testing activities. Whilst the approach is aimed at being generic to many types of artifacts, in this paper we have focused on Prototypes and Final UIs. In the following sections we present the conceptual background, an overview of the underlying process for using the approach and a case study that demonstrate its feasibility. Lately, we discuss related works and the next steps for this research.

## 2   Conceptual Background

Hereafter is a summary of the basic concepts to explain how the approach works.

### 2.1   User Stories and Scenarios

A large set of requirements can be expressed as stories told by the user. Nonetheless, the term User Story might have diverse meaning in the literature. In the Human-Computer Interaction (HCI) field, a User Story refers to a description of users' activities and jobs collected during meetings, which is close to the concept of Scenarios given by Rosson and Carroll [8]. Users and other stakeholders typically talk about their business process emphasizing the flow of activities they need to accomplish. These stories are captured in requirements meetings and are the main input to formalize a requirements artifact. These meetings work mainly like brainstorm sessions and include ideally several stakeholders addressing needs concerning features that may be developed. As stated by Lewis & Rieman, "...scenarios forced us to get specific about our design, [...] to consider how the various features of the system would work together to accomplish real work..." [9]. For Santoro [7], Scenarios provide informal descriptions of a specific use in a specific context of application, so a Scenario might be viewed as an instance of a use case. An identification of meaningful Scenarios allows designers to get a description of most of the activities that should be considered in a task model. Given task models have already been developed, Scenarios can also be extracted from them to provide executable and possible paths in the system.

In the Software Engineering (SE), the term User Stories is typically used to describe requirements in agile projects [4]. They are formatted to fulfil two main goals: (i) assure testability and non-ambiguous descriptions and (ii) provide reuse of business Scenarios. Figure 1 presents a template for formalizing User Stories.

```
Title (one line describing the story)
Narrative:
As a [role]
I want [feature]
So that [benefit]
Acceptance Criteria: (presented as Scenarios)
Scenario 1: Title
Given [context]
  And [some more context]...
When  [event]
Then  [outcome]
  And [another outcome]...
Scenario 2: ...
```

**Fig. 1.** Template for specifying User Stories as defined by North [3] and Cohn [4]

A User Story is thus described with a Title, a Narrative and a set of Scenarios representing Acceptance Criteria. The Title provides a general description of the story. The Narrative describes the referred feature in terms of role that will benefit from the feature, the feature itself, and the benefit it will bring to the business. The Acceptance Criteria are defined through a set of Scenarios, each one with a Title and three main clauses:

"Given" to provide the context in which the Scenario will be actioned, "When" to describe events that will trigger the Scenario and "Then" to present outcomes that might be checked to verify the proper behavior of the system. Each one of these clauses can include an "And" statement to provide multiple contexts, events and/or outcomes. Each statement in this representation is called Step.

In the Behavior-Driven Development (BDD) [10], the user point of view about the system is captured by User Stories described according to the template shown in Fig. 1. The BDD approach assumes that clients and teams can communicate using a semi-structured natural language description, in a non-ambiguous way (because it is supported by test cases).

In some extension, all approaches agree on that User Stories and Scenarios must provide a step-by-step description of tasks being performed by users using a given system. Nonetheless, there are some differences as illustrated by Table 1. This analysis gives us the opportunity to establish a correlation between requirements identified in User Stories, their representation in terms of tasks and the extracted Scenarios in both UCD and SE approaches. We can notice that the main difference lies in the degree of formality and their possible value to support automated test. Another remark we can make is about the type of tasks mapped to Scenarios in SE. As SE consider only tasks being performed by users when using an interactive system, User Stories in this context address only Scenarios extracted from Interaction Tasks in Task Models; Cognitive Tasks, for example, are not mapped to be SE Scenarios because they cannot be performed in the system.

**Table 1.** Approaches for describing User Stories and Scenarios

| Approaches | Key facts | Advantages | Shortcomings |
|---|---|---|---|
| User Stories and/or Scenarios by Rosson and Carroll [8] | Informal description of user activities contextualized in a story | Highly flexible and easily comprehensive for non-technical stakeholders | Very hard to formalize, little evolutionary and low reusability |
| Scenarios extracted from Task Models by Santoro [7] | Possible instance of execution for a given path in a Task Model | Highly traceable for Task Models | Dependency of Task Models and low testability |
| User Stories and/or Scenarios by North [3] and Cohn [4] | Semi-formal description of user tasks being performed in an interactive system | Highly testable and easily comprehensive for non-technical stakeholders | Very descriptive and time consuming to produce |

## 2.2 Acceptance Testing of Functional Requirements

In this paper, we are interested in testing functional requirements that users raise through the means of User Stories and Scenarios. In Software Engineering, the testing activity covers several levels of abstraction, from low level of tests such as Unit and Integration

Testing to high level ones such as System and Acceptance Testing [20]. Low level tests are focused on the quality of the code which we call White Box testing approach. On the other hand, high level tests are more interested in the quality of the final product as a whole which we call Black Box testing approach. Tests can also be focused on specific aspects of the system such as Functional, Usability, Scalability or Performance aspects.

Functional Testing identifies situations that should be tested to assure the correct working of the system under development in accordance with the requirements previously specified. The Acceptance testing are tests made under the client/user point of view to validate the right behavior of the system. For that clients might be able to run their business workflows and to check if the system behaves in an appropriate manner. Several techniques are employed to conduct functional testing such as Boundary Value Analysis, Equivalence Class Testing, Decision Table Base Testing, etc. [20]. These techniques support the development of test cases that might be specified to validate the right implementation of the requirements.

The big challenge is that requirements are dispersed in multiple artifacts that describe them in different levels of abstraction. Thus, tests should run not only in the final product, but also in the whole set of artifacts to assure that they represent the same information in a non-ambiguous way and in accordance with the whole requirements chain. Moreover, testing should be performed along the development process as clients and users introduce new demands or modify the existing ones all along the iterations. Regression Testing is crucial to assure that the system remains behaving properly and in accordance with the new requirements. However, manual Regression Tests are extremely time consuming and highly error-prone. Therefore, automated tests are a key factor to support testing in an ever-changing environment, allowing a secure check of requirements and promoting a high availability of testing.

## 2.3 Computational Ontologies

According to Guarino et al. [11], computational ontologies are a mean to formally model the structure of a system, i.e., the relevant entities and relations that emerge from its observation, and which are useful to our purposes. Computational ontologies come to play in this work as a mean to formalize the vocabulary and the concepts used in User Stories, Scenarios and other artifacts during the development process of interactive systems. Without a common agreement on the concepts and terms used it will be difficult to support traceability of user requirements across many artifacts. Nowadays, some approaches have tried to define languages or at least a common vocabulary for specifying UIs in interactive systems. Despite the fact there is no such a standard, a few ontologies are worthy of mention, including DOLPHIN [12], UsiXML [13] and W3C MBUI Glossary [14]. DOLPHIN [12] is a reference framework that formalizes concepts around task models and in particular provides a mean to compare task model notations. UsiXML (USer Interface eXtensible Markup Language) [13] is a XML-compliant markup language that describes the UI for multiple contexts of use such as Character User Interfaces (CUIs) or Graphical User Interfaces (GUIs). UsiXML consists of a User Interface Description Language (UIDL) that is a declarative language capturing the essence of what a UI is or should be independently of physical characteristics. UsiXML describes at a high level of abstraction the constituting elements of the UI of an application: widgets, controls, containers, modalities and interaction techniques. More recently, W3C has published a glossary of recurrent terms in the Model-based User Interface domain (MBUI) [14]. It was intended to capture a common, coherent terminology for specifications and to provide a concise reference of domain terms for the interested audience. The authors' initial focus was on task models, UI components and integrity constraints at a level of abstraction independent of the choice of devices to implement the models.

## 3   A New Approach for Multi-artifact Testing

The approach relies on the premise that user requirements expressed by the means of User Stories and Scenarios can be specified using a standard user interface ontology which will allow testing automation against multiple artifacts through the development process of interactive systems. To explain how this could be, two figures (Figs. 2 and 3) are presented hereafter. Figure 2 shows how User Stories support both Production Activities and Quality Assurance Activities. Client, Users and Stakeholders are the main source of User Stories that will be consumed by Requirements Analysts and User Interface (UI) designers in Production Activities and by Testing Analysts who are in charge of building test cases and assessing artifacts in Quality Assurance Activities. The Fig. 3 provides a workflow view of activities that have been grouped in Fig. 2.

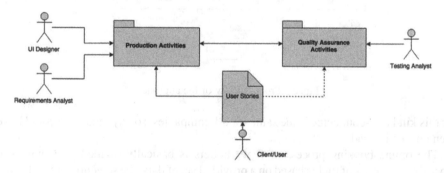

**Fig. 2.** Overview of the Requirements Model

The operationalization of the approach is made up in four main steps that are pinpointed by numbers as follows: (1) definition of the ontology, (2) writing testable requirements, (3) adding test cases, and (4) testing Prototypes and other artifacts. These steps are described herein. To illustrate the operationalization of each step, we have proposed a case study in the flight tickets e-commerce domain in a traditional airline company, showing how the approach can support the testing of Prototypes and Final UIs. This case was chosen because it is easily comprehensible and we believe it represents a common activity for the most part of readers. For the study, we have selected the American Airlines (AA) case to show these concepts. The AA model has been arbitrarily chosen to conduct this work. However, as we know, the core of business models

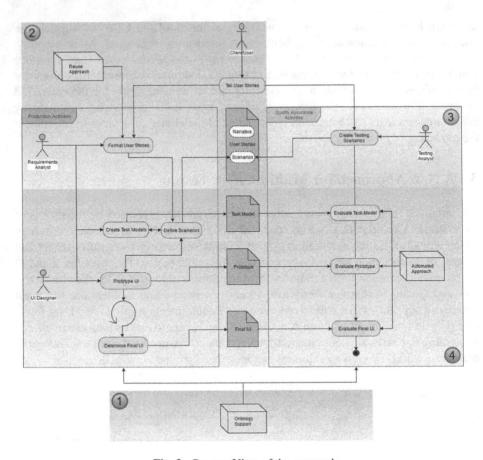

**Fig. 3.** Process View of the approach

for this kind of e-commerce is the same for all companies, so any other else could have been chosen instead.

The online booking process of flight tickets is basically divided in 3 main sub processes: searches of flights based on a provided set of data, the selection of the desired flight(s) in a list of flights resultant from the search, and finally providing passengers and payment data to conclude the booking. We have selected the two first processes for this study as they are the most interactive ones and represent the main source of cognitive efforts from users and designers. The third sub process is basically a data providing in forms so it is not so relevant to demonstrate the concepts presented in the paper, even though the whole process can be supported by this approach.

### 3.1 Step 1: Definition of the Ontology

The proposed ontology is largely inspired from existing languages and vocabularies already described in the Subsect. 2.3, but to make it operational we have created an OWL (W3C Web Ontology Language) specification covering concepts related to graphical components (presentation and behavior) used to build Web and Mobile applications. Figure 4 presents a general view of the ontology structure. We started modeling concepts describing the structure of User Stories, Tasks and Scenarios. Following this, we have modeled the most common Interaction Elements used to build Prototypes and Final User Interfaces (FUIs) in the Web and Mobile environments. The dialog component that allows us to add dynamic behavior to Prototypes and navigation to FUIs was modeled as a State Machine (highlighted in the Fig. 4b). In this level, a Scenario that runs on a given interface is represented as a Transition in the machine, while the interface itself and the one resultant of the action were represented as States. Scenarios in the Transition state have always at least one or more Conditions (represented by the "Given" clause), one or more Events (represented by the "When" clause), and one or more Actions (represented by the "Then" clause).

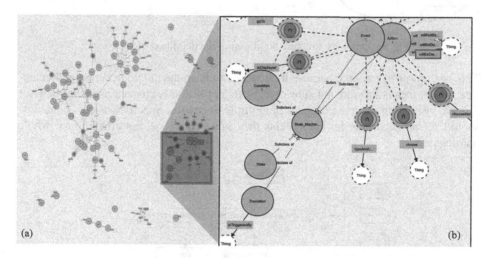

(a)                                                                                              (b)

**Fig. 4.** Ontology representation: (a) Overall View, (b) State Machine Concepts

Figure 5 provides an example on how behavior specification is defined in the ontology. In the example, the behavior "clickOn" (see bottom-left side of the figure) has been associated to the Interaction Elements "Button", "Menu_Item", "Menu" and "Link" to express that these ones are the elements that would be able to answer this behavior when it is triggered. The ontology also specify that the behavior "ClickOn" is triggered by objects Action ("Then" clause) and Event ("When" clause).

Figure 6 shows how a Behavioral Property (behavior of graphical components) is mapped to Interaction Elements (presentation of graphical components) of the ontology. Each behavior is suitable to receive (or not) two parameters as in the example "I choose $elementName referring to $locatorParameters", and to be triggered by the clauses "Given", "When" and/or "Then". In the example, whilst the first parameter is associated to a data for testing, the second parameter refers to the Interaction Element supported by this behavior: "Radio Button", "CheckBox", "Calendar" or "Link". The ontological model describes only behaviors that report Steps performing common actions directly in the User Interface through Interaction Elements. We call it Common Steps (see Sect. 4.2).

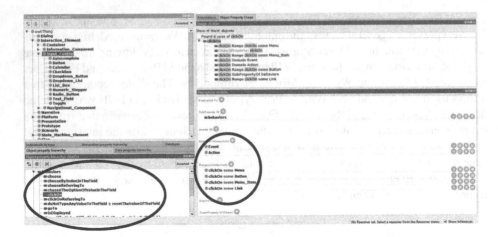

**Fig. 5.** Ontology structure highlighting the definition of behaviors

This is a powerful resource because it allows us to keep the ontological model domain-free, which means they are not subject to particular business characteristics in the User Stories, instigating the reuse of Steps in multiple Scenarios. Specific business behaviors should be specified only for the systems they make reference, not affecting the whole ontology.

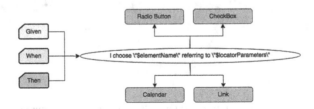

**Fig. 6.** Behaviors being mapped to UI Elements

Technically and with this structure, the current version of the ontology bears an amount of 422 axioms, being 276 logical axioms, 56 classes, 33 object properties, 17 data properties and 3 individuals.

## 3.2 Step 2: Writing Testable Requirements

The approach is focused on functional requirements. A functional requirement defines statements of services that the system should provide, how the system should react to particular inputs and how the system should behave in particular situations. To assure that the system behaves properly, requirements should be expressed in a testable way. Figure 7 presents the conceptual model that explains how testable requirements are formalized in the approach. A requirement is expressed as a set of User Stories (US) as in the template proposed by North [3] and Cohn [4]. User Stories are composed by a Narrative and a set of Acceptance Criteria. Acceptance Criteria are presented as

Scenarios and these last ones are composed by at least three main Steps ("Given", "When" and "Then") that represent Behaviors which the system can answer. Behaviors handle actions on Interaction Elements in the User Interface (UI) and can also mention examples of data that are suitable to test them. Notice that these concepts are part of the ontology shown in Sect. 3.1.

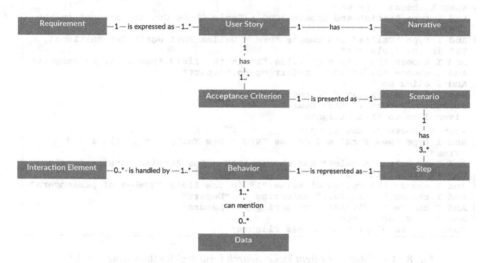

**Fig. 7.** Conceptual Model for testable requirements

Hereafter, we present two User Stories with their respective Scenarios to describe and test the features of our case study. Figure 8 presents the User Story for searching flights in which the user should provide at least: a type of ticket he wants (one-way or round trip), the airport he wants to depart and arrive, the number of passengers, and finally the date of depart and return. In the first Scenario ("One-Way Tickets Search"), it is presented a typical search of tickets concerning a one-way trip from Paris to Dallas for 2 passengers on 12/15/2016. According to the business rule, the expected result for this search is a new screen presenting the title "Choose Flights", in which the user might select the desired flight in a list of flights matching his search. The second Scenario ("Return Tickets Search") simulates a round trip from New York to Los Angeles for only 1 passenger, departing on 12/15/2016 and returning on 12/20/2016. For this case, the same behavior is expected from the system, i.e., a new screen presenting the title "Choose Flights", in which the user might select the desired flight in a list of flights matching his new search.

The User Story that selects the desired flight(s) is given in Fig. 9. The Scenario "Select a diurnal flight", using the Scenario "One-Way Tickets Search" already executed, simulates the selection in the list of available flights, a couple of diurnal flights, the AA6557 and the AA51. For this case, the behavior expected from the system is the presentation of a new screen with the "Optional log in" message, indicating the user is able to login in order to proceed to the booking, filling the passengers and payment data.

```
User Story: Flight Tickets Search
Narrative:
As a frequent traveler
I want to be able to search tickets, providing locations and dates
So that I can obtain information about rates and times of the flights.

Scenario: One-Way Tickets Search
Given I go to "Find flights"
When I choose "One way"
And I type "Paris" and choose "CDG - Paris Ch De Gaulle, France" in the
field "From"
And I type "Dallas" and choose "DFW - Dallas Fort Worth International,
TX" in the field "To"
And I choose the option of value "2" in the field "Number of passengers"
And I choose "12/15/2016" referring to "Depart"
And I click on "Search"
Then will be displayed "Choose Flights"
Scenario: Return Tickets Search
Given I go to "Find flights"

When I choose "Round trip"
And I type "New York" and choose "NYC - New York, NY" in the field
"From"
And I type "Los Angeles" and choose "LAX - Los Angeles International,
CA" in the field "To"
And I choose the option of value "1" in the field "Number of passengers"
And I choose "12/15/2016" referring to "Depart"
And I choose "12/20/2016" referring to "Return"
And I click on "Search"
Then will be displayed "Choose Flights"
```

**Fig. 8.** User Story for *Flight Ticket Search* formatted for the testing template.

```
User Story: Select the desired flight
Narrative:
As a frequent traveler
I want to get the list of flights and their rates and times
So that I can select the desired flight after a search of available
flights.

Scenario: Select a diurnal flight
One-Way Tickets Search
Given "Flights Page" is displayed
When I click on "Flights" referring to "AA flight 6557, AA flight 51"
Then "Optional log in" is displayed
```

**Fig. 9.** User Story for *Select the desired flight* formatted for the testing template.

## 3.3   Step 3: Adding Test Cases

Test Cases are represented as Testing Scenarios that specify potential error situations related to the Scenarios already defined to set Requirements. Testing Scenarios are the responsible component to describe the situations in which the system should be verified, covering as deeply as possible the largest set of features. Thereby, Scenarios and Testing Scenarios compose the User Stories, providing in the same artifact, descriptions of functionalities as well as the potential tests to verify the correct implementation of the requirements. As we have leading with functional testing in the acceptance level, the Black Box approach is used to check expected outcomes when predefined inputs are provided to the system. Figure 10 shows the Scenarios "Search for flights with more than one year in advance" and "Search for a return flight before a departure flight" that will be added to the User Story "Flight Ticket Search". They present specific business rules (and their tests) in the flight-booking domain. The expected outcome in both cases is the impossibility to search flights.

```
Scenario: Search for flights with more than one year in advance
Given I go to "Find flights"
When I choose "One way"
And I type "Paris" and choose "CDG-Paris Ch De Gaulle, France" in the
field "From"
And I type "Dallas" and choose "DFW-Dallas Fort Worth International, TX"
in the field "To"
And I choose the option of value "1" in the field "Number of passengers"
And I try to choose "12/15/2017" referring to "Depart"
Then the system should not allow performing this task
Scenario: Search for a return flight before a departure flight
Given I go to "Find flights"
When I choose "Round trip"
And I type "New York" and choose "NYC-New York, NY" in the field "From"
And I type "Los Angeles" and choose "LAX-Los Angeles International, CA"
in the field "To"
And I choose the option of value "1" in the field "Number of passengers"
And I try to choose "12/15/2016" referring to "Depart"
And I try to choose "12/10/2016" referring to "Return"
Then the system should not allow performing this task
```

**Fig. 10.** Two Scenarios added to the User Story for *Flight Ticket Search*.

## 3.4    Step 4: Testing Prototypes and Other Artifacts

The execution of testing in Prototypes and other artifacts is exemplified in Fig. 11. The top part presents the Step of a Scenario describing the behavior *"choose … referring to …"*. In the example, a user chooses the date of depart "12/15/2016" on the field "Depart" in a form. This task is triggered when an event "When" occurs in the Scenario. This task is associated to values for date of depart ("12/15/2016") and field ("Depart"), indicating a possible executable Scenario that can be extracted from that task. Following the ontology,

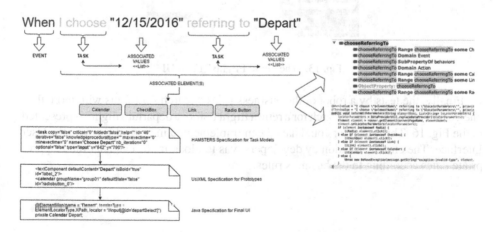

**Fig. 11.** Identifying behaviors through multiple artifacts

the behavior addressed by this task can be associated to multiple UI elements such as Radio Button, CheckBox, Link and Calendar components. The arrows in the right side of the figure indicate two implementations of this ontology, highlighting these associations. First in OWL version at the top and then converted in Java code in the bottom.

When the UI element Calendar is chosen, a locator is triggered to trace this element throughout the artifacts, thus allowing us to reach it for testing purposes. Figure 11 shows this trace being made through a HAMSTERS Specification for Task Models [24] (in the task "Choose Depart"), through a UsiXML Specification for Prototypes [13] (Calendar "Depart"), and finally through a Java Specification for Final UIs (@ElementMap "Depart" with the XPath reference "//input[@id='departSelect']" in a Calendar). For the purposes of the illustration when testing the User Story "Flight Tickets Search", Fig. 12 presents the mapping of a Prototype and the Fig. 13 the mapping of a Final User Interface. Figures 14 and 15 present respectively the mapping of the Prototype and the Final UI for the User Story "Select the desired flight".

**Fig. 12.** The "Find Flights" Prototype

**Fig. 13.** The "Find Flights" Final UI

Finally, the tests by a robot of the business rules "Search for flights with more than one year in advance" and "Search for a return flight before a departure flight" is presented in the Fig. 16. This behavior could have been implemented in several ways on the User Interface. The chosen solution by developers was to block in the calendar the inappropriate dates according to the business rules.

**Fig. 14.** The "Choose Flights" Prototype

**Fig. 15.** The "Choose Flights" Final UI

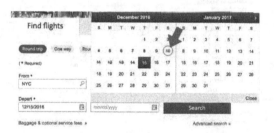

**Fig. 16.** An attempt to select a return date before the departure date

## 4 Tool Support

This section presents a technical description about how tests are implemented in both Prototypes and Final UIs artifacts. For operationalizing the test we employ tools like Webdriver, JBehave and JUnit. Nonetheless, in order to integrate tests into development process of Prototypes, other tools also have been developed.

### 4.1 Testing in the Prototype Level

For the test in the Prototype Level, we have developed a prototyping environment named PANDA (Prototyping using Annotation and Decision Analysis) [25]. The development of a Prototype using this tool is made thanks to a toolbar containing widgets automatically generated from the OWL Ontology as described in the Subsect. 3.1. Once the toolbar is generated, the user can create his Prototype by placing widgets, whose properties are described in the ontology and presented in the edition area as illustrated in the Fig. 17. Using this technique allows to have a mapping between the elements described in the ontology (and thus, their properties and supported behavior) and each widgets of the Prototype.

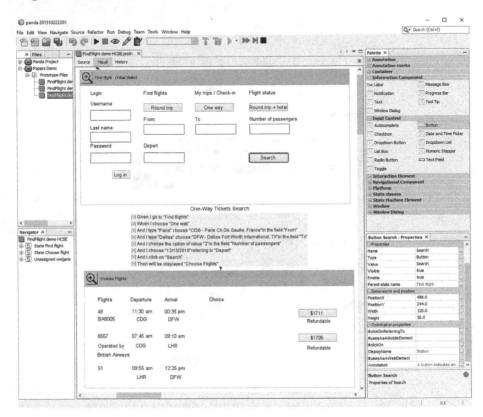

**Fig. 17.** PANDA screenshot

A PANDA Prototype features a state machine where states of the system are populated with the elements in the display when the state is active. By linking states with transitions, it is possible to specify the structure and the behavior of the Prototype. After having developed the Prototype, it is possible to replace a transition with a Scenario. Indeed, in the Fig. 17 we have a testing Scenario used as a transition in the state machine. This Scenario links together the state "Find Flight" represented by the rectangle with a grey header in the upper part of the Prototype with the state "Choose Flight" located in the lower part. The state "Find Flight" represents the initial condition (indicated by the "Given" clause) and the state "Choose Flight" represents the result of the Scenario execution (indicated by the "Then" clause).

PANDA supports Scenarios described in a text format which are imported in the edition area. When importing a Scenario, PANDA parses the different Steps and analyzes them by identifying the events, the tasks, the associated values and the targets of the task, as illustrated in the Fig. 11 in the Subsect. 3.4. This identification is done by splitting each line of the Scenario and identifying keywords like "Given" or "Then" and the quote character. Quoted segments are interpreted as values except for the last quoted element of each line, which is identified as the target of the task. Segments before the quoted elements are considered as actions related to the values read. Each line read is then registered as a Step of the Scenario. Figure 18 shows an example of a parsed Step. The value "Paris" is associated to the action "I type", "CDG – Paris Ch De Gaulle, France" is associated to the action "choose" and "From" is associated to the locator "in the field". Keywords are ignored except for the word « Given » and « Then » which introduce conditions and the final actions.

| And | I type | "Paris" | and | choose | "CDG - Paris Ch De Gaulle, France" | in the field | "From" |

**Fig. 18.** Example of a split Step during the parsing

Once the Scenario have been parsed and attached between an initial and a resultant state, it can be executed in order to find out if the Scenario is supported by the Prototype. This execution can be made step-by-step or with the whole set of Steps of the Scenario being executed at the same time. The system checks the state described in the Prototype and the properties defined in the ontology loaded, as well as if each Step is possible according to the task described in the Scenario. To do so, the system starts by making a mapping between the widgets of the Prototype and the target of the tasks during the execution, since Scenarios and states of the Prototype are independent. For the moment, this mapping is based on the name of the widget, but other mapping methods will be also considered. Then, for each Step whose target has been mapped, the system checks if each actions or properties matches with the properties of the widget which were defined in the ontology. As an example, in the Step "And I click on 'Search'", PANDA looks for any widget named "Search" in the initial state, and check if the description of the corresponding widget in the ontology support the behavior "ClickOn" (Fig. 19).

**Fig. 19.** Properties of a button in the tool PANDA with properties defined by the ontology

The results of the tests are displayed by a colored symbol next to each Step as shown in the Fig. 20. A red "X" represents failure, a green "V" represents success a black "?" represents an untested Step. There is currently no distinction between the different reasons of test failure (e.g. widget not found, property not supported, etc.). In our example, the button supports the event "#clickOn" which matches with the action "I click on" of the Scenario. However, none of the UI Elements (Calendar, CheckBox, Link or Radio Button) described in the ontology to support the behavior "chooseRefer-ringTo" was found.

[X] And I choose "12/15/2016"referring to "Depart"
[V] And I click on "Search"
[?] Then will be displayed "Choose Flights"

**Fig. 20.**  Example of results given during a Scenario testing

## 4.2    Testing in the Final UI Level

To test Final UI directly from User Stories, we use external frameworks (the so-called robots) to provide automated execution in the Final UI. Robots mimic user interactions with the Final UI by running Scenarios described in the User Stories. We use the robot Selenium WebDriver to run navigational behavior and JBehave and Demoiselle Behave to parse the Scenario script. Test results provided by the JUnit API indicate visually which tests passed and which ones failed and why. Execution reports of User Stories, Scenarios and Steps can be obtained by using the JBehave API.

Figure 21 presents the architectural model integrating tools and classes in the approach for testing the Final UI. The ontological model described in the Sect. 3.1 provides a pre-defined set of behaviors used at the Requirements Layer. Artifacts produced in Proto-typing and Task Layers are suitable to not only benefit from the ontology description to model better requirements, but also to contribute with the development of new User Stories. Pre-defined behaviors are mapped by the CommonSteps class that supports the development of specific behaviors not covered by the ontology, and subsequently mapped in the MySteps class. Both Steps are extracted from the User Stories that can be repre-sented in simple packages of text files. This structure composes the Requirements and Testing Layer. The Presentation Layer includes the MyPages class that describes the link between UI components defined in the ontology and the real UI components instantiated on the interface under testing. This link is crucial to allow the Selenium WebDriver robot and the other External Testing Frameworks to automatically execute the Scenarios in the right components on the UI. Finally, the MyTest class is a JUnit class responsible to trigger the tests, pointing which Scenarios should be executed and making the bridge between UI components in the Presentation Layer and executable behaviors in the Requirements and Testing Layer. Figure 22 shows the MyTest class automatically executing the "Return Tickets Search" Scenario presented in the case study.

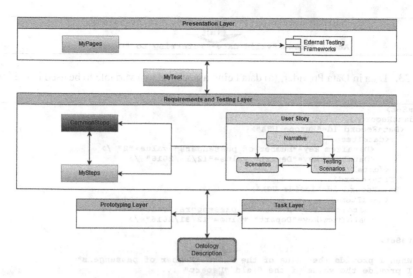

**Fig. 21.** Architectural representation of automated testing in the Final UI

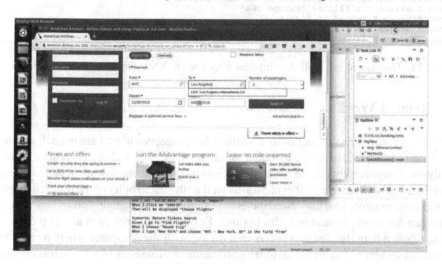

**Fig. 22.** Automated execution of the "Return Tickets Search" Scenario

Concerning the testing data, the approach offers two main strategies to set them out of Scenarios. The first one is establish Data Providers to store values for variables that can be used in the writing of Scenarios Steps. This mechanism is useful to render flexible the reuse of data dynamically and to hide data in Scenarios without losing readability. The second mechanism is the use of data storage in XML files. It is useful to work with a large set of data that should be introduced in Scenarios at runtime. Figures 23 and 24 illustrate these mechanisms.

```
        dataProvider.put("valid date", "12/30/2016");
                            ┌(a)┐
        And I choose "valid date" referring to "Depart" …
```

**Fig. 23.** Data in Data Provider: (a) data being associated to a variable to be used in the Step

```
<DataSet>
   <dataRecords>
      <DataRecord id="Europe USA">
         <dataItems>
            <DataItem key="Number of passengers" value="2" />
            <DataItem key="Depart" value="12/15/2016" />
         </dataItems>
      </DataRecord>
      <DataRecord id="Inside USA">
         <dataItems>
            <DataItem key="Number of passengers" value="3" />
            <DataItem key="Depart" value="12/31/2016" />
         ...
</DataSet>
                                  ┌(a)┐
... When I provide the value of the field "Number of passengers"
And I provide the value of the field "Depart" ...
                                  ┌(b)┐
Scenario: Search of flights stored in the dataset
When I search for flights "Europe USA"
Then "Choose Flights" is displayed
When I search for flights "Inside USA"
Then "Choose Flights" is displayed
```

**Fig. 24.** Data stored in a XML file: (a) data associated to XML file, (b) reference to dataset

## 5   Related Works

Efforts to specify requirements in a natural language, such as Language Extended Lexicon (LEL) [18], have been studied since the 90's. The authors propose a lexical analysis of requirements descriptions in order to integrate scenarios into a requirements baseline, making possible their evolution as well as the traceability of the different views of the requirements baseline. Nonetheless, requirements specified through an ATDD approach are recent in academic discussions. For example, Soeken et al. [1] propose a design flow where the designer enters in a dialog with the computer where a program processes sentence by sentence all the requirements creating code blocks such as classes, attributes, and operations in a BDD template. The template proposed by the computer can be revised which leads to a training of the computer program and a better understanding of following sentences. Some works [1, 18] use different approaches to process natural language; nonetheless none follow a User-Centered Design process.

Wolff et al. [5] proposes to link GUI specifications to abstract dialogue models. Specifications are linked to task models describing behavioral characteristics. Prototypes of interactive systems are refined and interactively generated using a GUI editor. The design cycle goes from task model to abstract user interfaces and finally to a concrete user interface. It is an interesting approach to have a mechanism to control changes in interface elements according to the task they are associated in the task models. However, the approach is not iterative and does not provide the necessary testing component to check and verify user interfaces against predefined behaviors from requirements.

Martinie et al. [6] propose a tool-supported framework for exploiting task models throughout the development process and even when the interactive application is deployed and used. The framework allows connecting task models to an existing, executable, interactive application thus defining a systematic correspondence between the user interface elements and user tasks. The problem with this approach is that it only covers the interaction of task models with Final UI, not covering other types of possible requirements artifacts that can emerge along the process. Another problem is it requires much intervention of developers to prepare the code to support the integration, making difficult to adopt in applications that cannot receive interventions in the code level.

Buchmann and Karagiannis [15] present a modelling method for the elicitation of requirements for mobile apps that enables semantic traceability for the requirements representation. Instead of having requirements represented as natural language items that are documented by diagrammatic models, the communication channels are switched: semantically interlinked conceptual models become the requirements representation, while free text can be used for requirements annotations/metadata. The authors claim that the method can support semantic traceability in scenarios of human-based requirements validation, but using an extremely heavy modeling approach which is not suitable to check requirements in a high level of abstraction. Besides that, the method is not focused in providing a testing mechanism through common artifacts, but only in validating the requirements modeled within the approach.

Käpyaho and Kauppinen [2] explore how prototyping can solve the challenges of requirements in an agile context. Authors suggest that prototyping can solve some problems of agile development such as the lack of documentation, poor communication tools, but it also needs complementary practices such as the use of ATDD (Acceptance Test-Driven Development). The authors conclude that one of the biggest benefits from prototyping is that the prototypes act as tangible plans that can be relied on when discussing changes.

# 6 Conclusion and Future Works

In this paper we have presented an approach aiming test automation that can help to validate functional requirements through multiple artifacts used to build interactive systems. For that, an ontology was provided to act as a base of common ontological concepts shared by different artifacts and to support traceability and test integration along the project. When representing the behaviors that each UI element is able to answer, the ontology also allows extending multiple solutions for the UI design. We have focused in this paper in the testing of Prototypes and Final UIs, but the same solution can be propagated to verify and validate other types of artifacts like Task Models and others, integrating the testing process and assuring traceability through artifacts. The degree of formality of these artifacts, however, can influence the process of traceability and testing, making it more or less tricky to conduct. These variations should be investigated in the future.

This approach also provides important improvements in the way teams should write requirements for testing purposes. Once described in the ontology, behaviors can be freely reused to write new Scenarios in natural language, providing test automation with little effort from the development team. Another important advantage is that multi-artifact testing is provided with no intervention in the source code of the application. It is also important to note that the concepts and definitions in the ontology presented herein are naturally only one of the possible solutions to address and describe behaviors and their relations with UIs. The ontology is provided ready to use for a new development project, but it is not changeless and could be replaced for other behaviors, concepts and relationships eventually more representatives for some contexts of development. Future discussions might consider having ontologies as knowledge bases, keeping specific behaviors for specific groups of business models. It would give us the possibility to also reuse entire business Scenarios in systems sharing similar business models.

We have also presented tools that demonstrate the feasibility of the approach. So far, PANDA supports automated testing only in the Medium-Fidelity Prototypes. However, like Task Models, Low-Fidelity Prototypes can also be checked on their XML files to validate if the interaction components referred in the Scenarios were considered in the Prototype. Considering that High-Fidelity Prototypes and Final UIs are built using the same level of fidelity for their interaction components, they both can also be tested by equivalent means. Doing so would allow us testing Prototypes at different periods of the design process, especially since the early phases, following their cycle of evolution and successive refinements, while ensuring that the tests on different artifacts share the same goals in terms of requirements.

The approach is still under development, so although the results of the first case studies are promising, we have no more data yet about the difficulty to implement it in different contexts (or platforms), neither about the time consumed to run it. Ongoing work is currently being conducted to verify potential problems and inconsistencies when working with multiple design options and manipulating more complex task models. We are also refining the set of developed tools to better support the creation, visualization and execution of the tests. Future works include experiments to evaluate the effectiveness and the workload when running the approach in real cases of software development, as well as establishing other case studies including mobile platforms.

# References

1. Soeken, M., Wille, R., Drechsler, R.: Assisted behavior driven development using natural language processing. In: Furia, C.A., Nanz, S. (eds.) TOOLS 2012. LNCS, vol. 7304, pp. 269–287. Springer, Heidelberg (2012)
2. Kapyaho, M., Kauppinen, M.: Agile requirements engineering with prototyping: a case study. In: IEEE International on Requirements Engineering Conference (RE) (2015)
3. North, D.: What's in a story? (2016). http://dannorth.net/whats-in-a-story/
4. Cohn, M.: User Stories Applied: For Agile Software Development. Addison-Wesley Professional, Reading (2004)
5. Wolff, A., Forbrig, P., Dittmar, A., Reichart, D.: Linking GUI elements to tasks: supporting an evolutionary design process. In: Proceedings of the 4th International Workshop on Task Models and Diagrams, pp. 27–34. ACM (2005)

6. Martinie, C., Navarre, D., Palanque, P., Fayollas, C.: A generic tool-supported framework for coupling task models and interactive applications. In: Proceedings of the 7th ACM SIGCHI Symposium on Engineering Interactive Computing Systems, pp. 244–253 (2015)

7. Santoro, C.: A Task Model-based Approach for Design and Evaluation of Innovative User Interfaces. Presses Univ. de Louvain (2005)

8. Rosson, M.B., Carroll, J.M.: Usability Engineering: Scenario-Based Development of Human-Computer Interaction. Morgan Kaufmann, San Francisco (2002)

9. Lewis, C., Rieman, J.: Task-Centered User Interface Design: A Practical Introduction. University of Colorado, Boulder (1993)

10. Chelimsky, D., Astels, D., Helmkamp, B., North, D., Dennis, Z., Hellesoy, A.: The RSpec book: Behaviour driven development with Rspec, Cucumber, and friends. Pragmatic Bookshelf (2010)

11. Guarino, N., Oberle, D., Staab, S.: What is an ontology? In: Handbook on Ontologies, pp. 1–17. Springer, Heidelberg (2009)

12. Limbourg, Q., Pribeanu, C., Vanderdonckt, J.: Towards uniformed task models in a model-based approach. In: Johnson, C. (ed.) DSV-IS 2001. LNCS, vol. 2220, pp. 164–182. Springer, Heidelberg (2001)

13. Limbourg, Q., Vanderdonckt, J., Michotte, B., Bouillon, L., López-Jaquero, V.: USIXML: a language supporting multi-path development of user interfaces. In: Feige, U., Roth, J. (eds.) DSV-IS 2004 and EHCI 2004. LNCS, vol. 3425, pp. 200–220. Springer, Heidelberg (2005)

14. Pullmann, J.: MBUI - Glossary - W3C (2016). https://www.w3.org/TR/mbui-glossary/. Fraunhofer FIT

15. Buchmann, R.A., Karagiannis, D.: Modelling mobile app requirements for semantic traceability. Requirements Eng., 1–35 (2015)

16. Nair, S., de la Vara, J.L., Sen, S.: A review of traceability research at the requirements engineering conference re@ 21. In: 2013 21st IEEE International Requirements Engineering Conference (RE), pp. 222–229. IEEE (2013)

17. Uusitalo, E.J., Komssi, M., Kauppinen, M., Davis, A.M.: Linking requirements and testing in practice. In: 16th IEEE International Requirements Engineering, RE 2008, pp. 265–270. IEEE (2008)

18. Leite, J.C., Oliveira, A.P.: A client oriented requirements baseline. In: Proceedings of the Second IEEE International Symposium on Requirements Engineering (1995)

19. Ebert, C.: Global Software and IT: A Guide to Distributed Development, Projects, and Outsourcing. Wiley, New Jersey (2011)

20. Myers, G.J., Sandler, C., Badgett, T.: The Art of Software Testing. Wiley, New Jersey (2011)

21. Lindstrom, D.R.: Five ways to destroy a development project. IEEE Softw. **10**, 55–58 (1993)

22. Pugh, K.: Lean-Agile Acceptance Test-Driven-Development. Pearson Education, Upper Saddle River (2010)

23. Adzic, G.: Specification by Example: How Successful Teams Deliver the Right Software. Manning Publications, Westampton (2011)

24. Martinie, C., Palanque, P., Winckler, M.: Structuring and composition mechanisms to address scalability issues in task models. In: Campos, P., Graham, N., Jorge, J., Nunes, N., Palanque, P., Winckler, M. (eds.) INTERACT 2011, Part III. LNCS, vol. 6948, pp. 589–609. Springer, Heidelberg (2011)

25. Hak, J.L., Winckler, M., Navarre, D.: PANDA: prototyping using annotation and decision analysis. In: Proceedings of the 8th ACM SIGCHI Symposium on Engineering Interactive Computing Systems, EICS 2016, Brussels, Belgium, 21–24 June, pp. 171–176. ACM (2016). ISBN: 978-1-4503-4322-0

# Socio-Technical and Ethical Considerations

# Communication in Teams - An Expression of Social Conflicts

Jil Klünder[1]([⊠]), Kurt Schneider[1], Fabian Kortum[1], Julia Straube[2],
Lisa Handke[2], and Simone Kauffeld[2]

[1] Software Engineering Group, Leibniz Universität Hannover,
Welfengarten 1, 30167 Hannover, Germany
{jil.kluender,kurt.schneider,fabian.kortum}@inf.uni-hannover.de
[2] Department of Industrial/Organizational and Social Psychology, Technische
Universität Braunschweig, Spielmannstraße 19, 38106 Braunschweig, Germany
{julia.straube,l.handke,s.kauffeld}@tu-bs.de

**Abstract.** The more members a team has, the more information needs
to be shared with single team members or within the whole team. Sufficient information sharing is difficult to ensure, since a project leader
will not be fully aware of all on-going information and communication
within the team. In software engineering, information flow is essential
for project success. In each part of the process, information like requirements or design decisions needs to be communicated with appropriate
persons. Neither missing nor wrong implemented requirements are desirable, since extra working hours or incomplete working results need to
be paid. Therefore, the right amount of information sharing is highly
desirable. To ensure this, communication is a mandatory requisite. Furthermore, knowing about social conflicts is suitable, since these influence
the information flow.

In an experiment with 34 student software projects, we collected data
referring to internal team communication and mood. In these projects, we
could show a correlation between chosen communication channels, social
conflicts and mood. Since social conflicts foster an insufficient information flow, knowing about these helps software developing teams to reach
higher quality and a higher customer satisfaction.

## 1 Introduction

Ensuring the right amount of information sharing with all involved persons is
often difficult. Some information only needs to be communicated with a few team
members, while other information needs to be shared within the whole team.

In software engineering, the impact of "appropriate" communication on
project success has been discussed frequently (e.g. [23,28]). Both, the communication with the customer and the inner team communication require special

© IFIP International Federation for Information Processing 2016
Published by Springer International Publishing Switzerland 2016. All Rights Reserved
C. Bogdan et al. (Eds.): HCSE 2016/HESSD 2016, LNCS 9856, pp. 111–129, 2016.
DOI: 10.1007/978-3-319-44902-9_8

attention to provide high quality project results with well performing functionalities [16]. Communication is important for working in groups. Furthermore,
motivated by the importance of information sharing within the project team,
communication has been proven to be a determinant of project success [19].

In software developing teams, wrong or insufficiently transmitted requirements often cause wrong or not implemented parts of the software [27]. Therefore, insufficient communication can threaten project success. Otherwise, adequate communication can foster project success. Hence, a good working communication is desirable for all project members: The developer team that does
not want to spend time on implementing unnecessary program code, the project
leader who wants to complete the tasks, and lastly the customer who wants a
successful project. But not only requirements need to be shared within the team.
Also design decisions, customized standards, reports about bugs and many other
information need to be transported to the relevant persons.

As Stapel [30] pointed out, not only the intensity of communication, but also
the chosen communication channel is important for transmitting the desired
information. In the "Modes of Communication", Cockburn [5] rated different
kind of communication channels by their effectiveness and richness. Among other
characteristics like synchronicity, the perceptions addressed by the media channels are one factor for the grading. For example, meetings with face to face
communication – in physical support with a white board – are the most effective
way to communicate [1,5]. As teams often do not have the opportunity to meet
regularly and since meetings often do not suffice for conveying the entire information at hand, other ways of information sharing need to be used. In practice,
common alternatives are services like email, video chat, telephone or group and
single chat.

Schneider et al. [26] developed an approach to combine communication channels and the intensity. They used *FLOW distance*, which is defined to be a measure for the collaboration in teams.

In this contribution, we want to motivate the usage of FLOW distance by
achieving a relationship between FLOW distance, and hence communication
behavior, mood and social conflicts in software developing teams.

Along with the findings of Watson et al. [35], mood can be described using
positive and negative affect. While persons in a state of high negative affect
feel anger, disgust and fear, persons in a state of high positive affect feel active,
enthusiastic and alert [35]. The affects of persons working in groups converge
over time, meaning that the mood of all team members assimilate [6,32]. This
assimilation influences team performance as well as important process variables:
For example, Barsade [3] was able to prove that positive group mood is associated
with better performance and less conflicts.

This paper concentrates on the positive affect dimension, as we assume that
positive group mood facilitates action (cf. [21]) and will thus be beneficial, especially at the beginning of the project.

We are able to show that summarizing the chosen communication channels
and the communication intensity using FLOW distance has a relation to social

conflicts and mood. The FLOW distance between two members measures the indirections and barriers hampering the information flow when they communicate. Given by the intuitive comprehension of distance, FLOW distance increases with a decreasing collaboration and with the usage of non-direct communication channels and vice versa.

In an experimental study on 34 student software projects, we show a correlation between FLOW distance, social conflicts and mood at certain stages of the project. Therefore, an increasing FLOW distance can be seen as indication for difficulties within the team. Therefore, observing FLOW distance may be helpful for the project leader. It helps assuming problems within the developing team and working against lack of information sharing. In the case of a well-working communication, the project leader finds out that there is no reason to modify or adjust the used media channels.

The structure of this article is as follows: In the following Sect. 2, we give an overview of related work in similar topics. In Sect. 3, we motivate and give the definition of FLOW distance with its properties and the way of calculation. Afterwards, we validate our approach in Sect. 4, followed by Sect. 5, in which we discuss the results. Section 6 summarizes our work.

## 2 Related Work

The relationship between communication intensity, communication channels and project success has been studied for a long time in software engineering. This chapter gives an overview about already existing approaches in certain topics which are related to this paper: The combination of *social network analysis* with the *FLOW method* to analyze information flows and the *distance*, i.e. *collaboration*, within the team referring to the communication intensity of a co-located working software developing team.

The idea of combining *social network analysis* and communication intensities is not entirely new. In the context of the collaboration within a team, Damian et al. [8] studied the awareness among team members in global software development teams using methods of social network analysis. They found a positive correlation between communication and awareness within so-called requirements-centered social network analysis.

Additional work often refers to team communication centralization that indicates the degree to which communication is focused on a subset of participants or even a single person. High centralization can be considered as an indication of unequal communication participation (for other network measures of participation, such as Maverick score, see [24]). Centralization of communication compiles structural and quantitative elements (weights) into an indicative number. It is a widely-used metric in social network analysis.

Sauer et al. [25] applied social network analysis to team interaction. They investigated the calculation of centralization for various kinds of small group interactions. After having conceptualized group discussions as networks, they were able to present a metric calculating a centralization for these networks using extensions of Freeman's metrics for centrality measures [11]. In the end, they examine the relationship between team performance and centralization of the interactions during the meeting.

In software engineering, Wolf et al. [38] also applied social network analysis to team communication structures. They wanted to indicate the importance of developer communication for software integrations. In order to reach this aim, they used well-elaborated measures like density and centrality in general as metrics.

The *FLOW method* serves for visualizing and analyzing information flows in project teams. It was introduced and presented by Stapel et al. [31]. The general structure of communication within the team is extended about the state of information flow: *Solid* information summarize all information that is repeatable, long term accessible and comprehensible for third parties, whereas *fluid* information is everything which is not solid.

Although most research concerning the *distance* in teams refer to distributed software developing teams, there are some approaches that are comparable to our approach, which focuses on co-located teams.

Bjarnason [4] identified different variants of distance in software engineering literature. She stated that distance plays an important role in both, distributed and co-located software development. In her systematic literature review, she found eight different distances between people, i.e. within the team, also including the geographical distance. In the context of this contribution, Bjarnason's results concerning the *socio-cultural distance* including among other things organizational and national culture, language and individual motivations, *opinion distance* and *organizational distance* are important. The most important results are those related to the *psychological distance*. Prikladnicki [24] has denoted psychological distance as a "measure of the perceived psychological (subjective) effort of an actor to communicate with another actor" [4].

There have already been various researches relating to *FLOW distance*. Schneider et al. [26] presented a first approach of defining and using FLOW distance. The authors evolved the idea of a "perceived distance" generated by the communication intensity and a certain weighting of the used communication media. Schneider et al. considered FLOW distance as "the number of weighted indirections between source and target of an information flow" [28]. In the present contribution, we will refine the definition and motivate this approach by pointing out a relation between FLOW distance, social conflicts and mood.

## 3    FLOW Distance

FLOW distance is a metric combining communication intensity and used media. Exploring the information flow within a project, FLOW distance simplifies the detection of the wrong amount of communication and therefore indicates problems in information sharing. Considering the FLOW distance enables strategic changes in the way of communication (for example by adding an obligatory meeting each week) and hence a better flow of relevant information.

In this contribution, we want to elaborate the already existing definition of FLOW distance (cf. [26, 28]) restricted to a static network of a single software developing team consisting of three to five co-located working members. We want the measure to consider the used media and the subjective communication intensity between two persons within these teams. FLOW distance can also be used to analyze the structure of a team using social network analysis.

The requests and restrictions can be summarized as follows:

- FLOW distance should consider the communication intensities and the used media.
- It shall increase with a decreasing collaboration and vice versa.
- It has to be practicable, i.e. it needs to be easy to calculate and the input data need to be collectable with low effort.
- For later research, it needs to be extendable towards bigger software developing teams and to FLOW models[1].

Fulfilling these requests yields to a few more definitions and analyses before giving the definition of FLOW distance.

1. Creating a mathematical model of FLOW distance which allows a precise and well-founded definition.
2. Weighting the used media with respect to their effectiveness and richness. This needs to be done at least for the common used communication channels "meetings (F2F)", "video chats", "chats", "emails" and "phone calls".
3. Defining and calculating the communication intensity only using easily collectable data.
4. Giving the definition of FLOW distance and using it for calculation.

These steps will be executed in the course of this chapter.

## 3.1 Mathematical View

We consider FLOW distance as a mapping $d\colon A \times A \to [0, 1]$, where $A$ denotes the set of all team members and $[0, 1]$ is the unit interval[2]. We understand FLOW distance as a metric from a mathematical point of view, i.e. it is (i) positive definite, (ii) symmetric and (iii) the triangle-inequality holds:

(i) *positive definite:* The measure is always greater than or equal to zero. It vanishes if and only if the two persons are the same, i.e. $d(i, i) = 0$ and $d(i, j) \neq 0 \, \forall \, i \neq j$.

This is useful, since there is no interpretation for negative distances between two members and having a FLOW distance of zero between to different members would mean that they spend the whole time together exchanging each thought.

---

[1] This extension will not be part of this contribution.

[2] The restriction of the image of $d$ to the unit interval helps comparing the FLOW distances of different teams.

(ii) *symmetric:* Along the lines of Watzlawick's findings [36], one cannot not communicate, meaning that also if only $i$ sends many emails to $j$ without receiving an answer, $j$ communicates with $i$ by receiving the emails. Therefore, the mapping $d$ should be symmetric, even if the communication is one-directional.

(iii) *triangle-inequality:* The FLOW distance between two team members $i$ and $k$ should be greater than or equal to the sum of the FLOW distances between $i$ and $j$ and $j$ and $k$, i.e. $d(i, k) \geq d(i, j) + d(j, k)$. In the context of communication, this means that communicating via a third person let the distance between the two other persons increase.

## 3.2  Media Richness and Effectivity

We consider the common used communication media "email", "phone call", "video chat", "chat" and "meeting". Intuitively, the intensity and efficiency are the largest in meetings, followed by video chat, chat, phone and email. There are proper justifications to use this or a very similar grading of the media [10].

First of all, the more human senses the media addresses, the more information can be transported. One does not only communicate by speaking; the facial expression, the gestures and the voice are not less important than the used words [7]. In meetings and video chats, most senses are addressed. In chats, emails and in phone calls, there is only written or heard text. This way, we get the following weighting:

$$\text{meetings} = \text{video chat} > \text{email} = \text{chat} = \text{phone call}$$

Furthermore, we should consider the synchronicity of the media [9]. Meanwhile meetings, chats, video chats and phone calls are instantaneous, emails often need much time until the receiver answers them. Therefore, the weighting of emails should be smaller than the weighting of chat and phone calls, i.e.

$$\text{meetings} = \text{video chat} > \text{chat} = \text{phone call} > \text{email}$$

Due to the direct face-to-face communication without screens or bandwidth (potentially limiting the information flow) and the interactions of team members in one room, the importance of meetings should be bigger than the importance of video chats. Therefore, we get the following final order of the efficiency and effectivity of the media:

$$\text{meetings} > \text{video chat} > \text{chat} = \text{phone call} > \text{email}$$

Table 1 reflects the weighting of media gained by starting with 1 and increasing the weighting about one unit at each jump in the previous ordering. These weights will be used for calculating FLOW distance.

Cockburn's [5] and Ambler's [1] reflections support this ordering. In his "Modes of Communication", Cockburn proposes a grading of various communication channels referring to their "richness" and "effectiveness". Figure 1 represents these findings, which can be retrieved in the grading above.

**Table 1.** Media weighting for calculating FLOW distance

| meeting | 4 |
|---|---|
| video chat | 3 |
| chat | 2 |
| phone call | 2 |
| email | 1 |

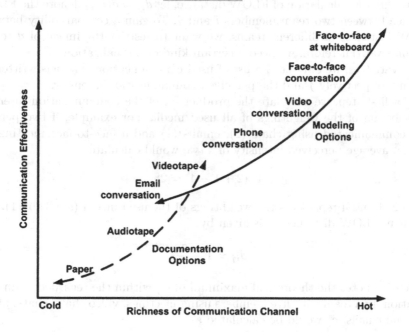

**Fig. 1.** Modes of communication [1]

### 3.3 Communication Intensity

Calculating the FLOW distance requires a certain kind of communication intensity. Therefore, each team member is asked to estimate the intensity of communication with respect to each other team member. This way, we gain a matrix of the following structure:

$$\begin{bmatrix} 0 & a_{12} & a_{13} & a_{14} & a_{15} \\ a_{21} & 0 & a_{23} & a_{24} & a_{25} \\ a_{31} & a_{32} & 0 & a_{34} & a_{35} \\ a_{41} & a_{42} & a_{43} & 0 & a_{45} \\ a_{51} & a_{52} & a_{53} & a_{54} & 0 \end{bmatrix}$$

where each $a_{ij}$ has a value between 0 and $4^3$. Ideally, this matrix is symmetric, i.e. $a_{ij} = a_{ji}$ for all team members $i, j \in A$. But since the statements concerning the

---

[3] This area was fixed by the study design and may be adapted to other study designs.

intensity are all subjective and there does not exist a (non-technical) objective reference, this matrix will probably never be symmetric. Therefore, we calculate the average of each $a_{ij}$ and $a_{ji}$ to gain the resulting communication intensity between $i$ and $j$.

### 3.4   Calculation

To simplify the calculation of FLOW distance, let $d_{ij} = d(i,j)$ denote the FLOW distance between two team members $i$ and $j$. To gain a comparability between FLOW distances of different teams, we want to restrict the image of $d$ to the unit interval. Therefore, we need a certain kind of normalization.

As variables, we only need a list of used communication channels written by person $i$ respectively $j$ and the perceived communication intensity.

In a first step, we calculate the product $c_{ij}$ of the communication intensity and the sum of the weightings of all used media. For example, if two persons have communicated using chats (2), emails (1) and a face-to-face meeting (4) with an average perceived intensity of 4, we would calculate

$$4 \cdot (2 + 1 + 4) = 28,$$

where 2, 1 and 4 represents the weightings of the used media (see Table 1).

Then, FLOW distance $d_{ij}$ is given by

$$d_{ij} = 1 - \frac{c_{ij}}{c^*},$$

where $c^*$ denotes the theoretical maximum of $c_{ij}$ within the regarded team constellation. In a team with five members using meetings, video chats, chats, phone calls and emails, $c^*$ would be calculated as

$$c^* = 4 \cdot (4 + 3 + 2 + 2 + 1) = 48,$$

where 4 is the maximal possible communication intensity.
Looking at the example of above, the FLOW distance is

$$d_{ij} = 1 - \frac{28}{48} \approx 0,4167.$$

The FLOW distance of the whole team, $d$, is given by the average of the FLOW distances of the team members, i.e.

$$d = \mathrm{avg}\{d_{ij} : i \neq j \in A\}.$$

### 3.5   FLOW Centralization

Using FLOW distance calculation, we can create the *FLOW centralization* which gives an overview for the structure of the team. As centralization and centrality are common measures in psychology and social network analysis to analyze team structures and the collaboration, FLOW centralization can be applied to further calculations in social network analysis.

We start with an upper triangular matrix $D$, where the entry $d_{ij}$ is given by the FLOW distance between the members $i$ and $j$. The FLOW centralization is then calculated as follows:

We get the *FLOW centrality* of a person $j$ by summing up over all FLOW distances between this person and all other team member, i.e.

$$\text{centrality}(j) = \sum_{i \in A} d_{ij},$$

where $A$ again denotes the set of all team members and $d_{ij}$ is the FLOW distance (respectively the entries in $D$). The higher a person's centrality, the closer he or she is generally to the other team members.

Let now $\text{centrality}_{\max}$ denote the score of the team member who has the maximum centrality, i.e.

$$\text{centrality}_{\max} = \max\{\text{centrality}(j) : j \in A\}.$$

Then, we calculate the FLOW centralization by

$$\text{centralization} = \sum_{j \in A} \frac{\text{centrality}_{\max} - \text{centrality}(j)}{\text{centrality}^*}, \qquad (*)$$

where $\text{centrality}^*$ denotes the theoretical maximum of centrality.

Calculating $\text{centrality}^*$ bases on considering the star shape as network [11]. The star network has the largest centralization, which is why it is used to normalize the FLOW centralization. In this network, we weight each edge with $c^*$,

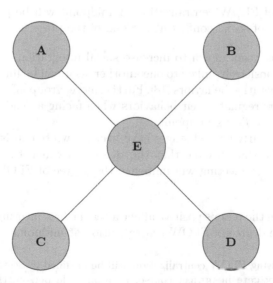

**Fig. 2.** The star shape network with five persons. In this example, person E is the most central team member.

which is defined to be the most possible communication interaction (gained by using all media with the most perceived intensity). Figure 2 shows the star shape network with five persons.

Considering not an individual's centrality, but the group centralization allows conclusions about the team internal structure[4]: The higher the centralization, the more individual members communicate via one dominant actor rather than directly to one another.

## 4    Empirical Validation

To motivate the use of FLOW distance and FLOW centralization, we want to show the relationship between communication channels, perceived communication intensity and social conflicts.

As several studies have shown, a low degree in centralization appears to be beneficial for team performance [25, 28]. As software projects are considered to be highly dynamic entities, communication structures may also be expected to vary over time [2]. The project's midpoint may be particularly relevant in this case, as teams have been shown to display increased effort at this time [12, 34]. Furthermore, at this stage of the project, team structures also seem to change, as individual expectations and perceptions transform into shared group goals and understandings [12, 13]. Considering that team development during this point in time also involves conflict resolutions [15], we assume that it will be influential on how teams deal with relationship conflicts throughout the rest of the project. We thus hypothesize that a higher degree of FLOW centralization in the middle of the project will also be associated with increased social conflicts later on.

H1: The degree of FLOW centralization at midpoint will be positively related to the degree of social conflict at the end of the project.

Positive affect has been known to increase social integration, i.e. the extent to which people are positively linked to one another, as it can be linked to approach-oriented and cooperative behaviors [18]. Furthermore, group affect seems to influence how members regulate their behaviors when facing a deadline [17], such as a quality gate[5] at project's midpoint.

Interactions in early project stages have been shown to consist of long-lasting effects [12, 39]. We thus assume that the degree to which the team's positive affect after their first meeting will influence the degree of FLOW centralization at midpoint.

H2: The degree of the team's positive affect after the first meeting will negatively influence the degree of FLOW centralization at midpoint.

---

[4] The benefit of using FLOW centralization will be outlined in Sect. 5.2.

[5] Within a quality gate in project course, a responsible person, the so-called gate keeper, decides about the release of the next project step on the basis of clearly determined quality criteria [29].

In line with Totterdell et al.'s [33] assertion that social networks act like conduits for affect to flow and converge through, we furthermore assume that positive group affect after the first team meeting will decrease the incidence of social conflicts at the end of the project via decentralized communication structures at midpoint.

H3: Centralization will mediate the relationship between positive affect after the first team meeting and social conflicts at the end of the project.

To validate these hypotheses, we conducted a study with 34 student software projects.

## 4.1 Student Software Projects

At Leibniz Universität Hannover, the Software Engineering Group offers a yearly repeating course called Software-Project (SWP), which is scheduled in the last (third) year of the computer science bachelor curriculum. Participating in this course is a requisite in order to complete the undergraduate studies.

In this course, the teams mostly consist of five students developing a software for a customer, who is usually part of the software engineering group and who has a real interest in project success. The projects resemble industrial projects, but also consider the academic environment[6]. The students need to organize themselves, i.e. they need to coordinate the meetings with the customer, within their team, and with the advisors at the right time and in an appropriate way. The teams get supported by a coach who is part of the software engineering group.

Within the 15 weeks of the fall semester, the students learn to work in a team, talk to the customer and organize the internal communication. To support them and to get the ability to obtain feedback, the teams had to pass three quality gates – after the requirements elicitation, after the design and at the end of the project.

The students are free to choose time and location for their meetings. They also autonomously decide on how often they meet and which communication channels they use.

With regards to the technical experiences in executing a project, teams need to elicit requirements, design, implement, and test their product. Thus, they pass through all common phases of the waterfall model. They need to write a requirements specification and either create a design or implement a prototype of the product. Co-located in the process, they furthermore make a review of the design respectively the prototype of another team. In the last step, they develop the software, which needs to be approved by the customer.

---

[6] A german description of all tasks can be found at http://www.se.uni-hannover.de/pages/de:lehre_fungate.

## 4.2  Study Design

In 2012 and 2013, a total of 165 students participated in the Software-Project. They worked in 34 teams mostly consisting of five persons. There was only one team consisting of four students, and two teams with three students. Each team worked together for a period of 15 weeks. Due to missing data, we had to exclude one team from the analyses. The final sample therefore consisted of 33 teams (160 individuals).

During the course, the students were asked to fill in questionnaires at three specific dates: after the initial meeting with the customer, after half of the project duration and at the end of the project. Questionnaires contained items on e.g. positive affect and social conflicts. We did not ask the students to report on the cause of conflict, but the mostly arising conflicts have been caused by different attitudes to work, reliability and different abilities to work in a team. Additionally, the team members filled out a weekly online-questionnaire referring to the interactions with other team members.

To assess the communication within the teams, we asked each team member to record his or her communication with each other member of the team. They were free to choose gradations between "not communicated at all" and "very high". We did not raise the frequency of the used communication media. During a whole week, the frequency influences the perceived intensity, so that measuring perceived intensity is sufficient for our approach. Furthermore, each team member stated the used communication media with respect to every other team member. The channels "in one room", "video", "chat", "telephone" and "email" were available. Additionally, the project leader was asked to state the duration of all meetings and the presence of each team member.

## 4.3  Ethics Committee

The ethics committee at Leibniz Universität Hannover authorized this elevation of data. We informed the students about the collection of data and the further usage. All data records were anonymized and the data did not influence the success of passing the course.

## 4.4  Methodology

**Measures.** Within the scope of this contribution, we used the following data:

*FLOW centralization* at midpoint of each project's total duration was measured using a communication score derived from data obtained via the self-report in week 7. Using the individual ratings of intensity and media, an undirected communication matrix for each team and for every week was obtained by averaging the two scores for communication intensity and by determining the maximum value for media use for each communication pair, and then multiplying these two scores (see Sect. 3.5). As described by the formula (*) in Sect. 3.5, FLOW centralization was computed in adding up the differences between the most central team member's centrality and centralities of all other team members and subsequently dividing them by the theoretical maximum score of 576 (288 and 96 for the teams with four or three members respectively).

*Social conflict* was measured using the German version of Jehn's [14] intragroup conflict scale by Lehmann-Willenbrock, Grohmann and Kauffeld [22], adapted to the context of teams. The scale consisted of four items with a six-level range from 1 = "never/none" to 6 = "very often/very much". An exemplary item was "How much friction is there among members in your team?" The measurement was taken at the end of the project. The reliability value for this scale was $\alpha = .87$.

*Positive affect* was measured using the German translation of the positive and negative affect scale (PANAS) [35] by Kroehne et al. [20]. The response format ranged from 1 = "not at all" to 5 = "extremely". The questions were answered after the first team meeting in week 1. The scale, which consisted of ten items, showed a reliability of $\alpha = .85$.

To obtain group level constructs for social conflict and positive affect, individual scores were mean-aggregated to the team level.

**Data Analysis.** Statistical procedures were performed using SPSS 22 (IBM Corp.). In order to avoid alpha error inflation, all three hypotheses were tested in one mediation model. The PROCESS-macro for SPSS by Andrew F. Hayes[7] was employed for the mediation analysis.

While the path from the mediator (FLOW centralization) to the dependent variable (social conflict) was used to test the first hypothesis, the path from the predictor (positive affect) to the mediator (FLOW centralization) served to test the second. As both of these hypotheses are directed, we will later report the results of one-tailed hypothesis tests. The third hypothesis was tested in

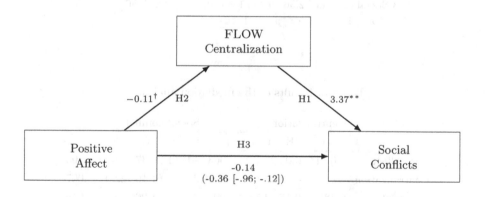

$^\dagger p < .1, {}^* p < .05, {}^{**} p < .01$

**Fig. 3.** Mediation model

---

[7] For further information see http://www.afhayes.com.

calculating the indirect effect from positive affect via FLOW centralization to social conflict. Figure 3 shows the hypothesized mediation model[8].

## 4.5 Results

Table 2 shows descriptive statistics and intercorrelations among the variables under study. As Table 3 shows, the unstandardized coefficient between FLOW centralization and social conflict was statistically significant ($p = .007/2 \approx .004$). The first hypothesis was thus supported. Showing a clear negative tendency, the relationship between positive affect and FLOW centralization also reached statistical significance ($p = .063/2 \approx .03$). The second hypothesis was thus also corroborated. The relationship between positive affect and social conflict was mediated by FLOW centralization. We tested the significance of this indirect effect using bootstrapping procedures. Unstandardized indirect effects were computed for each of 1000 bootstrapped samples, and the 95 % confidence interval was computed by determining the indirect effects at the 2.5th and 97.5th percentiles. The bootstrapped unstandardized indirect effect was $-.3551$, and the 95 % confidence interval ranged from $-.9553$ to $-.0169$. Thus, the indirect effect was statistically significant, supporting hypothesis 3.

**Table 2.** Descriptive statistics and intercorrelations among variables

|  | M | SD | Min | Max | 1 | 2 | 3 |
|---|---|---|---|---|---|---|---|
| 1 Pos. affect | 3.16 | 0.33 | 2.60 | 3.86 | - |  |  |
| 2 Centralization | 0.15 | 0.11 | 0.01 | 0.51 | $-.31^a$ | - |  |
| 3 Social conflict | 2.36 | 0.75 | 1.35 | 4.19 | $-.22$ | $.50^{**}$ | - |

$^a p < .1, {}^* p < .05, {}^{**} p < .01$

**Table 3.** Results of the mediation analysis

|  | Centralization | | | | Social conflict | | | |
|---|---|---|---|---|---|---|---|---|
|  | Coeff. | SE | t | p | Coeff. | SE | t | p |
| Pos. Affect | $-0.11^a$ | 0.05 | $-1.93$ | .063 | $-0.14$ | 0.37 | $-0.38$ | .705 |
| Centralization | - | - | - | - | $3.37^{**}$ | 1.16 | 2.90 | .007 |
| Constant | $0.48^{**}$ | 0.17 | 2.78 | .009 | $2.31^a$ | 1.26 | 1.84 | .076 |

$^a p < .1, {}^* p < .05, {}^{**} p < .01$

---

[8] In order to ensure a better understanding of the results, coefficients are also included in the model.

# 5   Discussion

In this section, we consider the study's limitations and threats to validity before interpreting and discussing our findings.

## 5.1   Limitations and Threats to Validity

Referring to our evaluation with students, we had to make some limitations with regards to the real world. These limitations may threaten the validity of the collected data and therefore influence the results of our calculations. Along with the classifications of threats to validity by Wohlin et al. [37], we divide the threats into *construct*, *external* and *internal* validity and *reliability*.

*Internal validity:* We wanted to consider the changes over the course of the projects. Therefore, all threats concerning the internal validity (e.g. maturation, internal interactions and talking about the project, the questionnaires and the collected data) were desired and to some extent even necessary.

*External validity:* Although there are some modifications of the student projects towards industrial standards, the academic environment still influences the scope and the duration of the projects. The ability of working together in a room each week was supported by the academic environment, since all students mostly worked at university and have been there five days per week. Project leader were not able to access to a big pool of experiences, since they possessed the same amount of experiences as the rest of their team. Therefore, a coach of the software engineering group supported the teams, when any social, i.e. interpersonal, problems occurred. Furthermore, we only considered projects with a duration of 15 weeks with small teams (3–5 members). Almost all participants had the same background in theory and the team internal experiences and knowledge was comparable in all teams. This was given by forming the teams deliberately. Beside these threats, there are no more relating to the external validity.

*Construct validity:* We formulated the questionnaires for the students in a general manner and used reliable gradations and items. But we still cannot ensure that our comprehension of the items correspond with the student's comprehension. We tried to minimize the impact of this wrong understanding through the presence of one of the researchers involved in the project while the students filled out the extensive questionnaires. This threats arose by comparing the perceived communication intensities (the communication matrices have not been symmetric), for instance. We respected these irregularities in the definition of FLOW distance. The weekly report was formulated in a very general manner, so that we do not expect any deviations in the understanding.

*Reliability:* The study's results are statistically significant. But there are still a few threats concerning the reliability of the study. Different projects have different scopes and the knowledge and experience base of each team is different from the other teams. These factors can restrict the reliability of this study.

## 5.2   Interpretation

With our approach of using FLOW distance, we propose a way to comprehend the influences of different communication channels on project success. Along with the findings of our study, we are able to show two things:

(i)  The mediation model consisting of FLOW centralization, social conflicts and mood.
(ii) The appropriateness of using FLOW distance to combine the communication channels and the perceived communication intensity.

The experiment supports our three hypotheses:

1. The degree of FLOW centralization at midpoint is positively related to the degree of social conflict at the end of the project. (H1)
2. The degree of the team's positive affect after the first meeting negatively influences the degree of FLOW centralization at midpoint. (H2)
3. Centralization mediates the relationship between positive affect after the first team meeting and social conflicts at the end of the project. (H3)

A suitable amount of information sharing is necessary for project success. Therefore, ensuring information flow is very important for the project leader. Exchanging information goes along with communication – often in meetings, via e-mail, phone or in (video) chats.

Using certain communication channels can foster and ensure information sharing. Obligatory meetings each week can guarantee a minimum of information exchange. Phone calls, e-mails, conversations and chats in addition to the meetings are also mandatory, since they can minimalize loss of information.

Along with our findings, asking each team member about the perceived communication intensity and the used communication channels is a good way to monitor the information flow.

Combining these data using FLOW distance also indicates social problems and conflicts at the end of project. As shown in H1 and H2, high positive mood influences FLOW centralization, which depends on FLOW distance and thus on communication behavior. The FLOW centralization again has an impact on social conflicts which can influence the project success.

As the deadline approaches, collaboration is very important. Social conflicts at this point may impair project success, i.e. the successful completion of the overall project. FLOW distance is an indicator for that kind of conflicts. Knowing about conflicts arising with an increasing probability can help solving them before they occur.

Therefore, we are not only able to support the hypothesis that communication is important for project proceeding, for example because of its influence on information sharing. Our approach of using FLOW distance as a metric for the collaboration in teams is also target-oriented with respect to ensure an appropriate amount of information flow.

# 6    Conclusions

This work introduces an approach of using FLOW distance to foster a suitable amount of information flow in software development teams and therefore project success.

Internal team communication is very important for project success: In each part of the project, information needs to be shared within the whole team or with certain team members.

FLOW distance is a measure combining communication intensities and the used communication channels, which is much easier to assess than surveying every interaction between two or more team members. Furthermore, based on the calculation of FLOW distance, FLOW centralization can be calculated. It can be applied to methods in social network analysis supporting the recognition of team internal structures.

Using the data collection of 33 comparable software projects with 160 participants, we are able to show the relationship between FLOW centralization, social conflicts and mood at certain stages of the project. The degree of FLOW centralization at midpoint is positively related to the degree of social conflicts at the end of the project, which means that the chosen communication channels and the perceived communication intensity at midpoint are indicators for social conflicts at project's end. Furthermore, the degree of the positive affect negatively influences the degree of FLOW centralization at midpoint: Positive mood in the developing team (for example reducible to a successful start of the project) has a negative impact on FLOW centralization which depends on communication in the middle of the project. Moreover, the FLOW centralization mediates the relationship between positive affect after the first team meeting and social conflicts at the end of the project meaning that FLOW centralization – and hence communication – links good mood at the start of the project and social conflicts at project's end.

Therefore, considering FLOW distance helps the project leader to get an overview about possibly existing social conflicts and mood, which influence the information flow and therefore project success. Considering the FLOW distance can foster project success with respect to different metrics: requirement compliance [27], customer satisfaction, and the team mood by preventing unnecessary work through a sufficient information flow.

Future work will inter alia focus on the application of FLOW distance and FLOW centralization in social network analysis to analyze internal team structures and indicate critical interpersonal combinations.

**Acknowledgements.** This work was funded by the German Research Society (DFG) under grant number *263807701* (Project TeamFLOW, 2015–2017).

# References

1. Ambler, S.W., et al.: Agile modeling (2002)
2. Balijepally, V.: Collaborative software development in agile methodologies - Perspectives from small group research. In: AMCIS 2005 Proceedings (2005)

3. Barsade, S.G.: The ripple effect: emotional contagion and its influence on group behavior. Adm. Sci. Q. **47**(4), 644–675 (2002)
4. Bjarnason, E.: Distances between requirements engineering and later software development activities: a systematic map. In: Doerr, J., Opdahl, A.L. (eds.) REFSQ 2013. LNCS, vol. 7830, pp. 292–307. Springer, Heidelberg (2013). http://dx.doi.org/10.1007/978-3-642-37422-7_21
5. Cockburn, A.: Agile Software Development: The Cooperative Game. Pearson Education, London (2006)
6. Collins, A.L., Lawrence, S.A., Troth, A.C., Jordan, P.J.: Group affective tone: a review and future research directions. J. Organ. Behav. **34**, 43–62 (2013)
7. Daft, R.L., Lengel, R.H.: Information richness. A new approach to managerial behavior and organization design. Technical report, DTIC Document (1983)
8. Damian, D., Marczak, S., Kwan, I.: Collaboration patterns and the impact of distance on awareness in requirements-centred social networks. In: 15th IEEE International Requirements Engineering Conference, RE 2007, pp. 59–68. IEEE (2007)
9. Dennis, A.R., Fuller, R.M., Valacich, J.S.: Media, tasks, and communication processes: a theory of media synchronicity. MIS Q. **32**(3), 575–600 (2008)
10. Figl, K.: Team and media competencies in information systems. Oldenbourg Verlag (2010)
11. Freeman, L.C., Roeder, D., Mulholland, R.R.: Centrality in social networks: II. Experimental results. Soc. Networks **2**(2), 119–141 (1979)
12. Gersick, C.J.: Time and transition in work teams: toward a new model of group development. Acad. Manage. J. **31**(1), 9–41 (1988)
13. Jarvenpaa, S.L., Shaw, T.R., Staples, D.S.: Toward contextualized theories of trust: the role of trust in global virtual teams. Inf. Syst. Res. **15**(3), 250–267 (2004)
14. Jehn, K.A.: A multimethod examination of the benefits and detriments of intragroup conflict. Adm. Sci. Q. **40**, 256–282 (1995)
15. Jehn, K.A., Mannix, E.A.: The dynamic nature of conflict: a longitudinal study of intragroup conflict and group performance. Acad. Manage. J. **44**(2), 238–251 (2001)
16. Kauffeld, S., Lehmann-Willenbrock, N.: Meetings matter effects of team meetings on team and organizational success. Small Group Res. **43**(2), 130–158 (2012)
17. Knight, A.P.: Mood at the midpoint: affect and change in exploratory search over time in teams that face a deadline. Organ. Sci. **26**(1), 99–118 (2013)
18. Knight, A.P., Eisenkraft, N.: Positive is usually good, negative is not always bad: the effects of group affect on social integration and task performance. J. Appl. Psychol. **100**(4), 1214 (2015)
19. Kraut, R.E., Streeter, L.A.: Coordination in software development. Commun. ACM **38**(3), 69–82 (1995)
20. Krohne, H.W., Egloff, B., Kohlmann, C.W., Tausch, A.: Untersuchungen mit einer deutschen Version der "Positive and Negative Affect Schedule" (PANAS). DIAGNOSTICA-GOTTINGEN- 42, 139–156 (1996)
21. Kuhl, J., Kazén, M.: Volitional facilitation of difficult intentions: joint activation of intention memory and positive affect removes stroop interference. J. Exp. Psychol. Gen. **128**(3), 382 (1999)
22. Lehmann-Willenbrock, N., Grohmann, A., Kauffeld, S.: Task and relationship conflict at work. Eur. J. Psychol. Assess. **27**, 171–178 (2011)
23. Pikkarainen, M., Haikara, J., Salo, O., Abrahamsson, P., Still, J.: The impact of agile practices on communication in software development. Empirical Softw. Eng. **13**(3), 303–337 (2008)

24. Prikladnicki, R.: Propinquity in global software engineering: examining perceived distance in globally distributed project teams. J. Softw. Evol. Process **24**(2), 119–137 (2012)
25. Sauer, N.C., Kauffeld, S.: Meetings as networks: applying social network analysis to team interaction. Commun. Methods Measures **7**(1), 26–47 (2013)
26. Schneider, K., Liskin, O.: Exploring FLOW distance in project communication. In: Proceedings of 8th International Workshop on Cooperative and Human Aspects of Software Engineering (CHASE 2015), ICSE 2015 (2015)
27. Schneider, K., Liskin, O., Paulsen, H., Kauffeld, S.: Requirements compliance as a measure of project success. In: Proceedings of the 4th IEEE Global Engineering Education Conference (EDUCON 2013) (2013)
28. Schneider, K., Liskin, O., Paulsen, H., Kauffeld, S.: Media, mood, and meetings: related to project success? ACM Trans. Comput. Educ. (TOCE) **15**(4), 21 (2015)
29. Sondermann, J.P.: Interne Qualitätsanforderungen und Anforderungsbewertung. Handbuch Qualitätsmanagement/Masing, München 2007, pp. 387–404 (2007)
30. Stapel, K.: Informationsflusstheorie der Softwareentwicklung. Dissertation, Gottfried Wilhelm Leibniz Universität Hannover, München, April 2012
31. Stapel, K., Knauss, E., Schneider, K.: Using FLOW to improve communication of requirements in globally distributed software projects. In: Collaboration and Intercultural Issues on Requirements: Communication, Understanding and Soft-skills, 2009, pp. 5–14. IEEE (2009)
32. Totterdell, P.: Catching moods and hitting runs: mood linkage and subjective performance in professional sport teams. J. Appl. Psychol. **85**(6), 848 (2000)
33. Totterdell, P., Wall, T., Holman, D., Diamond, H., Epitropaki, O.: Affect networks: a structural analysis of the relationship between work ties and job-related affect. J. Appl. Psychol. **89**(5), 854 (2004)
34. Waller, M.J., Zellmer-Bruhn, M.E., Giambatista, R.C.: Watching the clock: group pacing behavior under dynamic deadlines. Acad. Manag. J. **45**(5), 1046–1055 (2002)
35. Watson, D., Clark, L.A., Tellegen, A.: Development and validation of brief measures of positive and negative affect: the PANAS scales. J. Pers. Soc. Psychol. **54**(6), 1063 (1988)
36. Watzlawick, P., Bavelas, J.B., Jackson, D.D., O'Hanlon, B.: Pragmatics of Human Communication: A Study of Interactional Patterns. Pathologies and Paradoxes. WW Norton & Company, New York (2011)
37. Wohlin, C., Runeson, P., Höst, M., Ohlsson, M.C., Regnell, B., Wesslén, A.: Experimentation in Software Engineering. Springer Science & Business Media, New York (2012)
38. Wolf, T., Schroter, A., Damian, D., Nguyen, T.: Predicting build failures using social network analysis on developer communication. In: Proceedings of the 31st International Conference on Software Engineering, pp. 1–11. IEEE Computer Society (2009)
39. Zijlstra, F.R., Waller, M.J., Phillips, S.I.: Setting the tone: early interaction patterns in swift-starting teams as a predictor of effectiveness. Eur. J. Work Organ. Psychol. **21**(5), 749–777 (2012)

# Exploring the Requirements and Design of Persuasive Intervention Technology to Combat Digital Addiction

Amen Alrobai[✉], John McAlaney, Huseyin Dogan, Keith Phalp, and Raian Ali

Faculty of Science and Technology, Bournemouth University, Poole, UK
{aalrobai,jmcalaney,hdogan,kphalp,rali}@bournemouth.ac.uk

**Abstract.** Digital Addiction (DA) is an emerging behavioural phenomenon that denotes an obsessive and problematic usage of digital media. Such usage could meet various criteria of an addictive behaviour such as salience, conflict, tolerance and withdrawal symptoms and, hence, it would raise new challenges and ethical considerations on the way we engineer software. Luckily, software as a medium for such addictive usage could be also a medium for enacting a behaviour change and prevention strategy towards a regulated usage. However, due to the recentness of such software-based interventions, we still need a body of knowledge on how to develop them. In this paper, we conduct empirical research, through a diary study and an online forum content analysis, to understand users' perception of such emerging systems. The results shed the light on a range of design aspects and risks when building and validating such persuasive intervention technology.

**Keywords:** Digital addiction · e-Heath design · Design for behavioural change

## 1  Introduction

The wealth of information and digital connectivity is a characteristic of a modern society but its excessive and obsessive use may result in a less sustainable society and create social and mental well-being problems. The consequences of such Digital Addiction (hereafter DA) on individuals and collectively, include poor academic performance, reduced social and recreational activities, relationships breakups, low involvement in real-life communities, poor parenting, depression and lack of sleep [1–3]. DA manifests psychological characteristics and along with dependency, the user can experience withdrawal symptoms (e.g. depression, cravings, insomnia, and irritability). Estimates of DA vary according to country and according to the definition of DA and the metrics used to measure it in the studies. Such estimates of internet addiction suggest that 6 %–15 % of the general population test positive on signs of addiction; this figure rises to 13–18 % among university students who have been identified as most at risk for DA [4]; at 18.3 % UK has a relatively high prevalence of DA amongst university students [5].

The existing literature on DA has focused mainly on users' psychology. There is a paucity of research that positions software and its developers as primary actors in the development of DA. Notable exceptions are the research in [6, 7] which advocates that by developing DA-aware architecture and design, software developers can minimise

© IFIP International Federation for Information Processing 2016
Published by Springer International Publishing Switzerland 2016. All Rights Reserved
C. Bogdan et al. (Eds.): HCSE 2016/HESSD 2016, LNCS 9856, pp. 130–150, 2016.
DOI: 10.1007/978-3-319-44902-9_9

addictive usage and thereby prevent or intervene early with DA. Software developers, together with users, can use inputs from technology and psychology to create DA-aware software and facilitate a healthy use of digital technology.

Technology-assisted behaviour change is an emerging topic and we are witnessing an increase in its adoption in several domains and for different addictive and problematic behaviours. For example, online intervention is being used for alcohol addiction and encouraging a responsible drinking [8]. Also, the advances in information technology and Web 2.0 have enabled a new range of possibilities including a more intelligent, context-aware, continuous and social online intervention. As evidence, the use of mobile applications for behaviour change is now a possibility, e.g. for smoking cessation [9], medication adherence [10], diet and eating disorder [11], to name a few.

Despite the trend, there are still few principles and design guidelines on how technology-assisted behaviour change should be engineered. Amongst other aspects, we lack studies on users' views and their requirements, personal and collective [12]. In general, there is a limited amount of theory-based solutions and this deters their acceptance, efficiency, usability and sustainability. In developing such solutions, there seem to be interesting intersections amongst several disciplines. For example, topics like personalisation, either based on automatic adaptation or user's direct modifications [13], social norms and social comparisons [8] which fall within a psychology remit, would be familiar concepts in computing areas such as requirements personalisation [14] and persuasive technology [15].

Software design can play a key role in facilitating addictive behaviours. Certain interactivity can trigger preoccupation and an escalation of commitment and tendency to allocate additional time and to a chosen task, e.g. in forum or email conversation. Other can trigger the fear of missing out events that maybe currently happening, e.g. newsfeeds in a social network. At the same time, we argue that software enjoys capabilities that can offer breakthrough solutions to manage such addictive behaviour. This includes being transparent to users and providing real-time traceability of their usage and intelligent and personalized feedback messages. Unlike other addictive mediums, e.g. tobacco and alcohol, software can aid users to take an informed decision of their usage more actively.

In this paper, we study a set of commercial e-health persuasive applications to combat DA and collect evidence of their capabilities, design defects and their potential to cause adverse impact. We explore such persuasive intervention technology (hereafter PIT) from their users' perspective. This will inform software engineering about the relevant requirements and design facets and concerns and paradoxes to cater for. We follow a qualitative approach and analyse users' online feedback on a set of popular PIT and conduct a diary study with a group of users having a problematic usage style to capture their experience with such technology for a period of time. We conclude with a set of recommendations to follow and risks to avoid when designing PIT for combatting DA.

The paper is structured as follows. We first present our method in Sect. 2. Then we present the results in four categories of features related to PIT in Sect. 3. We then reflect on the results from both design and psychological perspectives with the aim to inform their development in Sect. 4. Study limitations presented in Sect. 5. Finally, we draw conclusion and presents our future work in Sect. 6.

## 2    Method

We followed a qualitative method to understand users' perception of PIT for combatting DA. Overall, multiple data sources were used to increase coverage and credibility of the study. The first was the diary study to collect data in naturalistic settings. The second was the follow-up individual interviews to develop a better understanding of the data collected from the diary studies. The third was the analysis of an online forum to gather more contextual knowledge about these applications. For an exploratory study, we treated the data coming from the three sources equally and made the content analysis under the assumption that such diversity will reveal more concepts.

We began with reverse engineering three popular smartphone application designed to aid users regulate their usage and reduce their DA to extract their notable features. An extra application (App.4) has been included later in the study. The reason will be discussed in the following paragraph. Table 1 outlines the features of these applications and categorises them based on their support dimension [16]. The popularity was measured through the number of installs (over 1 M) and feedback provided (over 5 K). We then aimed to get users' perception of these features. This helped to decide the prominent and significant features and to look at the requirements and contextual factors that can influence their effectiveness and deficiencies.

**Table 1.** The features and design principles of the selected applications

|  | Features | App.1 | App.2 | App.3 | App.4 |
|---|---|---|---|---|---|
| Task support | Monitoring & tracking | ● | ● | ● | ● |
|  | Coercive techniques | ● | ● | ● | ● |
|  | Goal settings | ● | ● | ● |  |
|  | Tunnelling |  |  |  |  |
| Social support | Competition |  | ● |  | ● |
|  | Normative influence |  |  | ● |  |
|  | Recognition |  |  | ● |  |
|  | Social support |  | ● | ● | ● |
|  | Comparisons | ● |  |  |  |
| Dialogue support | Rewarding | ● | ● | ● | ● |
|  | Reminders | ● | ● | ● |  |
|  | Addiction scoring |  | ● | ● |  |

In the diary study, 14 participants were recruited (5 females and 9 males, with ages ranging between 18 and 50). They were asked to use the three commercial PIT to combat DA for two weeks and write down their observations and feelings about them and their usage style. They were also asked to take snapshots of significant moments during the usage and share that with the research team at least once every two days. The data gathered was then used to support our interviews with those participants after the two weeks. The interviews were audio recorded and transcribed. The studies followed the principles and guidelines presented in [17]. The recruitment was based on convenience sampling. The inclusion criterion was that the participants should have the feeling that the smartphones or social media is used in an excessive and obsessive way. Participants who met that criterion were then sent an invitation email with a short questionnaire to complete.

The research indicates that self-reports in which participants are simply asked if they thought they have DA are strongly correlated with available psychometric measures to assess DA [18]. However, CAGE questionnaire [19] was also used as a self-assessment instrument for further validity check. The participants all declared at least one aspect of problematic usage of their smartphones; they passed a pre-selection survey test which was designed based on the CAGE questionnaire which is a screening self-report instrument to detect addictive behaviours by examining the addiction symptoms such as conflict, tolerance, withdrawal symptoms, mood modification and salience.

The other data source utilised users' online feedback and review on the same three applications. However, we noticed from the analysis of the diary study data that users wanted to be motivated by some sort of rewarding systems that reinforce their sense of accomplishments and care of some virtual object of character. As such, we analysed one more application that represents users' achievements metaphorically by providing them with virtual experience of looking after something, e.g. a tree or a pet, which would become less healthy or less happy when they are busy with their usage of digital technology.

In the analysis of users' online reviews and feedback, we analysed 733 informative comments out of 5 K on the four applications (the three which were used in the diary plus the added one). The ignored comments were mainly related to the technicality of the applications or adding no value to our analysis by being so generic, e.g. "I uninstalled this app, it exhausted the phone battery", "this is absolutely a nice app". 347 comments were made by male users, 254 by female users and 105 by users with undeclared gender.

Three main behaviour change theories guided the analysis of the selected applications; Control Theory [20], Goal-Setting Theory [21] and Social Cognitive Theory [22]. Control Theory suggests that the behaviour is regulated based on the person's intended behaviour seen as a goal. The control system will then compare the actual behaviour with that intended behaviour and actuate interventions if a deviation happens. Goal-Setting Theory emphasises the relationship between the goals and performance. Challenging goals appear to promote higher and persistent effort through motivating people to develop strategies that are more effective. The accomplishment will then reinforce further motivation due to individuals' satisfaction. Social Cognitive Theory suggests that behaviours are influenced by environmental aspects such as observing others. As such, changing learning conditions can promote behavioural change. Overall, these theories were selected as they have been widely implemented in behaviour change research and had an evidence base [23]. In the data analysis phase, these established theories served as a conceptual basis for the priori coding approach to identify potential coding categories [17]. Hence, other theories have emerged during the process of the analysis such as Transtheoretical Model (TTM) [24]. Therefore, our methodology utilized behaviour change theories to explain the data analysed rather than controlling the analysis.

Qualitative content analysis was used. Although subjectivity is a common risk in this type of studies, the content analysis process included three researchers, two as evaluators and the third to take decision when a consensus was not reached.

# 3 Results

In this section, we will present the results of our analysis of the popular PIT, their features and how these features are seen by users and what concerns their usage would raise. The taxonomy which represents the results is shown in (Fig. 1). We concluded four main categories of features in this technology and we detailed that in the next four subsections. This thematic map reflects the features that are considered by users as important. The PIT studied could also contain other features, which we omitted mainly because of the lack of relevance and influence from the users' perspective. we also elaborated on users' different views on the features.

## 3.1 Monitoring

Monitoring is an essential functionality of any self-regulation system. Measurement, comparison and the monitor are the core building blocks of the monitoring activity, while verifiability and transparency are monitoring-related principles that require a high degree of details to increase trustworthiness and reliability from a users' perspective especially for personal and behaviour-related information.

**Measurement.** Tracking time on-screen, i.e. *duration*, was the predominant method to calculate the addiction scores in all the reviewed applications. However, different applications rely on different metrics to measure time on screen. Users commented that these applications lack users' goals identification. As such, all types of usage are included in the measurement model without a special consideration of the intention and the reason for that usage. Time spent is perhaps not a meaningful measure for judging addiction if certain contextual factors are ignored and this requires intelligent and context-aware monitors that also look at the requirements and goals of the usage.

A time-based measurement model can be affected by the so-called *passive usage*. An example is the time between closing an application and screen auto-lock. Users commented that they would like not to have passive usage counted against them. On the other hand, receiving notifications, against their will including those coming from PIT, is a debatable case. Some commented that this would still be a type of usage as it requires additional cognitive load.

*Frequency* measurement is also used to estimate users' engagement with software products. The reviewed applications provided some frequency-based stats, e.g. screen unlocks. Calculating addiction scores is the quantification of a wide range of frequency-based and time-based stats to provide indications to the degree of usage. However, applying non-validated methods will lead to false conclusions.

The use of quantifying methods that are not validated will lead to false assertions. In more extreme bias users can use such misleading information to claim spontaneous recovery, which is a defensive mechanism known as the flight into health tactic [25]. For example, a user commented: *"I did not ever know how often I checked my phone, I was using it about 200 times a day. Now I check it about 200 times a week thanks to much for curing me"*. Adopting factual and objective approaches, such as in the

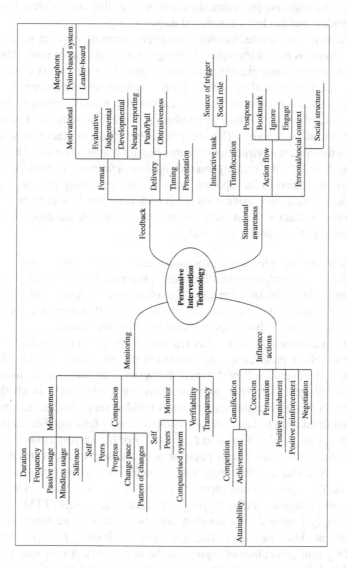

**Fig. 1.** Content analysis of users' views of PIT to combat digital addiction

comment above, could provide more persuasive effect. Yet, careful feedback is still essential to avoid any misleading conclusions.

*Mindless usage* is another factor that can also influence the measurement models. It can be characterised by the lack of conciseness and awareness during the present interaction with smartphones. This type of usage cannot be identified by duration or frequency. A technique like eye tracking might be able to identify this behaviour assuming that eye movements, which are guided by cognitive processes, during normal reading, are different from that during mindless reading and this helps automated detection.

Designing systems that can capture, measure and even intervene with the state of preoccupation, i.e. *salience*, is one of the open challenges for the design of interactive e-health and ICT-facilitate behaviour change. Salience attribute is one of the six clinical criteria proposed in [26] to identify addictive behaviours. It refers to the state when users are not actually engaged in the behaviour, yet they cannot stop thinking about it. For example, a user commented *"I got so tired of thinking in Facebook statuses. Fellow addicts know what I am talking about"*. The challenge stems from the fact that such events do not occur in the system environment *"points-based systems are a good motivational approach but how will [the system] monitor off-line behaviour or preoccupation"*. Thus, designers may need to incorporate users in the monitoring process and feedback loops in order to enable the system to react to such violation. However, proactive and intelligent masseurs that require stimulus identification and minimisation would be more advantageous from the usability perspective.

**Comparison.** All monitoring and feedback processes need to adopt some comparison approaches, or benchmarks, in order to measure users' progress. The overall findings indicate that users may need to be involved in the design phase to understand what would work well for them to avoid providing comparisons in a form that may negatively influence the user or cause them to disengage with the intervention system.

While the system can compare the user to his *self*-past, this can be done at different levels of granularity to reflect preferences on visualising the progress. For example, instead of comparing to the overall self-past usage, the system can compare the usage on each application individually. Such an approach was not implemented in all the reviewed applications. In fact, one of the applications provided very detailed stats but they were not in a quantified form to facilitate self-comparisons *"I have not figured out yet how to see specifics of the applications that I do use ... just the overall usage!"*.

While comparing the performance with peers or self can help to motivate users progressive change, this social element may lead to negative experience, such as unhealthy competition. We argue that this approach can provide better outcomes when considering the stage of change according to the Transtheoretical Model (TTM) [24] stage of addiction, i.e. early, intermediate and severe and also the stage of treatment pre-, post- and during treatment. Also, the competition between peers is likely to impact self-esteem and self-efficacy (our perception of regulating the behaviour). A user who is in the early stages of the change, e.g. contemplation, may be compared to others in the advanced stages, e.g. maintenance. Although this upward social comparison is suggested to inspire those who are in worse off condition [27], it may also severely lower their self-esteem. For example, a user commented that gamifying the systems can be effective with caution "*fun is needed but what about non-addicts appearing in a leaderboard?!*". In other words, having users with different degrees of addiction in the comparison can have adverse effects. This also applies for those who are in the better off as they may use it as a defensive mean by using it and ignoring the other symptoms of addiction such as salience and conflict.

Showing the *progress* while performing the comparison can provide more meaningful information to users. This is a subtype of self-comparison by which users can compare themselves according to their own goals. It can also be a subtype of social-comparison when the goals setting is performed collaboratively as a group activity such as in surveillance systems.

The monitoring system can also compare the pace of users' progress toward the healthy usage. We labelled this as monitoring the *changing pace*. For example, one of the applications uses a metaphorical system in which users were enabled to grow trees to represent the progress towards healthier use. This application can be enhanced by monitoring the time between planting trees or how many trees planted in a given period of time to assess the pace of change. While planting trees entails implicit peers- or self-comparisons, the *changing pace* will be assessed by monitoring the outcomes. As such the reference point to compare with will keep changing in a progressive form.

As a follow-up, it may be argued that monitoring the *pattern of changes* can empower stage-based intervention systems. These systems are mainly built upon the TTM which takes pragmatic approach by focusing on "how" rather than "why" users progress through stages of change [24]. While there is still a lack of concrete evidence of its effectiveness on behavioural change [28], improving the tailoring system to take into consideration the unique motivational characteristics and trigging cues of each stage, provided promising outcomes [29]. The gap here is to identify the influential elements of the personalised information led to that improvement. This on its own is an indication of the applicability of stage-based interventions. However, one of the open challenges is collecting the evidence to confirm the stage transition to identify the current stage and then provide the right stage-matched interventions (SMI) [30]. In PIT, the monitorability of software-mediated interactions can help to facilitate monitoring that *pattern of changes* in order to assess the current stage and inform the tailoring system to provide effective and personalised interventions.

**Monitor.** This component refers to the agent who will do the monitoring activity itself. It can be performed by the *users* themselves, by *peers* or by a *computerised system*. Selecting one of those agents will have an influence on the other requirements and design choices. For example, the design of peer groups monitoring will require careful feedback engineering to avoid damage to social relationships or the development of maladaptive peer norms of usage. In groups' dynamics, the conformity effect can be a threat when a user temporary changes their behaviour only to conform and to avoid any contrary actions from peers. While this is considered a positive behaviour [31], this could be only positive in tasks adopted within a group to speed up achieving collective goals. In group-based treatment, however, this can be a threat as the relapse will be inevitable afterward, i.e. when users detach.

**Verifiability.** PIT need to provide means to verify the accuracy of their measurements and judgement of users' usage and behaviour in order to maximise their credibility and acceptability. Some of the reviewed applications provide detailed reports of usage. Such information can be used to support the claims of self-regulatory systems. One user criticised the subjectivity of the measurement of their addiction score or level: *"The application allows seeing usage by time and some arbitrary addiction score"*. Our study indicated that the ability to verify the measurement process itself is much needed for such PIT especially if we consider the tendency of addicts to tolerate the increasing usage and deny reality.

**Transparency.** Transparency has been highlighted as a key requirement. Users commented that they would like to see how scores are calculated and how the judgement on their usage is made. However, there was a wide range of scenarios that these systems utilize in the addiction scoring. Yet, users felt uncomfortable with not being involved in deciding them or even knowing them. This is a typical attitude in health-related interaction when patients require knowing details even if they may not fully understand them. One of the scenarios is the aforementioned "passive usage". Some of the passive usage cases were not identified by the designers. A user commented: *"I didn't realise it counts the time the screen is left on even if you aren't using any of the applications"*. Thus, transparency requires carful elicitation and modelling to reach to an acceptable level. Participatory design and lifelong personalization approaches can support transparency by which users can be part of the decision-making process. This could increase adoption of the decisions and judgements made by the PIT but also introduce the risk of being biased and ineffective.

### 3.2 Feedback

Feedback is mainly to inform users about their performance and can take different forms. Feedback is one of the main pillars in self-regulation systems, which function to express users' status and to act as a motivational tool. The users' comments show that feedback techniques among these applications should be given a special considered in terms of the timing, format, delivery method and presentation.

**Format.** This refers to the type of content included in the feedback system. Feedback design can play a very important role to help different type of users to track their progress, yet should not conflict other design principles to avoid creating an addictive experience by itself. For example, a user criticised one of the applications *"this application is addictive as well. Actually made me use my [mobile] more"*.

*Motivational* feedback is a complex type of feedback that visualises users' progress in a meaningful and gamified form to enrich their experience. Users commented that they would like to have point-based and metaphorical-based systems as well as leaderboards for this type of feedback *"why can't I connect to Facebook? I wanted to compare the high scores"*. A user suggested that the metaphorical system could be improved by adding *"a delay before the tree dies when using other applications. A notification could say, quickly, your tree is dying"*. Leaderboards, however, could have a contradictory characteristic as they "*may encourage unhealthy competition while they should be more about supporting each other not beating each other*" especially in e-health solutions.

*Evaluative* feedback uses reference points to compare with, such as *benchmarking, social or group's norms*, but most importantly to show them how their performance scores were derived. Allowing users to set up their own reference points to compare with can be effective "*I wish this application would allow me to set a time limit I feel is appropriate. If I use my phone for work, it is almost impossible to get [good] score which is pretty irritating when I have really cut down [time wasted] on my phone*". The *self-set reference point* is linked to the concept of "goal choice" which is influenced heavily by past experience, past performance and some social influences [32]. A follow-up of this feedback is to guide the users to what areas they should improve in their usage and potentially enlighten them to think of what steps to take, e.g. using reductions and tunnelling [15]. This feedback needs to be timely to show the user the causes of the provided feedback when the usage contextual properties and cues are still fresh in their minds. However, users' feedback also indicated that timeliness might not be always appreciated especially if the user is still in a mental status of preoccupation about what they did or are doing on their smartphones.

*Judgemental* feedback can take an assessment manner in terms of judging the usage style to be right or wrong, healthy or addictive, etc. While this type can still carry some evaluative feedback attributes, it can be loaded with some emotive and judgmental terminologies, such as "you had an unusual and unhealthy usage style today" or "your usage is above the average time we expected for you today", etc. Users differ in terms of their motivations to accept and follow self-regulation systems. Sometimes this genuinely relates to their usage goals and other contextual factors, e.g. those who engage heavily with technology but still do not show addiction symptoms or those stating they are the "digital native" generation. As such, judgemental feedback messages may not suit all users "*I just want data about how I use my phone, not silly platitudes about living my life to the fullest. This application was not for me*". Techniques like authority and social proof [33] as well as basing the judgement on the measure or goal given by the user [21] would potentially help in increasing users' acceptance of such kind of feedback.

*Developmental* feedback can be used to offer fitting suggestions and tailored achievable plans, which can have greater persuasive powers. In terms of higher education, this maps to the *formative assessment*, which aims to constructively and iteratively evaluate performance and give suggestions for the next steps. A user commented that PIT would help them "*to realise what they need to prioritise*".

Some users preferred *neutral reporting* feedback, which only reports their usage stats without any further assessment and judgement "*don't really like the score thing. Showing more real stats would be more useful*".

**Delivery.** Self-regulation systems can communicate feedback messages following *push* or *pull* approaches. Designers need to understand users' requirements in terms of when to apply covert and overt feedback. The pull approach does not require the user to check their status as long as that will be prompted automatically following specific predefined event-based or interval-based modes. The push approach entails that the user is triggered to check their status. The pull approach can lead also to further addictive habits. For example, a user commented about an application uses trees metaphor *"it seems counterintuitive to be building a forest on your phone, meaning you will inevitably keep coming back on to check your progress"*. The push approach, also, has a side effect by acting as a stimulus to initiate unnecessary usage *"I love this application! But they should do something about getting notifications because those are tempting me"*. This approach may work for certain personality types and cultures. The pull approach could increase the sense of ownership and the fact that the user leads the querying process would encourage commitment and consistency [33] and hence the success of the change. We still do not have designated approaches for validating these design options when implemented in software systems.

*Obtrusiveness* can be, but not necessarily, one of the accompanying attributes when implementing the push approach, which may then affect users' experience. Obtrusive feedback, which can take a form of popup notifications, demands high attention and positions itself as a priority. Many users highlighted that feedback mechanisms were very obtrusive due to the lack of contextual considerations *"this application doesn't let me define what works for me. Feels like a nosy parent ... there's a problem when a note pops up saying that I have spent too much time."* However, as most interventions, obtrusiveness is still essential and participants stated that a *"wake-up call"* could be needed occasionally even if it violates some usability requirements.

**Timing.** The reviewed applications applied different usage-related timing strategies to deliver the feedback. Some were criticised of being very distractive, while others were very preferable. Feedback can be delivered during users' interaction with their mobile, after the usage (i.e. immediately after locking the screen or closing a specific application), while the user is away from the mobile, i.e. offline, or immediately after unlocking the screen. Users also commented that right timings are highly likely to motivate users. A user commented: *"I like the fact that when I go to unlock my phone it tells me how many times I've unlocked it. Then I can think no I don't need to check"*.

**Presentation.** Presentation not only relates to the visual appearance of the feedback but also to what extent the information is consistent with users' attitudes and preferences, e.g. whether the message is a gain- or loss-framed, its friendliness, strictness, personal, etc. A user commented *"there was a graph of how much I used my phone during the week. I found that quite useful because I could compare the days. Which ones I used it the most"*. In the systems that allow users to set their own plans, the colour coding can have a negative influence on how users set their own plans especially within social settings *"If I am enabled to decide myself the maximum time I can use my phone, I am more likely to put high numbers. So in worst case, I'll get the orange colour. So I don't look that bad"*. As such, using statistical figures rather than colour coding in the intervention systems that enable self-setting of goals, can be more effective to eliminate self-bias. That bias can be used as a mechanism to minimize perceived impact on the self-image.

### 3.3 Influence Actions

This component aims at helping users regulating their usage by implementing behavioural change theories and techniques.

**Punishment.** Positive punishment can discourage behaviour by delivering a punishment when that behaviour is performed. Negative punishment, on the other hand, can discourage behaviour by removing positive stimulus when that behaviour is performed. Our study shows that these two forms of conditioning can strength likelihood of a healthier digital life style, e.g. *"when I pick up my phone and get distracted, I get a notification telling that my tree died. This motivates me to stay focused next time"*. The tree is the symbolic object a user cares of and reduces the usage to avoid causing harm to it.

**Positive Reinforcement.** The system can be improved by implementing a rewarding scheme to assign specific rewards to different actions. Secondary actions linked to stimulus control such as a deliberate disabling Internet connection can be also rewarded *"I wish you could get points for putting it in airplane mode or something"*.

**Gamification.** Self-regulation systems can be empowered by implementing some gaming elements to create a more engaging experience. Amongst the different game mechanics, competition and achievements seem to be predominant, still with potential for misuse.

*Competition* can be individual-based or even team-based to maximise users' experience. Any decline in the team performance can be perceived as an individual reasonability. Proper design of competition-based gamification can increase users' engagement significantly *"I would suggest is if you added a 'buddy/friends list' so you can compete with your friends"*. The risk here is that the competition can take an adverse form, i.e. towards more use, or becomes itself addictive. For example, a user commented, *"I can see making it competitive to worsen the addiction, would members want to get better and therefore get addicted to the points/rewards/making their avatar better?"*.

Providing users with tangible *achievements* can increase the likelihood of long-term engagement, which will particularly help to sustain users' behavioural change. Achievements are normally provided to users on an individual basis. However, users can be provided with individual achievement experience within the group context. As such, achievements can be provided to peers to gain social recognition. This is just an example to show how social and achievement aspects can be combined to create a very engaging experience, yet to be supported by consistency and commitment principles as a powerful social influence [33] to avoid relapse. A user commented: *"I really like this application. Rather just sounding alarm or something, it gives a sense of accomplishment"*.

Some users criticised the rewarding system in some of the PIT. They pointed out that the long time and efforts needed to progress in the levelling system made it significantly difficult to get the rewards and this was very disappointing. On the other hand, the applications provide more *attainable* rewards seem to motivate users substantially *"the little rewards or accomplishments I get are nice little reinforcements for low phone use"*. One approach that can be taken into consideration is to increase the difficulty as the user progress in the behavioural change stages, e.g. those of the Transtheoretical Model.

**Coercion.** The converge of the monitoring processes can have a significant impact on users' experience. We mean by coverage what can be included in the monitoring, e.g. application usage, lunches, device unlocks or even within-application interactions such as likes, posts and sharing. For example, some of the reviewed applications provided functionality to exclude applications from the monitoring process or to allow user specify monitoring preferences *"there should be a new feature in which the phone will close on its own after a certain time period which can be set by the users"*. Such flexibility is required to avoid unnecessary coercive interventions. Users normally have the tendency to exclude work-related applications such as email clients and navigation applications. However, this flexibility would certainly need to be implemented with high caution, as addicts tend to deny reality and invent untrue reasons for excluding an appli-cation *"Some people like me need to not be able to manually [stop the monitoring]"*. Other applications provide "snoozing" feature to support task continuity or even to pause the monitoring activity *"a pause feature would be amazing because sometimes I want to get food while studying and I don't want to spend time on the app"*.

**Persuasion.** Persuasion is a very important principle to influence users' intentions and behaviours. Tunnelling, social comparison, reminding, rewarding and suggestion were the most requested techniques by the users *"it would be better to get software recom-mendations for planning the allowed time of usage and to update this based on my actual usage"*. Research on evaluating effectiveness and sustainability of the technology-assisted version of such techniques in general, and for DA in particular, is still to be done. For example, personality traits besides the type and stage of addiction could have a high impact on the acceptance and effectiveness of persuasion and also coercion.

**Negotiation.** Users' conflicting requirements require carful identification and resolu-tion. The question here is how to intelligently negotiate requirements in a way that considers the peculiarities in addicts' behaviour such as tolerance and denial of reality. For example, most of the PIT enable users to exclude certain applications from the monitoring activity and this was perceived as a desirable functionality *"I wish this application would allow you to set a time limit you feel is appropriate for green, or have certain applications like e-mails and phone calls do not count against you"*. We argue, here, that it would be more efficient to exclude them in the influence layer, but not monitoring and feedback according to (Fig. 1). This is to alert users when addiction patterns are identified in one of the excluded applications. In some scenarios, however, coercive approaches can be used when such patterns are detected as these systems should perceive users as two interconnected personas; current user and user-to-be.

### 3.4  Situational Awareness

Situation includes a wide range of variables related to the performed task. The lack of knowledge about tasks' context as well as poor elicitation of a user's mental models, can affect user experience when implementing self-regulation systems. Thus, expanding the exploratory investigation to include contextual factors is essential to provide empirical rational needed to inform the design of software-based interventions and promote the intended behavioural change. Data analysis of the collected comments highlighted the critical principles below.

**Interactive Task.** Users highlighted that the system should distinguish between tasks in terms of their nature, e.g. seriousness "*I just uninstalled this after I nearly had an accident. Upon setting GPS map route the reminder pop out blocking my map in the midst of driving*", another commented "*fails to meaningfully distinguish between productive phone use and addiction*", and also who initiated it, i.e. *triggered by* attribute "*only counts the interactions initiated by the phone user. If a call comes in, it should not be counted*". Again, there seems to be a grey area between the two cases, e.g. receiving a message on Facebook as a result of sharing a post and the escalating commitment on social networks. Here, we propose the *severity* as an important quantifiable task-related attribute to enrich measurements models. In order to achieve this, different interactions need to be categorised based on their implications on the usage style. In the previous example, the sharing a post is likely to cause a high volume of responses, which can aggravate habitual checking. This is unlike other tasks which can be categorised as human to machine interactions. Such interactions can be less problematic as the social element is messing. This also suggests categorising interactions based on their *social roles* which denote the notion of the extent to which interaction motivate or demotivate face-to-face interactions. For example, interactions that encourage face-to-face communications, such as organising events using software-mediated tools, may need to be treated as positive interactions that should be promoted by the system rather than those encouraging online participation which can still be counted against addiction score. Thus, understanding the goal of the interactions and the task being done is essential for decision-making, e.g. on the type of feedback to give and measurement to apply.

**Time/Location.** The system should enable users to decide when and where they want to be monitored. These contextual variables can be very sensitive when it comes to feedback messages. Time, location and tasks can also be combined to identify problematic usage. For example, users can be enabled to select the morning as a working period and any Facebook usage during that time whether it is exempted from monitoring or not will be counted in the addiction score. However, implementing such scenario for users who do not want coercion approaches can create conflicting requirements.

**Action Flow.** In less coercive settings, the design of PIT is required to minimise affecting user experience. One way of doing that is by providing users with more flexibility to support taking appropriate decisions as intuitively as possible. Research has shown that self-control has very limited resources for tasks involving a strong desire. So, when users utilise the power of self-control in the initial task, subsequent tasks are compromised due to "*self-control depletion*" [23]. A user commented "*It needs a strong mechanism to prevent us from simply turning off [digital addiction] rules. This is because self-control is a limited resource that depletes as the day goes by. So when it's late in the afternoon won't have the energy to stop myself from simply disabling the* *rules"*. As such, the software must use up this valuable resource intelligently to avoid *"ego depletion"*. One way of doing that through intervention systems is to use self-control resources for the high problematic tasks only such as entirely blocking certain applications. Bolstering self-control through software means is an important aspect to promote behavioural change. For this, we propose the *postponing* and *bookmarking* techniques to supports task continuity for users who do not like strict coercive approaches. The former technique enables the user to postpone a promoted desired task to be performed later but at the right time. As such the spontaneous urge to perform the task will be controlled with minimum use of self-control resources since the task can be performed later. The bookmarking technique is to maintain the point of usage before the intervention happened. A user commented: *"the application will not kick me out when time is up. However, it will prevent me from starting it again if I have used it already for longer than the allowed time"*. While both techniques could be particularly the case with gaming addicts, implementing such interaction is irrelevant to multiplayer video games where more than one player engaged in the same game simultaneously. This highlights the need for consideration of conflicting requirements, which can be addressed by an ontology supported by behavioural change theories and domain reasoner to help designers mapping the interaction artefacts to the application domain.

The intervention software can prompt all muted notifications or those were postponed during the controlled time. One way of strengthening self-efficacy is by utilising the actions taken towards these notifications. Simply by counting the *ignored* ones for the user not against him and to reflect that positively on his addiction score. As users are still expected to *engage* with those notifications, they should not be penalised when that is performed out of the controlled time. This emphasises the importance of having considerate interventions which can be categorised as a special form of considerate requirements for social software proposed in [34]. For example, a user commented, *"I don't look at my phone when I drive so it would be nice to [reward me]"*. This class of requirements seems to be fundamental and should be advocated to allow evaluating such interactions against addicts' perception of consideration to avoid any potential harms resulting from interventions.

**Personal/Social Context.** Personal context relates to the innate feeling and status of the user, e.g. mood. Social context refers to the both the position of the user within a group either in the real world or on a social network. Sensitivity to such context is hard to achieve but with advances in sensing mechanisms, e.g., smart watch, and machine intelligence, we speculate this would become eventually a reality. Social elements can influence users' perceptions towards intervention mechanisms. Yet, what is accepted and being effective in human-to-machine interactions, might be harming in social settings due to different factors such as digital identity. We looked at how social context would affect users' willingness to use this type of intervention systems. User raised the importance of having a space that is free of criticism *"I think it needs to be a safe space that people can feel free to explore their issues without fear of criticism"*. Having the social elements would also influence what feedback format should be adopted. For example, judgemental feedback is not preferable in such settings *"I wouldn't consider any group which labelled an individual's use of a medium or set of media in such a* *sweepingly judgemental way to be an efficient mode of help"*. In terms of being within an online social network, users also raised the need for considering the *social structure* within social intervention system. A user commented, *"I prefer groups in which members know each other. Nothing is against family members being in the group. But they might be still seen as strangers by others and this may influence how they communicate with me, e.g. when my daughter is in the group"*.

## 4   Designing PIT to Combat Digital Addiction

Our analysis in Sect. 3 demonstrated the need for careful considerations and design principles when using PIT in the domain of DA. In this section, we discuss those aspects in light of the literature and other relevant study and then highlight the need for testing and validating methods for this technology. Finally, we pinpoint the main issues and challenges in designing PIT for DA and where the future research studies are needed.

PIT is an example of how technology is enabling individuals to engage with the field of behaviour change in a way that has in the past primarily been restricted to health educators and policy makers. Researchers and practitioners working in behaviour change have developed an extensive research literature on theories of behaviour change, and an evidence base to support the efficacy of different techniques. This knowledge is reflected in sources such as NICE (National Institute for Health and Care Excellence) guidelines on behaviour change for individuals (https://www.nice.org.uk/Guidance/PH49), which advise on best practice. It is interesting how many of the characteristics of the selected PIT mirror the NICE recommendations for behaviour change in other potentially addictive behaviours such as alcohol and tobacco use. For example, as noted, all of the applications include some form of monitoring, which is the first step of many behaviour change approaches in alcohol and drug use.

Nevertheless, behaviour is determined by a multitude of factors, and as such, there can be a discrepancy between the behaviour change strategies, which should be expected to work according to theory and those which have an actual impact. PIT may or may not have some basis in behaviour change theory, but even if designed with the best of intentions and some relevant knowledge it may not provide any benefit to users, and may even have harmful effects. There are several examples of large-scale behaviour change campaigns that have been unsuccessful, such as the DARE (Drug Abuse Resistance Education) programme in the USA that failed to bring about change and was alleged to inadvertently reduce the self-esteem of participants [35].

Even simple and apparently commonsensical strategies such as suggesting that the individual avoids thinking about certain behaviour may be harmful. For example, it has been noted that advising people to try and avoid thinking about certain behaviour, as often done for instance in relation to smokers and avoiding thinking about cigarettes, can actually increase the compulsion to engage in that behaviour [17]. Care must also be taken that a behaviour change strategy is not chosen simply because it is opportune. PIT is especially suited to social comparisons that allow users to see how their usage compares to that of their peers, with the assumption being that those who behave in an excessive way will reduce their usage. However as noted with regards to alcohol use in

American college students individuals may base their identity of being the most extreme amongst their group, in which case highlighting to them how they compare to their peers may on reinforce that behaviour [36]. Finally, in any behaviour change, there is the issue of reactance. This refers to when individuals feel that they are being manipulated and respond by engaging more actively in the behaviour that they feel they are being dissuaded from. Overall it could be argued that behaviour change is easy to achieve, but ensuring that the change occurs in the intended direction is much more challenging.

We can conclude that the requirements engineering and design for PIT introduce challenges in several areas including the decision on the relevant stakeholders and their decision rights and priorities. The failure stories of traditional behaviour change practices send also an alarm on the need for novel testing and validation for PIT. Testing for long-term consequences, e.g. decreased self-esteem, and collective side effects, e.g. creating certain norms of usage, would necessitate novel ways on validating whether such software does meet the requirements sustainably and without unpredictable side effects. This requires a joint effort of multiple disciplines including requirements engineering, human-computer interaction and psychology.

The term universal design describes the concepts of designing for all regardless of their age, gender and abilities [37]. As such, PIT should not be designed with the mind-set of one

**Table 2.** Design concerns and their potential sources in PIT to combat DA

| UX concerns | Source of concerns |
|---|---|
| Lack of interest | Experience fails to engage, ineffective rewarding system, poor levelling design, willingness and readiness to change |
| Lack of trust | Unreliable addiction scoring, lack of verifiability and transparency, uncertainty of agenda of application's developer(s) |
| Lowering self-esteem | Peer-pressure, upward social comparisons, low sense of self-efficacy, assigning to non-matched groups |
| Creating misconceptions | Addiction scoring, minimising the seriousness of the addicting, providing non-stage matched interventions |
| Biased decisions | Downward social comparisons, self-set goals, flight into health, denial of reality, influence from past experience and performance |
| Creating addictive experience | Pull and push feedback approaches, gamified experience, creating pre-occupation with targeted behaviour, poor stimulus control |
| Impacting user experience | Obtrusiveness, distraction, coercive techniques, affecting workflow, lack of requirements negotiations, neglect personalised experience |
| Unsustainable change | Social elements (e.g. conformity effect), losing interest |
| Self-image impact | Identification as addict, experience of relapsing |

size fits all and should cater for complex inter-related networks of variables. We view the domain of behavioural change, as an important effort to provide reactive approaches to deal with this issue. However, there is an evident lack of test frameworks to validate the effectiveness of intervention systems built based on the theories of behavioural change. Validating the effectiveness of such technology requires a unique set of pre-conditions such as *willingness to change, openness* to shortcomings, being free from *denial of reality* and also the *seriousness* of the condition. The challenge here is how to measure these factors, e.g. change readiness, to control their influence on the validity of the intervention system.

Also turning the system into social software by including peers in the monitoring activity requires assessing the long-term outcomes and their sustainability. The validity of such change might be distorted due to various confounding factors arising from peer pressure and other negative influences such as the short-term change only to conform to the group's norms. Table 2 summarizes the findings of the paper from the perspective of users' experience (UX) and what could be the source of concerns from the design perspective and also psychological and contextual perspectives.

## 5  Study Limitations

The study has two main limitations that may have an influence on how the features in PIT were seen by the participants. Firstly, in the measurement of participants' level of addiction, we used the CAGE questionnaire as a simple and inexpensive instrument that does not cater for the wide spectrum of cases and levels of addiction. Generally, psychometric measures have major issues in the addiction criteria itself such as the lack of considering the context of use, the aspects related to the temporal dimension such as compensating relationship breakdown [38] and preoccupation which has been highlighted in the results section of this paper. This explains why "no gold standard" for diagnosing and assessing DA yet exist [39]. The second limitation relates to the fact that those who installed the apps were help-seekers only. Apparently, non-help seekers may have different views and perception about features in PIT. Finally, an additional limitation is about the choice of the apps. Analysing extra apps might lead to discovering additional concepts and risks of this technology in the domain of DA.

## 6  Conclusions and Future Work

In this paper, we explored users' perception of PIT for combating DA and argued the need for a more careful and holistic approach to technology-assisted behaviour change in DA. The unique contribution of this work derives from its attempt to analyse various views, potentials and risks related to a dual use and dual effect of such technology.

Throughout the analysis of the users' comments and the developers' feedback to those comments on the online forum, we noticed the rush to embrace this technology in order to cope with the market demand without careful consideration of its adverse effects. A prominent example is dealing with fundamental issues such as the measurement of DA, which requires extensive research, as merely a technical problem promised to be addressed in the next updates. Hence, the outcome of technology designed for behavioural change is currently doubtful at least in the area of DA. We argue that more research is needed in the area of testing and validating the effectiveness of this technology on the intended behaviour in the short and long terms. For example, how can we assess the threats of users' rejection of the interactive intervention systems? Another example is the negative feelings that can be evoked, such as guilt and obligation, of certain design elements. The former may reinforce the relapse behaviours and the latter may aggravate addiction-related behaviours such as fear of missing out. While trade-offs is a common observation in HCI research, in the domain of addictive behaviours such compensation may propose undesirable effects.

The participatory approach can help to reduce unpredictable effects. However, there is a need to devise methods and guidelines supported by best practices to govern and engineer the users' involvement itself especially for the digital addicts user groups who may exhibit a denial of reality. Hence, more research is still needed to utilize user-centred and participatory approaches for designing PIT to combat DA. For example, it is not clear whether and how to involve ex-addicts in the design and test processes. While ex-addicts may have more empathy for addicted users, they might dictate their opinion due to their bias and their own experience.

In our future work, we will define metrics for addictive software and addictive behaviour to make DA subject to a more accurate monitoring and adjustment process. We will study the design of software-based behaviour change at the precautionary and recovery stages. In particular, we will focus on motivational approaches and the use of their software-based version, for example, persuasive technology and entertainment computing [40]. We aim to investigate the requirements engineering and software validation for DA-related behavioural change and their challenges, such as the denial of requirements of addicts and their conflicts. We will investigate the stakeholders set and their decisions rights in the engineering process, including addicts, the ethical issues around the engineering process and the sustainability of software-facilitated prevention and early-intervention for DA and their potential short and long-term side-effects. This will obviously require an inter-disciplinary research.

**Acknowledgements.** This research has been partially supported by Bournemouth University through the Fusion Investment Fund and PGR Development Fund and also by StreetScene Addiction Recovery. We would like also to thank Yasmeen Abdalla for her valuable contribution in conducting the diary study in the early stages of this research.

# References

1. Kuss, D.J., Griffiths, M.D.: Online social networking and addiction—a review of the psychological literature. Int. J. Environ. Res. Public Health 2011 **8**, 3528–3552 (2011)
2. Echeburúa, E., de Corral, P.: Addiction to new technologies and to online social networking in young people: a new challenge. Adicciones **22**(2), 91–95 (2009)
3. Young, K.S.: Internet addiction: symptoms, evaluation and treatment. In: Innovations in Clinical Practice: A Source Book (1999)
4. Young, K.S., de Abreu, C.N.: Internet Addiction: A Handbook and Guide to Evaluation and Treatment. Wiley, Hoboken (2011)

5. Kuss, D.J., Griffiths, M.D., Binder, J.F.: Internet addiction in students: prevalence and risk factors. Comput. Hum. Behav. **29**, 959–966 (2013)
6. Ali, R., Jiang, N., Phalp, K., Muir, S., McAlaney, J.: The emerging requirement for digital addiction labels. In: Fricker, S.A., Schneider, K. (eds.) REFSQ 2015. LNCS, vol. 9013, pp. 198–213. Springer, Heidelberg (2015)
7. Alrobai, A., Phalp, K., Ali, R.: Digital addiction: a requirements engineering perspective. In: Salinesi, C., Weerd, I. (eds.) REFSQ 2014. LNCS, vol. 8396, pp. 112–118. Springer, Heidelberg (2014)
8. Bewick, B.M., Trusler, K., Mulhern, B., Barkham, M., Hill, A.J.: The feasibility and effectiveness of a web-based personalised feedback and social norms alcohol intervention in UK university students: a randomised control trial. Addict. Behav. **33**, 1192–1198 (2008)
9. Bricker, J.B., Mull, K.E., Kientz, J.A., Vilardaga, R., Mercer, L.D., Akioka, K.J., Heffner, J.L.: Randomized, controlled pilot trial of a smartphone app for smoking cessation using acceptance and commitment therapy. Drug Alcohol Depend. **143**, 87–94 (2014)
10. Dayer, L., Heldenbrand, S., Anderson, P., Gubbins, P.O., Martin, B.C.: Smartphone medication adherence apps: potential benefits to patients and providers. J. Am. Pharm. Assoc. **53**, 172–181 (2013)
11. Pagoto, S., Schneider, K., Jojic, M., DeBiasse, M., Mann, D.: Evidence-based strategies in weight-loss mobile apps. Am. J. Prev. Med. **45**, 576–582 (2013)
12. Dennison, L., Morrison, L., Conway, G.: Opportunities and challenges for smartphone applications in supporting health behavior change: qualitative study. J. Med. **15**, e86 (2013)
13. Dumas, B., Signer, B., Lalanne, D.: Fusion in multimodal interactive systems: an HMM-based algorithm for user-induced adaptation. In: EICS, pp. 15–24 (2012)
14. Sutcliffe, A.G., Fickas, S., Sohlberg, M.M.: Personal and contextual requirements engineering. In: RE, pp. 19–30 (2005)
15. Fogg, B.J.: Persuasive Technology: Using Computers to Change What We Think and Do (Interactive Technologies) (2002)
16. Torning, K., Oinas-Kukkonen, H.: Persuasive system design: state of the art and future directions. In: Persuasive, article no. 30 (2009)
17. Lazar, D.J., Feng, D.J.H., Hochheiser, D.H.: Research Methods in Human-Computer Interaction. Wiley, New York (2010)
18. Widyanto, L., Griffiths, M.D., Brunsden, V.: A psychometric comparison of the internet addiction test, the internet-related problem scale, and self-diagnosis. Cyberpsychology Behav. Soc. Networking **14**, 141–149 (2011)
19. Ewing, J.A.: Detecting alcoholism: the CAGE questionnaire. Jama **252**(14), 1905–1907 (1984)
20. Carver, C.S., Scheier, M.F.: Control theory: A useful conceptual framework for personality-social, clinical, and health psychology. Psychol. Bull. **92**, 111–135 (1982)
21. Locke, E.A., Latham, G.P.: A theory of goal setting & task performance (1990)
22. Bandura, A.: Social cognitive theory: an agentic perspective. Annu. Rev. Psychol. **52**, 1–26 (2001)
23. Webb, T.L., Sniehotta, F.F., Michie, S.: Using theories of behaviour change to inform interventions for addictive behaviours. Addiction **105**, 1879–1892 (2010)
24. Prochaska, D.J.O.: Transtheoretical model of behavior change. In: Gellman, M.D., Turner, J.R. (eds.) Encyclopedia of Behavioral Medicine, pp. 1997–2000. Springer, New York (2013)
25. Frick, W.B.: Flight into health: a new interpretation. J. Humanistic Psychol. **39**, 58–81 (1999)
26. Griffiths, M.: A "components" model of addiction within a biopsychosocial framework. J Subst. Use **10**, 191–197 (2005)
27. Taylor, S.E., Lobel, M.: Social comparison activity under threat: downward evaluation and upward contacts. Psychol. Rev. **96**, 569–575 (1989)

28. West, R.: Time for a change: putting the transtheoretical (stages of change) model to rest. Addiction **100**, 1036–1039 (2005)
29. Borland, R., Balmford, J., Hunt, D.: The effectiveness of personally tailored computer-generated advice letters for smoking cessation. Addiction **99**(3), 369–377 (2004)
30. Sutton, S.: Back to the drawing board? A review of applications of the transtheoretical model to substance use. Addiction **96**(1), 175–186 (2001)
31. Toseland, R.W., Rivas, R.F.: An Introduction to Group Work Practice. Pearson Education Limited, Boston (2005)
32. Locke, E.A., Latham, G.P.: New directions in goal-setting theory. Curr. Dir. Psychol Sci. **15**, 265–268 (2006)
33. Cialdini, R.B.: Influence. HarperCollins, New York (2009)
34. Ali, R., Jiang, N., Jeary, S., Phalp, K.: Consideration in software-mediated social interaction. In: RCIS, pp. 1–11 (2014)
35. Lynam, D.R., Milich, R., Zimmerman, R., Novak, S.P., Logan, T.K., Martin, C., Leukefeld, C., Clayton, R.: Project DARE: no effects at 10-year follow-up. J. Consult. Clin. Psychol. **67**, 590–593 (1999)
36. Carter, C.A., Kahnweiler, W.M.: The efficacy of the social norms approach to substance abuse prevention applied to fraternity men. J. Am. Coll. Health **49**, 66–71 (2000)
37. Center for Universal Design: The Principles of Universal Design. https://www.ncsu.edu/ncsu/design/cud/about_ud/docs/use_guidelines.pdf
38. Griffiths, M.: Internet addiction - time to be taken seriously? Addict. Res. **8**, 413–418 (2000)
39. Kuss, D.J., Griffiths, M.D., Karila, L., Billieux, J.: Internet addiction: a systematic review of epidemiological research for the last decade. Curr. Pharm. Des. **20**, 4026–4052 (2014)
40. Jiang, J., Phalp, K., Ali, R.: Digital Addiction: Gamification for Precautionary and Recovery Requirements. In: REFSQ Workshops, pp. 224–225 (2015)

# Do You Own a Volkswagen? Values as Non-Functional Requirements

Balbir S. Barn(✉)

Middlesex University, Hendon, London NW4 4BT, UK
b.barn@mdx.ac.uk

**Abstract.** Of late, there has been renewed interest in determining the role and relative importance of (moral) values in the design of software and its acceptance. Events such as the Snowden revelations and the more recent case of the Volkswagen "defeat device" software have further emphasised the importance of values and ethics in general. This paper posits a view that values accompanied by an appropriate framework derived from non-functional requirements can be used by designers and developers as means for discourse of ethical concerns of the design of software. The position is based on the Volkswagen "Dieselgate" case study and a qualitative analysis of developers views from Reddit discussion forums. The paper proposes an extension of an existing classification of requirements to include value concerns.

## 1 Introduction

Values are a key driver of human behaviour and are seen as an important component in societal and environmental sustainability. However, current software engineering practice does not pay sufficient attention to the notion of values given the role of software and systems in so-called "smart city" sustainability actions. Critically, there is no sufficiently expressive machinery to describe how values such privacy and security are elicited, negotiated, mediated and accommodated in systems design beyond either early stages such as contextual design. For the purposes of this paper, values are what Friedman refers to: ownership and property; privacy, freedom from bias, universal usability, trust, autonomy, informed consent and identity. She defines values as: what a person or group of people consider important in life [13].

The paper's position is motivated by the recent so-called "Dieselgate" media story concerning Volkswagen. On 18th September 2015, Volkswagen, USA was accused by the US Environment Protection Agency (EPA) of installing an illegal "defeat device" software that dramatically reduces nitrogen oxide (NOx) emissions - but only when the cars were undergoing strict emission tests.

This paper advances the notion that (moral) values are distinct from non functional requirements or even *softgoals* as in goal oriented requirements engineering (GORE) approaches but can benefit from being incorporated into Non-Functional Requirements (NFR) frameworks. In order to present this position,

© IFIP International Federation for Information Processing 2016

Published by Springer International Publishing Switzerland 2016. All Rights Reserved
C. Bogdan et al. (Eds.): HCSE 2016/HESSD 2016, LNCS 9856, pp. 151–162, 2016.
DOI: 10.1007/978-3-319-44902-9_10

the paper takes a case example approach. Firstly, a summary outlining the key issues arising from the Volkswagen "defeat device" is presented in Sect. 2. The case example is analysed with respect to value concerns. In contrast to other recent analyses of the Volkswagen case [29], the paper augments the analysis by taking concrete views from developers. Evidence is drawn from the Reddit discussion forum section on Coding where developers posted 80 items over a four day period [25]. Section 3 presents this analysis. In doing so, this paper concretely proposes how an existing classification mechanism for requirements can be extended. Section 4 draws on the academic literature on values, ethics and non functional requirements to provide further support for the proposition that values can be classified as a special case of non-functional requirement. In Sect. 5, the paper concludes by offering a roadmap for further research.

## 2    Case Study and Approach

Interpretative, exploratory case study research is a first step to understanding phenomena as input for further research. The Volkswagen case study is important from two perspectives: Firstly, its impact on environmental pollution and secondly, the subsequent apportioning of blame on software engineers responsible for the "defeat device" software and their (implicit) unethical actions. A descriptive (non-value laden) account of the Volkswagen case study is presented next using the investigative reports from two quality newspapers, the Guardian and the New York Times.

### 2.1    Volkswagen Case Study

The story was first reported in the media on the 18th of September, 2015 with a claim that around 482,000 cars were affected in USA. However this story begins much earlier. In 2014, a non-profit group, the International Council on Clean Transportation worked with the California Air Resources Board and researchers at West Virginia University to conduct on-road diesel emissions tests of cars including two Volkswagens and a BMW X5. The researchers found that when tested on the road some cars emitted almost 40 times the permitted levels of nitrogen oxides yet performed flawlessly in lab conditions. Subsequently the federal body and the Environmental Pollution Agency (EPA) were both involved in negotiations with Volkswagen. Eventually in September 2015, when delays on announcing new 2016 models could not be explained, the EPA announced the violation of the Clean Air Act [33]. The basis of this violation was the discovery of software sub-routines that detected when the car was being tested and then activated equipment that reduced emissions. But the software turned the equipment off during regular driving, increasing emissions far above legal limits, possibly to save fuel or to improve the car's torque and acceleration. Note that while all cars undergo strict emission tests, manufacturers have always been able to manipulate the settings of the parameters for emission tests. The story developed and up to 11 million cars were affected [26] leading to around 25 billion Euro being wiped off the company's market value [3]. Eventually, the CEO,

Martin Winterkorn resigned but denied personal wrongdoing. At the same time. VW's CEO in USA, Michael Horn in a testimony before US Congress identified the true authors of his company's deception [7]: "This was a couple of rogue software engineers who put this in for whatever reason."

As a further justification, he described the "defeat device" as a line of code "hidden in millions of software code". Since then, following investigations in Germany, other senior managers appear to have been implicated and were suspended. Huber, the acting head of VW's supervisory board, called the crisis a "moral and policy disaster" and went on to say: "The unlawful behaviour of engineers and technicians involved in engine development shocked Volkswagen just as much as it shocked the public" [1].

Since initial reporting of this case, Federal and California regulators have begun an investigation into a second computer program in Volkswagen's diesel cars that also affects the operation of the cars' emission controls.

## 2.2   Approach

A notable aspect of the media reporting of the Volkswagen defeat device story is the lack of discussion of ethical considerations that engineers are subject to, in the act of engineering a system. Both US and Germany have strong engineering codes of ethics yet these have not featured in any reporting. Given the relationship between ethics and values, this paper analyses this case study from that perspective and by drawing upon a qualitative analysis of the Reddit discussion forum section on coding. The thread, entitled: "'Rouge'(sic) Software Engineers blamed for VW emissions (would this be a bug or feature?)" received 80 items that were posted over a over four day period (12 October to 15 October)[25].

The approach presented has reliability limitations of the analysis of the Reddit posts. A single developer forum was identified through search queries. Various forums such as StackOverflow were investigated but there were no discussions about the Volkswagen "defeat device". There are a limited number of participants who posted discussion items. Although there are over 65,000 readers who subscribe to the coding forum, 27 participants posted comments, from which 7 posted at least twice. The data is is largely indicative and an appropriate future research avenue would be to explore developer's perspectives.

## 3   Case Study Analysis

The first question is one of ethics and its relationship to (software) engineering and the section begin with a provocative prompt:

"Engineers are the un-acknowledged philosophers of the postmodern world." [21].

In part, the reason for this is straightforward: an engineer may not ask about what they should be doing, or may find that a solution that cannot be achieved by technical expertise alone. From this it follows that ethical judgements such as responses to questions of environmental protection following violations of the

Clean Air Act are required. Hence, philosophy is an internal practical need. So did the "rogue" engineers alluded to by Horn seek this ethical judgement? A more complex explanation is also offered by Mitcham: engineering is *modelling* a new philosophy of life. One interpretation of this is: we have moved from a natural environment to one where we increasingly present humans as information-centric entities whose production and consumption of information occurs through engineered artefacts. Such a world demands continuous evaluation of ethical concerns.

The codes of engineering ethics such as that developed by the Association of German Engineers [8][1] provide some insight as to what is expected in terms of norms of behaviour from engineers. For example:

- Engineers are responsible for their professional actions and tasks corresponding to their competencies and qualifications while carrying both individual and shared responsibilities.
- Engineers are aware of the embeddedness of technical systems into their societal, economic and ecological context, and their impact on the lives of future generations.
- Engineers apply to their professional institutions in cases of conflicts concerning engineering ethics.

The Engineering ethics principles also give guidelines on how to resolve conflicting values. In cases of conflicting values, engineers give priority: to the values of humanity over the dynamics of nature; to issues of human rights over technology implementation and exploitation; to public welfare over private interests; and to safety and security over functionality and profitability of their technical solutions. It would appear that the software developers responsible for developing and installing the "defeat device' violated a normative code of conduct. What is not known is whether the developers concerned were able to escalate it to their managers, their professional body and in the last resort, directly inform the public or refuse co-operation altogether as directed in paragraph 3.4 of the VDI code of ethics for engineers [8]. Both the media reporting and the posts on the Reddit Coding forum by developers find no mention of ethical concerns directly. For the latter, there are references and extensive dialogue that tries to account for defensive actions and how to minimise potential fallout:

*gullibleboy*: I agree. Thankfully, I have never been asked to write code that was blatantly illegal. And I would like to think I would have enough integrity to say no. But, I certainly would make sure to get written confirmation, from my superiors, to ensure that I was not made the patsy. Any seasoned developer would do the same.

Retaining evidence of written confirmation such as in email, while potentially difficult and desirable raises other legal issues.

*LongUsername*: Will be surprising to see if they have written evidence. It happened at least 5 years ago, and I know many companies with an automatic email deletion policy of

---

[1] http://www.vdi.eu/engineering/.

about 2 years. Even if there were explicit instructions, unless the engineer thought enough to archive the email off (in violation of data retention policies), it may be gone.

Resolving conflicting values appears to be core philosophical action that engineers will always have to deal with. While the VDI code of ethics provides rules to apply in cases of conflict, it may not always be appropriate to recourse to the professional body. Some times conflict of values are also a proxy for conflicting goals. The comment by *frezik* below makes that point. It might be the case that the requirements specifications are poorly specified and the design process does not allow for the conflict resolution. It could also be possible that "requirements creep", created un-wanted changes that should not have got through an approval process.

*mallardtheduck*: In a "normal" vehicle, all profiles should conform to the relevant emissions standards. In this case, my suggestion is that VW's programmers/engineers started with "good" profiles and over the process of tweaking/improving them, ended up making the more common profiles violate said standards. Whether this was done deliberately or not is hard to say. Either way it's something that should have been caught and probably was, but was "hushed up" by persons higher up the chain.

The idea of a "rogue" software engineer is also interesting when observed from different perspectives. A "rogue" engineer could have inserted the software that did exactly what the company required against the express wishes of her manager. In which case, the problem is even bigger in terms of questioning the entire software engineering practice at Volkswagen.

*PCLoad_Letter*: From this you can draw the conclusion that there are no software audits on the code running millions of these cars and no one in QA or the engineering divisions even questioned when the emissions tests came back much lower that expected? That is a much bigger problem than a Rogue engineer.

Conversely, in his testimony to Congress, Michael Horn, although implausible, may have meant to imply that the engineers were "rogue" because they had not reported the software behaviour as required by the engineering codes of practice and their company. A notion gently supported by a developer:

*MuonManLaserJab*: For it to be "rogue engineers", they would have had to decide to keep the facts a secret while writing the cheat...

It is constructive to consider why the developers on Reddit have focussed on defence rather than ethical concerns. Partly, it is explained by how engineers work. The way that engineering (and code development) happens as reported in [21] by Louis Bucciarelli in his ethnographic studies of engineers: when students are doing engineering problems it is generally thought that they "*ought not to get bogged down in useless 'philosophical' diversions*" [6, pp. 105–106]. At this stage of their engineering career, students are practicing to be engineers. The developer's world (when they are engaged in problem solving) is also highly abstract. It is one of programming syntax, data structures, and program comments that refer only to functional requirements. Such an abstract world does not leave room for ethical concerns that might have serious implications for society at large. The question arises: where and how in the process of design can these critical diversions be accommodated? The problem is further compounded by deadline pressures resulting in poor decisions and is also offered as an explanation.

*frezik*: The situation I'm thinking of here is when the programmer is told "we need the ECU tweaked on this car to make x mpg highway while passing emissions tests, and we need it by date y". They make a profile that makes the mpg requirement, and they make another profile that makes the emissions requirement. They try to combine them to meet both goals, but they run out of time. Under pressure, they do something stupid and illegal, and make the emissions test run when test mode is detected, and mpg mode otherwise.

Following on from ethical concerns, is a consideration of who else was involved the chain of decision making that led to the insertion of the "defeat device" software. The developers point out that software running the engine control unit would have gone through numerous code reviews.

*rfinger1337*: VW has a responsibility to know whats in the code. It wouldn't get past testing, code review...

*GuyNamedNate2*: It really depends on what their code reviewing /auditing practices are...I would hope and expect an organization as big as VW would have avionics-quality processes.

*AllGloryToHypno-Toad*: if this company is writing engine management software without code reviews and testing, then that's another issue. This should have come up and many, many times.

Modern software engineering can also create spaces whereby an engineer may not be aware that he has violated his engineering ethics codes. For example, component based design mandates black box design through well defined interfaces that supports specific functional requirements. Developers may end up writing code for a software component without an awareness of the wider context of where that component may be used. Thus we see:

*LongUsername*: Unfortunately, The real coders may not have known what they were doing. Tell the programmer who does the emissions system to "disable the emissions system when this flag over here is set... It's for test-purposes only." and tell the guy working on the steering system "when the wheel doesn't change position for X amount of time, set this global flag over there that says we're on a Dyno".

Cultural issues within the organisation are also of concern. The engineering community either chose deliberately to not report the rogue engineers to the organisation or even outside, or were not able to because of the cultural climate. A Reuters report published in the Guardian on 10th October described the culture under the former CEO, Martin Winterkorn [1] as authoritarian. Bernard Osteloh was quoted as saying: "We need in future a climate in which problems aren't hidden but can be openly communicated to superiors...We need a culture in which it's possible and permissible to argue with your superior about the best way to go.". The reality as presented by the developers is different:

_ *Toranaga* _: I dunno, fall guys get fired... Whistle-blowers get exiled to Siberia.

# 4    Values Versus Non Functional Requirements

In this section, it becomes apparent that a common implicit position in current software engineering practice is that of non functional requirements (NFR) being used as a proxy for accounting for values. The literature is examined and used to argue that existing approaches for managing NFRs would not have sufficed to prevent the Volkswagen case. A further argument advanced is that values need to be unpicked in order for them to be used effectively by engineers. Simply, we want to provide engineers with the necessary machinery to allow them to externalise their philosophical deliberations as they practice their craft.

## 4.1    Non Functional Requirements

NFRs have been extensively studied by the software engineering community as they are recognised as important factors to the success of a software project [12, for example]. Despite their importance, NFRs are poorly understood and often neglected in the software design process. A satisfactory understanding of NFRs remains elusive and is attributed to three key problems: lack of a workable definition; difficulties of classifying types of NFRs; and representing NFRs in the design process [15]. Further, once NFRs have been identified, they need to be assigned properties (attributes) which can be measured. Not all NFRs have attributes and notably, the systematic review by Mairiza et al. shows that of the 252 types of NFR identified, over 50 % were without attributes [18]. This is relevant to values.

One consistent view of NFRs is: they are a *quality* attribute of a system that its stakeholders care about and hence will affect their degree of satisfaction with the system. These qualities end up being referred to as *"ilities"*. Examples include: reliability, testability, usability, portability etc. Mairiza et al. identify 115 such quality characteristics [18]. Such sayilities are hard to characterise in ways that can support rigorous engineering and are ultimately subjective and stakeholder specific [11]. Further, implementations of sayilities may be cross-cutting across many software components and may also impinge on the meta-systems used for constructing a system under question.

An inspection of several empirical studies all omit any consideration of treating values as NFRs [16,18,19,31]. While security and privacy are both moral values, their treatment as NFRs are from a system perspective and not from that of the end user's moral concerns. A survey of software architects to consider NFRs conducted by Ameller et al. also found that values as we define them do not feature as NFRs even in a category of non-technical NFRs (i.e. not those such as performance etc.) [2]. Overall, this implies a conclusion where, either values are systematically ignored in the practice of NFR elicitation or values may not be NFRs. Certainly, the ethics/values discussions did not feature strongly in the media reporting and the coder's comments on Reddit.

We now consider the relevance of techniques of requirements engineering to values. Over recent years, goal oriented requirements engineering (GORE) [22] has began to dominate practice [16] particularly with respect to NFRs with the

NFR Framework [9] being the most widely cited. In the NFR Framework, NFRs or goals that are hard to express (*softgoals*), and their decisions are captured in goal graphs and refined into detailed concrete goals. Others following the GORE tradition include i* [35]. GORE based techniques present a variety of options for analysis such as providing a more formal basis of how goals realise other goals, conflict between goals and the positive and negative contributions goals make to other goals and ultimately tradeoffs between goals. GORE approaches would appear to be a promising area for further examination from a values perspective.

## 4.2 Values and Value Sensitive Concerns

Investigating the intertwining and entailment of values and technology development has been an ongoing area of research mostly originating in the domain of human-computer interaction (HCI) [30]. In the HCI literature, values are identifiable entities that are built in by design or accident through the affordances of the technology [13]. These considerations have been termed Value Sensitive Design (VSD) by Friedman [13], who refers to: ownership and property; privacy, freedom from bias, universal usability, trust, autonomy, informed consent and identity.

This is contrasted with sociology and social psychology where values are criteria that are used to evaluate or make judgements about events or people encountered, helping explain individual and collective behaviour [5]. As social interactions become increasingly mediated by technology then these two interpretations of values merge and in doing so, they govern user action or non-action within technology [17]. Thus design choices that explicitly consider values can change the affordances of resulting technologies [14,27].

The problem of identifying and qualifying values has many facets: their individual or shared nature; their realisation in concrete features; their subjective or objective location; their accidental or intended role with respect to system functionality [28]. A further complexity is that all these facets operate along a continuum so an intended or accidental property is not simply two possible states of a value. These complexities prevent their widespread acknowledgement and treatment. In particular, there is no general theoretical framework to allow stakeholders in the design process to identify, qualify and successively map into usable data the relevant values for the application at stake. In short, the understanding of values and their contribution to technology acceptance is not theoretically grounded into the entire software development lifecycle. As discussed earlier, GORE approaches (particularly, the use of softgoals) have the potential to represent values. However, softgoals cannot be directly linked to direct or indirect stakeholders. Further, '"Values are not goals, they are assumptions (more precisely, evaluations). A value is a judgment, though very general and vague. It says of something that it is good or bad. A goal is a regulatory state in someone's mind" ([20] reported by Pommeranz et al. [23]). It would appear that values and their multi-dimensional nature requires new GORE-like approaches that allow designers to engage in a philosophical discourse about their systems and their shaping of society.

## 4.3 Value Architectures

In summary, values are not referenced in meta reviews of NFRs, nor are example values listed as an "ility". So either values are systematically ignored in the practice of NFR elicitation or values may not be NFRs. The complexity of values cannot be accounted for by simple attributes and importantly, typical NFR elicitation approaches do not allow designers to engage in a necessary philosophical dialogue about those "...*problems that engineers admit cannot be resolved simply with engineering methods alone....professional ethical issues.*" [21, p.31].

It is also clear that GORE based approaches, particularly the notion of *softgoals*, is a promising area of research for incorporating values as these provide qualitative mechanisms for resolution that are sufficient. Thus we propose the following:

1. Extend the Glinz classification to include a values category;
2. Develop processes and the necessary vocabularies to allow ethical discussions of the impact of values of design decisions that can contribute a *"value architecture"* in much the same way as functional requirements contribute to *application* architectures and NFRs lead to *technical* architectures of system.

Glinz proposed a classification of requirements based on concerns - something that is a matter of interest to a system. A concern is a performance concern if timing or volume is a matter of interest. The set of all requirements are partitioned into functional requirements, performance requirement, specific quality requirements and constraints. Alongside the classification, are a set of rules that are applied in order in order to classify a given requirement. We propose extending this classification and rule base as follows.

We introduce *Value* defined as: a requirement that pertains to value concern. Such a concern is classified by the introduction of an additional classification rule. "...a specific moral value that the system or component shall either support or prevent erosion of.". The resulting classification and rule set is shown in Fig. 1. The benefits of this extension allows us to specifically consider values as a concern in the requirements process. While it is relatively straight forward to develop measures for attributes such as Performance, defining a measure for value is much harder and requires agreement amongst stakeholders. By interacting with stakeholders using the trigger question, we open a channel for that necessary philosophical dialogue alluded to by Mitcham and necessary for the agreement.

Having addressed the requirements classification concern, the next stage is to develop value sensitive processes that can take advantage of the classification. The proposal here is to adapt the work of Yoo et al. [34] to support value elicitation, ethical discussions of the impact of values of design decisions and their capture suitable for engineers. Their work develops a framework for accounting for values using participatory design approaches. Evaluations on the efficacy of this approach have been reported elsewhere [4] but the technical machinery to support this remains an ongoing research challenge. For example, can a value expression language be used to both specify value requirements, and provide input for technology acceptance models such [32]? Such models use survey

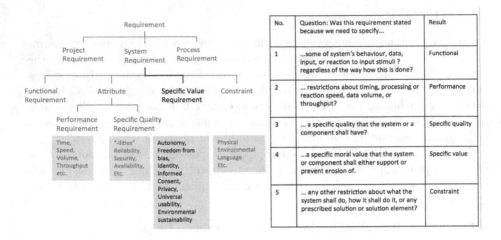

**Fig. 1.** Extension of Glinz's concern-based taxonomy and classification rules

based research instruments that do not have questions about values. Practical considerations can be dealt with as functional requirement specifications are developed and be part of the descriptive frameworks used in requirement specification. A greater challenge is during the design of the software interactions. It is proposed that the trigger question can be integrated in processes that check if a requirement has been implemented. With regard to the original case study, stages where the trigger question could have been invoked include: code reviews, and componentisation of software.

## 5    Conclusion

The Volkswagen case study illustrates the importance of the role of ethics and its subsuming notion of values in software practice. Developers currently do not appear to engage in meaningful discussions about values that are explicit or those that emerge through the use of systems. It is notable, that the developers on the Reddit platform were relatively subdued in their discussion of ethical / value concerns. This paper has proposed that such hesitancy is partly linked to how functional and non functional requirements are managed. On the surface, values appear to have similarities with NFRs but the view is taken that just as NFRs present problems of representation, definition and classification, values may generate similar issues. Hence an extension of Glinz's concerns-based taxonomy for requirements that accounts for values is presented. In doing so, a channel for necessary dialogue with stakeholders about the ethics of decisions that programmers and designers is opened. Epistemological study to develop the necessary frameworks for such a dialogue is an important first step. Future research plans include: empirical data collection of values and their importance to relevant communities such as developers; the development of informal, semi-formal and formal conceptual models of values and related concepts; and experimental evidence of evaluation of such models. Identifying where trigger questions can be incorporated is also a critical element in any processes. In today's hyper-connected world where systems are increasingly delivered in a pervasive form, such as through "apps" on smart phones, the risk to erosion of values, as well as, threats to social and societal sustainability are paramount. Values need to be formally accounted for in software engineering practice.

# References

1. Reuters Agency. Volkswagen executives describe authoritarian culture under former ceo (2015). http://www.theguardian.com/business/2015/oct/10/volkswagen-executives-martin-winterkorn-company-culture
2. Ameller, D., Ayala, C., Cabot, J., Franch, X.: How do software architects consider non-functional requirements: an exploratory study. In: 2012 20th IEEE International on Requirements Engineering Conference (RE), pp. 41–50. IEEE (2012)
3. Arnett, G.: The scale of the volkswagen crisis in charts (2015). http://www.the guardian.com/news/datablog/2015/sep/22/scale-of-volkswagen-crisis-in-charts
4. Barn, B., Barn, R.: Resilience and values: antecedents for effective co-design of information systems. In: 23rd European Conference on Information Systems (ECIS 2015), AISNet Library (2015)
5. Bennett, R.: Factors underlying the inclination to donate to particular types of charity. Int. J. Nonprofit Voluntary Sect. Mark. **8**(1), 12–29 (2003)
6. Bucciarelli, L.L.: Designing Engineers. MIT press, Cambridge (1994)
7. C-SPAN.org. Hearing on volkswagen emissions violations (2015). http://www.c-span.org/video/?328599-1/hearing-volkswagen-emissions-violations
8. Christ, H.: Fundamentals of engineering ethics. VDI the Association of Engineers, Dusseldorf (2002)
9. Lawrence Chung, B., Nixon, E., Mylopoulos, J.: Non-functional requirements. Softw. Eng. (2000)
10. Dardenne, A., Van Lamsweerde, A., Fickas, S.: Goal-directed requirements acquisition. Sci. Comput. Program. **20**(1–2), 3–50 (1993)
11. Dou, K., Wang, X., Tang, C., Ross, A., Sullivan, K.: An evolutionary theory-systems approach to a science of the ilities. Procedia Comput. Sci. **44**, 433–442 (2015)
12. Ebert, C.: Putting requirement management into praxis: dealing with nonfunctional requirements. Inf. Softw. Technol. **40**(3), 175–185 (1998)
13. Friedman, B.: Value-sensitive design. Interactions **3**(6), 16–23 (1996)
14. Friedman, B., Nissenbaum, H.: Bias in computer systems. ACM Trans. Inf. Syst. (TOIS) **14**(3), 330–347 (1996)
15. Glinz, M.: On non-functional requirements. In: 15th IEEE International on Requirements Engineering Conference 2007, RE 2007, pp. 21–26. IEEE (2007)
16. Franco, A.J.: Requirements elicitation approaches: a systematic review. In: 2015 IEEE 9th International Conference on Research Challenges in Information Science (RCIS), pp. 520–521. IEEE (2015)
17. Locke, E.A.: The motivation sequence, the motivation hub, and the motivation core. Organ. Behav. Hum. Decis. Process. **50**(2), 288–299 (1991)

18. Mairiza, D., Zowghi, D., Nurmuliani, N.: An investigation into the notion of non-functional requirements. In: Proceedings of the 2010 ACM Symposium on Applied Computing, pp. 311–317. ACM (2010)
19. Matoussi, A., Laleau, R.: A survey of non-functional requirements in software development process. Departement dÕInformatique Universite Paris, 12 (2008)
20. Miceli, M., Castelfranchi, C.: A cognitive approach to values. J. Theory Soc. Behav. 19(2), 169–193 (1989)
21. Mitcham, C.: The importance of philosophy to engineering. Teorema: Revista Internacional de Filosofía, pp. 27–47 (1998)
22. Mylopoulos, J., Chung, L., Yu, E.: From object-oriented to goal-oriented requirements analysis. Commun. ACM 42(1), 31–37 (1999)
23. Pommeranz, A., Detweiler, C., Wiggers, P., Jonker, C.: Elicitation of situated values: need for tools to help stakeholders and designers to reflect and communicate. Ethics Inf. Technol. 14(4), 285–303 (2012)
24. Raymond, E.S.: The Cathedral & the Bazaar: Musings on Linux and Open Source by an Accidental Revolutionary. O'Reilly Media Inc., Sebastopol (2001)
25. reddit. "rouge" software engineers blamed for vw emissions (would this be a bug or feature?) (2015). https://www.reddit.com/r/coding/comments/3ogtqw/rouge_software_engineers_blamed_for_vw_emissions/?
26. Ruddick, G.: Vw scandal: chief executive martin winterkorn refuses to quit (2015). http://www.theguardian.com/business/2015/sep/22/vw-scandal-escalates-volks wagen-11m-vehicles-involved
27. Shilton, K.: Values levers: building ethics into design. Sci. Technol. Hum. Values 38(3), 374–397 (2012)
28. Shilton, K., Koepfler, J.A., Fleischmann, K.R.: Charting sociotechnical dimensions of values for design research. Inf. Soc. 29(5), 259–271 (2013)
29. Spinellis, D.: Developer, debug thyself. IEEE Softw. 33(1), 3–5 (2016)
30. Suchman, L.: Do categories have politics? the language/action perspective reconsidered. In: Human Values and the Design of Computer Technology, pp. 91–106. Center for the Study of Language and Information (1997)
31. Svensson, R.B., Höst, M., Regnell, B.: Managing quality requirements: a systematic review. In: 2010 36th EUROMICRO Conference on Software Engineering and Advanced Applications (SEAA), pp. 261–268. IEEE (2010)
32. Venkatesh, V., Morris, M.G., Davis, G.B., Davis, F.D.: User acceptance of information technology: toward a unified view. MIS Q. 27(3), 425–478 (2003)
33. Wikipedia Clean air act (United States) (2015). https://en.wikipedia.org/wiki/Clean_Air_Act_(United_States)
34. Yoo, D., Huldtgren, A., Woelfer, J.P., Hendry, D.G., Friedman, B.: A value sensitive action-reflection model: evolving a co-design space with stakeholder and designer prompts. In: Proceedings of the SIGCHI Conference on Human Factors in Computing Systems, pp. 419–428. ACM (2013)
35. Yu, E.S.K.: Towards modelling and reasoning support for early-phase requirements engineering. In: Proceedings of the Third IEEE International Symposium on Requirements Engineering 1997, pp. 226–235. IEEE (1997)

# Human Error and Safety-Critical Systems

# A Core Ontology of Safety Risk Concepts
## Reconciling Scientific Literature with Standards for Automotive and Railway

Hermann Kaindl[1]([⊠]), Thomas Rathfux[1], Bernhard Hulin[2], Roland Beckert[1], Edin Arnautovic[1], and Roman Popp[1]

[1] Institute of Computer Technology, TU Wien, Vienna, Austria
kaindl@ict.tuwien.ac.at
[2] Berner & Mattner Systemtechnik GmbH, Munich, Germany

**Abstract.** Safety is a major concern for both automobiles and railway vehicles. The related standards provide definitions of the same concepts such as *Risk*, *Harm*, *Hazard*, etc., which we consider here as the core concepts. However, related conceptual models existing in the scientific literature either are inconsistent or do not cover the core concepts comprehensively.

We modeled the core of these safety concepts ourselves both in meetings and with tool support, based on the definitions given in the related standards. As a result, this paper presents a small core ontology of safety risk concepts for reconciling the scientific literature with standards. Since it matches the terminology of the related standards, it may serve as a reference model in the future. In fact, we already used it ourselves for systematically studying where human error may compromise safety.

## 1 Introduction

In the context of our overall effort to support reuse in safety risk analysis (see, e.g., [18], we have been working on tool support. Such a tool needs to allow for input, handling and storing information on concepts like *Hazard*. Our chosen approach to generate parts of such a tool using Eclipse, a related *metamodel* has to be defined.

So, we looked up standards and related scientific literature to gather information for such a metamodel. Unfortunately, we found inconsistencies between the terminology of the standards with conceptual models in the literature. In addition, we could not find any conceptual model in the literature that would cover the core concepts comprehensively.

In particular, we investigated this issue in the context of automobiles and railway vehicles. In general, all such vehicles are covered by the generic standard IEC 61508 [3], which has the scope of Electrical / Electronical / Programmable Electronic Safety-related Systems (E/E/PE) and is based on ISO/IEC Guide 51 [5]. For practical reasons, more specific standards apply:

© IFIP International Federation for Information Processing 2016
Published by Springer International Publishing Switzerland 2016. All Rights Reserved
C. Bogdan et al. (Eds.): HCSE 2016/HESSD 2016, LNCS 9856, pp. 165–180, 2016.
DOI: 10.1007/978-3-319-44902-9_11

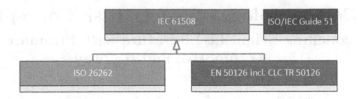

**Fig. 1.** Taxonomy of standards under investigation

– ISO 26262 [4] for automobiles, and
– EN 50126 [1] & TR 50126-2 [2] for railway systems.

Figure 1 depicts the relationships between these standards in the notation of the Unified Modeling Language (UML) [22], see omg.org for the current version. The arrow head points from the specific standards to the more general one (IEC 61508), which is also associated with ISO/IEC Guide 51.

ISO/IEC Guide 51:2014 [5] provides requirements and recommendations for the drafters of standards for the inclusion of safety aspects. This standard is applicable to any safety aspect related to people, property or the environment, or to a combination of these.

ISO 26262 is the functional safety standard for road vehicles and is derived from the generic functional safety standard IEC 61508. It deals with the possible hazards that could result from function failure in the electrical/electronic system in automotive vehicles.

EN 50126 is relevant for the whole railway system and not limited to railway vehicles. In contrast to IEC 61508 and ISO 26262, the railway standard EN 50126 is not limited to hazards resulting from malfunctioning of E/E/PE.

Primarily based on the terminology of these standards as defined in their glossaries, we started modeling of what we consider the core safety concepts. In addition, we employed tool support for finding relations between these concepts. In the course of several iterations over model versions in meetings, the models were most importantly extended and refined by expert knowledge from both the automotive and railway domains. We present here the resulting core ontology.

While it may have various applications in practice as a reference model in the future, we already used it for a preliminary but systematic study on where *human error* may compromise safety. This involved both traversing the graph of ontology concepts and looking at it as a whole.

The remainder of this paper is organized in the following manner. First, we motivate our work explicitly and discuss related work in the scientific literature. Then we elaborate on our effort on conceptual modeling of terminology from standards. Based on that, we explain our resulting core ontology of risk concepts. In addition, we sketch its fit into an *upper ontology*. As a possibility to make use of our ontology, we sketch how human error may compromise safety.

## 2   Motivation

While we originally strived for a metamodel for our tool support, our motivation for creating such a core ontology soon became more fundamental. In fact, safety assessment is in many ways subjective, partly because of individual risk perception, experience, education, cultural pressure and habits.

To reduce the arbitrariness of safety assessment, experts defined safety concepts such as *Risk, Hazard* and *Accident.* However, definitions in natural language are inherently ambiguous. With an ontology, at least the relations among the concepts contained can be made precise. They can also be visualized in figures as shown below, and such figures can support a common understanding of safety concepts.

In addition, even the definitions of safety core concepts such as *Risk* are not consistent between different safety standards. For example, while it is defined in the ISO 26262 standard [4] for the automotive domain as "combination of the probability of occurrence of harm and the severity of that harm", for the railway domain it is defined as "the rate of occurrence of accidents and incidents resulting in harm (caused by a hazard) and the degree of severity of that harm" [2]. For creating our core ontology, we made an ontological decision in favor of the former definition, since it is actually derived from the ISO/IEC Guide 51 [5].

Being precise and consistent in this regard is actually a major concern in practice. This was, for instance, a major lesson learned by the author of this paper who is a safety expert in the railway domain, in an international project for the installation of a people mover. According to this real-world experience, if understandable and consistent definitions are not introduced in an early project phase, later much time will be wasted with discussions and with the reformulation of documents for the safety case.

Moreover, the consistency of definitions of safety concepts may become important after an accident in legal courts. Interpretations of safety concepts may be discussed there and related questions raised, such as the following:

- What was the interpretation of the safety concept $x$ for the safety case?
- What are other interpretations of this safety concept (in the standards used or other similar ones)?
- Would the other interpretation have led to additional safety requirements?
- Could the accident have been avoided if such additional safety requirements were taken into account?

Our core ontology of safety risk concepts may help to answer such questions consistently.

## 3   Related Work in the Literature

Ambiguity of safety standard terminology and the problems resulting are discussed in [12,23]. Models of safety standards can contribute to avoid misunderstandings and conflicting views on the concepts behind the terminology.

Such a model for IEC 61508, with the focus on creating a chain of evidence for safety compliance demonstration, is proposed in [21]. Unfortunately, as explained below, there are ontological problems with this model, in particular its *Risk* concept. Another model of a few concepts from ISO/IEC Guide 51, from which IEC 61508 takes many of the core glossary definitions, can be found in [23]. It only centers around a model of *Risk*, but also this model has ontological problems as explained below. Hence, we could not base our core ontology on either of these papers.

A discussion of evolving definitions of the concepts *Risk*, *Hazard* and *Mishap* in military standards is discussed in [28]. As a result, a formalized model for calculating hazard and mishap occurrence probabilities is presented. The ontological view of risk-related concepts in these military standards is quite different from the one in automotive and railway standards. Hence, it was not possible to base our core ontology on this work, either. However, the increasing importance of the *Mishap* concept in the evolution of military standards suggests to us the importance of the related *Accident* concept. As explained below, the inclusion of *Accident* into our core ontology was only in the course of an evolution of our conceptual models.

The closest attempt to our ontological modeling in this paper can be found in [13], where we focused on the differences in automotive and railway standards and unified them conceptually as far as possible. In contrast, the current paper provides a core ontology of the common safety concepts. In addition, there was no model of *Risk* yet in [13].

Our development of a core ontology of safety risk concepts may be considered as a simple application of *Ontology Engineering* (OE) [8]. OE represents "the set of activities that concern the ontology development process, the ontology life cycle, and the methodologies, tools and languages for building ontologies" ([9], as cited in [25]. Typical activities in OE are Domain Analysis and Specification (knowledge acquisition, and the definition of ontological purpose, including its use cases, users, etc.), Conceptualization (structuring of domain knowledge), and Implementation (expressing the ontology using an appropriate ontology representation language). On top of the activities for ontology building are the activities for ontology utilization and application (e.g., building tools for the defined use cases). Another important activity in OE is ontology *evaluation*. The goal of ontology evaluation is to estimate the quality of the ontology, and it includes ontology *validation* (investigation if the ontology represents the real-world domain concepts and their relationships appropriately, and if it fulfills the ontology use case and purpose), and *verification* (proving consistency and that the ontology is correctly constructed according to the language used, etc.) [10]. However, most of the ontology evaluation approaches [6] deal with large, complex and more or less formally represented ontologies (e.g., in OWL or description logic) and are not suitable for our case.

Since we have used a semi-formal representation in UML without constraints, logic formalisms, etc., and having in mind the current size of our core ontology, explicit ontology verification is not feasible. Regarding validation, we iteratively reviewed the results from ontology development steps using expert knowledge. In our future work, we plan to validate the ontology against use cases. Another option for ontology validation would be to automatically create an ontology from standards and (or) scientific literature and qualitatively compare it to our manually created ontology. Sfar et al. [24] use a similar comparison to evaluate automatically created ontologies against a "gold-standard" ontology created by humans. So, using ontology learning [27] for the validation of our core ontology would be a valid goal for our future research. We already gained first experience in comparing semi-automatically created taxonomies (light-weight ontologies) to manually created domain models in requirements engineering [7].

## 4    Conceptual Modeling of Terminology from Standards

Conceptual modeling is, in general, not that simple. Regarding models of safety concepts in the literature, we particularly found inconsistencies in [23] and in [21]. In both cases, these are supposedly related to misunderstandings of the *aggregation* relationship of UML.

In [23], a categorization of the concept *Risk* is correctly modeled using *generalization* of the classes representing the subconcepts in UML. However, "Damage" (supposedly used here as a synonym of *Harm*) is modeled there as an aggregation of three special cases of *Harm*, and this should rather be modeled as well using *generalization*.

In [21], the concept *Risk* is modeled as class with a few UML *attributes*, including "likelihood" and "consequence". Assuming that they correspond to *Probability* and *Severity* according to the standards that we model below, there is an interesting modeling issue. In the specification of UML, an attribute is said to be "semantically equivalent to a composition association". When considering this statement more precisely, the question arises, in which sense an attribute is part of an object. In the UML *metamodel*, *attribute* is part of *class* in a composition. In this sense, an attribute is an entity of its own, which defines UML. But in the specification of UML as well as in [22], attributes are also said to be "composition relationships between a class and the classes of its attributes". In this sense, an attribute would model the same relationship as a composition. A simple example shows that this view is questionable. The region of a wine can be modeled as its attribute (as one of possibly several), but this does not mean that any particular region is "part of" a particular wine. Already in [26], "attribution" was said to be often confused with a whole-part relationship. The argument that these are different relationships was another simple example: "While towers have height as one of their attributes, height is not a part of a tower."

Therefore, it is rather the class representing the concept *Harm* that may have (among others) the attributes *Probability* and *Severity*, see Fig. 2. While we think that this is a 'true' model of these concepts (according to the standards under consideration), this way of modeling raises yet another issue. How would it be possible in such a model to represent that this combination of *Probability* and *Severity* of *Harm* is *Risk*? All this justifies the ontological decision to model this inner core as given below (using aggregation).

**Fig. 2.** Harm class with attributes

For the actual modeling involved for achieving our proposed core ontology, we pursued two different ways. We employed tool support for getting automated suggestions for association relationships, and we had a series of expert meetings, i.e., meetings involving two safety experts. Note, that the tool run was only after the second of a total of four meetings. So, it was not intended to bias the whole effort but only to see more exactly what can be extracted directly from the given glossaries.

### 4.1   Tool-Supported Modeling

After the second meeting (as sketched below), we tried tool-supported modeling. We were interested in getting suggestions for (binary) association relations between any two of the core concepts under discussion in the meetings, based on their glossary definitions in the standards under investigation. Our major interest was to see what exactly these definitions say about potential relations between the concepts defined.

More precisely, we employed the tool RETH (Requirements Engineering Through Hypertext), a tool for requirements specification according to the method with the same name. RETH combines object-oriented technology and hypertext. It was developed under the guidance of the first author of this paper some time ago, see, e.g., [16].

For tool-supported modeling in the course of creating our core ontology of safety risk concepts, we used the RETH tool to automatically generate *glossary links*, see [17]. More generally, it is a semi-automated generation that allows the user to reject a suggested link, but we refrained from this option in order not to influence the result. Based on such links, we let the tool automatically generate (binary) association relations in a second step, see [15]. According to the heuristic behind that, RETH simply generates an association, if and only if there is a glossary link in either direction. Of course, such proposed associations can be deleted manually, e.g., if they are transitive and, therefore, may be considered redundant. Again, we refrained from this option in order not to influence the result. Note, that this tool can also propose generalizations, e.g., for *Risk* being more general than *Individual Risk* (based on an obvious linguistic clue), but we did not have such a case here.

Let us show an example of an entry for a concept and its definition as an excerpt from a linearized tool output:

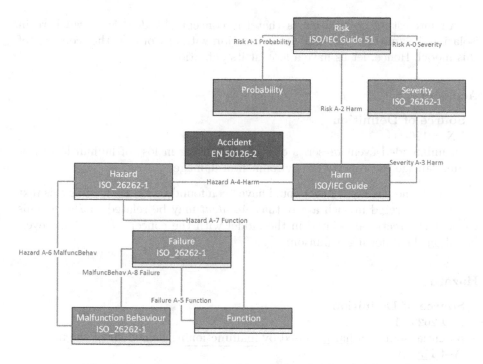

**Fig. 3.** Conceptual model with tool-generated associations

**Risk**

- **Source of Definition**
  ISO/IEC Guide51:2014
- combination of the <u>probability</u> of occurrence of <u>harm</u> and the <u>severity</u> of that <u>harm</u>
- **A-0** Severity
- **A-1** Probability
- **A-2** Harm

The link to "harm" was already given in this standard, but not the one to "severity", which was generated by the tool. The associations in this case only correspond to out-going links from this concept and are shown here through a generated name and a link to the associated concept.

The resulting model from the tool run is shown in UML in Fig. 3. With respect to our inner core of concepts around the concept *Risk*, the association A-2 is a typical case of a redundant transitive relation, which can be deleted in order not to clutter the diagram. A-0 and A-1 are simply shown here as associations, while they may be modeled as their special case of an aggregation in UML. However, the tool does not have any clue for such a distinction. (Note, that the UML definition of an aggregation is vague, and attempts to formalize them in logic are difficult.)

An interesting observation is that the concept *Accident* is shown here in isolation, i.e., without any association relation with any of the other concepts of this model. Hence, let us have a look at its definition:

## Accident

- **Source of Definition**
  EN 50126-1
- an unintended event or series of events resulting in loss of human health or life, damage to property or environmental damage

In fact, there is no link that could have been found by the tool, while this text can be interpreted in such a way that *Accident* may be related to *Harm*. This concept is directly associated in the model with the concept *Hazard*, however, based on the following definition:

## Hazard

- **Source of Definition**
  ISO 26262-1
- potential source of <u>harm</u> caused by <u>malfunctioning behaviour</u> of the item
- **A-4 <u>Harm</u>**
- **A-6 Malfunctioning Behaviour**
- **A-7 <u>Function</u>**

The reader is encouraged to compare this model with the ones created and elaborated at the meetings as sketched below, especially regarding this direct association. Note, in addition, that the concept *Malfunctioning Behaviour* was finally not included into our core ontology, although it would make sense, but it seemed to be less important in the standards under investigation.

## 4.2 Expert Meetings

As indicated above, we had four expert meetings including two safety experts, one primarily in the railway domain, the other in automotive. The other participants have primarily background in software and symbolic modeling, in particular also on ontologies. Note, that all participants of these meetings are also authors of this paper. Each meeting had five to six participants, and the duration was, on average, approximately seven hours. Between these meetings, we aligned ourselves via email and telecommunication, while we primarily worked on different tasks.

The starting point was a metamodel intended to create an Eclipse-based tool for supporting reuse of safety risk analyses. This metamodel included among other classes for requirements, etc., the following ones: *Function, Failure, Hazard, Severity* and *Tolerable Hazard Rate* (see also [18]).

Since this metamodel was considered insufficient by these authors, the relevant standards were consulted, first IEC 61508 and ISO Guide 51. Since the

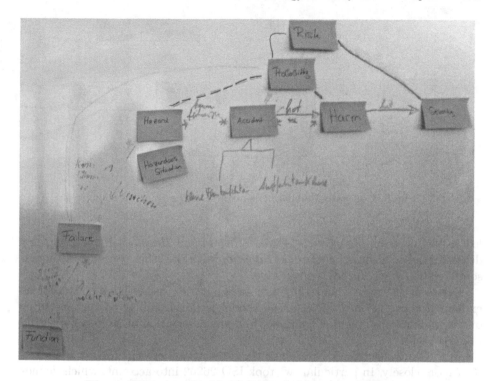

**Fig. 4.** White board with sticky notes from second meeting

terms in these standards are not unambiguously defined, we decided to look for conceptual models that we could adopt for the metamodel needed. Unfortunately, as explained above, we could not find a comprehensive model of the core safety terms as needed in the scientific literature. It even contained conceptual models that are inconsistent with the terminology of these standards.

In the course of a first meeting of all the authors, we primarily discussed an integration of a *Risk* model with the concepts corresponding to the classes of our previous metamodel. Immediately after this first meeting, however, the safety expert of the railway domain criticized that *Accident* was missing in our model and pointed to the definition according to EN 50126. Additionally, he proposed to introduce *Hazardous Situation* for representing preconditions that could lead to an *Accident*.

In our second meeting, we discussed possible inclusions of these concepts into our model. Even though neither IEC 61508 nor ISO 26262 define *Accident* explicitly, we decided to extend our model with this concept. In order to determine reasonable associations between the given concepts, we used sticky notes with a concept name per note, and arranged them on a white board (for the result see Fig. 4). As shown above, an association between *Accident* and *Harm* is obvious, but what causes the occurrence of such an unintended event? The definitions do not clarify that. So, the safety experts' knowledge was brought in and

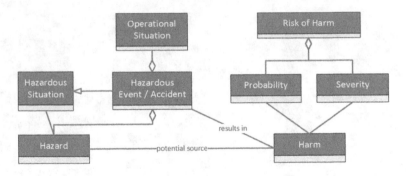

**Fig. 5.** Conceptual model in the course of the third meeting

led to the inclusion of *Accident* between *Hazard* and *Harm*. Still, we could not determine associations of *Hazardous Situation* with the other concepts, although some relation with *Hazard* is suggestive.

Between the second and the third meetings, we used the RETH tool as explained above. While the resulting model is fairly similar to the one after our second meeting, the tool could not find any association of *Accident* with the other concepts.

In the third meeting, we examined the association between *Hazard* and *Accident* more closely. In particular, we took ISO 26262 into account, which defines *Hazardous Event* as the combination of a *Hazard* and an *Operational Situation*. According to the glossary definitions, there is a missing link between *Hazard* and *Accident*, because an *Accident* is a result of a single event or a series of events. After long discussion, we erroneously decided to add both the concepts *Hazardous Event* and *Accident* as one named *Hazardous Event / Accident* due to their apparent similarity, resulting in the conceptual model given in Fig. 5.

After even more discussion in the course of the third meeting, we split *Hazardous Event* and *Accident*, and defined an association named "may cause" between them.

In the fourth meeting, we reviewed the resulting model from the third meeting and did not find a flaw, while there are always options for other ontological decisions. The only change was adding *Triggering Event*, with an association named "triggers" with *Accident*. This model intends to reflect that both *Hazardous Event* and *Triggering Event* are preconditions of an *Accident*.

## 5  Our Core Ontology

The resulting conceptual model is shown in Fig. 6. We consider it as a core ontology of safety risk concepts. While our sketch of its evolution above should already serve as an explanation, a few more explanations are still necessary for the rationale of some of its parts.

The ontological decision for the aggregation of *Risk* (instead of attributes) is explained above in detail. Such an aggregation relation in UML is shown as a

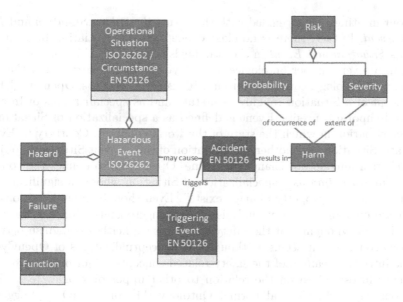

**Fig. 6.** Resulting conceptual model defining a core ontology of safety risk concepts

diamond, see Figs. 5 and 6. The rationale for the aggregation of *Hazardous Event* is by analogy. In fact, both underlying definitions in the standards use the same formulation "combination of".

The name of the association between *Accident* and *Harm*, "results in", suggests that every accident results in harm. Otherwise, this unintended event or series of events would not be considered an accident according to the definition of *Accident* in EN 50126 (see also above). Instead of naming it "may results in", which somehow involved yet another probability, our railway expert suggested to assign *Severity* 0 in case there is no resulting human *Harm*. In this way, our model resolves the very narrow and conflicting definition of *Harm* in the ISO 26262 standard, which is restricted to human health but not to goods or the environment.

The concepts *Function* and *Failure* are only relevant for 'Functional Safety', i.e., when assessing *Harm* based on analyzing potential failures of each function of a system. This has to be done according to ISO 26262 in the automotive domain. For other kinds of safety analyses, these concepts may be ignored.

Overall, this core ontology is an interesting combination of both the automotive and the railway domains. The concepts shown in blue are common, while the others are based on terminology from ISO 26262 and EN 50126, respectively.

## 6   Upper Ontology

For such an ontology, also its fit into a so-called *upper ontology* is important. Upper ontologies represent general concepts to be used for creating more specific domain ontologies such as ours. In this regard, let us focus on a specific problem.

In our meetings, we struggled with the terms *Hazardous Situation* and *Hazardous Event*. In fact, there is no clear conceptual differentiation between the concepts *Situation* and *Event* in the standards that we used. To clarify this, we looked into several upper ontologies. OpenCyc [19] is the largest and the best known upper ontology, containing around $10^5$ generic concepts. OpenCyc defines the concept of a Situation roughly as a state and as specializations of Intangible and Temporal concepts. Event is defined as a specialization of Situation (a dynamic situation in which the state of the world changes). Contrary to Event, in a Static Situation (as another specialization of the concept Situation), objects and their relations do not change over time. OpenCyc also defines the concept of *DangerousSituation* as a specialization of Situation where "a significant risk of death, injury, or property damage exists". Even though these definitions are not precise enough for safety analysis (e.g., DangerousSituation has the word "Hazard" as a synonym, but the safety standards explicitly distinguish between these two concepts), it seems as though the conceptualizations of OpenCyc fit well the intrinsic meaning of the safety-related concepts of our ontology.

Deeper investigation on the relation to other upper ontologies (e.g., ABC upper ontology [14], General Formal Ontology [11], or SUMO — Suggested Upper Merged Ontology [20]) will be part of our future work.

# 7    Human Error

Human error may compromise safety in the context of safety-critical systems. Let us sketch how our core ontology of safety risk concepts can be used for a systematic analysis of human error.

First, the graph of ontology concepts can be traversed systematically, where each concept is investigated regarding human error. In particular, additional hazards caused by human error are important. They may lead to additional hazardous events and accidents as well. With respect to user errors, e.g., especially the triggering events of accidents are of interest. Design and development errors as well as manufacturing, construction and installation errors seem to be more related to functions and related failures. Also maintenance errors are to be studied in this context.

With the help of the ontology, human error can be identified or classified systematically, see Table 1. The three concepts *Function*, *Failure* and *Hazard* at the left of Fig. 6 are relevant for human error analysis if an operator or maintainer is involved in fulfilling or supporting a function, respectively. For example, a train driver of certain railway vehicles has to fulfill part of the so-called Parking function. For the analysis of human error in such a case, the acting humans are considered part of the system. Such an analysis is especially important in degraded modes with more intensive use of human capabilities. In general, the traversal of the ontology guides from each instance of *Function* to analyzing it with regard to *Failure* and *Hazard*. This functional safety analysis has to investigate which failures may be caused by such a human error, and which hazards may result. Analogously to operator error, errors of maintainers can be analyzed in this way. For example, in a railway vehicle the generation of pressurized air is safety-relevant, since many functions such as braking are implemented based on it. Filtering of dust and dirt in the pressurized air is a crucial point, since air pipes may become locked by dust and dirt. Hence, the dust filters have to be changed after at least one year. If this does not happen, e.g., caused by human error in maintenance, these filters will lose their required function.

**Table 1.** Classification of human error related to concepts of the ontology.

| Role of human | Related concepts | Possible reason |
|---|---|---|
| Operator | *Function, Failure, Hazard* | Operator involved in *Function* |
| Maintainer | *Function, Failure, Hazard* | Maintainer supporting *Function* |
| Person at risk | *Hazardous Event, Accident* | Self rescue |
| User | *Triggering Event, Accident* | Misuse |

Affected persons of operator errors can, of course, be the operator who caused the hazard, but also others, such as passengers of a train. Related to persons at risk, i.e., all involved humans that may suffer *Harm* from a given *Hazard*, the concepts *Hazardous Event* and *Accident* are particularly important for the analysis of human error. Their instances need to be analyzed especially regarding possibilities for escaping or avoiding any instances of *Harm*, e.g., through self rescue, and what kind of human error may happen in this course. The avoidance of harm must be recognizable, understandable, possible and desirable. For example, in case of large and abnormal vibrations in a wagon of a train, pulling the emergency brake may be the most appropriate action to be taken by a passenger. However, there are some problems involved in such a situation. First of all, the passenger needs to recognize that these vibrations are abnormal. Given that, the passenger has to understand that it is reasonable or necessary for him or her to act. In addition, the passenger needs to figure out which actions are possible, e.g., pulling the emergency brake or moving to another part of the train. Finally, the passenger needs to judge that such an action is desirable, since unjustified pulling an emergency brake is also subject to being punished, and decide to actually perform such an action. In particular, such an analysis of human error needs to take into account that humans involved in an accident are usually under stress, and the more stressed humans are the more likely they commit errors.

The concept of a *Triggering Event* related to an *Accident* is relevant in the context of unintended or intended misuse. An example of a triggering event is pushing the button for opening doors of a train during the *Operational Situation* in a tunnel at high speed (say, 300 km/h). In such a situation, the aerodynamic forces can be strong enough to pull a passenger out of the train if a door in the vicinity opens. This human error of misuse is covered by electronic locking of the doors, where unlocking a door in such a situation would be an instance of *Hazard*.

Such a systematic analysis of human error may, in turn, suggest an integration of additional technical assistance systems. These are intended to reduce the possibilities of human error or its negative effects. The overall safety assessment needs to find a balance between human and technical aspects related to hazards and risks.

Another potential use of our core ontology related to human error is to look at it as a whole. After all, it is currently fed into a tool for supporting reuse of risk analyses (through a related metamodel). When risk analyses with all the related information according to our model will be reused for similar cases, e.g., previous hazards will be taken into account that otherwise may be overlooked by human error.

Even regarding standards, both their creation and their application, there is some potential use of our core ontology. After all, it is based on ISO 26262, EN 50126 and IEC 61508. Problems often arise from contradicting or arbitrary definitions, or even missing definitions. For example, in ISO 26262 the term "accident" is not defined even though it is used in some of its parts. For the creation of future (versions of) standards, human error may be reduced through this and enhanced ontologies.

## 8 Conclusion and Future Work

Primarily based on the glossaries of standards for automotive and railway, we created conceptual models, both using tool support and in a series of expert meetings. Especially in these meetings, of course, expertise of two safety experts played a major role in the evolution of these models. We consider the resulting model a core ontology of safety risk concepts covering both domains, which also fits into a major upper ontology. As a preliminary application of this core ontology, we used it for systematically studying possibilities of human error compromising safety.

In on-going and future work, we base a corresponding metamodel for tool creation using Eclipse on this core ontology. This metamodel will also include requirements-related concepts, which we have sufficient previous experience with. Using the resulting tool, and indirectly our core ontology, we will perform case studies, focusing on reuse of risk analyses. In this course, we will particularly investigate whether this reuse can help to reduce human error of omitting important information on previously known hazards, etc. All this will be important for the sake of validation of our proposed approach. Also extending the scope, e.g., to avionics or healthcare will be of interest.

**Acknowledgment.** Part of this research has been carried out in the RiskOpt project (No. 845610), funded by the Austrian BMVIT (represented by the Austrian FFG).

## References

1. EN 50126-1, Railway applications – The specification and demonstration of reliability, availability, maintainability and safety (RAMS). Part 1: Basic requirements and generic process, September 1999

2. CLC/TR 50126-2, Railway applications – The specification and demonstration of reliability, availability, maintainability and safety (RAMS). Part 2: Guide to the application of EN 50126-1 for safety, February 2007
3. IEC 61508, Functional safety of electrical/electronic/programmable electronic safety-related systems, May 2010
4. ISO 26262, Road vehicles - Functional safety, November 2011
5. ISO/IEC Guide 51 - Safety aspects - Guidelines for their inclusion in standards (2014)
6. Brank, J., Grobelnik, M., Mladenić, D.: A survey of ontology evaluation techniques. In: Proceedings of 8th International Multi-conference Information Society, pp. 166–169 (2005)
7. Casagrande, E., Arnautovic, E., Woon, W.L., Zeineldin, H.H., Svetinovic, D.: Semi-automatic system domain data analysis: a smart grid feasibility case study. IEEE Trans. Syst. Man Cybern. Syst. **PP**(99), 1–11 (2016)
8. Fernandez-Lopez, M., Gomez-Perez, A., Juristo, N.: Methontology: from ontological art towards ontological engineering. In: Proceedings of the AAAI 1997 Spring Symposium, Stanford, USA, pp. 33–40, March 1997
9. Gómez-Pérez, A., Fernández-López, M., Corcho, O.: Ontological Engineering: With Examples from the Areas of Knowledge Management, e-Commerce and the Semantic Web. Advanced Information and Knowledge Processing. Springer, New York Inc. (2007)
10. Hajdu, M., Skibniewski, M.J., Bilgin, G., Dikmen, I., Birgonul, M.T.: Selected papers from creative construction conference 2014 ontology evaluation: an example of delay analysis. Procedia Eng. **85**, 61–68 (2014). http://www.sciencedirect.com/science/article/pii/S1877705814018955
11. Herre, H.: General formal ontology (gfo): a foundational ontology for conceptual modelling. In: Poli, R., Obrst, L. (eds.) Theory and Applications of Ontology, vol. 2. Springer, Berlin (2010)
12. Hogganvik, I., Stolen, K.: Risk analysis terminology for IT-systems: does it match intuition? In: 2005 International Symposium on Empirical Software Engineering 2005, p. 10, November 2005. http://dx.doi.org/10.1109/ISESE.2005.1541810
13. Hulin, B., Kaindl, H., Rathfux, T., Popp, R., Arnautovic, E., Beckert, R.: Towards a common safety ontology for automobiles and railway vehicles. In: European Dependable Computing Conference (2016, to appear)
14. Hunter, J.: Enhancing the semantic interoperability of multimedia through a core ontology. IEEE Trans. Circ. Syst. Video Technol. **13**(1), 49–58 (2003)
15. Kaindl, H.: How to identify binary relations for domain models. In: Proceedings of the Eighteenth International Conference on Software Engineering (ICSE-18), pp. 28–36. IEEE, Berlin, March 1996
16. Kaindl, H.: A practical approach to combining requirements definition and object-oriented analysis. Ann. Softw. Eng. **3**, 319–343 (1997)
17. Kaindl, H., Kramer, S., Diallo, P.S.N.: Semiautomatic generation of glossary links: a practical solution. In: Proceedings of the Tenth ACM Conference on Hypertext and Hypermedia (Hypertext 1999), Darmstadt, Germany, pp. 3–12, February 1999
18. Kaindl, H., Popp, R., Raneburger, D.: Towards reuse in safety risk analysis based on product line requirements. In: 2015 IEEE 23rd International Requirements Engineering Conference (RE), pp. 241–246, August 2015
19. Lenat, D.B.: Cyc: a large-scale investment in knowledge infrastructure. Commun. ACM **38**(11), 33–38 (1995). http://doi.acm.org/10.1145/219717.219745

20. Niles, I., Pease, A.: Towards a standard upper ontology. In: Proceedings of the International Conference on Formal Ontology in Information Systems, FOIS 2001, vol. 2001, pp. 2–9. ACM, New York (2001). http://doi.acm.org/10.1145/505168.505170

21. Panesar-Walawege, R.K., Sabetzadeh, M., Briand, L., Coq, T.: Characterizing the chain of evidence for software safety cases: conceptual model based on the IEC 61508 standard. In: 2010 Third International Conference on Software Testing, Verification and Validation, pp. 335–344, April 2010. http://dx.doi.org/10.1109/ICST.2010.12

22. Rumbaugh, J., Jacobson, I., Booch, G.: The Unified Modeling Language Reference Manual. Addison-Wesley, Reading (1999)

23. Schnieder, L., Schnieder, E., Ständer, T.: Railway safety and security —two sides of the same coin? In: International Railway Safety Conference 2009 (2009). http://www.intlrailsafety.com/bastad/20090928/09-stander/paper.pdf

24. Sfar, H., Chaibi, A.H., Bouzeghoub, A., Ghezala, H.B.: Gold standard based evaluation of ontology learning techniques. In: Proceedings of the 31st Annual ACM Symposium on Applied Computing, SAC 2016, pp. 339–346. ACM, New York (2016). http://doi.acm.org/10.1145/2851613.2851843

25. Simperl, E.P.B., Tempich, C.: Ontology engineering: a reality check. In: Meersman, R., Tari, Z. (eds.) OTM 2006. LNCS, vol. 4275, pp. 836–854. Springer, Heidelberg (2006). http://dx.doi.org/10.1007/11914853_51

26. Winston, M.E., Chaffin, R., Herrmann, D.: A taxonomy of part-whole relations. Cogn. Sci. **11**, 417–444 (1987)

27. Wong, W., Liu, W., Bennamoun, M.: Ontology learning from text: a look back and into the future. ACM Comput. Surv. **44**(4), 20:1–20:36 (2012). http://doi.acm.org/10.1145/2333112.2333115

28. Zhao, N., Zhao, T.: An event-chain risk assessment model based on definition evolution in safety criterions. In: 2011 9th International Conference on Reliability, Maintainability and Safety (ICRMS), pp. 573–578, June 2011. http://dx.doi.org/10.1109/ICRMS.2011.5979333

# Complementary Tools and Techniques for Supporting Fitness-for-Purpose of Interactive Critical Systems

Dorrit Billman[1], Camille Fayollas[2], Michael Feary[3],
Célia Martinie[2(✉)], and Philippe Palanque[2]

[1] San Jose State University, San Jos, USA
`dorrit.billman@nasa.gov`
[2] ICS-IRIT, University of Toulouse, Toulouse, France
`{fayollas,martinie,palanque}@irit.fr`
[3] NASA Ames Research Center, Mountain View, USA
`michael.s.feary@nasa.gov`

**Abstract.** Sound design of complex, interactive, safety critical systems is very important, yet difficult. A particular challenge in the design of safety-critical systems is a typical lack of access to large numbers of testers and an inability to test early designs with traditional usability assessment tools. This inability leads to reduced information available to guide design, a phenomenon referred to as the Collingridge dilemma. Our research proposes to address parts of this problem with the development of tools and techniques for generating useful information and assessing developing designs early, to minimize the need for late change. More generally, we describe a set of three tools and techniques to support the process of ensuring fitness-for-purpose of complex interactive systems, helping designers focus on interaction across different functions of an overall system. These different tools and techniques support different parts of the overall design and evaluation process, but are focused on improving the coverage and effectiveness of evaluating interaction.

**Keywords:** Work analysis and representation · Interactive systems behavior · Complementary approaches · Safety-critical systems · Aviation

## 1 Introduction

Design of complex, interactive, safety critical systems requires an analysis of both the purpose (mission) the technology is intended to support, the users, and the environmental and social context in which the technology is to be used to determine whether the concept or prototype is fit for its purpose. Early in the process it is easy to make changes to the requirements or design concept, but it may be difficult to determine whether a candidate design or requirement specification will in fact meet the work needs. Later in the process

The rights of this work are transferred to the extent transferable according to title 17 § 105 U.S.C.

© IFIP International Federation for Information Processing 2016 (outside the US)
Published by Springer International Publishing Switzerland 2016. All Rights Reserved
C. Bogdan et al. (Eds.): HCSE 2016/HESSD 2016, LNCS 9856, pp. 181–202, 2016.
DOI: 10.1007/978-3-319-44902-9_12

there is much more information available, but the cost of change is much greater. This is known as the Collingridge Dilemma [11], which states that when change is easy, information to guide change is scarce; when information is available, change is difficult.

In the context of critical systems, the Collingridge Dilemma manifests in two broad challenges, which we will refer to as coverage and effectiveness. The *coverage challenge* concerns adequacy or sufficiency of the technology to support the work for which it was designed. For example, is the information needed for the task provided and are the actions to be taken supported? Are the needed tasks available at the right time without being locked out? Are actions specified for all reachable conditions? The *effectiveness challenge* concerns how much of the technology is actually necessary for the work, versus technology which is not needed for the work. For example, are information and operators provided that do not support the work? Are multiple, redundant methods provided that do not benefit the work? Does operation of the technology itself add excessive overhead? Quality of how the effectiveness challenge has been addressed might be measured in terms of unnecessary "features" and lines of code or in terms of end user time or effort to accomplish work. Finally, even for technology that roughly provides capabilities sufficient to get the job done, without a great deal of unnecessary elements, the technology can differ in how well the elements are organized or configured. When any of these aspects are poor, the technology will not be well-aligned with the work, and will not be well fit for purpose.

Where work domains are simple, it may be feasible to develop technology that is aligned with the work informally, by relying on design skill and prior experiences. As work and supporting technology becomes more complex, systematic methods supported by appropriate tools become increasingly valuable. In this paper, we propose a process, and three tools and techniques for ensuring that the requirements, design, and resulting system in fact support the intended work missions, and are fit for purpose. The tools and techniques address the Collingridge Dilemma through their intended use early in the design process.

This article is structured as follows. Section 2 presents, after an overview and analysis of the existing development processes, a new process for ensuring fitness for purpose of interactive critical systems prototypes. Section 3 presents three tools and techniques for supporting this process, along with its detailed description when using these tools. Section 4 presents the application of the proposed development process to an illustrative example from the commercial aviation domain. Section 5 discusses the complementarity of the three tools and techniques and the perspectives of the proposed approach. Finally, Sect. 6 concludes the paper.

## 2   Development Processes for Ensuring Fitness for Purpose of Interactive Critical Systems Prototypes

This section first presents an overview of the existing development processes. From the analysis of these existing processes, we then propose a new process for ensuring fitness for purpose of Interactive Critical Systems prototypes.

## 2.1 Related Work

Three research strands are relevant to our work. Most of the existing system and software development processes do not include prototyping activities. User centered-design does include prototyping as a key activity in design processes. Work-centered design focuses on analysis of the needs dictated by the work, rather than those based on technology or the user.

**Development Processes.** Early development process models [21, 28] promoted the construction of reliable software by building the "system right". To try to address the concern of building the "right system", the spiral development process promoted by Boehm [5] has introduced the production of specific artifacts called prototypes in order to first identify the adequacy of the current version of the software with clients' requirements, and second provide a framework for handling explicitly iterations. Such iterative processes were not delivering as expected, as demonstrated by a thorough study of more than 8000 project [6]. As identified in this study, the main drawback of these early software development processes (beyond the inherent difficulty of building large and complex system products) was the difficulty of identifying user needs and of producing software meeting user needs while encompassing ever evolving new technologies. Iterative or agile approaches, such as Scrum [29], advocate that requirements tuning is performed by means of rapid and systematic iterations. However, even in the last version of Scrum[1], there is still no reference to the end user. This has been clearly stated and identified in [30] where User Centered and Agile approaches where compared and assessed. Beyond that, task/artifact life cycle, as identified in [10], introduces a different perspective on user needs evolution. It argues that providing users with a new tool (even if the tools are perfectly in line with their needs) will change the needs as the work and practice of users will evolve due to this particular new tool. This demonstrates the need to involve end users throughout the development process to validate the systems and to redefine their needs [18]. Another very different problem lies in the iterative nature of the agile and spiral processes. Software can be hard to manage, test, and modify because it has been built by frequently adding new functionalities without following a global and thorough design. While this might not be a big problem when small and rather simple applications are considered, when it comes to large scale and complex systems (as aircraft flight decks) this might have significant impacts both in term of development costs and resources but also in terms of reliability and dependability. To handle such complexity model-based approaches such as UML or [24] provide abstraction and domain specific notations. However, approaches such as Scrum or the Spiral model reject the use of models due to the cost in terms of effort and time.

**User-Centered Design Processes.** Even though it took a long time to make its way in the area of system and software engineering, the necessity of designing systems and software compliant with user needs and user capabilities recognized much earlier in the area of Human-Computer Interaction. The User Centered Design approach (introduced in [23]) has promoted user-related consideration to the center of the development

---

[1] https://www.scrum.org.

processes. Several processes have since been proposed to take into account usability while designing an interactive system. Hartson et al. [17] and Collins [12] identified mandatory steps to design usable system. Curtis & Hefley [13] first tried to match software development processes with usability engineering and techniques. Rauterberg [27] identified more precisely design steps to involve end-users in an iterative-cyclic development process. Goränsson et al. [16] proposed a design process centered on usability: "The usability design process is a UCSD approach for developing usable interactive systems, combining usability engineering with interaction design, and emphasizing extensive active user involvement throughout the iterative process". This work emphasizes that design processes for interactive systems must be highly iterative and must promote multiple designs through evolvable prototypes in order to accommodate requirement changes that result from usability evaluations. However, such processes have put too much emphasis on the user side, forgetting the complex reality of software development.

Further, user involvement and prototyping activities are not enough to ensure that the technology is fit for the intended purpose. Users' goals and work has to be described and compared with system functions in a systematic way.

**Work-Centered Design.** Work Focused Design emphasizes the importance of understanding the work to be supported. Cognitive Work Analysis [26, 31] emphasizes the importance of Work Domain Analysis as the first and fundamental step of ecological design [7]. Work Centered Design [8, 14] and related approaches [2, 3] also emphasize the importance of work analysis and representation to guide technology design. Our work shares this orientation, and in this paper we aim to lay out a specific design process and associated tools and methods to provide explicit, structured guidance for designing to fulfill work needs.

### 2.2 A Process for Ensuring Fitness for Purpose of Interactive Critical Systems Prototypes

The proposed process takes into account several inputs, namely, the extant systems, the work environment, and the mission that has to be performed by the operator. Figure 1 presents an abstract view of this process. It makes explicit the three phases (detailed in the following subsections) that have to be performed before the evaluation, development, and deployment of the interactive critical system:

- Work and task analysis loop;
- Early prototyping loop;
- Full-scale software prototyping loop.

The proposed process is complementary with other HCI techniques such as user evaluations. As each of these phases is iterative, several version of prototypes are produced and can be iteratively tested with users before being refined in the next iteration of the loop.

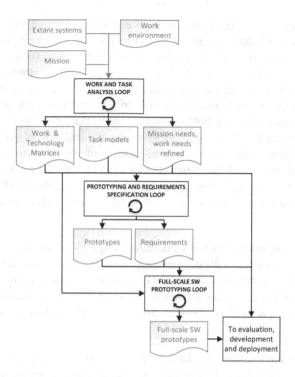

**Fig. 1.** Process for ensuring fitness for purpose of Interactive Critical Systems prototypes

**Work and Task Analysis Loop.** The work and task analysis loop aims to specify the scope of work that technology is intended to support (work analysis) and to specify the more specific sequences of actions that will accomplish that work (task analysis). Design and evaluation of technology for safety critical work should be based on the functionality needed for the work. If work needs are not specified, there is no basis to assess whether the technology is fit for the intended purpose. To represent work needs at this level requires specifying the component functions across the scope of work relevant to the design/evaluation goal. An analysis for a flight deck design or evaluation needs to be of broader scope than for (re)design of one part. A component function maps onto a high-level task, or goal, to be accomplished to carry out the needed work.

For work analysis, the level of specification must be fairly abstract, in order to be applicable across alternative technology designs. To see why applicability across alternative designs is important, consider what is needed from a design and from an evaluation perspective. From the design perspective, a characterization of the work that the technology should support should apply across the space of possible designs. The characterization should allow a designer to understand what the space of appropriate solutions might be and consider alternative possibilities; it should provide high-level guidance to the designer during development to ensure that the design does support the work needs. From the evaluation perspective, a characterization of the work needs should allow assessment of how and how well one particular design meets the various needs but it should also allow comparison of alternative designs with respect to fitness for purpose.

For task analysis, it is valuable to build a more specific representation of tasks needed to accomplish the work, once technologies and policies for accomplishing the work are specified. A task analysis typically specifies how particular technology (radio communication with ATC) or policies (pointing so co-pilot can verify action) are used to build a sequence of actions carrying out a particular work function. The task analysis and task modeling phase aims at understanding and describing user activities. It precisely identifies goals, tasks, and activities that have to be done by the operator. Task models bring additional advantages to task analysis: representing the structure of the gathered information about operators' activities and enabling use of software tools to compute, analyze and simulate these models. When supported by (a) a task modeling notation and (b) a tool featuring human task-refinement (cognitive, motor, perceptive tasks) and complex activity editing and simulation, this step enables qualitative analysis of user or operator tasks.

**Prototyping and Requirements Specification Loop.** The prototyping and requirements specification loop is usually done by designers. This phase aims at rapidly building first versions of the interactive system and at evaluating and modifying early designs of user interfaces. The result of the evaluation of the final version enables requirement specification for the final device. These requirements will then be used as inputs for the full-scale prototyping loop.

**Full-Scale Software Prototyping Loop.** The full-scale software prototyping loop is usually done by developers. This phase aims at refining the requirements from the prototyping and requirement specification loop by refining them in a precise and unambiguous way.

The full-scale software prototyping loop produces very high-fidelity prototypes, thus specifying a complete and unambiguous description of the interactive system. This description enables fine tuning these prototypes.

This loop also supports the activity of ensuring conformance and compatibility between the different representations of the interactive system (e.g., the tasks models or work representations and the systems models). Indeed, the full-scale prototype can be compared to the work and task representations of the interactive system, thereby ensuring that the system's behavior will be fully compatible with user tasks.

The final full-scale software prototype can then be used for the evaluation, development, and deployment of the interactive system.

This process helps to ensure in a systematic way that prototypes are developed taking into account the critical tasks that the users will have to perform, even numerous and complex. With this process, the focus is set on the reliability of the developed interactive system with regards to the work that has to be performed. This process may be applied to safety-critical as well as non-safety-critical systems but, in terms of costs and benefits, is more intended to be applied to interactive systems for which functions are numerous and complex.

# 3 Tools and Techniques Supporting the Proposed Process

In this section, we first preview the set of tools and techniques that we use to support the proposed process. We first present the MAESTRO work and technology representation. Second we present the ADEPT prototyping tool. Third, we present the CIRCUS development environment and its associated notations for full-scale prototyping. The illustrated in Fig. 1 is then expanded to show how these tools and techniques support its different phases.

## 3.1 MAESTRO Work and Technology Representation

Matrix-Assisted Exploration of Structured Task-Technology Relations and Organization (MAESTRO) is a process and representation to guide development of the (formal or informal) requirement specification. It characterizes what work needs to be done, what information is needed to do the work, and what changes as a result of doing the work. Broadly, it focuses on "usefulness" rather than "usability." Thus, it is not intended to cover all aspects needed in requirements. It provides guidance both for design and evaluation, helping ensure that designers are building to the criteria on which the result will be evaluated [4].

We decompose work into a set of constituent work functions (roughly, abstract tasks), and into a set of the domain variables, both the information needed as input and the control variables changed as output. The input variables represent the information and resources needed by a function (to accomplish a goal). The output variables represent the changes that are intentionally produced as the result of carrying out the function. In cognitive work, the input variables are primarily information needed for the task and the output variables are actions taken as the result of some decision. In piloting, information such as current wind or airspeed are examples of input variables and control settings such as target altitude or flap position are examples of output variables. The work functions, domain variables, and their relationship can be represented in a matrix. Work functions form one dimension and the input/output variables form the second dimension. Cells in this binary matrix code whether or not a particular variable is relevant to a particular work function as 1 s or 0 s.

## 3.2 ADEPT

The Automation Design Evaluation and Prototyping Tool (ADEPT) is intended to help designers rapidly build, evaluate and modify interactive prototype automated devices and their user interfaces [15]. It is intended to fill a gap between early storyboarding of a device, and a full-scale software prototype. ADEPT relies on a table based formalism to enable domain experts, who may not have formal programming expertise to define the behavior of the prototype technology. The ADEPT tool can produce a software prototype, but the prototype is only intended to be used to test the behavior of the device, and the result of the evaluation is intended to define the specification for the final device.

### 3.3   CIRCUS Integrated Development Environment

CIRCUS, which stands for Computer-aided-design of Interactive, Resilient, Critical and Usable Systems, is an integrated development environment embedding both system and task modeling functionalities. The CIRCUS environment targets the following user types: engineers, system designers, and human factors specialists. It aims at helping them to achieve their specific tasks during the design and development of interactive critical systems. CIRCUS embeds features for the formal verification of the system's behavior as well as features for assessment of compatibility between the user's task and the system's behavior. The CIRCUS environment integrates three tools for task modeling, system modeling and their synergistic validation:

- The HAMSTERS (Human-centered Assessment and Modeling to Support Task Engineering for Resilient Systems) notation and its tool (named the same) have been designed to provide support for ensuring consistency, coherence, and conformity between user tasks and interactive systems at the model level [1]. The HAMSTERS notation (a) enables structuring users' goals and sub-goals into a hierarchical tasks tree in which qualitative temporal relationship among tasks are described by operators [20] and (b) encompasses notation elements including a wide range of specialized tasks types, explicit representations of data and knowledge, device descriptions, genotypes and phenotypes of errors, and collaborative tasks. The HAMSTERS tool provides means for editing and simulating HAMSTERS task models.
- The PetShop (Petri Net workshop) tool [25] provides support for creating, editing, simulating and analyzing system models using the ICO (Interactive Cooperative Objects) notation [22]. The ICO notation is a formal description technique devoted to specify interactive systems. Using high-level Petri nets for dynamic behavior description, the notation also relies on an object-oriented approach (dynamic instantiation, classification, encapsulation, inheritance and client/server relationships) to describe the structural or static aspects of systems.
- The SWAN (Synergistic Workshop for Articulating Notations) tool enables the co-execution of the ICO system models with the corresponding HAMSTERS user's task models [1]. This is done through the editing of correspondences between system and task models and their co-execution. This co-execution presents several advantages such as helping in guaranteeing the application effectiveness and can be partially automated as presented in [9].

### 3.4   Process Instantiated with the Set of Notation and Tools

Figure 2 presents the expansion of the process illustrated in Fig. 1 and shows how the tools and techniques we use support its different phases. The work analysis is supported by the MAESTRO tool and technique and this phase leads to work and technology matrices. These matrices can be used as inputs for the task analysis phase, helping by giving a description of work functions that can be used as a high-level representation of user tasks. The task analysis phase is supported by the HAMSTERS tool, and leads to the creation of tasks models. These two representations must be checked in order to ensure their completeness and consistency. Once this is achieved, these two representations are used to refine the work and mission needs and are used as inputs for the prototyping and requirements specification loop.

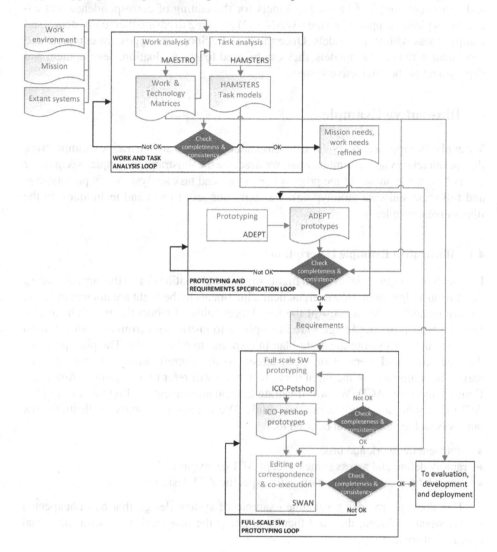

**Fig. 2.** Process for ensuring fitness for purpose of Interactive Critical Systems prototypes instantiated with the set of notation and tools

The prototyping and requirements specification loop is supported by the ADEPT tool. The resulting ADEPT prototypes are analyzed and verified and, once their consistency and completeness is checked, are used to define the requirements for the interactive system specification. These requirements and ADEPT prototypes are used as inputs for the full-scale software prototyping loop.

The full-scale software prototyping loop is first supported by the PetShop tool (and ICO notation) for the prototyping task. Once the ICO-PetShop prototypes are complete and consistent, they can be used as inputs for the editing of correspondence and co-execution phase (supported by the SWAN tool) enabling to ensure their consistency and completeness with tasks models. Once the ICO-PetShop prototypes are complete and consistent with the tasks models, they can be used for the evaluation, development and deployment of the interactive system.

# 4   Illustrative Example

We apply the proposed three-phase development process to an illustrative example from the commercial aviation domain. First, we describe the illustrative example. Second, for each of the three phases of the process (*i.e.,* work and task analysis, early prototyping, and full scale software prototyping), we apply our set of tools and techniques, to the illustrative example.

## 4.1   Illustrative Example Description

For much of a commercial aviation flight, airplane automation draws the targets guiding flight from a flight plan. However, tactical adjustments to the flight are not unusual, and require manual, in-flight entry of the new target values. Frequently, these changes in lateral, vertical, or speed targets are in response to instructions from air traffic control (ATC) to deviate to from the flight plan in response to other traffic. The pilot provides the changed lateral, vertical or speed targets to the aircraft automation through one particular component of the flight deck, which we will refer to as a generic Autoflight Control Interface (ACI). We will illustrate tactical adjustments to flight and use of the ACI to carry out this work as our case study. We use this case study to illustrate how our tools and techniques can be used to:

- represent the work and tasks,
- rapidly define and assess some concept ACI behavior, and
- represent and assess interaction with a specific ACI design.

This domain provides a valuable example of system design that had unexpected effects when deployed, due to difficulty aligning the imagined work with the actual operational context.

**Work Function Studied in this Illustrative Example.** We focus on the descent phase of flight because it has greater the likelihood of deviations from the flight plan, producing higher workload for the pilot. Arrival processes are becoming increasingly complex, in turn imposing increasing workload on the pilot. As airliners near their intended destination to a busy airport, they are usually cleared to fly along a prescribed route known as a Standard Terminal Arrival Route (STAR) to provide an orderly flow of aircraft. The STAR contains lateral and vertical path flight plan information that pilots can enter into the aircraft automation to provide precise navigation. If all goes according to plan, the aircraft will fly the exact lateral and vertical path specified in the STAR, however, in busy airspace it is not uncommon to receive amendments to the flightplan instructions; these clearances specify new limits and restrictions for the airliner. A frequent example is to receive an altitude restriction to ensure that aircraft are safely separated vertically. For our example we will suppose an aircraft is cruising at 33000 ft/10000 m, and is cleared for a STAR which contains vertical flightplan information to 10000 f/3000 m, but is interrupted by Air Traffic Control requesting to not descend below 26000 ft/8000 m.

**The ACI Device.** In order to select and engage an altitude limit value, the pilot will use the ACI device. The one used in this illustrative example is depicted in Fig. 3. With this particular device, the pilot selects an altitude value by rotating the altitude selection knob. This value appears within the altitude selection display area. When the pilot decides that the desired value is selected, s/he engage it as the altitude limit value by pushing the altitude limit engagement pushbutton. This causes the altitude limit to be displayed within the altitude limit display area and passes this value to the aircraft automation which restricts the airliner's descent.

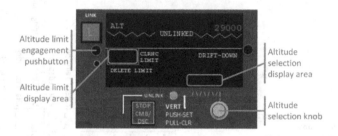

**Fig. 3.** Panel for altitude management of the ACI device used in this paper.

### 4.2   Work and Task Analysis

The work and task analysis loop aims to specify the scope of work that the ACI is intended to support (work analysis) and to specify the more specific sequences of actions that will be accomplished with it (task analysis). Both our work analysis and task analysis use the idea of *abstract* characterizations. Concerning work analysis, an abstract level of representation means that work functions and variables are characterized at a level of abstraction that a subject matter expert would naturally adopt when asked to describe work to be performed at a high-level. Concerning task analysis, an abstract task is one that can be refined in a set of concrete activities. Abstract representation pulls back from the details of how work is done with a specific interface or technology, allowing this to be specified at a later or lower analysis. This is important because it allows comparison across alternative technologies and interfaces and it provides guidance before such details are specified.

**Work Analysis.** MAESTRO is a process for gathering the work functions and work variables needed in a work domain and representing their relationships in a matrix. Matrix rows represent work functions, columns represent variables (information input or output controls), and cells represent whether or not the column variable is relevant to the row work function. We use a binary matrix because we want to start with the "simplest possible" representation and because this enables certain methods for finding structure in the relationships between work functions and variables. Of course, other processes and representations could be developed; one extension of our matrix representation would be using cells to code richer information about functions and variables than simply relevant/nonrelevant.

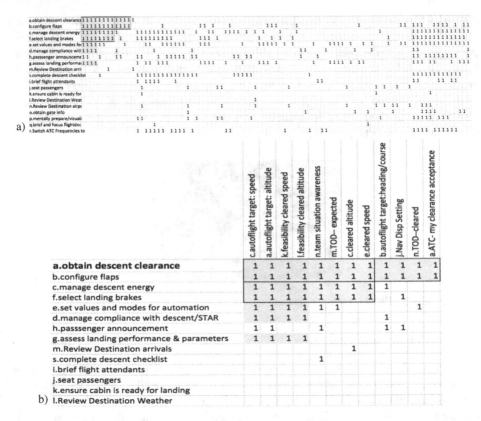

**Fig. 4.** (a) A high level view of a work matrix showing the patterns of relevant variables (cells with "1"s). Rows show all 19 work functions in Descent phase, and several dozen of the 189 variables as columns. (Variables are truncated.) The intact matrix provides a census of all the information and control variables used in the domain and all the component work functions. The matrix is sorted to focus on the first work function, obtain-descent-clearance (ODC), with rows ordered by how many of ODC's variables are also relevant to that row's work function. The matrix also shows that work functions vary greatly in their number of relevant variables. Highlighting shows overlapping clusters of relevant variables. (b) A detail view showing the content of the variables and functions in this group.

Our example matrix shows work functions and variables for the descent phase of flight, with 19 work functions and 189 variables of which 68 are shown. Figure 4-a provides a "bird's eye view" of the distribution of "1's" in the matrix showing where a variable is relevant to a work function. The rows and columns in this matrix view have been manually sorted to place a focal work function, obtain descent clearance, in the first row, to sort the variables this function uses to the left, and to sort the other work functions so that those that also use these variables move to the top. This shows a cluster of work functions and variables that have similar usage. Figure 4-b shows the content of this example cluster. Informally, one can see that there are multiple clusters of mutually relevant variables, throughout the matrix. While manual sorting is shown here, we also use clustering and biclustering methods to find related groups [4]. For example, clustering shows that target speed and altitude and cleared speed and altitude are used together in many tasks, which also share additional variables. Note that not all cockpit interfaces group this information together, or clearly distinguish been cleared and current-control altitude across autoflight modes.

To build the matrix in this example, three domain experts (pilots) generated the functions and variables. A human factors expert reconciled the alternative terms and the domain experts reviewed the resulting standardized row and column names. Then the pilots filled in the cells of the standard matrix. We provided a browser-based interface to an underlying database, so users could scroll through sets of variables, selecting those relevant to a work function. The work functions and variables were grouped into labeled categories to aid presentation in the interface, but the categories were not part of the underlying work matrix.

Work analysis can provide input to task analysis by identifying the functions that need to be translated into tasks, accomplished within assumptions about the particular technology and resources available. The variable census could be used to check whether or to what degree the needed information and controls are provided for.

The work matrix provides several ways of providing guidance and of assessing an interaction design. The assessment is made possible because the variables provide a 'common language' linking the work and the technology. Just as variable sets are needed for the work, technology provides variable sets for the work, both as input to the operator through displays, and by providing the operator with the means of affecting change through controls. Technology can also be represented in a matrix with variables as columns; matrix rows represent elements within the technology such as a panel on the ACI, or a page on a display for the flight management computer.

The fit of technology to work can be evaluated at the level of individual variables and work functions, or in terms of clusters. Not all relevant variables are necessarily provided by the technology. For example, the ACI panel in Fig. 3 represents several related variables: the currently controlling altitude, the source of the currently controlling altitude or mode (i.e., from flight plan or from pilot's adjustment), the current altitude clearance limit, and a "scratch pad" holding a value (such as an issued but not in-use clearance) the pilot has noted but not commanded. The fact that all these variables are represented, and represented together, is a strength of this interface. Alternative designs may not distinguish a "planning" value from a commanded value; or information needed together maybe provided in different components, such as the ACI showing only the mode requested by the pilot but not showing the mode actually controlling the airliner. This example illustrates how a technology assessment can be made at the level of an individual work function.

**Tasks Analysis.** The tasks analysis phase leads to several tasks models representing the different activities that have to be performed by the pilots in order to fly the plane. In the current example, we are more interested in the activities that have to be performed during the descent phase. Figure 5 presents an extract of the task model describing the activities that have to be performed during the descent phase. This model enables to see that the pilot flying the plane (PF) has to perform several concurrent tasks. For readability purposes, we only described here the following tasks: "Manage descent energy", "Manage compliance with decent/STAR", "Monitor performance to clearance limit", "Review destination weather". These tasks can be further detailed and are thus represented in Fig. 5 as folded abstract tasks. While performing these tasks, the pilot can be interrupted by the reception of a clearance ("Manage an ATC clearance" folded abstract task). This task is the one we are focusing on in this example and is detailed in Fig. 6.

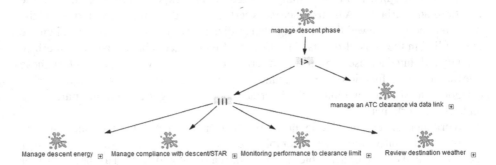

**Fig. 5.** "Manage descent phase" task model

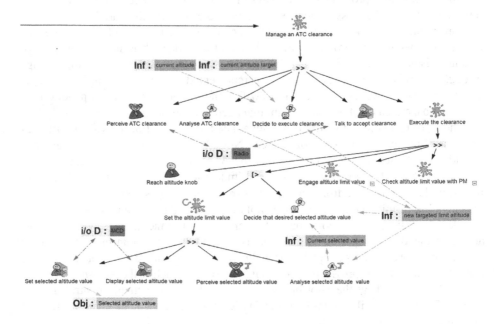

**Fig. 6.** Details of "Manage an ATC clearance" task

In this task, first the pilot perceives (from the radio) the ATC clearance ("Perceive ATC clearance" perceptive task in Fig. 6), analyzes it, decides to execute it ("Analyze ATC clearance" and "Decide to execute clearance" cognitive tasks in Fig. 6) and notifies the ATC of the clearance acceptance through the radio ("Talk to accept clearance" interactive input task in Fig. 6). Then, the pilot executes the clearance: s/he first set the altitude limit value ("Set the altitude limit value" abstract iterative task) by (in the case of the ACI device presented in Fig. 3) turning the altitude selection knob (bottom right in Fig. 3 and "set selected altitude value" interactive input task in Fig. 6) until the desired value is obtained ("Decide that desired selected altitude value is OK" cognitive task in Fig. 6). Finally, the pilot has to engage the selected altitude value as the limit value ("Engage altitude limit value" abstract task in Fig. 6) and then to check with the pilot monitoring if this value is correct ("Check altitude limit value with PM" in Fig. 6).

Both work analysis and task analysis can aid assessment and refinement of the needs at the level of the work domain. This can be done in terms of coverage, overhead, and organization.

Concerning coverage, for each work function, the technology can be assessed for whether the variables needed for that work function are provided. Generally, higher coverage means that more aspects of the work can be supported by the technology; less, then, must be done in the head, with paper and pencil, or through means outside the technology. Providing a census of the tasks and variables is the simplest and most direct way a work matrix can contribute to design and evaluation. In complementary way, HAMSTERS task models bring an additional support to assess whether all the temporally ordered user actions can be performed with the system functions.

Concerning overhead, technology typically requires variables specific to managing that technology and not directly related to the work per se. For example, most require a control for turning the technology on or off. While some overhead is likely necessary, a large number of distinctions and operations in the technology that are unrelated to the work and to the tasks add extrinsic complexity and usually weaken the design.

Concerning organization, the "just right" collection of variables should not only be included in the technology, but they should be organized to align with the work. Ideally, the variables needed for a single work function or task should be accessible together, in space and time. For visual displays, this typically would mean co-location of information in space. For information presented in a multi-page interface, it would mean minimal navigation time. For controls and displays used together, it means that the perception and action modalities do not conflict. The hand and gaze can coordinate. While multiple effectors–hand, voice, feet–might be used on different controls, their use should not conflict, nor make displayed information inaccessible. For simple domains, perhaps a bank teller machine, it may be possible to provide a near-ideal design for each work function. However, for complex domains, the needs of one work function will likely compete with those of another: the ideal grouping of variables for one work function may be different from that of another. Clustering methods can identify groups of variables and of tasks that behave similarly; such clusters can prioritize support for variables with similar groupings of variables. Biclustering methods simultaneously group rows by columns and columns by rows, provide a useful way of identifying structure, particularly where there are multiple, overlapping groups, possibly with exceptions.

### 4.3   Prototyping and Requirements Specification

ADEPT is used for the early development of testable prototypes to support designers in the specification of requirements. ADEPT uses an object-oriented tabular format to specify software input conditions and resulting behaviors to reduce programming language knowledge requirements. This enables the domain-expert designer to focus on the development of the prototype. The ADEPT interface (Fig. 7) consists primarily of a software logic editing tool combined with a Graphical User interface editing tool. In the Logic Editor, each set of input conditions and corresponding behavior is represented as a column, and can be read vertically as an "IF" (input condition) "THEN" (software behavior) with "OR" conditions represented as thin grey row dividers, and "AND" conditions as thick grey row dividers associated with variables. ADEPT allows the designer to drag and drop graphical objects from the User Interface editor into the Logic Editor to enable development of prototype interfaces.

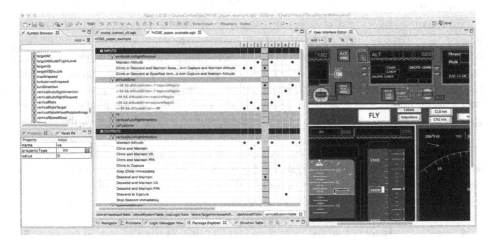

**Fig. 7.**   ACI represented in ADEPT

Specifying the ACI device in ADEPT allows us to start to think about requirements for the device. For example, should the device need an altitude to be set below the aircraft altitude before the start of the descent? What should happen if the altitude is set above the aircraft altitude while descending? The ADEPT prototyping environment lets designers with domain knowledge explore these questions, and provides automatic tools to confirm that prototype addresses each combination of input conditions, and that there are no duplicate software behaviors that might lead to confusion when addressing each situation identified.

### 4.4   Full-Scale Software Prototyping

The full-scale software prototyping loop is divided into two steps: (i) the full-scale software prototyping using the ICO notation (and the PetShop tool), leading to the creation of ICO prototypes and (ii) its validation through the co-execution of the tasks and systems models. The result of these two steps, in the case of the ACI illustrative example are detailed in the following subsections.

**ICO-Petshop Prototypes.** Figure 8. presents the ICO model of the behavior of the ACI device (which is presented in Fig. 3). It is important to note that this model is completed by two functions (the activation and rendering functions) that define the connections between this model and the ACI device elements: the activation function defines the connection from the ACI input elements to the model transition firing and the rendering function defines the connection from the state of the model to the ACI output elements. Here we will focus just on the part of the model corresponding to the work presented in Sect. 4.1 and detailed in the task model presented in Fig. 6.

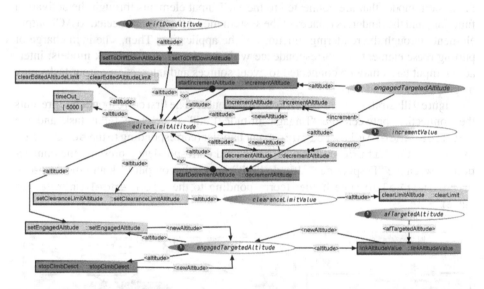

**Fig. 8.** ICO model of the ACI behavior for altitude management–Rectangles represent transitions (purple ones are enabled and light gray one are disabled); ellipses represent places; purple circles within places represent tokens (the number is the number of tokens in the place). (Color figure online)

The ICO notation is based on high-level Petri nets, its complete definition can be find in the following paper [22]. When the pilot sets the selected altitude value (i.e., using the altitude selection knob of the ACI depicted in Fig. 3), the startIncrementAltitude transition is fired (if the pilot has incremented the altitude; otherwise, the startDecrementAltitude transition is fired). This firing leads to the creation of a token (containing the value of the current selected value) in the editedLimitAltitude place. The presence of a token in this place leads to the display of the selected altitude value within the altitude selection area. Therefore, the incrementAltitude (resp. `decrementAl-titude`) transition is fired when the pilot turns the knob in order to increment (resp. decrement) the current selected value, leading to the modification of the value contained in the token within the `editedLimitAltitude` place. When the pilot pushes the altitude limit engagement pushbutton, the `setClearanceLimitAltitude` transition is fired, leading to the shifting of the token contained by `editedLimitAlti-tude` place to the `clerenceLimitValue`. This token shifting leads to the clearing of the altitude selection area and to the display of the selected altitude value within the altitude limit display area.

**Editing of Correspondence and Co-Execution.** Once the ICO-PetShop prototype is obtained, the "editing of correspondence and co-execution" step is performed using the SWAN tool. This iterative step leads to a list of correspondences between task-model elements and system-model elements, enabling the co-execution of both task and system models.

To define this list, the developer has first to identify the event sources (transitions of the system model that are connected to the ACI input elements through the activation function) and the renderers (places of the system model that are connected to ACI output elements through the rendering function) of the application. Then, s/he is in charge of putting these elements in correspondence with the elements of the task models: interactive input tasks may be connected to event sources and interactive output tasks may be connected to renderers.

Figure 9 illustrates this editing of correspondences. The first correspondence presents the connection between the "Engage altitude limit" interactive input task and the `setClearanceLimitAltitude` event handler (corresponding to the `setClear-anceLimitAltitude` transition. The second correspondence presents the connection between the "Display new altitude limit" interactive output task and the `clear-anceLimitValue` state holder (corresponding to the `clearanceLimitValue` place).

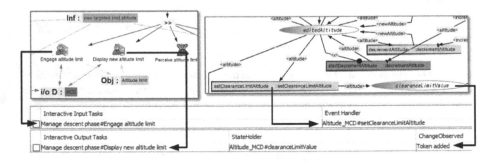

**Fig. 9.** Correspondence editing between HAMSTERS models and ICO models

Once this correspondence editing step is done, the developer is able to co-execute the tasks and systems models and check if there are inconsistencies between them (e.g., a task that should be available according to the task model but that is not within the system model). S/he is then able to correct iteratively the tasks or the systems models according to the detected discrepancy. This step helps in guaranteeing the application effectiveness and can be partially automated as presented in [9]. If the effectiveness requirements are met, the ICO-PetShop prototypes can then be used for the evaluation, development and deployment of the interactive system.

# 5 Discussion

The process presented here integrates complementary approaches and this integration builds on the strength of each approach and mitigates their weaknesses. Altogether, they cover a wider range of design and evaluation needs, and provide better assurance that technology will be fit for purpose.

## 5.1 Complementarity

MAESTRO provides an integrated perspective in terms of the resources needed across the domain, spanning both the information and controls needed. Overall, this representation is distinctive, however, a compiled list of information needed (as in the columns of the matrix) is similar to the information census proposed within the ecological interface approach [7]. The work functions, enumerated in the rows, can provide input to a task analysis, as used by HAMSTERS or ADEPT. Although it provides a broad representation of work needs, MAESTRO leaves out many aspects of work, including temporal structure and means-ends relations, even when these are inherent in the work and not a consequence of a particular technology choice. HAMSTERS, in turn provide support for describing and analyzing temporal relationships between the tasks, as well as means-ends relations between required devices to perform an action (or a temporally ordered set of action). While potentially using work matrices as input, HAMSTERS can also provide feedback to the work analysis, for example, by indicating places where a more specific level of representation would help with the design task at hand.

ADEPT can check the logical structure of a design based on a very early prototype. The result of this check can provide assurance that it is worth developing a more complete and detailed prototype, and can guide specification of formal requirements for the finished system. PETSHOP in turn, links prototype development with early evaluation. SWAN, uses PETSHOP input to feed tools for an analyst to link task descriptions to the operations being carried out by automation (or other computational system), through its interface. This allows the analyst to determine how tasks map onto the capabilities of the technology, what is covered or omitted, and by what means.

## 5.2 Perspectives

For each approach that has been integrated in the process, many improvements are envisioned. For instance, for MAESTRO, we have applied and extended biclustering and associated visualization tools to examine the organization implicit in a matrix. However, ways of filtering, comparing, and evaluating clusters would aid interpretation at the organization level. Methods for systematic comparison of the structure in the work matrix with the structure in technology matrix could be implemented in future work. For CIRCUS, integration of tasks and system descriptions could be used for automatic generation and execution of test scenarios. Analysis of what functions can be automated is an important topic for future research. The proposed overall process and representation flow is novel, and has no integrated use or evaluation has been done. Some individual components have been used helpfully to guide system development, providing an informal evaluation of that component. For example, ADEPT has been used to prototype concepts in aviation automation research and development.

At the process level, providing support (e.g., guidelines and related tools) to the information flow between the phases would help ensure that all the outputs from a phase are taken into account in an appropriate manner and in a systematic way.

## 6  Conclusion

This article presents a tool-supported approach that aims at ensuring that the require-ments, design, and resulting system support the intended work missions, and are fit for purpose. The proposed suite of tools and methods that are proposed for instantiating this process, collectively support design and development of safety-critical software systems. This set of integrated complementary approaches allows designers and devel-opers identify information and behaviors that might have been otherwise missed. The approach also supports storage of information gathered and proposes analysis tools to reason about it. Knowledge gained from applying the approach can then be re-injected in the design process to improve the interactive system.

This approach has been defined and applied using a simple case study from the interactive cockpit. Each technique integrated in the approach has been applied to much larger case studies, but work remains to be done to ensure that the approach can scale to operational systems.

It is important to note that interaction techniques in cockpits are going beyond the WIMP paradigm used in the case study, and the approach should be extended to address new interaction techniques for future cockpits such as multi-touch, gestures, and audio feedback.

## References

1. Barboni, E., et al.: Beyond modeling: an integrated environment supporting co-execution of tasks and systems models. EICS 2010, pp. 165–174 (2010)
2. Billman, D., et al.: Benefits of matching domain structure for planning software: the right stuff. In: ACM Press, p. 2521 (2011)
3. Billman, D., et al.: Needs analysis and technology alignment method: a case study of planning work in an international space station controller group-part 1. J. Cogn. Eng. Decision Making 9(2), 169–185 (2015)
4. Billman, D., et al.: Representing work for device design and evaluation using biclustering. In: Presented at the Human Factors & Ergonomics Society, Washington, D.C. (2016)
5. Boehm, B.: A spiral model of software development and enhancement. ACM SIGSOFT Softw. Eng. Notes 11(4), 14–24 (1986)

6. Boehm, B.: A view of 20th and 21st century software engineering. Invited talk, IEEE International Conference on Software Engineering 2006. http://www.isr.uci.edu/icse-06/program/keynotes/boehm.html

7. Burns, C.M., Hajdukiewicz, J.R.: Ecological interface design. CRC Press, Boca Raton (2004)

8. Butler, K.A. et al.: Work-centered design: a case study of a mixed-initiative scheduler. In: Proceedings of the SIGCHI Conference on Human Factors in Computing Systems, pp. 747–756. ACM (2007)

9. Campos, J.C. et al.: Systematic automation of scenario-based testing of user interfaces. In: EICS 2016, pp. 138–148 (2016)

10. Carroll, J.M., et al.: The task-artifact cycle. In: Carroll, J.M. (ed.) Designing Interaction: Psychology at the Human-Computer Interface. Cambridge University Press, Cambridge (1991)

11. Collingridge, D.: The Social Control of Technology. Palgrave Macmillan, London (1981)

12. Collins, D.: Designing Object-Oriented user interfaces. Benjamin Cummings, Redwood City (1995)

13. Curtis, B., Hefley, B.: A WIMP no more: the maturing of user interface engineering. Interactions 1(1), 22–34 (1994)

14. Eggleston, R.G.: Work-centered design: a cognitive engineering approach to system design. In: Proceedings of the Human Factors and Ergonomics Society Annual Meeting, vol. 47(3), 263–267 (2003)

15. Feary, M.: Automatic detection of interaction vulnerabilities in an executable specification. In: Harris, D. (ed.) HCII 2007 and EPCE 2007. LNCS (LNAI), vol. 4562, pp. 487–496. Springer, Heidelberg (2007)

16. Göransson, B., et al.: The usability design process - integrating user-centered systems design in the software development process. Softw. Process Improv. Pract. 8(2), 111–131 (2003)

17. Hartson, H., Hix, D. Human-computer interface development: concepts and systems for its management. ACM Comput. Surv. 21(1) 1989

18. Hussain, Z., Slany, W., Holzinger, A.: Investigating agile user-centered design in practice: a grounded theory perspective. In: Holzinger, A., Miesenberger, K. (eds.) USAB 2009. LNCS, vol. 5889, pp. 279–289. Springer, Heidelberg (2009)

19. Martinie, C., et al.: Multi-models-based engineering of collaborative systems: application to collision avoidance operations for spacecraft. EICS 2014, pp. 85–94 (2014)

20. Martinie, C., Palanque, P., Winckler, M.: Structuring and composition mechanisms to address scalability issues in task models. In: Campos, P., Graham, N., Jorge, J., Nunes, N., Palanque, P., Winckler, M. (eds.) INTERACT 2011, Part III. LNCS, vol. 6948, pp. 589–609. Springer, Heidelberg (2011)

21. McDermid, J., Ripken, K.: Life cycle support in the Ada environment. ACM SIGAda Ada Lett. III(1) (1983)

22. Navarre, D., et al.: ICOs: a model-based user interface description technique dedicated to interactive systems addressing usability, reliability and scalability. ACM TOCHI 16(4), 1–56 (2009)

23. Norman, D., Draper, S. (eds.): User Centered System Design: New Perspectives on Human-Computer Interaction. Lawrence Erlbaum Associates, Hillsdale (1986)

24. Palanque, P., et al.: Supporting usability evaluation of multimodal man-machine interfaces for space ground segment applications using petri net based formal specification. In: SpaceOps 2006 (2006)

25. Palanque, P., Ladry, J.-F., Navarre, D., Barboni, E.: High-fidelity prototyping of interactive systems can be formal too. In: Jacko, J.A. (ed.) HCI International 2009, Part I. LNCS, vol. 5610, pp. 667–676. Springer, Heidelberg (2009)

26. Rasmussen, J., et al.: Cognitive Systems Engineering. Wiley, New York (1994)
27. Rauterberg, M.: An iterative-cyclic software process model. In: SEKE 1992 (1992)
28. Royce, W.: Managing the development of large software systems. In: IEEE Wescon, pp. 1–9 (1970)
29. Schwaber, K.: Agile Project Management with Scrum. Microsoft Press, Redmond (2004)
30. Sy, D., Miller, L.: Optimizing agile user-centred design. In: CHI 2008 extended abstracts on Human Factors in Computing Systems (CHI EA 2008), pp. 3897–3900. ACM (2008)
31. Vicente, K.J.: Cognitive work analysis: toward safe, productive, and healthy computer-based work. Lawrence Erlbaum Associates, Mahwah (1999)

# Demon Hunt - The Role of Endsley's Demons of Situation Awareness in Maritime Accidents

Tim Claudius Stratmann$^{(\boxtimes)}$ and Susanne Boll

Carl von Ossietzky Universität Oldenburg, Oldenburg, Germany
{tim.claudius.stratmann,susanne.boll}@uni-oldenburg.de

**Abstract.** Human Error is the cause of most maritime accidents. In a majority of the cases the source of the Human Error is a lack of Situation Awareness. Endsley et al. have identified eight causes that corrupt the Situation Awareness of human operators, the so-called Demons of Situation Awareness (SA Demons). We analyzed over five-hundred maritime accident reports for each of the eight SA Demons to provide a ranking of the causes and to identify the most prominent ones. Addressing these SA Demons enables maritime system designers to enhance the Situation Awareness of maritime operators and thereby improves the safety at sea.

**Keywords:** Situation awareness · Accident analysis · Maritime · Human Error

## 1 Introduction

Human Error accounts for 80–85% of maritime accidents [2]. The type of Human Errors are diverse, however they can be classified. Prior work of Grech et al. showed that a lack of Situation Awareness causes about 71% of all Human Error related accidents [9]. Similar findings have been made in other transportation domains. The problem of a lack in Situation Awareness was extensively investigated in the aviation domain.

Mica R. Endsley has defined Situation Awareness as "the *perception* (level 1) of the elements of the environment within a volume of time and space, the *comprehension* (level 2) of their meaning, and the *projection* (level 3) of their status in the near future" [6]. In 1999 Endsley introduced a taxonomy of Situation Awareness errors [7]. This taxonomy later led to the definition of the so-called Demons of Situation Awareness (SA Demons) [8]. The SA Demons stand for eight common causes for a lack of Situation Awareness. They address all three levels of Situation Awareness.

The aim of our work is to classify maritime accidents by Endsley's SA Demons. Moreover we provide our corpus of 1376 maritime accident reports and perform our analysis on a subset of it. We investigate the occurrences and

© IFIP International Federation for Information Processing 2016
Published by Springer International Publishing Switzerland 2016. All Rights Reserved
C. Bogdan et al. (Eds.): HCSE 2016/HESSD 2016, LNCS 9856, pp. 203–212, 2016.
DOI: 10.1007/978-3-319-44902-9_13

distribution of the eight SA Demons in a corpus of 535 maritime accident reports. Information about occurrences and distribution of the SA Demons enables maritime system designers to adjust their systems to the SA related needs of the operator and to build assistance systems that focus on mitigating the specific cause of SA errors.

## 2    Related Work

Most scientific accident analyses in the maritime domain focus on the statistical classification of error causes, whereas the investigations of safety authorities focus on deriving guidelines to prevent the same accidents from happening again. Human Error as cause of maritime accidents is no new phenomenon. As long ago as 1987 Wagenaar et al. analyzed 100 maritime accidents, of which 96 were caused by Human Error [13].

In 2005 Baker et al. published their three year enduring analysis of maritime accidents from the United States, Australia, Canada, Norway and the United Kingdom. Their results show that the frequency of accidents is declining, but that Human Error continues to be the dominant factor in approximately 80 to 85 % of maritime accidents [2,3]. According to their findings failures in Situation Awareness are a causal factor in the majority of accidents attributed to Human Error. They identified some significant factors associated with Situation Awareness failures which include: Cognitive and decision errors, Knowledge-Skill-Ability errors, task omissions and risk taking. They expect most of them to be artifacts of fatigue.

Endsley et al. determined eight types of causes for failures in Situation Awareness, the so-called Demons of Situation Awareness (SA Demons) [8]. The following list[1] describes each SA Demon and states the Situation Awareness levels it affects.

SAD1 **Attention Tunneling** (*SA level 1*)
> Good Situation Awareness is dependent on switching attention among multiple data streams. Locking in on certain data sources and excluding others is attention tunneling.

SAD2 **Requisite Memory Trap** (*SA level 2*)
> The working memory processes and holds chunks of data to support Situation Awareness level 2. The working memory is a limited resource. Systems that rely on robust memory do not support the user.

SAD3 **Workload, Anxiety, Fatigue, and other Stressors** (*SA level 1 and 2*)
> Stress and anxiety are likely issues in the warning environment. *WAFOS* taxes attention and working memory.

SAD4 **Data Overload** (*SA level 1*)
> There is more data available than can be processed by the human "bandwidth".

---

[1] Based on: http://www.au.af.mil/au/awc/awcgate/noaa/anti_situation_awareness. pdf.

SAD5 **Misplaced Salience** *(SA level 1)*
Salience is the "compellingness" of a piece of data, often dependent on how it is presented.
SAD6 **Complexity Creep** *(SA level 1, 2 and 3)*
Complexity slows down the perception of information and it undermines the understanding and the projection of information.
SAD7 **Errant Mental Models** *(SA level 2 and 3)*
Wrong mental model may result in incorrect interpretation of data.
SAD8 **Out-of-the-loop syndrome** *(SA level 1)*
For example: Automated systems that do not involve the human until there is a problem.

Antão et al. used BNN models to analyse maritime accidents [1]. Other work dealing with human error in maritime accidents is [4,5,10,12].

## 3   Corpus

Performing an analysis on specific SA error causes requires a data source with a high level of detail. Therefore we retrieved full-text reports of maritime accident investigations. The full corpus consists of 1376 maritime accident reports from five transportation safety authorities between the years 1987 and 2015. The reports were gathered from the British Marine Accident Investigation Branch (MAIB)[2], the American National Transportation safety Board (NTSB)[3],the United States Coast Guard (USCG)[4], the Australian Transportation safety Board (ATSB)[5] and the Transportation safety Board of Canada (TSBC)[6](Table 1).

**Table 1.** This table gives an overview of the retrieved corpus. The table shows the total number of available full-text reports, the time period covered by the reports and the country of origin. *(last update: April 15, 2016)*

| Authority | MAIB | NTSB | USCG | ATSB | TSBC |
|---|---|---|---|---|---|
| # Reports | 535 | 152 | 202 | 80 | 407 |
| Period | 1989–2015 | 1994–2015 | 2005–2015 | 1987–2015 | 1990–2015 |
| Country | Great Britain | USA | USA | Australia | Canada |

We specifically chose authorities from these countries, because they have English as their first language and a high number of available full-text reports. We share

---

[2] https://www.gov.uk/government/organisations/marine-accident-investigation-branch.
[3] http://www.ntsb.gov/investigations/accidentreports/pages/accidentreports.aspx.
[4] http://www.uscg.mil/.
[5] https://www.atsb.gov.au/marine/.
[6] http://www.tsb.gc.ca/eng/rapports-reports/marine/index.asp.

our full corpus on request to support further research in this area. For our following analysis we focused on the MAIB sub-corpus, but we intend to apply the same method of analysis to the whole corpus in the future (Fig. 1).

## 4   Analysis

The MAIB corpus consists of over five hundred accident reports. In order to classify these accident reports we applied a request-oriented classification approach. We used boolean queries to perform a full-text search on all documents in the corpus. Beforehand the corpus had to be prepared and a list of keywords had to be created in order to build meaningful queries. The preparation of the corpus is described in the following. Thereafter we describe the generation of keywords and our classification method.

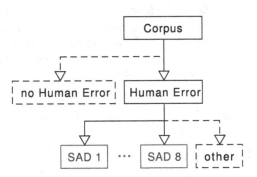

**Fig. 1.** This chart shows a segmentation of the corpus in relevant subsets. The SA Demons are colored in blue. (Color figure online)

### 4.1   Preparation

In order to perform an analysis on the gathered corpus of accident reports some pre-processing of the corpus is necessary. We gathered full-text maritime accident reports in English and PDF-format from five transportation safety authorities. As preparation for the analysis we extracted the plain-text from the reports in PDF-format and performed simple cleaning of the reports by removing the front page and fixing character encoding issues. Further we converted the reports to lowercase in order to simplify case-insensitive search. As some reports consisted of several files we merged these documents into one. After this preparation one document represents one accident.

For the exploration of the corpus we created a document-term-matrix

**Fig. 2.** This is a word cloud of the one hundred most frequent terms in the MAIB Corpus. The terms have been reduced to their stem using the SnowballC stemming algorithm.

of the corpus and checked the most frequent terms. Furthermore this enabled us to check term correlations in the corpus. We used R version 3.2.4 with a number of text-mining packages to perform this. The creation of the document-term-matrix requires some further pre-processing in R. The following pre-processing steps were conducted on the data-frame in R, only. We removed URLs, punctuation, numbers, standard English stop-words and some custom stop-words from the corpus. From the pre-processed corpus we created a tf-idf-weighted document-term-matrix. Figure 2 shows a word cloud of the one hundred most frequent terms in the corpus.

## 4.2 Generation of Keywords

A list of keywords for each SA Demon was created. The selected keywords were derived from the description of the SA Demons and examples from [8] and keywords identified during the exploration of the corpus. The keyword list was complemented with fitting synonyms of the keywords using wordnet [11].

A meaningful choice of keywords and the proper construction of the boolean queries is critical to the success of the retrieval. Adjusting the query based on the exploration of the corpus always bears the danger of overfitting the queries to the specific corpus. Furthermore the composition of the queries directly influences the precision and recall of the retrieval. Although we did not measure the recall, we tried to achieve a good balance between precision and recall.

The iterative exploration of the corpus showed unexpected usage of keywords, such as 'fatigue' in 'fatigue wear' of machine parts. The identification of these negative keyword combinations helped us to increase the precision of our search queries. We increased the recall of the query be reducing the keywords in the queries to their stems. The aim was to create a list of queries that can be applied to any set of maritime accident reports in English.

The generation of fitting keywords is a semi-automated process that highly relies on the judgment of a human analyst. In summary, the process consists of the following steps:

1. derive keywords from definitions and examples
2. find fitting synonyms for keywords using wordnet
3. explore corpus, find term-correlations for the keywords, and add new keywords
4. reduce some keywords to their stems to increase the recall based on human judgment

Furthermore we added keywords for Situation Awareness and Human Error to be able to search on a meta level if none of the keywords for a SA Demon returns any results. Table 2 shows the resulting list of generated keywords for each of the SA Demons.

## 4.3 Retrieval Method

We classified the documents into the SA Demon categories by using boolean queries constructed from the SA Demon keywords. We performed test queries to

**Table 2.** This table shows the generated keywords for each SA Demon. Some of them are reduced to their stem to increase their recall.

| SA Demon | Keywords |
|---|---|
| SAD1 | Preoccupied (himself/herself), pre-occupied (himself/herself), focus, not attent, no attent, fixate, concentrate, not note |
| SAD2 | Forget, forgot, not remember, no memory |
| SAD3 | Fatigue, workload, stress; |
| | *Negative keyword combinations:* |
| | Fatigue crack, fatigue wear, unlikely, distress, rope stress |
| SAD4 | Occupied, data overload |
| SAD5 | Caught attention, attracted attention, draw attention, distract, mislead attention |
| SAD6 | Misinterpret, not understand, complex |
| SAD7 | Misinterpret, misunderstand, misunderstood, not correct |
| SAD8 | Not aware, unaware |
| Human Error | Human error, human element, human factor |
| Situation Awareness | Situation, aware |

**Table 3.** This table shows the composition of the boolean search queries for each SA Demon.

| SA Demon | Query |
|---|---|
| SAD1 | $(preoccupied \land (himself \lor herself)) \lor (pre\text{-}occupied \land (himself \lor herself)) \lor (attent \land not) \lor focus$ |
| SAD2 | $(human \land error) \lor (human \land element) \lor (human \land factor) \lor (situation \land aware)$ |
| SAD3 | $fatigue \land \neg crack \land \neg wear \land \neg not \land \neg unlikely \lor workload$ |
| SAD4 | $occupied$ |
| SAD5 | $(human \land error) \lor (human \land element) \lor (human \land factor) \lor (situation \land aware)$ |
| SAD6 | $(human \land error) \lor (human \land element) \lor (human \land factor) \lor (situation \land aware)$ |
| SAD7 | $misinterpret$ |
| SAD8 | $not \land aware$ |

identify the keyword combinations with the best balance of precision and recall. Table 3 shows the final queries we used to retrieve the accidents caused by the SA Demons.

For SAD2, SAD5, and SAD6 we could not find a fitting query that specifically retrieves them. Queries constructed from SAD6 keywords always delivered SAD7 problems, as the keywords are to similar. The keywords for SAD5 are often used by the authors of the accident reports to emphasize their findings and recommendations, e.g. "[...] draw the attention of Owners, Skippers, Mates and crews to [...]". We therefore used a more general query for these SA Demons.

We applied the *pipeline and filters* design pattern to implement the boolean queries as a unix pipeline combining the unix programs *find* and *grep*. The advantage of this approach over using an indexing search engine is the support of full-text search. To remove false positives, the query results were inspected manually in the context of the sentences containing the positive keywords. If we were unsure, the sentence before and after the finding was also inspected.

## 5 Results

The SA Demons with the highest proportion in the investigated sample were *WOFAS* with fatigue as main cause, *errant mental models*, and *attention tunneling*. We were not able to find accidents caused by *requisite memory trap*, *misplaced salience* or *complexity creep*. Not all Situation Awareness related accidents can be explained by the SA Demons. During analysis we found some accidents caused by a lack of Situation Awareness that could not be derived directly from a SA Demon, such as insufficient trip planning.

**Table 4.** Retrieved occurrences of SA Demons in MAIB Corpus. The Percentage behind the absolute counts indicates the count relative to the corpus size.

| SA demon | Description | True positives | Query precision |
|----------|-------------|----------------|-----------------|
| SAD1 | attention tunneling | 36 (7 %) | 0.14 |
| SAD2 | requisite memory trap | not found | - |
| SAD3 | WOFAS | 216 (40 %) | 0.87 |
| SAD4 | data overload | 34 (6 %) | 0.17 |
| SAD5 | misplaced salience | not found | - |
| SAD6 | complexity creep | not found | - |
| SAD7 | errant mental models | 40 (7 %) | 0.93 |
| SAD8 | out-of-the-loop syndrome | 7 (1 %) | 0.02 |
| Total | | **333 (62 %)** | |
| Expected | | *300–321 (56–60%)* | |

Table 4 shows the results of our request-oriented classification. The table lists the absolute count of retrieved accidents and the precision of the query for each SA Demon. The query precision is the positive predictive value of the query-request on the corpus.

It is calculated as follows:

$$query\ precision = \frac{number\ of\ true\ positives}{number\ of\ true\ positives\ +\ number\ of\ false\ positives}$$

Moreover we calculated an estimate of the total number of results based on statistics from related work. This provides us with a weak sanity check of the total number of retrieved accidents related to SA problems. For the MAIB corpus this estimate amounts to 300–321 accidents. We based the estimate on the results of Baker et al. stating that in about 80–85% of maritime accidents Human Error is the dominant factor [2]. Further Grech et al. have stated that about 71 % of maritime accidents caused by Human Error are caused by a lack of Situation Awareness [9]. We combined these two statistics in the following calculations:

$$estimate_{lower} = 535 \times (71\% \times 80\%) = 535 \times 56\% = 300$$
$$estimate_{higher} = 535 \times (71\% \times 85\%) = 535 \times 60\% = 321$$

## 6   Discussion

The relationship between documents and SA Demons is a many-to-many relationship. That means more than one SA Demon could have lead to the accident. Our previously introduced weak sanity check suggests that our retrieval was quite successful. However, without knowing the number of false negatives and the recall of our retrieval this is just an educated guess.

We did not find any accidents caused by *requisite memory trap, misplaced salience* or *complexity creep*. However, the fact that we were not able to find them does not mean they do not exist. We expected these demons to be hard to find. Endsley has already stated in her definition of the SA Demons that "complexity is a subtle SA Demon" [8]. *Requisite memory trap* is an internal processing problem that is hard to observe. The same applies to *misplaced salience*. As our source of data are accident reports, the completeness of the data regarding SA failures depends on the ability of the respective inspector conducting the investigation to identify human errors and their causes. The completeness therefore varies from inspector to inspector depending on their interpretation abilities and work experience.

The most frequent found SA Demons all affect Situation Awareness Level 1. This confirms prior work by Grech et al. identifying Situation Awareness Level 1 as most prominent cause for a lack of Situation Awareness [9].

## 7   Conclusion

Our results confirm that Situation Awareness Level 1 is the most prominent source of Human Error in maritime accidents. Likewise it is the most prominent one of the three levels of Situation Awareness. All in all, the SA Demons with the highest proportion in the investigated sample were *WOFAS* with fatigue as main cause, *errant mental models*, and *attention tunneling*. We were not able to find accidents caused by *requisite memory trap, misplaced salience* or *complexity creep*, however we still think that these exist. Unfortunately detecting these SA Demons in maritime accident investigation reports will remain difficult, unless it becomes part of the investigation itself. We advise taking special care of the SA Demons *WOFAS, errant mental models, data overload* and *attention tunneling* when designing new interfaces for ship bridges. Our findings might also be beneficial for the design of user interfaces for Vessel Traffic Management (VTM) centers. We intend to improve our retrieval method by labeling ship personnel in the corpus using a custom-built tool for named-entity-recognition of maritime personnel such as the 'master' or the 'OOW'[7]. This will enable us to use higher level queries such as *PERSON* ∧ *fatigue*. Also, we intend to apply our method of analysis to our full corpus of retrieved reports with refined keywords and queries in the future. We expect to get similar results in relation to the corpus size and to find further examples of SA failures caused by SA Demons.

**Acknowledgments.** We thank the Ministry of Science and Culture of Lower Saxony for supporting us with the graduate school *Safe Automation of Maritime Systems (SAMS)*.

# References

## All links were last followed on April 15, 2016.

1. Antão, P., Guedes Suares, C., Grande, O., Trucco, P.: Analysis of maritime accident data with bbn models. In: Martorell et al. (eds.) Safety, Reliability and Risk Analysis: Theory, Methods and Applications. Taylor & Francis Group, London (2009)
2. Baker, C., McCafferty, D.: Accident database review of human element concerns: what do the results mean for classification?. In: Proceedings of the International Conference Human Factors in Ship Design and Operation, RINA Feb. Citeseer (2005)
3. Baker, C.C., Seah, A.K.: Maritime accidents and human performance: the statistical trail. In: MarTech Conference, Singapore (2004)
4. de la Campa Portela, R.: Maritime casualties analysis as a tool to improve research about human factors on maritime environment. J. Marit. Res. **2**(2), 3–18 (2005)
5. Chauvin, C., Lardjane, S., Morel, G., Clostermann, J.P., Langard, B.: Human and organisational factors in maritime accidents: analysis of collisions at sea using the hfacs. Accid. Anal. Prev. **59**, 26–37 (2013)
6. Endsley, M.R.: Toward a theory of situation awareness in dynamic systems. Hum. Factors J. Hum. Factors Ergon. Soc. **37**(1), 32–64 (1995)
7. Endsley, M.R.: Situation awareness and human error: designing to support human performance. In: Proceedings of the High Consequence Systems Surety Conference, pp. 2–9. Lawrence Eribaum Associates (1999)
8. Endsley, M.R., Jones, D.G.: SA demons: the enemies of situation awareness. In: Designing for Situation Awareness: An Approach to User-Centered Design, chap. 3, pp. 31–41. CRC Press (2011)

---

[7] Officer of the watch.

9. Grech, M.R., Horberry, T., Smith, A.: Human error in maritime operations: analyses of accident reports using the leximancer tool. In: Proceedings of the Human Factors and Ergonomics Society Annual Meeting. vol. 46, pp. 1718–1721. SAGE Publications (2002)

10. Koester, T.: Human error in the maritime work domain. In: Proceedings of 20th European Annual Conference on Human Decision Making and Manual Control, pp. 149–158 (2001)

11. Miller, G.A.: Wordnet: a lexical database for english. Commun. ACM **38**(11), 39–41 (1995)

12. Rothblum, A.M.: Human error and marine safety. In: National Safety Council Congress and Expo, Orlando, FL (2000)

13. Wagenaar, W.A., Groeneweg, J.: Accidents at sea: Multiple causes and impossible consequences. Int. J. Man Mach. Stud. **27**(5), 587–598 (1987)

# User and Developer Experience

# Are Software Developers Just Users of Development Tools? Assessing Developer Experience of a Graphical User Interface Designer

Kati Kuusinen[1,2(✉)]

[1] University of Central Lancashire, Preston, Lancashire PR1 2HE, UK
kkuusinen@uclan.ac.uk
[2] Tampere University of Technology, Tampere, Finland

**Abstract.** Software developers use software products to design and develop new software products for others to use. Research has introduced a concept of developer experience inspired by the concept of user experience but appreciating also the special characteristics of software development context. It is unclear what the experiential components of developer experience are and how it can be measured. In this paper we address developer experience of Vaadin Designer, a graphical user interface designer tool in terms of user experience, intrinsic motivation, and flow state experience. We surveyed 18 developers using AttrakDiff, flow state scale, intrinsic motivation inventory and our own DEXI scale and compare those responses to developers' overall user experience assessment using Mann-Whitney U test. We found significant differences in motivational and flow state factors between groups who assessed the overall user experience either bad or good. Based on our results we discuss the factors that construe developer experience.

## 1 Introduction

Software development, especially the design and development of the graphical user interface (GUI) strongly benefits from the developers' ability to emphasize with the user and understand user needs. Simultaneously, it requires numerous technical skills to create GUIs. Traditionally GUI development has been done manually via application programming interfaces (APIs) which generally are interfaces to components often represented as libraries. Thus, when using APIs, developers program the GUI by calling required widgets and components via the API and giving parameters for them manually. The resulting GUI is only visible after it is runnable. Often in such approach, GUI is first designed and drawn by UI (user interface) designers separate from front-end developers. The design is often communicated to developers as ready-made static images of the future GUI, which might not be fully implementable as such [10, 11, 25].

Considering notation, we will use "*GUI designer*" throughout the paper to refer to software and "*UI designer*" to refer to a person.

Another approach for designing and developing GUIs is to use a GUI designer which often is a WYSIWYG (what you see is what you get) editor that allows the

© IFIP International Federation for Information Processing 2016
Published by Springer International Publishing Switzerland 2016. All Rights Reserved
C. Bogdan et al. (Eds.): HCSE 2016/HESSD 2016, LNCS 9856, pp. 215–233, 2016.
DOI: 10.1007/978-3-319-44902-9_14

designer/developer to produce GUIs by dragging and dropping UI elements on screen layout. This approach can, for instance, help those UI designers who are less experienced in programming to produce more implementable design and developers would only need to refactor the produced code [23]. Or it could help a developer somewhat knowledgeable in user experience (UX) issues to produce design that a UX specialist could only review to ensure the quality of use.

Although qualities of both software developers and development work have been studied, developers have rarely been seen as users of development tools in the research. As developers are users of, for instance, GUI designers, all that is true to any user according to UX definitions (e.g. [19]), should apply also to developers. However, the dualistic role of the developer both as user of development tools and designer of new software products makes the developer special: Besides being users of GUI designers, developers should be able to understand the human user to be able to fulfill their needs with the GUI under development. A concept of developer experience (DX) has been suggested to address the particularities to software development [9]. The concept of DX is influenced by the concept of UX [9]. Moreover, DX consists of aspects related to cognition, affect, and conation and understanding of the concept should help practitioners in improving project environments with respect to developers' perceptions and feelings [9].

This paper has two main contributions. First, we present our DEXI scale developed for assessing the particularities of DX. Then we explore which factors of UX, flow state experience and intrinsic motivation correlate with developers' overall UX assessment regarding the assessed GUI designer (Vaadin Designer, https://vaadin.com/designer) thus contributing towards increased understanding of developer experience. Finally, we discuss these findings in relation to both related research and our previous findings on DX of integrated development environments.

The rest of this paper is organized as follows. Section 2 introduces background and related work. Section 3 describes the survey study method including description of the procedure and participants. Section 4 presents survey results. Section 5 discusses the results and Sect. 6 discusses the validity and possibilities for future work. Finally, Sect. 7 gives concluding remarks to the paper.

## 2  Background

Traditional GUI development has based on desktop screen model born in 1980's [31]. The model, based on windows and menus on a desktop computer screen used with a physical keyboard and a mouse was dominant from 1980's to around millennium when handheld devices started to become more common [31]. In fact, the desktop GUI generally still works in a similar fashion it was introduced in the 1980's. Mobile devices, however, have introduced new design challenges with their small-sized screens, virtual keyboards on touch screens, voice control mechanisms etc. [24, 31]. In addition, interoperability demands of cross-platform environments introduce additional requirements for GUI design: The variety of platforms and operating systems has never been as massive as it is today. Furthermore, embedded systems and internet of things bring totally new kind of considerations on the research field of human-computer interaction.

## 2.1  GUI Designers

Commonly used GUI designers, sometimes called also GUI builders, include Eclipse Window Builder, Flex Builder, JetBrains Swing GUI designer, Netbeans Swing GUI Builder, Sencha Architect, and Vaadin Designer. GUI designers offer a visual interface to the underlying component and widget libraries. Therefore, designing the UI with GUI designer software can help to mitigate the problem with unimplementable design often seen when UX designers produce UI design as static UI images that developers need to interpret and amend for implementation. Such problems have been reported, for instance in [10, 11, 25].

In general, GUI designers help reduce the number of lines of code developers need to write for the GUI since those tools generate part of the code [31]. They also make GUI development faster [31] and can help UI designers and developers cooperate better and the designer to produce more implementable design compared to the use of static UI images as design artefacts [22, 23]. In cross-platform environments where GUI needs to be designed for several platforms, creating design manually is time-consuming [31]. The variety, functionality, and use of GUI design tools has grown rapidly during the mobile era. Moreover, digital prototyping and design tools have replaced paper prototyping in many organizations because of their fastness to use, repeatability, and detailed look and feel [22, 23]. In addition, responsive design (design that scales based on the screen size of the device) makes the use of paper prototypes difficult as the designer cannot design fixed-sized screens and with paper prototypes it is hard to understand what will be visible for the user at once [23].

In addition to actual GUI designer software, there are numerous prototyping tools available for rapid prototyping before the GUI building. Those include, for instance, Balsamiq, InVision, and Pencil. These tools differ from GUI designers in that they are mostly intended for sketching and making mock-ups and prototypes instead of creating the production version of the UI.

## 2.2  User Experience

The standard definition of user experience (UX) is as follows: a *"person's perceptions and responses resulting from the use and/or anticipated use of a product, system or service"* [19]. Commonly, UX is understood as subjective, context-dependent, and dynamic [29]. It is affected by user's expectations, needs and motivation, system's characteristics such as purpose and functionality, and the context of use including physical, organizational and psychological aspects [18]. One of the most commonly referred models of UX, the hedonic-pragmatic model divides user experience into hedonic or non-utilitarian dimension and pragmatic or instrumental dimension [15]. Hassenzahl [15] further divides hedonic quality into two sub dimensions of identification and stimulation while instrumental quality contains mostly items related to usability and usefulness. Usability is often seen as a necessary precondition for good UX [16, 28].

## 2.3    Developer Experience

Developer experience (DX) is a recent concept addressing the experience of software development [9]. Whereas UX occurs in relation to the use of software, DX addresses the creation of new software. Consequently, UX does not cover all aspects of DX [8]: Developers use development tools in order to create software that provokes experience in the user. On the other hand, developers are users of development software and thus it can be argued that the concept of UX can be applied also to software developers. What makes the developer special, however, is the dualistic nature of being simultaneously both producer and user of software.

Fagerholm's concept of DX [8] presents that DX is the sum of cognitive, affective, and conative mental processes of developer in a context consisting of social and technical environments in which they interact with other developers and numerous technical artefacts (Fig. 1).

The concept of DX aims at providing an intuitive abstraction of the vast variety and quantity of human factors that influence developers and the outcomes of software development [9]. While UX considers the context of use, DX considers the context of development. DX includes also aspects beyond software tools, such as development processes, modeling methods, and other means of structuring development tasks. Some of these aspects are embedded in tools such as GUI builders while others are part of organizational practices. The software development activity and environment differ in significant ways from other information-intensive activities and environments. For example, software development requires a nested understanding: developers use software installed on a computer system to build another software system that is to be used by users to accomplish their task in their particular domain providing them desired UX. Also, developers frequently configure and extend their tools, and are in effect continuously developing both the development environment and the end product at the same time.

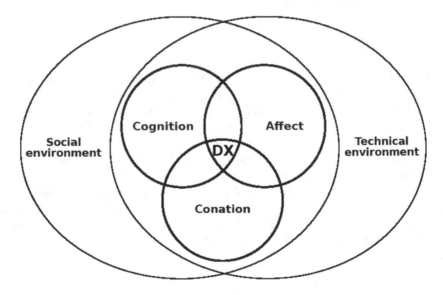

**Fig. 1.** Concept of developer experience [8]

## 2.4 Motivation and Flow State Experience in Software Development

One of the current influential theories of motivation is the self-determination theory from Deci and Ryan [7]. They distinguish between intrinsic and extrinsic motivations. Intrinsic motivation refers to engaging in a task because of it is inherently pleasurable and satisfying whereas extrinsic motivation refers to engaging in a task because of its outcomes, the task is used as a means to lead to the outcome [7].

Developer motivation is as an important factor in software development. Majority of studies on motivation in development context report that developers are distinct from other occupational groups with respect to motivation [1]. "The work itself" is the most commonly cited motivator, but there is a lack of detail regarding what aspects of the work is motivating, how motivational processes occur, and what the outcomes of motivating developers are [1, 12]. Investigations into affective aspects of software development show the importance of considering also affect. The presence and variation of developers' emotions over time has been documented [36]. Programming tasks are influenced by mood [21], and happiness has been found to have productivity benefits [14]. This underlines the importance of considering affective aspects both for purposes of well-being and outcomes.

Flow experience refers to a state of concentration so focused that it amounts to absolute absorption in an activity [4]. Applicable to both work and leisure [5], flow builds on intrinsic motivation and internal reward over the achievement rather than on external goal or recognition. Its effect can be characterized as being totally focused on a particular task at hand, so that the person becomes fully immersed in a feeling of energized focus, full involvement, and enjoyment in the process of the activity. While immersed, three conditions have to be met to achieve a flow state [6]:

1. One must be involved in an activity with a clear set of *goals and progress*;
2. The task at hand must have clear and immediate *feedback*;
3. One must have a good balance between the perceived *challenges* of the task at hand and their own perceived *skills*, so that there can be confidence in one's ability to complete the task at hand.

These three conditions of flow state experience are comparable with what the literature has found focal for software developers and development work. For example, clear goals, technically challenging work, knowing the purpose of tasks, making good use of skills, and getting feedback are widely reported motivators of software developers [1, 35]. In addition, the core of software development work is writing the program code, which demands the ability to concentrate and work alone for several hours [2]. Both these motivators of developers and the nature of development work makes the concept of flow state experience interesting in the context of software development.

## 3 Method

Our research has an overall goal to increase understanding of DX. We aim to clarify how flow state experience, intrinsic motivation, and UX are intertwined in software development and with developer experience. This will enable improvement of development tools to better support developers' ability to experience flow in their work and to enhance developers' intrinsic motivation towards their work. Our hypothesis is that these factors make developers' work more enjoyable and increases their productivity. We have previously conducted a similar study in the context of integrated development environments [26].

This paper reports a survey study that was organized for two main reasons. (1) To examine the relationship of flow state experience, intrinsic motivation, and developer experience and (2) to evaluate the DX of a commonly used GUI designer called Vaadin Designer. The survey was organized together with Vaadin Ltd, the provider of the GUI designer under evaluation.

We present the following research question:

*What kind of relation does developer experience and the ability of Vaadin designer to fulfill developers' needs have with flow state experience and intrinsic motivation?*


### 3.1   Survey Contents

We conducted a survey study measuring developers' self-reported experiences considering a particular GUI designer. Our web survey consisted of the following four scales:

1. the Short Dispositional Flow State Scale (SDFS-2) [20] used in its entirety,
2. parts of the Intrinsic Motivation Inventory (IMI) [34] including questions related to interest/enjoyment, perceived competence, effort/importance, and perceived choice, and
3. the short version of the AttrakDiff-2 (SAD-2) [17] used in its entirety, and
4. our own Developer Experience Scale (DEXI) [26]. The scales, except DEXI, were selected since they are widely used and validated. They are also short enough to be combined in a survey.

In addition, we asked for overall UX assessment (OUX) and overall ability of the GUI designer to fulfill the needs of the respondent (NFS) as follows:

"*How would you rate the overall user experience of Vaadin Designer?*" using a seven-point Likert scale from "Bad" (1) to "Good" (7), and

"*How well does Vaadin Designer respond to your needs?*" using a seven-point Likert scale from "Not at all" (1) to "Completely" (7). All other measurements are compared to OUX assessment. NFS has no special role in this paper, it is used only as one of the independent variables.

Furthermore, we asked the following open-ended questions considering the use of GUI designers: "*In your opinion, what are the best qualities of Vaadin Designer?*", "*How could Vaadin Designer better support your development work?*", and "*Describe the ideal way of creating UI*".

Finally, we also asked demographics including experience of software development in years, experience of the particular GUI designer (seen it in use, used it [once or twice, a few times, several times, regularly for less than a month, regularly for over a month but less than a year, regularly for over a year]), age, country the respondent was based in (list of countries provided), size of the organization they were working for (individual developer, micro organization (< 10 employees), small (10–100), medium-sized (100–1000), large (over 1000 employees)), and the user group of the GUI designer they belonged (UI designer [they design the UI, someone else does the coding], UI developer [they produce the code], evaluator [typically architect or lead developer who assess the feasibility of different technologies for the organization], other).

Next we present the used scales in detail. We measured the frequency with which developers experience different dimensions of flow during software development activities by using the **Short Dispositional Flow State Scale (SDFS-2)** [20]. We used a 7-level Likert scale, ranging from 1 (never) to 7 (always). The instructions for the questions were *"Please evaluate how often (from 1 = never to 7 = always) you experience the following while you are doing development work with Vaadin Designer"*. The SDFS-2 measures nine dimensions of flow, each with one item (Table 1). In addition to the nine SDFS-2 items, an additional item was included to measure the experience of frustration: *"I feel frustrated"*.

**Intrinsic Motivation Inventory (IMI)**. Since the original IMI is long and partially repetitive, and shorter versions have been commonly used [30], we used a shortened version (Table 2). Utilized scale included selected items from the following IMI subscales: interest/enjoyment (the actual self-report measure of intrinsic motivation), perceived competence, effort/importance, and perceived choice. Framing of the question and assessment scale was according to IMI. Thus, the question was as follows: *"For each of the following statements, please indicate how true it is for you, using the following scale"*, and we utilized a seven-level scale ranging from 1 (not at all true) to 7 (very true).

**DX and UX assessment**. Both **DEXI** scale and **Short AttrakDiff 2** were used in the survey to assess DX or UX of the particular GUI designer tool. The wording from AttrakDiff [15] was used with both scales as follows: *"With the help of the word-pairs, please enter what you consider the most appropriate description for Vaadin Designer:"* The short version of AttrakDiff-2 (SAD-2) was used as such [17]. It contains four items

Table 1. SDFS-2 scale. Dimensions of state of flow and related survey items [20]

| Flow item | Survey question |
| --- | --- |
| Challenge-skill balance | I feel I am competent enough to meet the high demands of the situation |
| Action awareness | I do things spontaneously and automatically without having to think |
| Clear goals | I have a strong sense of what I want to do |
| Unambiguous feedback | I have a good idea while I am performing about how well I am doing |
| Concentration on task | I am completely focused on the task at hand |
| Sense of control | I have a feeling of total control |
| Loss of self-consciousness | I am not worried about what others may be thinking of me |
| Transformation of time | The way time passes seems to be different from normal |
| Autotelic experience | The experience is extremely rewarding |

**Table 2.** Selected subscales and survey items of IMI [34]

| Subscale | Survey item |
|---|---|
| Interest/Enjoyment | I enjoy UI creation very much |
| | I think UI creation is a boring activity |
| | I enjoy using Vaadin Designer very much |
| Perceived competence | I am satisfied with my performance at UI creation |
| | I am pretty skilled in UI creation |
| | I am pretty skilled in using Vaadin Designer |
| Effort/Importance | It is important to me to do well in UI creation |
| Perceived choice | I use Vaadin Designer because I have no choice |

**Table 3.** Short AttrakDiff 2 [17]

| Measurement | Word-Pairs |
|---|---|
| SAD_General | Bad–Good |
| SAD_General | Ugly–Beautiful |
| SAD_Practical | Confusing–Structured |
| SAD_Practical | Practical–Impractical |
| SAD_Practical | Unpredictable–Predictable |
| SAD_Practical | Simple–Complicated |
| SAD_Hedonic | Dull–Captivating |
| SAD_Hedonic | Stylish–Tacky |
| SAD_Hedonic | Cheap–Premium |
| SAD_Hedonic | Creative–Unimaginative |

**Table 4.** DEXI scale

| Quality | Survey question | Source |
|---|---|---|
| DEXI_G | Recommendable–Not recommendable | [33, 37] |
| DEXI_P | Efficient–Inefficient | [13, 37] |
| DEXI_P | Flexible–Inflexible | [13] |
| DEXI_P | Easy to learn–Difficult to learn | [13, 37] |
| DEXI_P | Limited–Extensive | [13] |
| DEXI_P | Uninformative–Informative | [37] |
| DEXI_H | Motivating–Discouraging | [9, 37] |
| DEXI_H | Increases respect–Decreases respect | [37] |
| DEXI_H | Enjoyable–Unenjoyable | [37] |
| DEXI_H | Promotes creativity–Suppresses creativity | [2, 37] |
| DEXI_H | Engaging–Uninvolving | [2, 37] |
| DEXI_H | Brings me closer to others–Separates me from others | [2, 9, 13, 37] |

(word-pairs) for both practical (PQ) and hedonic quality (HQ), and one for measuring goodness and beauty each (general quality GQ) (Table 3).

We formed our own DEXI scale for measuring additional items related to developers' UX, or DX. Thus, we aimed at construing a scale that would be relevant for software development. We selected word-pairs for DEXI from the dataset of a meta-study considering the often used UX items in research tailored for work-related systems [37], amongst concepts that have been used to describe DX [9], and amongst those characteristics of development platforms developers find beneficial [13]. We utilized the structure and wording of AttrakDiff in DEXI. We selected 5 items (DEXI_P) measuring pragmatic quality and 6 items (DEXI_H) measuring hedonic (non-utilitarian) quality. One item (DEXI_G) measured general quality (Table 4). DEXI scale was piloted with students in a code camp experiment and used in a study reported in [26].

## 3.2  Procedure

We organized an online survey to evaluate Vaadin Designer, a commonly used GUI designer. The survey was organized together with Vaadin ltd, the provider of Vaadin Designer. The survey had a front page presenting informed consent statements adopted from World Health Organization's Informed consent form template for qualitative studies [38]. Participants were informed of the organizer, purpose, target respondents, contents, and confidentiality of the survey as well as of the expected completion time and treatment of the information they will provide. We instructed only those who have been using the GUI designer to respond to the survey, and to respond only once. The survey was available for the respondents for four weeks. However, no notifications were sent for the request of the company.

## 3.3  Respondents

In total, we got 20 responses of which 18 were valid. Organizations of the 18 respondents were as follows, individual developers: 4, micro businesses: 4, small businesses: 3, middle-sized businesses: 4, and large businesses: 3. Mean experience from software development was 10 years ranging from 1 to 25 (SD: 7 years). Three of the respondents considered themselves UI designers, 9 were UI coders, 4 were evaluators and 2 were full-stack developers. Regarding the experience of the assessed GUI designer, one respondent had only watched a demonstration or somebody else using the GUI designer, 4 had tried it once or twice, 4 had used it a few times, 4 several times, 2 had used it regularly for less than a month, and 3 had used it regularly for more than a month but less than a year. Given this, respondents can be considered experts in software development but novices in using the GUI designer. Respondents' mean age was 36, SD 10 years, range 21 to 59 years. The respondents were from all over the world: Germany: 4 respondents, India: 2, Spain: 2, US: 2, and 1 from each of the following: Belgium, Columbia, Ecuador, Hungary, Indonesia, Italy, Portugal, and Romania. Thus, 11 respondents were from European countries, 3 from Americas, and 3 from Asian countries.

### 3.4 Analysis

The design of data analysis was finalized after the data gathering to suit the small data set of 18 valid responses. Thus, we approach the research question *"what kind of relation does developer experience and the ability of Vaadin designer to fulfill developers' needs have with flow state experience and intrinsic motivation?"* from two angles with two statistical methods using SPSS. First we run a more robust statistical test, namely Mann-Whitney U test on the data and compare between those respondents who assessed their overall UX with Vaadin Designer high and those who assessed it low. Second, we run Kendall's Tau correlation analysis on the data to address which items in each scale correlate with the overall UX assessment. Both Mann-Whitney U test and Kendall's Tau correlation analysis are nonparametric methods suitable for smaller and non-normal datasets. In Kendall's Tau correlation analysis, we calculate the correlation between OUX and each item in SDFS-2 and IMI. In using Mann-Whitney U, we test for equality of means to compare responses of those developers who assessed OUX in the seven-point scale 3 or lower (close to "bad") and those who assessed OUX 5 or higher (close to "good"). In the valid dataset, there were 8 respondents that considered the OUX of the GUI designer bad (ratings 1–3) and 9 who considered it good (ratings 5–7), thus one of the respondents assessed OUX with four, neutral, and this assessment was discarded from the analysis. We name the respondent groups "OUX_bad" (ratings 1–3) and "OUX_good" (ratings 5–7), respectively. Our null hypothesis for Mann-Whitney U is as follows:

H: *"The distribution of [each survey item] is the same across respondent groups OUX_bad and OUX_good."*

The hypothesis states that respondents assessing OUX as bad (group OUX_bad) cannot be significantly separated from those assessing it good (group OUX_good) in their responses to DX, UX, intrinsic motivation, and flow state experience. If the hypothesis is not supported, it means that there is statistically significant difference in responses between those groups.

### 3.5 Impact of Demographics

We ran Kendall's Tau and Mann-Whitney U test between OUX and demographic variables where feasible. There were no significant correlations and the null hypothesis remained for all demographics: there were no statistically significant differences in the demographics between groups of OUX_good and OUX_bad, i.e. between those who assessed overall UX high (good) and those who assessed it low (bad).

## 4   Results

We present first the Mann-Whitney U test results, continue with Kendall's Tau correlation analysis and end the results section with answers to the open-ended questions.

## 4.1 Mann-Whitney U Test Results

Table 5 presents only statistically significant values of Mann-Whitney U test to save space. These are the items for which the null hypothesis is not supported. Thus, for all the items in Table 5, there is a statistically significant difference between those respondents who considered the overall UX of the GUI designer bad (1–3) and those who considered it good (5–7 on a seven-point scale from bad to good). It means these items can also be used to differentiate between those groups of respondents. For example, respondents who do things spontaneously and automatically without having to think also consider the overall UX good significantly more often than those who do not, and vice versa. These results indicate that it is important to support developer flow and prevent frustration to ensure good developer experience.

Participants who assessed UX of Vaadin Designer high enjoyed using the Designer more and considered themselves more skilled with the Designer significantly more often than participants who assessed UX low. Furthermore, they were more spontaneous in their tasks and felt frustration significantly less than low assessors. Thus, in this data set, flow state experience (challenge-skill balance in particular) and intrinsic motivation towards the tool had an impact on user experience assessment.

Of the UX items in SAD-2 and DEXI, the null hypothesis was not supported for 2 of 3 word-pairs measuring general quality, for 5 of 9 word-pairs measuring practical quality and 2 of 10 measuring hedonic quality. In DEXI scale 6 out of 12 word pairs (50 %) were able to differentiate between OUX_bad and OUX_good whereas SAD_2 was able differentiate between those only with 3 word pairs out of the total 10 (30 %).

**Table 5.** Statistically significant Mann-Whitney U test results between respondent groups OUX_good and OUX_bad for NFS and all subscales (OUX, SDFS-2, IMI, SAD-2, DEXI). N = 17

| Survey item per subscale | U | p | r |
|---|---|---|---|
| How well does Vaadin Designer respond to your needs? | 3.50 | <.001 | 0.77 |
| I do things spontaneously and automatically without having to think | 8.50 | <.01 | 0.65 |
| I feel frustrated | 6.00 | <.01 | 0.71 |
| I enjoy using Vaadin Designer very much | 8.50 | <.01 | 0.65 |
| I am pretty skilled in using Vaadin Designer | 11.00 | <.05 | 0.61 |
| SAD_G Bad–Good | 2.00 | <.001 | 0.81 |
| SAD_P Unpredictable–Predictable | 12.00 | <.05 | 0.58 |
| SAD_P Practical–Impractical | 7.00 | <.01 | 0.69 |
| DEXI_G Recommendable–Not recommendable | 6.50 | <.01 | 0.70 |
| DEXI_P Easy to learn–Difficult to learn | 10.00 | <.05 | 0.62 |
| DEXI_P Flexible–Inflexible | 9.00 | <.01 | 0.64 |
| DEXI_P Efficient–Inefficient | 5.50 | <.01 | 0.73 |
| DEXI_H Motivating–Discouraging | 1.00 | <.001 | 0.83 |
| DEXI_H Enjoyable nenjoyable | 6.00 | <.01 | 0.71 |

Moreover, no word-pairs measuring hedonic quality in Short AttrakDiff 2 were able to differentiate OUX_good and OUX_bad whereas two word-pairs, namely motivating–discouraging and enjoyable–unenjoyable in DEXI were. However, larger datasets are required for further evaluation of the scales.

## 4.2 Kendall's Tau Correlation Analysis

As expected, overall UX assessment (OUX) strongly correlated with need fulfillment (NFS), $r_\tau = .84$, $p = < .001$. This finding is in line with Hassenzahl's results [17]. Correlations between OUX and individual items in Short AttrakDiff 2 and DEXI scales are presented in Table 6. What is notable is that 9/12 (75 %) of word-pairs in DEXI scale significantly correlated with OUX while only 4/10 (40 %) of SAD2 had a significant correlation with OUX, all of the latter measuring pragmatic or general quality. Otherwise there is nothing surprising, the majority of the word-pairs correlate with OUX which can be anticipated as all the items are to address UX.

**Table 6.** Results of Kendall's Tau ($r_\tau$) correlation analysis between overall UX (OUX) assessment and individual items of SAD2 and DEXI scales. Legend: SAD = Short AttrakDiff 2, G = general quality, P = practical quality, H = hedonic quality, n.s. = not significant. N = 18

| Measure | Items | $r_\tau$ | p |
|---------|-------|------|---|
| SAD_G | Bad–Good | .770 | <.001 |
| SAD_P | Practical–Impractical | −.650 | <.05 |
| SAD_P | Confusing–Structured | .530 | <.01 |
| SAD_P | Unpredictable–Predictable | .470 | <.05 |
| SAD_H | Stylish–Tacky | v.330 | n.s. |
| SAD_P | Simple–Complicated | −.310 | n.s. |
| SAD_H | Dull–Captivating | .270 | n.s. |
| SAD_G | Ugly–Beautiful | .240 | n.s. |
| SAD_H | Creative–Unimaginative | −.130 | n.s. |
| SAD_H | Cheap–Premium | .090 | n.s. |
| DEXI_H | Motivating–Discouraging | −.780 | <.001 |
| DEXI_G | Recommendable–Not recommendable | −.750 | <.001 |
| DEXI_P | Efficient–Inefficient | −.680 | <.001 |
| DEXI_P | Flexible–Inflexible | −.630 | <.01 |
| DEXI_H | Enjoyable–Unenjoyable | −.620 | <.01 |
| DEXI_P | Easy to learn–Difficult to learn | −.570 | <.01 |
| DEXI_H | Increases respect–Decreases respect | −.440 | <.05 |
| DEXI_H | Promotes creativity–Suppresses creativity | −.430 | <.05 |
| DEXI_H | Engaging–Uninvolving | −.400 | <.05 |
| DEXI_H | Brings me closer to others–Separates me from others | −.360 | n.s. |
| DEXI_P | Limited–Extensive | −.230 | n.s. |
| DEXI_P | Uninformative–Informative | .170 | n.s. |

**Table 7.** Results of Kendall's Tau ($r_\tau$) correlation analysis between overall UX (OUX) assessment and individual items of IMI subscale. N = 18

| Intrinsic motivation item | $r_\tau$ | p |
|---|---|---|
| I enjoy using Vaadin Designer very much | .560 | <.01 |
| I am pretty skilled in using Vaadin Designer | .490 | <.01 |
| I think UI creation is a boring activity | .350 | n.s. |
| I use Vaadin Designer because I have no choice | −.290 | n.s. |
| It is important to me to do well in UI creation | −.150 | n.s. |
| I enjoy UI creation very much | .100 | n.s. |
| I am satisfied with my performance at UI creation | .090 | n.s. |
| I am pretty skilled in UI creation | .040 | n.s. |

**Table 8.** Results of Kendall's Tau ($r_\tau$) correlation analysis between overall UX (OUX) assessment and individual items of SDFS-2. N = 18

| Dispositional flow state scale item | $r_\tau$ | p |
|---|---|---|
| I feel frustrated | −.740 | <.001 |
| The experience is extremely rewarding | .570 | <.01 |
| The way time passes seems to be different from normal | .500 | <.01 |
| I have a feeling of total control | .490 | <.05 |
| I do things spontaneously and automatically without having to think | .460 | <.05 |
| I feel I am competent enough to meet the high demands of the situation | .420 | <.05 |
| I am completely focused on the task at hand | .290 | n.s. |
| I am not worried about what others may be thinking of me | .260 | n.s. |
| I have a good idea while I am performing about how well I am doing | .100 | n.s. |
| I have a strong sense of what I want to do | .090 | n.s. |

**Intrinsic motivation.** OUX had a significant correlation with both items that measure intrinsic motivation in relation to the assessed GUI designer, namely *I enjoy using Vaadin Designer very much* and *I am pretty skilled in using Vaadin Designer* (Table 7). The first mentioned measure interest/enjoyment while the second measures perceived competence, both related to the tool under evaluation. Other items had no significant correlations with OUX.

**Flow state experience.** Regarding flow state experience, OUX correlated with the following items. *I feel frustrated, the experience is extremely rewarding, the way time passes seems to be different from normal, I have a feeling of total control, I do things spontaneously and automatically without having to think, and I feel I am competent enough to meet the high demands of the situation* (Table 8). Thus, there was a significant correlation between OUX and perceived competence item both in IMI and SDFS-2 as well as between OUX and enjoyment in IMI and autotelic experience in SDFS-2. These findings are in line with our previous results considering integrated development environments [26]; perceived competence and items assessing enjoyment were correlated in that study too.

### 4.3 Responses to Open-Ended Questions

Respondents considered the GUI developer makes the GUI creation process faster compared to the traditional method. They also liked that the GUI developer enables rapid feedback gathering on the actual working UI. They desired for full support on drag and drop feature in that the whole UI could be created simply by placing components on screen. Moreover, they asked for proper support for web UIs and responsive design and that the GUI designer would create proper code based on the UI design on selected programming language instead of HTML. Ideally, the system should also offer support for user involvement in the UI design process.

## 5    Discussion

### 5.1    Research Question Revisited

This paper addressed the following research question:

> "What kind of relation does developer experience and the ability of Vaadin designer to fulfill developers' needs have with flow state experience and intrinsic motivation?"

We addressed the research question first in terms of scale items' ability to differentiate between respondent groups with low and high overall UX assessment (OUX_bad and OUX_good), respectively. The null hypothesis was rejected for flow state experience scale item "*I do things spontaneously and automatically without having to think*", the additional item "*I feel frustrated*", and intrinsic motivation inventory items "*I enjoy using Vaadin designer very much*", and "*I am pretty skilled in using Vaadin Designer*" which means that on these items, there is statistically significant difference between responses of those developers assessing OUX good (OUX_good) and those that assess it bad (OUX_bad). Second, we addressed the research question with a correlation analysis. The same IMI scale items resulted from both analyses: "*I enjoy using Vaadin designer very much*", and "*I am pretty skilled in using Vaadin Designer*" correlated with OUX assessment and could differentiate between OUX_bad and OUX_good. This result is in line with our previous finding: intrinsic motivation was a significant predictor of DX in [26]. A number of flow state scale items were correlated with OUX, including the two items that were able to differentiate between OUX_good and OUX_bad. Mann-Whitney U test is more powerful than correlation analysis and thus it is expected that the correlation analysis includes the results of the test.

### 5.2    Discussion on Related Research

We got similar results in two previous studies. In our study with integrated development environments, hedonic quality was on the borderline of being significant predictor of DX (p = .05) while DX could not be predicted from pragmatic or generic quality [26]. Moreover, in a study on work-related systems [27], we found that rather than the system being professional, respondents appreciated that the system made them feel professional about themselves. Similarly, in this study, system being creative was not associated with DX while the system making the developer feel creative was. In fact, many of the DEXI scale items measuring hedonic quality address the emotion the system evokes in the respondent rather than qualities of the system (motivating, promotes creativity, increases respect, and brings me closer to others). Furthermore, of word pairs measuring pragmatic quality, simple-complicated has been difficult to interpret in work-related context and it does not correlate significantly with DX in this study. Our explanation is that simple systems generally cannot address all the complexity many work-related activities require. For instance, software development has often been described as complex whereas constructing physical buildings is only complicated [3]. Similarly, it is not straightforward to interpret the word pair 'technical–human' of AttrakDiff [15] in development context which is both technical and human.

'Limited–extensive' and 'informative–uninformative' were important for DX considering IDEs [26] while they were uncorrelated with DX in this study. Our explanation is that IDEs unlike GUI designers need to be extensive because software systems often are unique and base on new technologies and their combinations whereas GUIs often are conventional and base on design conventions while more interesting solutions are hidden from the user beneath the presentation layer. Moreover IDEs are large development environments whereas GUI designers are inherently much more limited systems.

Research on GUI designers and GUI design tools is scarce. There are papers on developed designs on new GUI tools but research on their usage on this century seems to be nonexistent. To our knowledge, Myers [31] is still the most extensive article on the topic. There was a workshop on "The Future of User Interface Design Tools" in CHI conference in 2005 [32] but the extended abstract nor the few citing papers do not

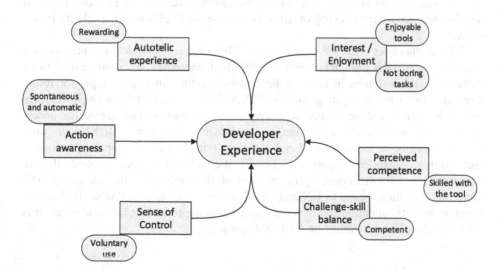

**Fig. 2.** Most relevant factors of intrinsic motivation and flow state experience to developer experience.

contain articles on GUI designers or developer work on GUI creation. Also research on developer experience is still scarce.

Figure 2 summarizes our statistical test results both from the study on GUI designers presented in this paper and on IDEs presented in [26]. Based on these studies, the most relevant factors of flow state experience and intrinsic motivation are enjoyment and reward the work offers.

Sense of control was a significant predictor of DX in [26]. Perceived competence and challenge-skill balance help the developer to manage with demanding tasks while working spontaneously and automatic without having to think is often understood as working under flow state experience. These are commonly mentioned motivation factors in related research [1] and our research connects them with development tools and developer experience of those tools. Advanced technologies motivate developers in their work [1] and development tools are often intertwined with utilized technologies.

## 6   Limitations and Future Work

The most obvious threat to validity is arguably the small respondent number, 18 software specialists. This is particularly critical for correlation analysis, especially considering the large number of connected variables. Small sample size can cause fluctuation in correlation values which makes the analysis less powerful and thus reduces the likelihood of reflecting a true effect. It also prevented us from using more powerful methods. For Mann-Whitney U test the respondent number is sufficient although the test would have benefitted from a larger sample size.

Further studies are needed to validate DEXI scale and to gain better understanding on the concept of DX. In addition, the population was diverse which can be seen both strengthening the results but also making the data incoherent. Our results however, are in line with our previous results considering another dataset on DX of integrated development environments [26] which is to increase the likelihood of reliability in this study.

The results cover only one GUI designer. Thus, larger respondent populations and users of several GUI designers ought to be studied. Moreover, to compare the DX of APIs and GUI designers in larger scale remains another interesting topic for future research. In addition, user groups such as UI/UX designers and UI/front-end developers and their needs could be studied separately or in comparison to increase the understanding of how designers and developers can better work together. DEXI scale could also be evaluated in the context of end user development and to compare developers' and end user developers' experiences. Finally, it could be interesting to study if there was a difference between developers' assessment of overall UX score and overall DX score and how those relate to UX and DEXI scales. To conclude, this study does not come without its limitations but it serves as one opening to further DX studies and it is also one of the scarce studies on GUI designer tools.

# 7  Conclusion

This paper presented a survey study on developer experience (DX) of a GUI designer tool. It introduced DEXI scale for assessing DX of development tools. We presented both quantitative and qualitative results on DX, measured with Short AttrakDiff 2 [17], a commonly used UX scale and DEXI scale specifically designed to assess DX. We found a statistically significant difference in responses between those developers who assessed the overall UX of the GUI builder good and those who assessed it bad considering both their flow state experiences and intrinsic motivation. Our results suggest that developer experience can be improved by fostering the developer's interest and enjoyment, offering rewarding experiences, supporting challenge-skill balance and feeling of competence. Finally, supporting action awareness and providing a sense of control are also key factors of good DX. Considering what software developers appreciate in GUI designer tools, we found that making the GUI design process faster and ensuring early feedback on the working version of the GUI under development were especially liked. Finally, the optimal way to create GUIs was often described as having full support on drag and drop and on responsive design, involving the user in the process, and the ability of the GUI designer tool to export the design into specific programming language instead of HTML code.

**Acknowledgment.** I want to thank all the survey respondents for their valuable contribution. I also want to thank Vaadin for making the study possible. I am grateful for my contact person in the company for their help in organizing the survey. This research has been conducted while I was working for Tampere University of Technology, Finland. My research has been supported by TEKES as part of the Need for Speed research program of DIGILE (Finnish Strategic Centre for Science, Technology and Innovation in the field of ICT and digital business).

# References

1. Beecham, S., Baddoo, N., Hall, T., Robinson, H., Sharp, H.: Motivation in software engineering: A systematic literature review. IST **50**, 860–878 (2008)
2. Capretz, L.F., Ahmed, F.: Making sense of software development and personality types. IT professional **12**(1), 6–13 (2010)
3. Coplien, J.O., Bjørnvig, G.: Lean Architecture: For Agile Software Development. Wiley, Hoboken (2011)
4. Csikszentmihalyi, M.: Flow: the psychology of optimal experience, vol. 41. HarperPerennial, New York (1991)
5. Csikszentmihalyi, M., LeFevre, J.: Optimal experience in work and leisure. J. Pers. Soc. Psychol. **56**(5), 815–822 (1989)
6. Csikszentmihalyi, M., Abuhamdeh, S., Nakamura, J.: Flow. In: Elliot, A.: Handbook of Competence and Motivation. The Guilford Press, New York pp. 598–698 (2005)
7. Deci, E., Ryan, R.M.: Self-Determination Theory. Handbook of Theories Of Social Psychology. SAGE, Los Angeles (2012). ISBN 9780857029607
8. Fagerholm, F.: Software developer experience: Case studies in lean-agile and open-source environments. Doctoral Thesis. Series of publications A, report A-2015-7. University of Helsinki (2015). ISBN 978-951-51-1747-2

9. Fagerholm, F., Münch, J.: Developer experience: concept and definition. In: Proceeding International Conference on Software and System Process, pp. 73–77. IEEE Press (2012)

10. Ferreira, J., Sharp, H., Robinson, H.: User experience design and agile development: managing cooperation through articulation work. Softw. Pract. Experience 41(9), 963–974 (2011). Wiley

11. Ferreira, J., Sharp, H., Robinson, H.: Values and assumptions shaping agile development and user experience design in practice. In: Martin, A., Wang, X., Whitworth, E., Sillitti, A. (eds.) XP 2010. LNBIP, vol. 48, pp. 178–183. Springer, Heidelberg (2010)

12. Franca, A.C.C., Gouveia, T.B., Santos, P.C.F., Santana, C.A., da Silva, F.Q.B.: Motivation in software engineering: a systematic review update. In: Proceeding Evaluation and Assessment in Software Engineering (EASE), pp. 154–163 (2011)

13. Gass, O., Meth, H., Maedche, A.: PaaS characteristics for productive software development: an evaluation framework. IEEE Internet Comput. 18(1), 56–64 (2014)

14. Graziotin, D., Wang, X., Abrahamsson, P.: Software developers, moods, emotions, and performance. IEEE Softw. 31(4), 24–27 (2014)

15. Hassenzahl, M.: The interplay of beauty, goodness and usability in interactive products. In: Proceeding HCI. Lawrence Erlbaum Associates, vol. 19, no. 4, pp. 319–349 (2004)

16. Hassenzahl, M.: User experience (UX): towards an experiential perspective on product quality. In: Proceeding of 20th International Conference of the Association Francophone d'Interaction Homme-Machine, pp. 11–15. ACM (2008)

17. Hassenzahl, M., Diefenbach, S., Göritz, A.: Needs, affect, and interactive products–facets of user experience. Interact. Comput. 22(5), 353–362 (2010)

18. Hassenzahl, M., Tractinsky, N.: User experience - a research agenda. Behav. Inf. Technol 25 (2), 91–97 (2006)

19. ISO 9241. Ergonomic requirements for office work with visual display terminals (VDTs) – Part 11: Guidance on usability. International Organization for Standardisation, Genève (1998)

20. Jackson, S.A., Martin, A.J., Eklund, R.C.: Long and short measures of flow: the construct validity of the FSS-2, DFS-2, and new brief counterparts. JSEP 30(5), 561 (2008)

21. Khan, I.A., Brinkman, W.-P., Hierons, R.M.: Do moods affect programmers' debug performance? Cogn. Technol. Work 13(4), 245–258 (2011)

22. Kuusinen, K.: BoB - A framework for organizing within-iteration UX work in agile development. In: Cockton, G., Larusdottir, M.K., Gregory, P., Cajander, Å. (eds) Integrating User Centred Design in Agile Development

23. Kuusinen, K.: Integrating UX work in agile enterprise software development. Doctoral thesis, Publication 1339, Tampere University of Technology (2015)

24. Kuusinen, K., Mikkonen, T.: On designing UX for mobile enterprise apps. In: Proceeding Software Engineering and Advanced Applications (SEAA) 2014, pp. 221–228 (2015)

25. Kuusinen, K., Mikkonen, T., Pakarinen, S.: Agile user experience development in a large software organization: good expertise but limited impact. In: Winckler, M., Forbrig, P., Bernhaupt, R. (eds.) HCSE 2012. LNCS, vol. 7623, pp. 94–111. Springer, Heidelberg (2012)

26. Kuusinen, K., Petrie, H., Fagerholm, F., Mikkonen, T.: Flow, intrinsic motivation, and developer experience in software engineering. In: Sharp, H., Hall, T. (eds.) XP 2016. LNBIP, vol. 251, pp. 104–117. Springer, Heidelberg (2016)

27. Kuusinen, K., Väätäjä, H., Mikkonen, T., Väänänen, K.: Towards understanding how agile teams predict user experience. In: Cockton, G., Larusdottir, M.K., Gregory, P., Cajander, Å.: (eds) Integrating User Centred Design in Agile Development

28. Lallemand, C., Gronier, G., Koenig, V.: User experience: a concept without consensus? Exploring practitioners' perspectives through an international survey. Comput. Hum. Behav. **43**, 35–48 (2015)

29. Law, E., Roto, V., Hassenzahl, M., Vermeeren, A., Kort, J.: Understanding, scoping and defining user experience: a survey approach. In: Proceeding of CHI 2009, pp. 719–728 ACM (2009)

30. McAuley, E., Duncan, T., Tammen, V.V.: Psychometric properties of the Intrinsic Motivation Inventory in a competitive sport setting: a confirmatory factor analysis. Res. Q. Exerc. Sport **60**, 48–58 (1989)

31. Myers, B., Hudson, S.E., Pausch, R.: Past, present, and future of user interface software tools. ACM Trans. Comput.-Hum. Interact. (TOCHI) **7**(1), 3–28 (2000)

32. Olsen Jr., D.R., Klemmer, S.R.: The future of user interface design tools. In: CHI 2005 Extended Abstracts on Human Factors in Computing Systems, pp. 2134–2135. ACM (2005)

33. Reichheld, F.F.: The one number you need to grow. Harvard Bus. Rev. **81**(12), 46–55 (2003)

34. Ryan, R.M.: Control and information in the intrapersonal sphere: an extension of cognitive evaluation theory. J. Pers. Soc. Psychol. **43**, 450–461 (1982)

35. Sharp, H., Baddoo, N., Beecham, S., Hall, T., Robinson, H.: Models of motivation in software engineering. Inf. Softw. Technol. **51**(1), 219–233 (2009)

36. Shaw, T.: The emotions of systems developers: an empirical study of affective events theory. In: Proceeding Computer Personnel Research: Careers, Culture, and Ethics in a Networked Environment, SIGMIS CPR 2004, pp. 124–126. ACM (2004)

37. Sundberg, H.-R.: The importance of user experience related factors in new product development – Comparing the views of designers and users of industrial products. In: 23rd Nordic Academy of Management Conference, 12–14 August 2015, Copenhagen, Denmark (2015)

38. World Health Organization, Informed consent form template for qualitative studies. http://www.who.int/rpc/research_ethics/informed_consent/enTools

# A Conceptual UX-Aware Model of Requirements

Pariya Kashfi[1,2(✉)], Robert Feldt[1,2,3], Agneta Nilsson[1,2],
and Richard Berntsson Svensson[3]

[1] Software Engineering Division, Department of Computer Science and Engineering,
Chalmers University of Technology, Gothenburg, Sweden
{robert.feldt,agneta.nilsson}@chalmers.se
[2] Gothenburg University, Gothenburg, Sweden
pariya.kashfi@chalmers.se
[3] Software Engineering Research Lab, School of Computing,
Blekinge Institute of Technology, Karlskrona, Sweden
{robert.feldt,richard.berntsson.svensson}@bth.se

**Abstract.** User eXperience (UX) is becoming increasingly important
for success of software products. Yet, many companies still face various
challenges in their work with UX. Part of these challenges relate to inadequate knowledge and awareness of UX and that current UX models are
commonly not practical nor well integrated into existing Software Engineering (SE) models and concepts. Therefore, we present a conceptual
UX-aware model of requirements for software development practitioners.
This layered model shows the interrelation between UX and functional
and quality requirements. The model is developed based on current models of UX and software quality characteristics. Through the model we
highlight the main differences between various requirement types in particular essentially subjective and accidentally subjective quality requirements. We also present the result of an initial validation of the model
through interviews with 12 practitioners and researchers. Our results
show that the model can raise practitioners' knowledge and awareness
of UX in particular in relation to requirement and testing activities. It
can also facilitate UX-related communication among stakeholders with
different backgrounds.

**Keywords:** Software quality · Quality requirements · User experience ·
Usability · Non-task-related · Hedonic · Non-instrumental

## 1 Introduction

To deliver a system that is consistent and of high quality, practitioners need to
take a large number of quality characteristics into account in development [1].
Some of these characteristics are internal or relate to the development process
and mainly concern developers (e.g., traceability) while others such as performance and usability are critical for end users [2]. Usability is defined as *"the*

© IFIP International Federation for Information Processing 2016
Published by Springer International Publishing Switzerland 2016. All Rights Reserved
C. Bogdan et al. (Eds.): HCSE 2016/HESSD 2016, LNCS 9856, pp. 234–245, 2016.
DOI: 10.1007/978-3-319-44902-9_15

*extent to which a system, product or service can be used by specified users to achieve specified goals with effectiveness, efficiency and satisfaction in a specified context of use.* " [3]. At a more abstract level, the actual experience of the end users with a piece of software also needs to be taken into account. This has led to introducing and studying the concept of User eXperience (UX): *a user's holistic experience and perception of functionalities and quality characteristics of a piece of software* [4]. Researchers emphasize that developers cannot necessarily create the intended experience for the end users (e.g. feeling scared in a video game, or motivated in an e-learning system) merely thorough assuring usability [5].

Nevertheless, studies show that software companies often face various challenges in their work with UX. Among other things, researchers relate these challenges to practitioners' low knowledge and awareness of UX and low industrial impact of UX theories [6,7]. This can be addressed at least partially by developing suitable practical UX models [1,7]. Models can be formal (e.g., analytical) or informal (e.g., conceptual). In this study, we developed a conceptual requirement model that presents the interrelation between UX, functional and quality requirements.

We focused on requirements because they play an important role in effective practice of UX. For instance, Ardito et al. [8] empirically show that if practitioners fail to include UX in requirements documents, UX practices often become neglected in projects [8]. Similarly, Lanzilotti et al. [9] argue that if UX is excluded from requirements documents, often limited or no resources get assigned to UX work.

Our model mainly targets software development practitioners, especially those who have little or no UX background and experience. The main goal of the model is to (i) help increasing practitioners' knowledge and awareness of UX, and (ii) facilitate overcoming current UX-related communication gap among practitioners. We aim to achieve these goals through providing a common terminology that is familiar to and understandable for practitioners with both Software Engineering (SE) and Human Computer Interaction (HCI) backgrounds.

Admittedly, various UX models have been developed so far, mainly in the field of HCI [4,10]. But such models are often too complex and use terminologies less familiar to practitioners with SE or similar technical backgrounds [11]. In addition, these models do not clearly present the interrelation between UX and other software quality characteristics and their corresponding models (e.g., ISO/IEC 25010). For instance, Hassenzahl [4] discusses how utility (i.e., relevant functionality) and usability contribute to achieving a better UX. However, his model lacks references to other quality characteristics and makes no explicit connection to other software quality models or standards. Through mapping UX models and concepts to models and standards in SE and using similar terminologies as them, we can facilitate a better understanding of UX among practitioners with more technical backgrounds.

In the field of SE as well, there have been efforts to model the concept of UX as an emerging software quality characteristic. Some researchers have focused on extending ISO/IEC standards on software quality models to incorporate UX [12]. In ISO/IEC 25010, concepts related to UX are included in the definition of *Quality in Use* (QiU): *"the degree to which a product or system can be used by specific users to meet their needs to achieve specific goals with effectiveness, efficiency, freedom from risk and satisfaction in specific contexts of use."* Similar to UX, QiU also emphasizes users' personal (aka. non-task-related) needs and emotional reactions, and includes 'pleasure' (i.e., an emotional consequence of interacting with a piece of software) as a quality characteristic. In ISO/IEC 25010, usability is a part of *Product Quality* (PQ) model. This model includes properties of the software product and computer system that determine the quality of the product in particular contexts of use. According to this standard, PQ affects QiU, i.e., the experience of users.

Both Hasssenzahl's model of UX [4] and ISO/IEC 25010 software quality model [2] are well established in HCI and SE communities respectively. Therefore, our model is inspired by these two models. Our model presents a categorization of quality requirements based on whether they can be measured objectively or not. To the best of our knowledge, current requirements literature does not include such a categorization. Our model aims to be a descriptive, simple, practical, and actionable model for practitioners rather than a contribution to UX models and theories.

This paper presents our model and the results of its initial validation through interviews with researchers and practitioners. Section 2 describes our methodology. Section 3 presents the model and our analysis of the interview data. Section 4 includes the discussion and ends with our conclusion and suggestions for future research.

## 2   Research Approach

Our model was developed in close collaboration with industry. We followed the steps suggested by Gorschek et. al. [13] in their *technology transfer model*:

- **problem issue in industry:** as elaborated in Sect. 1, we were motivated by previous empirical findings on challenges with UX work in software industry; and that many of these challenges relate to practitioners' lack of knowledge and awareness of UX.
- **study state of the art and problem formulation:** the model was developed based on ample literature study on UX and software quality characteristics. Two main models that inspired our work are Hassenzahl's UX model [4] and the most recent ISO/IEC standard on software quality [2].
- **candidate solution:** in a series of workshops, the authors developed and refined a UX-aware model of requirements.
- **validation in academia:** validation in academia was performed through interviews with four researchers. Two of the researchers have a SE background and the other two a HCI background with focus on UX.
- **static validation in industry:** for initial industrial (i.e., static) validation in industry, we interviewed eight practitioners with different backgrounds, from four companies.

We selected our industrial interviewees based on their backgrounds and roles in the companies. Four of them represent technical roles (e.g., developers and management with technical background) and four represent design roles (e.g., interaction designers and management with design background). This served to validate the model from two different perspectives: SE and HCI. When quoting the interviewees, we did not include their role titles since we did not see a noticeable difference among the views in relation to the roles. Instead, to emphasize the views in relation to the two communities that our model targets, the quotes are marked with either SE or UX.

The interviews were performed individually, face-to-face, and lasted between 30 to 60 min. We chose semi-structured interviews [14] to collect more of the interviewees' viewpoints and reflections. For this purpose, an interview guide was developed that included five main questions about correctness and understandability of the model (e.g. are the definitions provided by the model clear? how do they relate to your understanding of these concepts?)

In our study, we also paid attention to validity threats [14]. To increase construct validity (i) we minimized selection bias by selecting the subjects based on their role and experience, and (ii) we minimized the influence of researcher's presence on the behavior and response of the subjects by guaranteeing the confidentiality of the data. To increase internal validity, we recorded the interviews in audio format, and in three cases in form of extensive notes. To increase external validity, we sampled a number of different organizations in different industrial domains. However, since the interviews are just a sample they should be interpreted with some caution.

## 3 Results and Analysis

As Fig. 1 depicts, our model introduces the concept of *UX requirements* and puts it in relation to two other requirement types: *objective Quality Requirements* (objective QRs) and Functional Requirements (FRs). The model also includes definitions of these different requirement types. UX requirements cover aspects such as usability, usefulness, emotions, aesthetics, motivations, and values. For instance, 'the end user shall feel in control' (emotions), 'the system shall have a minimalistic design' (aesthetics), 'the system shall facilitate getting quick access to trendy news' (motivations), 'the system shall advocate recycling' (values).

Our model is presented using a reverse pyramid to emphasize that higher layers emerge from and depend on requirements below. For example, an objective QR that describes performance needs to be stated in relation to some (or sets of) specific functions or features on which the performance is to be measured. Thus, it assumes some FRs have already been (or at least could have been) established. This is why QRs are often known to be *cross-cutting*. Similarly, a user's perception of the software (i.e., UX) can be constrained by UX requirements but implies some FRs or objective QRs that the perception is based on. UX literature emphasizes this by highlighting the emergent nature of UX [4]. We stress that the use of layers does not mean one should first consider or implement the lower levels of requirements. Also, the size of the areas do not reflect the quantity or significance of different requirement types.

In our model, we divide QRs into two categories of objective and subjective. We emphasize that both FRs and objective QRs can be evaluated objectively (i.e. measured/tested) without reference to a specific end user. On the contrary, a group of requirements are subjective and should be singled out among the QRs. Since these requirements always involve *users' subjective perception*, we call them UX requirements. We note that in practice, objective QRs often can also involve subjectivity since it is not cost-effective to specify them to a degree that they are fully objectively measurable. This means that the subjectivity of these requirements is *accidental*[1]. On the other hand, UX heavily relies on human perception and is essentially subjective [4].

The role of *human perception* (and therefore subjectivity) increases as we move upwards in the model. For instance, a user may perceive particular features of software to be secure while another user may perceive the same features as insecure. In addition, the level of *abstraction* typically increases as we move upwards in the model. For instance 'shall evoke a sense of trust' is a more abstract concept compared to 'shall be secure' (objective QR) or 'shall have a log-in function' (FR).

UX of a piece of software, among other aspects, emerges from underlying functionalities and objective quality characteristics (i.e., objective QRs), and the user's perception of them in each certain situation [4]. A designer can select a group of specific functionalities to increase the likelihood of creating a particular experience for the end users [4]. To emphasize the emergent nature of UX, we used a reverse pyramid in our model. Putting UX requirements on top highlights that UX emerges from the underlying functionalities and quality characteristics. For instance, in order to be trustworthy (abstract) the system provides a good overview of the functions available (concrete). This resembles the cross-cutting nature of other quality characteristics. Researchers emphasize that although practitioners may manipulate UX through these underlying elements, they still cannot guarantee a certain overall UX [4,10].

The model was validated through interviews with eight software practitioners and four researchers. All of the interviewees were positive regarding clarity and understandability of the model. For instance, one of the interviewees said: *"My first impression of the model is that it is clear and easy to read. It is easy to understand what UX is and what extra 'things' are needed to make more UX-aware decisions."* (SE). The participants had some suggestions regarding the terms and shapes used in the model. These suggestions were taken into account when revising the model to the version we have presented above. From the interviewees' perspective, the main potential use and benefits of the model are as follows:

---

[1] The terms essential and accidental were originally used by Aristotle, and later adopted in the context of software development by Brooks [15] in his classification of complexities in software engineering.

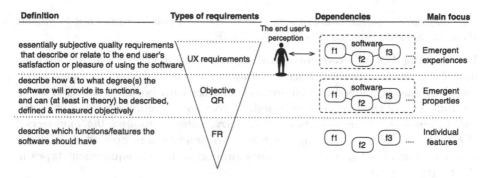

**Fig. 1.** A UX-aware model of requirements

**Raising knowledge and awareness of various requirement types.** The interviewees stated that the model can raise knowledge and awareness of the role of all requirement types in achieving the intended UX. Pointing to the two bottom layers of the model, one of the interviewees stated: *"You can define something that looks really cool [...] but to consistently deliver a good UX, we need to go the whole way down."* (HCI). Moreover, the interviewees generally agreed that to achieve the intended UX, FRs and objective QRs are important but not enough. In their view, the model clearly presents this matter. In addition, according to the practitioners, the two communities still disagree on the importance of viewing quality characteristics from not only the system perspective but also the end users' perspective. Regarding this a designer stated: *"We have quite an argument with technical people because [in our view] the perceived performance is more important than the actual performance, usually."* (HCI). Some practitioners with SE background believed UX requirements can be treated the same as other types of requirements: *"The practical application of discussions, elicitation, specifying UX goals and UX requirements, all of this is something we already do for any other goals and requirements."* (SE). This contradicts the view of practitioners with UX knowledge: *"[SE people] go through emotions and have it in their check lists, but it is not at the center of their effort [...]. That's perfectly fine when you work with the functional level, but there are tons of other complexities that you need to consider."* (HCI).

**Raising knowledge and awareness of UX-aware testing.** The concept of testing and its challenges was repeatedly brought up by the interviewees. They generally agreed that quantitative methods are insufficient for UX evaluation. For instance, one reason is that while they can identify the problem areas in design, they cannot explain why these problems exist. They, therefore, cannot sufficiently inform the re-design of the software. Nevertheless, as the interviewees highlighted, the field of SE puts more emphasis on quantitative methods. Regarding this, one interviewee stated: *"I think we have a problem that we have not addressed yet. When we write our requirements specifications we think all requirements should be testable either by a unit test, product test or system test;*

*and subjective requirements are very hard to test, so I think we tend not to include them in our requirements specifications."* (SE).

**Facilitating UX-related communication.** The interviewees highlighted the model can improve communication among stakeholders through a common terminology that is understandable for stakeholders with both SE and HCI backgrounds. One of the interviewees stated: *"a common terminology among the staff will improve the communication, particularly between us and the managers."* (HCI). In addition, presenting the model to practitioners opened up a series of discussions about how the companies support different requirement types in their current practices.

## 4  Discussion

Current software quality and UX models are evidently not practical or actionable [6,7,16]. Therefore, we saw a need for a practical model that can summarize and clarify the current UX models and connect them to software quality models. Requirements play an important role in effective UX work [8,9]; thus our model focuses on requirements.

In order to overcome the shortcomings of the current UX models, our model clearly situates UX requirements in relation to FRs and other QRs. The model is also simple, clear, and understandable for practitioners with both SE and HCI background as our initial validation shows.

The model also sheds light on UX-aware elicitation and documentation of requirements. By introducing the notion of *UX requirements* the model explicitly groups those quality requirements that are essentially subjective and relate to the end users' perception. We performed an initial validation of the model through interviews with researchers and practitioners. The validation confirmed correctness of the model, and that it can facilitate enhancing knowledge and awareness of UX and UX-related communication among practitioners.

In contrast to the approach taken in ISO/IEC 25010, we separated UX requirements from other QRs in our model. The reason was to emphasize that UX requirements are *essentially subjective*, and separate them from *accidentally subjective* quality requirements, what we call objective QRs. By doing so, the model can extend and complement the current models of UX and software quality. We have summarized our view on subjectivity and objectivity of different requirement types in Table 1.

FRs are objective by nature: we can objectively evaluate whether a piece of software satisfies a specific FR or not. This is a binary evaluation: either a functionality is implemented in the software or not. On the contrary, QRs (including usability) are known to be more difficult to evaluate. This has led practitioners to often evaluate QRs subjectively and based on their personal judgment [1]. Still, this does not mean that these requirements are not possible to be evaluated objectively. Therefore, in our model we call them 'objective QRs' and emphasize that they are essentially objective but still in practice accidentally subjective.

**Table 1.** Differences in subjectivity and objectivity of various requirement types, and how they are treated in practice

| | Functional requirements | UX requirements | Objective quality requirements |
|---|---|---|---|
| Essentially objective | Yes | | Yes |
| Essentially subjective | | Yes | |
| Accidentally subjective | | | Yes |
| Possible to evaluate objectively | Yes | | Yes |
| Objectively evaluated in practice | Yes | | Sometimes |
| Subjectively evaluated in practice | | Yes | Sometimes |

If a requirement is subjective by accident, this means that the subjectivity is not a result of its nature but other reasons such as lack of knowledge and awareness, tools and methods, or costs. In theory, it is possible and even recommended to evaluate these requirements objectively. Accidental subjectivity can be overcome as the field of requirements engineering matures. For instance, by developing more tools and methods to facilitate measuring these requirements objectively (e.g. [17,18]).

In contrast to FRs and objective QRs, UX requirements are essentially subjective. UX heavily relies on human perception and is therefore by nature subjective. Even in cases when UX is measured, the measurement is an approximation of the real experience of users. Especially since the phenomenon of experience is prone to fabrication and fading since it heavily relies on human memory [21]. Still, practitioners can approximately measure UX through gathering users' opinions, for instance using questionnaires (e.g. AttrakDiff, Self-assessment Manikin, the affect gird [20]). For an overview of various approaches to UX evaluation and measurement, we can refer to Law et al. [21] and Zimmermann [20].

When measuring UX, statistically significant number of heterogeneous users need to be involved to guarantee reliable results [21]. In contrast to UX requirements, practitioners can test objective QRs even without involving users (e.g., automatically). For instance, practitioners can automatically compute usability measures by running a user interface specification through some program [22]. UX requirements also differ from objective QRs in that their metrics and measures are not agreed upon or standardized yet; that makes their measurement even more difficult. On the other hand, for objective QRs (including usability) practitioners have access to relevant standards, e.g., ISO/IEC 9126 [23].

**Table 2.** Characteristics of UX and their implication for practice of software development and future research, especially concerning UX requirements

| Characteristics of UX | Implications for practice | Open research problems |
|---|---|---|
| *Abstract and emergent:* experience emerges from underlying functionalities and objective quality characteristics | – practitioner need to identify UX requirements and refine them into concrete FRs and objective QRs (sample method in [19]) <br><br> – practitioners need to evaluate UX both holistically and via evaluating its underling elements, i.e., users' perception of objective QRs and FRs (for a summary of evaluation methods see [20]) | – UX requirements are difficult to refine and translate into design solutions and more concrete requirements; there are limited guidelines to support that <br><br> – still, there is no standardized and agreed upon set of UX measures and metrics <br><br> – there are limited guidelines on how to choose suitable UX measures and metrics and interpret their findings to improve the overall UX |
| *Essentially subjective:* experience heavily relies on human perception therefore is essentially subjective | – qualitative user opinion should be used in evaluations (for a summary of evaluation methods see [20]) <br><br> – when measuring UX, practitioners need to involve statistically significant number of users to guarantee reliable data (for more information see [20, 21]) | – there are limited theories on the relationship between UX and memory |
| *Temporal:* experience can change over time | practitioners need to assure that the relation between time and experience is reflected in requirements testing activities | – current body of knowledge includes limited theories on the relationship between UX and time <br><br> – practitioners have limited access to tools and methods to handle temporality in evaluation |

The *emergent nature of UX* can partially explain why practitioners and researchers still do not agree on UX metrics and measures. For example, Law et al. [21] empirically show that often practitioners and researchers have two different attitudes towards UX measurement. They are either strongly convinced that it is "necessary, plausible and feasible" to measure UX through its finest underlying elements, or doubtful about the "necessity and utility" of measuring these elements. Law et al. further discuss that practitioners do not still have enough guidelines on how to choose suitable UX measures and metrics to measure these elements or to interpret the findings to better re-design the software [21].

We identified at least one more issue that relates to the abstract and emergent nature of UX: practitioners still do not have enough support for refining UX requirements to more concrete design solutions and requirements (i.e. FRs and objective QRs) [7]. One of the few existing methods for a UX-aware requirements work is developed by Hassenzahl [19]. Hassenzahl [19] emphasizes that, in their work with UX, practitioners should refine the abstract requirements into functionalities and concrete quality characteristics. He further emphasizes that this should be performed in close collaboration with the end users' representatives.

*Temporality* is another important characteristic of UX that differentiates UX requirements from objective QRs. Temporality implies that experience of a user with a piece of software can change over time [4]. Researchers therefore recommend practitioners to take the whole spectrum of interaction into account when designing or evaluating the UX of a piece of software [24]. Practitioners should pay attention to the users' experiences not only during, but also before and after the interaction [4,10]. Thus, UX requirements should also reflect the spectrum of experience. For instance, a UX requirement may concern users' first impression: *"average score of responses to questionnaire questions on initial impression and satisfaction should be higher than X."* Another requirement may concern users' overall experience: *"average score of responses to questionnaire questions should be higher than X."* In contrary, FRs and objective QRs are not dependent on time. For instance, practitioners get the same results if they repeat measuring performance or security of the software over time (providing that the software and the test context, e.g., CPU load, have not changed). Table 2 summarizes the main characteristics of UX and how they lead to differences between UX and other requirement types.

As a key initial step, to perform UX-aware requirements and evaluation work, practitioners require to understand the differences between UX requirements and objective QRs. But there are still a number of important issues that need attention to and plan for improvements. For instance, to facilitate a *UX-aware requirement elicitation*, practitioners require knowledge and awareness of human psychological needs and their relation to 'experiences'. They need to know what to look for and how to look for it. To facilitate a *UX-aware requirements documentation*, practitioners need to have access to tools, methods and guidelines on how to document and communicate the results of elicitation in form of various UX requirements. In addition, these tools and methods should be integrated into current requirements tools and methods. To facilitate a *UX-aware verification and validation*, practitioners need to have access to suitable tools, methods and guidelines that can help investigating whether these requirements are satisficed or not. Other open research problems concern traceability, conflict resolution, prioritization, and cost-estimation of UX requirements.

To start investigating how to better support UX requirements in practice, we suggest the communities to first investigate current tools, methods and guidelines for supporting usability in the above activities. We do not however claim that current tools, methods and guidelines for supporting usability are established and flawless; for the purpose we suggest here they do not need to be so. Since UX and usability are related, we believe we can get inspired by and learn from usability literature since it is comparatively more mature. Still, we need to pay attention to essential differences between the two concepts.

We hope to have convinced the reader that UX in general, and UX requirements in particular are worth pursuing in software development research and practice. We facilitate this through explicitly separating essentially subjective UX requirements from other requirement types, and raising knowledge and awareness of these requirements. However, as we mentioned, there are still a number of open research questions that the communities need to address. We also hope to have inspired extending current software quality and requirements models and standards to better support the concept of UX. Future research should introduce the model to software development companies, provide even more detailed advice and examples on how to elicit, document, and break down UX requirements and refine them to other more concrete requirement types.

# References

1. Chung, L., do Prado Leite, J.C.S.: On non-functional requirements in software engineering. In: Borgida, A.T., Chaudhri, V.K., Giorgini, P., Yu, E.S. (eds.) Mylopoulos Festschrift. LNCS, vol. 5600, pp. 363–379. Springer, Heidelberg (2009)
2. ISO: ISO 25010: Systems and software engineering - Systems and software Quality Requirements and Evaluation (SQuaRE) - System and software quality models. International Organisation for Standardisation, Geneva, Switzerland (2011)
3. ISO: ISO 9241: Ergonomics of human-system interaction - Part 210: Human-centred design for interactive systems. International Organisation for Standardisation, Geneva, Switzerland (2010)
4. Hassenzahl, M.: The thing and I: understanding the relationship between user and product. In: Blythe, M.A., Monk, A.F., Overbeeke, K., Wright, P.C. (eds.) Funology: from Usability to Enjoyment, pp. 31–42. Kluwer Academic (2003)
5. Hassenzahl, M.: Experience Design: Technology for All the Right Reasons. Morgan & Claypool, San Francisco (2010)
6. Lallemand, C., Koenig, V., Gronier, G.: How relevant is an expert evaluation of user experience based on a psychological needs-driven approach? In: Proceedings of the 8th Nordic Conference on Human-Computer Interaction: Fun, Fast, Foundational (NordiCHI 2014), pp. 11–20. ACM, New York (2014)
7. Kashfi, P., Nilsson, A., Feldt, R.: Integrating user eXperience practices into Software Development Processes: the implication of subjectivity and emergent nature of UX. PeerJ Computer Science (in submission) (2016)

8. Ardito, C., Buono, P., Caivano, D., Costabile, M.F., Lanzilotti, R.: Investigating and promoting UX practice in industry: an experimental study. Int. J. Hum. Comput. Stud. **72**(6), 542–551 (2014)

9. Lanzilotti, R., Costabile, M.F., Ardito, C., Informatica, D., Aldo, B.: Addressing usability and UX in call for tender for IT products. In: Proceedings of the 15h IFIP TC 13 International Conference Human-Computer Interaction (INTERACT 2015), pp. 1–8 (2015)

10. Wright, P., McCarthy, J.: Experience-Centered Design: Designers, Users, and Communities in Dialogue. Synthesis Lectures on Human-Centered Informatics. Morgan & Claypool, San Francisco (2010)

11. Kashfi, P., Nilsson, A., Feldt, R.: Supporting practitioners in prioritizing user experience requirements. In: Proceedings of 3rd International Workshop on Requirements Prioritization for Customer Oriented Software Development: (RePriCo 2012), vol. 19–23 (2012)

12. Bevan, N.: UX, Usability and ISO standards. In: Proceedings of the 26th Annual Conference on Computer Human Interaction (CHI 2008), pp. 1–5. ACM, New York, April 2008

13. Gorschek, T., Wohlin, C., Carre, P., Larsson, S.: A model for technology transfer in practice. IEEE Softw. **23**(6), 88–95 (2006)

14. Runeson, P., Höst, M.: Guidelines for conducting and reporting case study research in software engineering. Empirical Softw. Eng. **14**(2), 131–164 (2008)

15. Brooks, F.P.: No silver bullet essence and accidents of software engineering. Computer **20**(4), 10–19 (1987)

16. Folstad, A.: The relevance of UX models and measures. In: Proceedings of the 1st International Workshop on the Interplay between UX and Software Development (I-UxSED 2010), pp. 8–10 (2010)

17. Gilb, T., Brodie, L.: Competitive Engineering: A Handbook for Systems Engineering Requirements Engineering, and Software Engineering Using Planguage. Elsevier Ltd. (2005)

18. Berntsson Svensson, R., Regnell, B.: A case study evaluation of the guideline-supported QUPER model for elicitation of quality requirements. In: Fricker, S.A., Schneider, K. (eds.) REFSQ 2015. LNCS, vol. 9013, pp. 230–246. Springer, Heidelberg (2015)

19. Hassenzahl, M., Wessler, R., Hamborg, K.C.: Exploring and understanding product qualities that users desire. In: Proceedings of the 5th Annual Conference of the Human-Computer Interaction Group of the British Computer Society (IHM-HCI 2001), pp. 95–96 (2001)

20. Zimmermann, P.G.: Beyond usability-measuring aspects of user experience. Ph.D. dissertation, Swiss Federal Institute of Technology Zurich (2008)

21. Law, E.L.C., van Schaik, P., Roto, V.: Attitudes towards user experience (UX) measurement. Int. J. Hum. Comput. Stud. **72**(6), 526–541 (2014)

22. Nielsen, J.: Usability inspection methods. In: Conference Companion on Human Factors in Computing Systems - CHI 1994, pp. 413–414. ACM Press, New York (1994)

23. ISO: ISO 9126: Software engineering - Product quality - Part 4: Quality in use metrics. International Organisation for Standardisation, Geneva, Switzerland (2004)

24. Wright, P., McCarthy, J., Meekison, L.: Making Sense of Experience In: Blythe, M., Overbeeke, K., Monk, A., Wright, P. (eds.) Funology. Human-Computer Interaction Series, vol. 3, pp. 43–53. Springer, Netherlands (2005)

# Keep the Beat: Audio Guidance for Runner Training

Luca Balvis, Ludovico Boratto, Fabrizio Mulas, Lucio Davide Spano[✉],
Salvatore Carta, and Gianni Fenu

Department of Mathematics and Computer Science, University of Cagliari,
Via Ospedale 72, 09124 Cagliari, Italy
{luca.balvis,ludovico.boratto,fabrizio.mulas,davide.spano,
salvatore,fenu}@unica.it

**Abstract.** Understanding how to map the feedback by fitness apps into
concrete actions during the exercise performance is crucial for their effectiveness, for both inexperienced and advanced users. In this paper we
focus on audio feedback for running, describing a beat-rhythm representation of the target cadence for helping the user in keeping it. We
designed the feedback system in order to balance two conflicting objectives: its effectiveness in helping the user in reaching the training goal
and its intrusiveness with respect to concurrent activities (e.g., listening
to the music). We detail how we track the user's cadence through standard smartphone sensors, how and when we generate the audio messages.
Finally, we discuss the results of a user-study, showing effectiveness with
respect to the adherence to the exercise goal and the overall usability.

**Keywords:** Audio guidance · Beats · Running · Training · Evaluation ·
Fitness

## 1 Introduction

Smartphones have embedded sensors of increasing quality through the years,
which quickly substituted entry-level devices for different tasks, such as e.g. taking pictures, videos, recording audio, browsing the internet. In particular, inertial
sensors (accelerometers, gyroscopes, compass) and GPS receivers constituted the
basis for the entry level activity tracker, which is now represented by different
smartphone apps. The activity tracker applications are now spread also among
the entry-level users, since they are very cheap, if compared with professional
devices and applications.

Opening the market to such kind of users is a big opportunity for fitness
application providers, but it is also a big challenge: the design of dedicated
devices was targeted to professional users, which need many precise measures

© IFIP International Federation for Information Processing 2016
Published by Springer International Publishing Switzerland 2016. All Rights Reserved
C. Bogdan et al. (Eds.): HCSE 2016/HESSD 2016, LNCS 9856, pp. 246–257, 2016.
DOI: 10.1007/978-3-319-44902-9_16

they are able to interpret directly. Many app users are not experts instead, so they would need a more intuitive representation of the tracked data.

If we focus on the information needed *during* the exercise, this is even more difficult: the user not only has to understand what the tracked data means, but she has also to take decisions based on such data for continuing the session. In this paper we consider the running activity as an example of the latter case: while running, the user should keep a target cadence, and smartphone applications help her tracking and reporting its current value. During the training, the application cannot rely on the visual channel, so audio messages are usually preferred. However, many runners are used to listen to the music or other entertainment content that may require the audio channel (e.g., audiobooks). Therefore, it is important for the feedback system to provide the relevant information without prevent the user to carry-out such entertainment activities and taking the complete control of the audio channel [11,13].

Considering the information the system provides to the user, reporting the current cadence is useful, but what if its value is not in line with the target? Entry-level users may have difficulties in mapping the application reported difference between the target and the current cadence into a concrete running action. Professional users have less difficulties in interpreting the values, however they still need to repeatedly check the measures and to take decisions accordingly.

In this paper we describe a generic audio feedback engine for runners, whose architecture allows providing adaptable audio feedback, exploiting the audio channel only when needed. It is possible for designers to control the number and the type of the generated feedback messages, while users may override the notification frequency in order to fine-tune it to their needs. The feedback system relies only on built-in smartphone hardware for tracking the activity. We describe the software component that senses the user's cadence, together with the rule system that decides how and when the application generates the audio messages. We detail how we configured it for providing a beat-rhythm representation of the correct cadence, which helps the user in keeping the target for the current training. In order to keep it unintrusive, the beats are played only if the user is running out of range.

Finally, we provide the results of a user-study having a twofold objective. The first one was to compare the effectiveness of the beat feedback in helping the user in keeping the target pace, comparing it to providing natural language messages. The second goal was to collect a qualitative data on different usability dimensions for the proposed feedback, showing both a very good perceived precision and completeness for provided information.

## 2   Related Work

Mobiles have been used as activity trackers even before they were equipped with inertial sensors [1]. Since then, the tracking techniques have evolved and now it is possible to track the user's steps with a good level of precision using inertial sensors such as accelerometers [12] or gyroscopes [4], which are included in majority of smartphone models nowadays. For tracking the user's cadence, we built our prototype on top of such approaches, as many other commercial apps.

Even though several academic studies have been performed to support users in their running activities, finding applications that work in the real world and have an audio support is rarer. The three platforms that involve most users, i.e., *Endomondo*[1], *Runtastic*[2], and *Nike+*[3], all offer a form of audio support in which it is possible for the user to let the application read statistics when she covered a given distance or a specific amount of time has passed. These statistics involve common information, such as the average pace, speed, calories burned, heartbeat, etc. A form of support that provides the user with indications about the speed is provided by *u4fit* (previously known as Everywhere Run) [6]. Differently from the other applications, it checks the current pace of the user and compares it with the objective she had, and plays an audio support that tells the user to speed up or slow down.

The topic of providing effective audio feedback to users has been investigated under different perspectives in literature, especially considering mobile devices, which are often used while carrying-out different tasks. For this reason, different audio techniques have been developed for helping users in making selections without looking to the mobile screen [15]. Considering the particular application of audio feedback for providing guidance during physical activities, it is possible to find examples for different sports in literature. For instance, Nylander et al. [8] created an audio feedback for guiding the user in reaching the highest point of acceleration just before hitting the ball. Stienstra et al. [10] used a sonification technique for guiding professional skaters with a feedback on their performance in real time.

Considering running applications, we can find examples of auditory feedback in different work in literature. MPTrain [9] includes a set of sensing devices connected to a mobile phone, that are able to sense both the user's pace and physiological parameters, exploiting music for helping the user in achieving her goal. Our work focuses on built-in smartphone hardware and exploits an explicit feedback rather than on an implicit song selection. An evolution of this work, TripleBeat [2], introduced additional features like competition and a visual interface for motivating the user during the exercise.

Song playlists may be used as implicit feedback for helping users in keeping the target cadence. Indeed, music has different effects in the runner's performance, such as the synchronization of the cadence with the song tempo [11] and an overall higher performance and less perceived fatigue [13]. For instance, *RockMyRun*[4] is a commercial running application that selects songs from a playlist according to the user's hear rate, steps or target cadence, in order to increase the motivation and her performance. Even if this has been proven to be an effective support, it has two main drawbacks. Firstly, if the user is not willing to listen to

---

[1] https://www.endomondo.com/.
[2] https://www.runtastic.com/.
[3] https://secure-nikeplus.nike.com/plus/.
[4] http://www.rockmyrun.com/.

the music during the exercise, she cannot receive the application feedback. In addition, it may happen that the user would like to listen to specific song that maybe do not match with the feedback requirements. In contrast, our feedback mechanism exploits the audio channel only when needed and not for the whole duration of the exercise.

PaceGuard [3] exploits a pulse feedback, similar to the one exploited in this paper, played during the whole exercise and adapted to the current user's performance. Differently from PaceGuard, we provide the audio feedback only if the cadence is out of range. In the meantime, other smartphone applications may use the audio channel (e.g., music players, voice calls). Considering smartphone-based applications, the audio feedback has been exploited for providing a remote support for encouraging users during races [14]. RunRight [7] creates a visual representation of the running movement using the acceleration on the vertical and horizontal axis. Similarly to the approach proposed in this paper, the system provides also a metronome for communicating the running cadence to the user, which changed randomly after a predefined amount of time. Our approach combines the information coming from the inertial sensors with the audio feedback for helping the user in reaching the training goal.

## 3   Audio Support

In our work, we considered a scenario where the user should keep a target cadence, which is defined in advance according to the user's training goal (e.g., preparing for a competition) and the intensity not exceeding her capabilities. The target may be selected with the help of a trainer or by the user herself, but the application does not suggest it, since without heart-rate measures it would not be able to determine the correct intensity and this may lead to heart problems.

We designed the audio feedback support considering the trade-off between two aspects: the first one is the need to guide the user and to help her in keeping the correct cadence, while the second one is the intrusiveness of the support. On the one hand, sending messages each time we register a high difference between the current and the expected cadence guarantees the quickest possible user's reaction. On the other hand, if the user has difficulties in keeping the cadence, the feedback would be frustrating and it would take the complete control of the audio channel, preventing the users to perform other entertainment activities while running (e.g., listen to the music, radio or audio books).

Therefore, we designed a support able to adapt its behaviour to the user needs, which is configurable through different parameters, each one having a default value, which may be changed by the user for fine-tuning. The parameter set is the following:

- **Sampling interval** ($i_s$): the frequency for calculating the current cadence. The default value is 1 min.
- **Target cadence** ($k$): the cadence that our user should keep during the current activity (or the current part of it), expressed in terms of steps per minute.

- **Tolerance** ($\epsilon$): the number of steps per sampling interval that can be tolerated if a user is above or under the desired cadence, in order to consider her current cadence as correct. This allows us to define a tolerance range, as $k \pm \epsilon$. The $\epsilon$ default value is 5.
- **Feedback message duration** ($t_f$): the number of seconds the audio message should last. The default value is 15 s.
- **Frequency of positive feedback messages** ($\frac{1}{i_p}$): the number of minutes that should pass between an audio message and the next, when the user's cadence is correct. The default value for $i_p$ is 4 min.
- **Frequency of negative feedback messages** ($\frac{1}{i_n}$): the number of minutes that should pass between an audio message and the next, when the cadence of the user is out of range. The default value for $i_n$ is 1 min.

The audio feedback module contains two main components, separating the cadence tracking from the set of rules for generating the feedback messages:

1. **Cadence analyser.** This component analyses the current cadence of the user, in order to decide if it is correct, high or low.
2. **Feedback manager.** Given the decision of the cadence analyser and the current settings, this component decides whether a feedback message should be sent to the user and, if this is the case, it is responsible for creating it.

In the next sections, we describe in detail the two components.

### 3.1   Cadence Analyser

Given the current cadence of the user, i.e., the number of steps done in the last minute, this component determines if an audio message to support the user should be played, according to the constraints given as input to the application. It tracks the user's cadence exploiting the Step Counter Sensor[5] provided with the default Android SDK, which internally exploits the accelerometers.

The cadence analyser component is a simple state machine, depicted in Fig. 1. It classifies the user's cadence into three classes, corresponding to its internal states:

1. *Correct*, when the user's cadence $v$ is inside the target range $k \pm \epsilon$;
2. *High*, when the user's cadence $v$ is higher than the maximum of the range $k + \epsilon$;
3. *Low*, when the user's cadence $v$ is lower than the minimum of the range $k - \epsilon$;

The state transitions are defined through the value of $\Delta$, which we calculate as follows ($v$ is the current user's cadence)

- if $|k - v| < \epsilon$, then $\Delta = 0$;
- if $v > k + \epsilon$, then $\Delta > 0$;
- if $v > k - \epsilon$, then $\Delta < 0$;

---

[5] http://developer.android.com/guide/topics/sensors/sensors_motion.html.

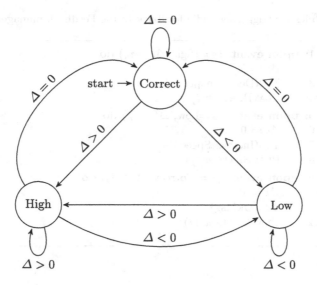

**Fig. 1.** The Pace Analyser state machine

In each state, if $\Delta = 0$ the machine fires a transition towards *Correct*, if $\Delta > 0$ the next state is *High*, otherwise the next state is *Low*.

Besides its internal state, the component exposes a variable $\Delta t$, that tracks how long the machine is in the current state. This variable is increased of $i_s$ each time the machine fires a transition towards the same state and reset to zero each time the transition is towards a different state. The component raises an event each time a transition is fired, passing as arguments the current state $s$ and $\Delta t$.

### 3.2   Feedback Manager

The feedback manager component registers to the events raised by the cadence analyser, and it contains a set of rules for generating the audio feedback. In the current configuration, we included three rules, which we summarise in Table 1.

The first rule (line 1) triggers while the user is running for a long time (longer than $i_n$) at a high cadence ($s$ is *High*). It resets $\Delta t$ to zero, renders a speech message for informing the user that her current cadence is too high, i.e. "Your cadence is too high. Try to follow this rhythm:" (line 3) and generates the beat feedback (line 4). The rules handling the other two cases, respectively low cadence (lines 5–8) and current cadence (lines 9–12) are similar: they render a different message through the text-to-speech, and we consider a different time in the correct case ($i_p$).

As already discussed while introducing the paper, we represent the cadence information as a rhythm, in order to allow the user to synchronize her steps with the beats. The PLAYBEATS procedure generates such feedback on the fly, creating and playing an audio stream containing a number of beat samples equally

**Table 1.** Rules for triggering audio feedback in the Feedback manager module.

---

1: **upon event**  $(s =\text{High}, \Delta t > i_n)$ **do**
2:     $\Delta t := 0$
3:     $\text{Tts}(\text{DecreaseSpeedMsg})$
4:     $\text{PlayBeats}(k, t_f)$
5: **upon event**  $(s =\text{Low}, \Delta t > i_n)$ **do**
6:     $\Delta t := 0$
7:     $\text{Tts}(\text{IncreaseSpeedMsg})$
8:     $\text{PlayBeats}(k, t_f)$
9: **upon event**  $(s = \text{Correct}, \Delta t > i_p)$ **do**
10:     $\Delta t := 0$
11:     $\text{Tts}(\text{OkMsg})$
12:     $\text{PlayBeats}(k, t_f)$

---

distributed in its duration. Such number $n$ is obtained according to two parameters: the target cadence $k$ and feedback message duration $t_f$, as defined in Eq. 1:

$$n = \frac{1}{60} \cdot k \cdot t_f \tag{1}$$

The peak of each beat is positioned exactly in each $n$-th fraction of $t_f$. The duration between two beats is filled with silence. The resulting message contains a simple click with the rhythm to be followed by the user. After $t_f$ seconds (15 by default), the audio channel is released by the feedback manager and it can be used again by other applications (e.g., the music player).

### 3.3   Discussion

We would like to point out here a set of relevant properties of the proposed audio feedback support. The first one is its flexibility: the separation of the two components makes it possible to provide different kinds of messages without changing the cadence tracking algorithm and vice versa. By maintaining the same communication protocol, it would be possible to exploit more sophisticated strategies for deciding if the cadence of our user is correct or not. The second important aspect is the possibility to configure the feedback messages through a set of rules, which may be defined differently by interface designers for increasing the effectiveness of the messages, and obtaining different types of feedback. As an example, we can consider the audio guidance provided by *u4fit* [6]. It exploits text-to-speech messages for informing the user in natural language, providing also quantitative information with messages such as e.g. "You're 10 s per km slower, speed up!". Such messages may be easily generated modifying the rules in Table 1, using $k - v$ as parameter for both the text to speech messages (increase ad decrease) and removing the calls to $\text{PlayBeats}$.

It would be possible to support a completely different feedback mechanism, such as for instance selecting a song from a playlist having a tempo that helps the user in increasing or decreasing her cadence, similarly to *RockMyRun*[6]. According to the difference between the current and the target cadence $(k - v)$, the rules in Table 1 would enqueue a song with a slower, faster or similar tempo for respectively decreasing, increasing and keeping constant the user's cadence.

The rules are also quite straightforward to understand even for users, if represented in natural language. This is very important, in order to enable the user's control over the feedback mechanism: if users have means for inspecting the rules and modify them (through guided procedures), it is more likely that they will be able to get the feedback they need. However, we are also aware that the large majority of the users are not willing to configure such aspects, therefore a good default mechanism is still crucial.

Finally, the parameters used for tuning the feedback and the run-time generation of the messages allows to exploit them in complex workouts, composed by different phases where the user should keep different cadences, or containing an adaptation of the target according to the current user's performance.

## 4   Evaluation

A user test has been carried out in order to evaluate the ability of the auditory support to guide the users in keeping a constant cadence during the workout, while maintaining the feedback unintrusive. Therefore, as baseline approach for providing feedback, we selected the approach among the currently available applications that we considered the most informative while keeping an unintrusive approach, which is the one used by *u4fit*. It exploits text-to-speech messages for informing the user in natural language, providing also quantitative information with messages such as e.g. "You're 10 s per km slower, speed up!".

It is worth pointing out that the experiment setting is different from the studies by Terry et al. [11] and by Waterhouse et al. [13], since in these studies the music stimulus was available during the whole exercise, causing the reported synchronization effect. Instead, we provide feedback messages (either in natural language or through the beats), only when the user is out of range or, if the user is in range, we provide confirmation feedback at regular time intervals. We study the effectiveness of two different feedback types in this context.

Besides the comparative study, we included in the evaluation a set of qualitative aspects for understanding the overall user experience with the proposed support, in order to assess whether unintrusive feedback techniques are acceptable for users.

### 4.1   Test Design

In order to perform the comparison between the two feedback types, we created two different prototypes, one providing feedback through voice ($V$) and one

---

[6] http://www.rockmyrun.com/.

through the beats $(B)$. In the $V$ condition we configured the rules for obtaining the feedback used in *u4fit*, while in the $B$ condition we used the rules described in this paper, with the default values for the parameters.

We recruited the participants among the students of the University of Cagliari, through both board notices and social networks, asking for people already following a training programme in running (at any level). Before starting the test, each user filled a demographic questionnaire and read a description of the experiment aim and organization. We explained them that the goal of the test was to evaluate the effectiveness of two types of feedback for helping them in keeping a constant cadence during the workout.

After that, each user started with a calibration phase, where we asked them to run at a sustainable cadence. We measured the user's cadence during a workout without providing any feedback and, in order to set a target speed that would be sustainable for him/her, we took the median value of the session. The cadence was measured using the same step-counter included in the two prototypes.

For the comparison phase we used a within-subject design: each user tried both prototypes during two different workouts. In order to avoid the carry-over effect, half of the users started from condition $V$ and half of them started from condition $B$. In both conditions we set the same target cadence, which we obtained during the calibration.

During the workout, the application logged the current cadence, expressed in number of steps per minute. With this data we were able to calculate the difference between the target and the current cadence for each minute of the workout, whose duration was fixed to 20 min.

At the end of each workout condition, we requested them to rate the following aspects of the audio feedback, in a 1 to 7 Likert scale (1 strongly disagree, 7 strongly agree). We also report the question asked:

- **Usefulness:** Please rate how useful the audio feedback was (1 useless, 7 very useful);
- **Timeliness:** Please rate how timely the audio feedback was (1 useless, 7 very useful);
- **Completeness:** I had all the information I needed.
- **Effort:** I did not have to reason on the feedback information in order to understand what it meant.
- **Satisfaction:** I was satisfied by the provided information.
- **Precision:** The provided information was precise.

In addition, we included an open-ended question for collecting suggestions and/or observations on the audio feedback.

### 4.2    Test Results

Twelve persons participated to the test, nine males and three females, their age ranged from 23 to 31 years old ($\bar{x} = 27.33$, $s = 2.46$). Most users have an average experience with running: three of them have a training once a month, one once every two weeks, two once a week, five twice a week and one once every two days. The experience with apps for running was quite low: half of them never used them, two use it once every ten trainings, while four use apps during every session. Instead, the experience with smartphone is high for all users, all of them use apps more than once a day.

In order to evaluate the effectiveness of the two designs, we measured how good it would be to fit the recorded cadence of the user during each session with the constant value obtained from the calibration phase. In order to measure the fitting quality we used the root-mean-square error (RMSE), defined in Eq. 2 as the standard deviation of the difference between the target cadence $c$ and the actual user's cadence $p_t$ at minute $t$ ($n$ is the duration in minutes of the workout).

$$RMSE = \sqrt{\frac{\sum_{t=1}^{n}(c - p_t)^2}{n}} \tag{2}$$

We registered a higher value of the RMSE in the vocal condition ($\bar{x}_V = 4.84$, $s_V = 3.79$), while in the beat condition we registered both a lower central and spread values ($\bar{x}_B = 2.33$, $s_B = 0.50$). The paired t-test highlighted a significant difference between the two means ($t(11) = 2.23$, $p < 0.05$), and the 95 % confidence interval of such difference is $2.50 \pm 2.48$.

This shows that the beat feedback is more effective for users and that they are able to better control their cadence while running also in the case feedback is provided only when they are out of range. The users were able to synchronize their cadence with the beats even if the stimulus was not continuous during the whole exercise.

The results of the qualitative assessment are shown in Fig. 2. The boxplot shows that the ratings expressed for the beats version are consistently higher than those for the voice version. In particular, we found a significant difference for the usefulness ($t(11) = 2.24$, $p < 0.05$, $CI = [0.02; 2.15]$) and a practical significance for the precision ($t(11) = 1.98$. $p < 0.07$, $CI = [-0.13; 2.48]$). It is also important to notice that the timeliness of the feedback received good ratings and there is no perceived difference between the two conditions (as expected, since the Cadence Analyser had the same settings in both cases).

In the open ended questions, the users asked for more feedback when their cadence was in line with the target in both versions. Increasing the number of audio messages is obviously possible, but we should find a good balance between this need and the usage of the audio channel for e.g., listening to the music. Providing too many messages may be annoying in that case. One of the users suggested to increase the number of messages through the time, especially at the end of the training, which would be easily supported with our engine.

Considering the vocal message condition, the users highlighted in the comments some difficulties in understanding how much they should increase or decrease their speed. Once the message communicated that the cadence was not in line with the target, it was not easy for them to articulate their inten tion into actions. Instead, in the beats condition the user recognized that it was

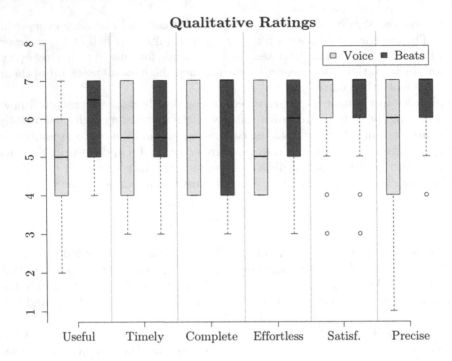

**Fig. 2.** Qualitative evaluation summary

easy to understand how much they should change their cadence. However, they suggested to complete such information with overall information on the training (duration, kilometers covered, average cadence, etc.).

## 5   Conclusion and Future Work

In this paper we discussed an audio feedback engine for providing cadence information to runners while training. We discussed how we tracked the current cadence and the rules for sending audio messages, trying to balance the trade-off between the timeliness and the effectiveness of the information and the disturbance for the user. We reported the results of a user-study comparing this technique with the one currently used in different smartphone apps in the market. Finally we reported a qualitative evaluation of its overall usability.

In future work, we aim to include such feedback system into a more complex training support, where the user may set different cadences for different parts of the workout. In addition, we would like to provide the feedback system to a larger number of users, and extracting different standard default configuration profiles. In addition, we would also enhance the feedback system in order to exploit data coming from more advanced sensors that runners may own (e.g., heart-rate sensors, GPS, etc.).

# References

1. Consolvo, S., McDonald, D.W., Toscos, T., Chen, M.Y., Froehlich, J., Harrison, B., Klasnja, P., LaMarca, A., LeGrand, L., Libby, R., Smith, I., Landay, J.A.: Activity sensing in the wild: a field trial of ubifit garden. In: Proceedings of CHI 2008, pp. 1797–1806. ACM (2008). http://doi.acm.org/10.1145/1357054.1357335
2. De Oliveira, R., Oliver, N.: Triplebeat: enhancing exercise performance with persuasion. In: Proceedings of MobileHCI 2008, pp. 255–264. ACM (2008). http://doi.acm.org/10.1145/1409240.1409268
3. Fortmann, J., Pielot, M., Mittelsdorf, M., Büscher, M., Trienen, S., Boll, S.: Paceguard: improving running cadence by real-time auditory feedback. In: Proceedings of MobileHCI 2012, pp. 5–10. ACM (2012). http://doi.acm.org/10.1145/2371664.2371668
4. Jayalath, S., Abhayasinghe, N.: A gyroscopic data based pedometer algorithm. In: Proceedings of ICCSE 2013, pp. 551–555 (2013)
5. Moens, B., Muller, C., van Noorden, L., Franěk, M., Celie, B., Boone, J., Bourgois, J., Leman, M.: Encouraging spontaneous synchronisation with d-jogger, an adaptive music player that aligns movement and music. PloS One 9(12), e114234 (2014)
6. Mulas, F., Carta, S., Pilloni, P., Manca, M.: Everywhere run: a virtual personal trainer for supporting people in their running activity. In: Proceedings of ACE 2011, pp. 70:1–70:2. ACM (2011)
7. Nylander, S., Jacobsson, M., Tholander, J.: Runright: real-time visual and audio feedback on running. In: CHI 2014 Extended Abstracts, CHI EA 2014, pp. 583–586. ACM (2014). http://doi.acm.org/10.1145/2559206.2574806
8. Nylander, S., Kent, A., Tholander, J.: Swing sound: experiencing the golf swing through sound. In: CHI 2014 Extended Abstracts, pp. 443–446. ACM (2014). http://doi.acm.org/10.1145/2559206.2574789
9. Oliver, N., Flores-Mangas, F.: Mptrain: a mobile, music and physiology-based personal trainer. In: Proceedings of MobileHCI 2006, pp. 21–28. ACM (2006). http://doi.acm.org/10.1145/1152215.1152221
10. Stienstra, J., Overbeeke, K., Wensveen, S.: Embodying complexity through movement sonification: case study on empowering the speed-skater. In: Proceedings of CHItaly 2011, pp. 39–44. ACM (2011). http://doi.acm.org/10.1145/2037296.2037310
11. Terry, P.C., Karageorghis, C.I., Saha, A.M., D'Auria, S.: Effects of synchronous music on treadmill running among elite triathletes. J. Sci. Med. Sport 15(1), 52–57 (2012)
12. Tomlein, M., Bielik, P., Krtky, P., tefan Mitrk, Barla, M., Bielikov, M.: Advanced pedometer for smartphone-based activity tracking. In: Proceedings of BIOSTEC 2012, pp. 401–404 (2012)
13. Waterhouse, J., Hudson, P., Edwards, B.: Effects of music tempo upon submaximal cycling performance. Scand. J. Med. Sci. Sports 20(4), 662–669 (2010)
14. Woźniak, P., Knaving, K., Björk, S., Fjeld, M.: Rufus: remote supporter feedback for long-distance runners. In: Proceedings of MobileHCI 2015, pp. 115–124. ACM (2015). http://doi.acm.org/10.1145/2785830.2785893
15. Zhao, S., Dragicevic, P., Chignell, M., Balakrishnan, R., Baudisch, P.: Earpod: eyes-free menu selection using touch input and reactive audio feedback. In: Proceedings of CHI 2007, pp. 1395–1404. ACM (2007). http://doi.acm.org/10.1145/1240624.1240836

# Models and Methods

# The Goals Approach: Enterprise Model-Driven Agile Human-Centered Software Engineering

Pedro Valente[1,2,3](✉), Thiago Rocha Silva[1], Marco Winckler[1], and Nuno Jardim Nunes[2]

[1] Institut de Recherche en Informatique de Toulouse (IRIT), Université Paul Sabatier, Route de Narbonne, 118, 31400 Toulouse, France
pvalente@uma.pt, {rocha,winckler}@irit.fr
[2] Madeira Interactive Technologies Institute (MITI), University of Madeira, Caminho da Penteada, 9020-105 Funchal, Portugal
njn@uma.pt
[3] Software Applications Development Office, University of Madeira, Colégio dos Jesuítas, 9000-082 Funchal, Portugal

**Abstract.** Business Process Improvement (BPI) is a key issue in the development of the enterprise competitiveness. However, achieving a level of software development performance that matches enterprise BPI needs in terms of producing noticeable results in small amounts of time requires the existence of a comprehensive and also agile Software Development Process (SDP). Quite often, SDPs do not deliver software architectures that can be directly used for in-house development, as specifications are either too close to the user interface design or too close to business rules and application domain modeling, and produce architectures that do not cope with software development concerns. In this paper we present the *Goals Approach*, which structures business processes to extract requirements, and methodologically details them in order to specify the user interface, the business logic and the database structures for the architecture of a BPI. Our approach aims in-house software development in small and medium enterprises.

**Keywords:** Enterprise engineering · Software engineering · Human-Computer Interaction · Agile software development process · Software architecture

## 1 Introduction

Software development within enterprises still lacks performance, and reports show that effectiveness is far from being achieved as software-project full-success rates in terms of time and budget are still as low as about 30 % [1]. Furthermore, there is still a long way until software development is achieved in a patterned and predictable way regarding development effort, so it can be established as a consistent source of revenue following investment within enterprises [2].

Nevertheless, the advances of Software Engineering (SE) have taken us at least from a chaotic state of the practice [3], to a more inspiring situation where enhanced

© IFIP International Federation for Information Processing 2016
Published by Springer International Publishing Switzerland 2016. All Rights Reserved
C. Bogdan et al. (Eds.): HCSE 2016/HESSD 2016, LNCS 9856, pp. 261–280, 2016.
DOI: 10.1007/978-3-319-44902-9_17

executive management support and increased user involvement in the Software Development Process (SDP) are appointed as factors for software project success [4].

In our research, we investigated whether it would be possible to establish a direct relation between concepts valuable for enterprise management and the implementation of a supporting Information System. And by stating the hypothesis that, it is possible if a cross-consistent definition of concepts is established between the enterprise concepts that model its human interaction, and if this interaction specification is evidenced in the architecture of a software system.

In this paper we present the *Goals Approach*. The Approach was empirically developed following the application of different methods in order to maximize software development performance in a medium sized enterprise, filling the gaps left by the used methods in terms of business specification and software architecting. *Goals* targets tailored in-house development of Information Systems for Small and Medium Enterprises (SMEs), which is characterized by needs of agility concerning the supportive Software Development Process (SDP) as a way to allow the achievement of observable organizational changes in limited amounts of time [5]. *Goals* defines a SDP that applies a straightforward methodology that analyses the enterprise in a top-down process in order to produce an Enterprise Structure of valuable business concepts as requirements. The methodology continues by means of the detail of the Enterprise Structure components, in order to design and structure, also in a top-down process, the user interface, the business logic and the database (given an MVC architectural pattern [6]), and compose a final Software Architecture that can be used for software implementation management.

In short, our approach aims at establishing a cross-consistent bridge of enterprise and software concepts, and applies a methodology to derive them, which can be summarized in the following way (back-bone components are underlined): the human interaction is represented by means of Business Processes, User Tasks, User Intentions and User Interactions; the User Interface is represented by Interaction Spaces and Interaction Components; its Business Logic by means of Business Rules, User Interface and Database System Responsibilities, and the database by means of Data Entities and Fields.

The *Goals Approach* SDP is presented in Sect. 2. Its methodology is presented in Sects. 3 (Analysis Phase) and 4 (Design Phase). The related work is presented in Sect. 5, conclusions are presented in Sect. 6, and future work in Sect. 7.

## 2    Software Development Process

Our approach Software Development Process (SDP) defines a Human-Centered Software Engineering (HCSE) methodology that integrates the Enterprise Engineering (EE) and Human-Computer Interaction (HCI) perspectives in the process of defining a Software Architecture for a given Business Process Improvement (BPI) problem.

The SDP defines an Analysis Phase that identifies Business Processes (BP, Step 1), User Tasks (UT, Step 2), Interactions Spaces (IS, Step 3), Business Rules (BR, Step 4) and Data Entities (DE, Step 5) in order to compose an enterprise model, the Enterprise Structure, by means of relating all the identified components of this Phase.

The Design Phase uses the Enterprise Structure in order to methodologically detail UTs using a Task Model (Step 6), an Interaction Model (in order to design the User Interface, Step 7), structure the Business Logic (Step 8) and the Database (Step 9), and elaborate a final Software Architecture (Step 10) of the Information System. Table 1 presents the SDP, including elements as inputs (I), output (O) or both (I/O) at each Step.

**Table 1.** *Goals* Software Development Process (I – Input. O – Output. IO – Input and Output.)

| Steps | Analysis Phase | | | | | Design Phase | | | | |
|---|---|---|---|---|---|---|---|---|---|---|
| | 1 | 2 | 3 | 4 | 5 | 6 | 7 | 8 | 9 | 10 |
| **Business Inputs** | | | | | | | | | | |
| Enterprise Functional Description | I | I | | | | | | | | |
| Business Regulations | | | | I | | | | | | |
| Business Concepts | I | | | I | | | | | | |
| User Collaboration | | | | | | I | I | | | |
| **Enterprise Structure Components** | | | | | | | | | | |
| Business Process (BP) | O | | | I | | | | | | I |
| User Task (UT) | | O | | I | | I | | | | I |
| Interaction Space (IS) | | | O | I | | I | I | | | I |
| Business Rule (BR) | | | | O | I | | | IO | | I |
| Data Entity (DE) | O | | | | IO | | | | IO | I |
| **User Behavior Specification** | | | | | | | | | | |
| User Intentions | | | | | | O | I | | | |
| User Interactions | | | | | | O | | | | |
| **Software Architecture Components** | | | | | | | | | | |
| Aggregation Space | | | | | | O | I | I | | I |
| Interaction Component | | | | | | O | I | I | | I |
| Interaction Object | | | | | | | O | I | | I |
| User Interface System Responsibility | | | | | | O | IO | | IO | I |
| Database System Responsibility | | | | | | O | IO | | IO | I |
| **Output Models** | | | | | | | | | | |
| Service Model | O | I | | | | | | | | |
| Business Process Model | | O | I | | | | | | | |
| UT – IS Relation | | | O | I | | | | | | |
| UT – IS – BR Relation | | | | O | I | | | | | |
| Enterprise Structure | | | | | O | I | | I | I | I |
| Task Model | | | | | | O | I | | | |
| Interaction Model | | | | | | | O | I | I | I |
| User Interface Design | | | | | | | O | | | |
| Business Logic Structure | | | | | | | | O | | I |
| Database Structure | | | | | | | | | O | I |
| Software Architecture | | | | | | | | | | O |

The Software Development Process (SDP) presented in Table 1 presents the information used in each Step. The "Business Inputs" provide unstructured information that must be available in the enterprise domain in any format. The "Enterprise Structure Components", "User Behavior Specification" and "Software Architecture Components" are elements that take part as inputs (I), outputs (O) or both (I/O) in the "Output Models" of each Step, and are used consecutively in the following steps, in a straight-lined process.

The application of the SDP presents a trade-off in terms of agility and traceability i.e. agility is constrained by the need to maintain traceability of all the elements as this is the primary foundation of the method. Traceability defines a structure between business and software concepts, that enables relating organizational changes in terms of changes in its supporting software system. Hence, the approach presupposes an initial effort for the documentation of a Software Architecture that later can be used to facilitate software development.

There are two distinct cases of changes. The ones that involve the Enterprise Structure, and the ones that are circumscribed to the Software Architecture. By the analysis of the SDP it is possible to identify both the Enterprise Structure (Step 5) and Interaction Model (Step 7) as core models of enterprise and of software respectively as both provide input for the final Steps (8, 9 and 10) of the SDP. Changes to the Interaction Model (Step 7) involve User Collaboration in order to specify interaction with the system, and involve a set of Software Architecture components that concern the support of a single User Task (UT). Oppositely, changes to the Enterprise Structure have a bigger impact in the Software Architecture, as this model also provides input for the Interaction Model (of Step 7) concerning a specific Business Process Improvement that involves Business Process and related UTs reorganization.

In any of the cases, the type of components (Enterprise Structure or Software Architecture) which are changed directly specifies the following Steps that need to be carried out. This is done means of the traceability of one Step components and Steps in which they are used as inputs when changed. In this way, by increasing the number of changed components the number of Steps that need to be carried out also increases, and consequently the software development effort also increases, providing a concrete perspective on the effort related to organizational and software changes.

In our approach, when the BPI does not imply the reorganization of the UTs of the BP, the method can be started from the Design Phase, which is the agile characteristic of the SDP. Directly relating our approach to the Agile Manifesto [7], it reduces the "need to follow a specific plan" other than the plan defined by traceability in Table 1. Defines "User Collaboration" (in Steps 6 and 7) for the specification of human interaction. And facilities the specification of a future architecture, with no need for further "comprehensive documentation", avoiding the chaos that can be generated in software development when carried out without architectural-documentation support.

Following the Analysis and Design Phases, the process continues with the Implementation and Testing Phases (which detail is out of the scope of the this paper), and use the Software Architecture to guide software development, and the User Interface Design, Task Model and User Stories to guide the Information System test before deployment.

## 2.1   Foundations

The *Goals Approach* was developed by means of the continuous application of the *Wisdom* method [8] and its extension Process Use Cases Model [9] for the elicitation of requirements from business processes as Essential Use Cases (based on the *Activity Modeling* (AM) [10] method), in the process of architecting software for purposes of in-house tailored development in a medium-sized enterprise. The applicability of the architectural *Wisdom* method, and the relevancy of the representation of business process flows as sequences of Use Cases led to the definitive establishment of the combined software development method (initially named Goals Software Construction Process [11]) as it supported the team needs in terms of producing a programmable software architecture. The model enabled dialogue among stakeholders on BPI decisions, and allowed the identification of patterns of reusability concerning implementation.

The relation between business and software was further complemented by means of the inclusion of the concept of the DEMO method Action Rule [12] as the business-specific component of the Business Logic of the Software Architecture. This introduced a new separation of concerns which positively contributed to the organization of the remaining software-specific components. The Approach further benefited in terms of the theoretical validation of the patterned structure that relates enterprise and software concepts, as the *Goals* Enterprise Structure is compatible with the DEMO concepts of Transaction, Action Rule and Object Class. *Goals* adds to those concepts the notion of Interaction Space (IS) and the Goal of each Business Process (BP) that build-up a structure that provides the back-bone of the final Software Architecture.

This consolidated relation between enterprise and software concepts provides the core structure that allows the application of a methodological process that focus on user needs by means of the application of the BDD method [13]. The detail provided by BDD extends the application of the architectural *Wisdom* method in terms of physical interaction between the user and computer (clicks, keys, etc.), providing the base

**Table 2.** Enterprise Structure components definition, origin and symbol.

| Component | Definition | Origin | Symbol |
|---|---|---|---|
| Business Process (BP) | *A network of UTs that lead to a Goal* | DEMO | |
| User Task (UT) | *A Complete Task within a BP* | AM | |
| Interaction Space (IS) | *The Space that supports a UT (with the same BRs and DEs)* | *Wisdom* | |
| Business Rule (BR) | *A Restriction over DEs Structural Relations* | DEMO | |
| Data Entity (DE) | *Persistent Information about a Business Concept* | *Wisdom* | |

mechanism that specifies the User Interface, Business Logic and Database components with a level of detail usable for system programming.

One particular view that matters concerning the methodology application, are the fundamental conceptual Enterprise Structure definitions on which it is based. The Enterprise Structure components, their definition, origin and symbol are presented in Table 2.

*Goals* defines as the top of the enterprise hierarchy, the Goal of the Business Process (BP). The BPs are composed by a series of User Tasks (UT), which once combined, lead the BP to the Goal. Those "Goals" are what names the approach. The human interaction between Actors that carry on, each his UT, happens in a given Interaction Space (IS) that makes available a series of Data Entities (DEs) that are subject to a number of Business Rules (BR) in order to be used by Actors. Each UT is considered complete when there is nothing that the Actor can do beyond his responsibility in order to further attain the Goal of the BP. This logic of the enterprise view provides the structure that is validated by means of the compatibility of concepts with the DEMO methodology, as every *Goals* component can be directly related or paternally derived from DEMO concepts. The difference between the two approaches is that DEMO does not consider the spaces where the human interaction happens, does not semantically structure the Business Process Goal, and cannot be directly related to the implementation parts of a Software Architecture, as DEMO defines separate ontologies for enterprise and software representation.

Figure 1 presents the relation between the main DEMO and *Goals* components, in which the DEMO concept of Business Process as an interrelated set of Transactions ("T1" and "T2" in the Figure) directly relates to the concept of BP of *Goals*. Furthermore, DEMO Transaction Acts ("rq", "pm", "st", "ac") related to *Goals* UTs in terms on consecutive Acts performed by the same Actor (e.g. sequence "T1 rq pm st ac" in "Pattern A", "T1 pm st" in A01 of "Pattern B" and "T1 pm T2 rq" in "Pattern C".

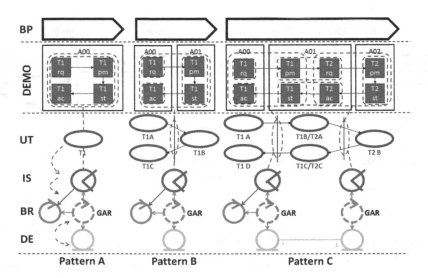

**Fig. 1.** Relation between DEMO and *Goals* main conceptual structures.

And the Interaction Space identification is based on the space that is used by (between) Actors in order to support their interaction of any two UTs.

The mechanism that derives ISs from UTs and relates them to BRs and DEs serves as a bridge that relates business conceptual definitions (the BP and the UT) with the business-and-software-recognizable concepts of IS, BR and DE. This mechanism, that relies on the architectural *Wisdom* method for the identification of the IS, and the application of principle of merging consecutive UTs based on the Essential Use Case (EUC) definition application, serves as a door to the identification of business regulations (BRs) and business concepts (DEs) that must be available for the ongoing transactional process between two Actors, defining as a basic logic and structure for the enterprise functional description.

# 3   Analysis Phase

The Analysis Phase develops the Enterprise Structure, in which the Interaction Space (IS) concept is the mechanism that establishes the relation between the User Tasks (UT) of the Business Process (BP), and Business Rules (BR) that constraint existing Data Entities (DE). Each component is identified in a top-down methodological process in five Steps: Step 1–Business Process Identification; Step 2–User Task Identification; Step 3–Interaction Space Identification; Step 4–Business Rule Identification; and Step 5–Data Entity Identification.

## 3.1   Step 1–Business Process Identification

*Goals* defines a Business Process (BP) as "*A network of User Tasks that lead to a Goal*". The Goal is the objective, and also names the BP. It is expressed as a unique set of related enterprise business concepts (Data Entities, DE) that support its execution, and compose the enterprise domain model. The establishment of a relation between the BP and the set of DEs that the Information System will manage provides an increased awareness on the problem begin solved, and also increased communication capability between project stakeholders. Stakeholders in-depth their knowledge of the specific part of the enterprise that is being evolved. This facilitates the BPI development, and in practical terms results in faster and more productive project meetings, increasing the probability of developing projects in less time.

The relation between BPs and DEs is also useful in order to design the BP Model, which relates BPs, Actors and DEs, increasing the perception on how a BP uses and produces certain business concepts from a higher level of abstraction. We present the relation by means of the application of the Process Use Cases Model [9] adapted to the current *Goals* notation. The meta-model and an example are presente in Fig. 2.

Figure 2 presents the meta-model of the BP Model, in which it can be read that only one actor can "Initiate" a BP, but an unlimited number of Actors can participate in it, and also, that an unlimited number of DEs can be used by a BP. It also presents an example where Actor "Customer" initiates the BP, Actors "Collaborator" and "Director" participate in it, and the DE "Request" is used and the DE "Approval" is produced.

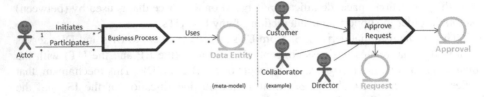

**Fig. 2.** Business Process Model meta-model, and BP Model example.

### 3.2 Step 2–User Task Identification

The User Task (UT) definition is derived from the concept of Essential Use Case (EUC) [10], which defines a Use Case as a "complete and meaningful task (carried out in relationship with a system)". This definition is adapted to the enterprise context based on the principle that the BP is a network of interrelated UTs, and that each UT is carried out by a single Actor, unless they are carrying out the same UT, performing cooperative work [14]. Since a BP always has a limited number of tasks, all UTs can be considered as meaningful, thus, we abandon the term "meaningful" and simply define a UT as a *"Complete Task within a BP"*. We also apply the principle that an Actor (a User) never carries on two UTs consecutively and separately, which is a restriction that aims user performance and software development efficiency, in order to induce the reduction of the articulatory distance of the UT i.e. the user's effort [15], and suggest that the necessary tools should be provided using as little User Interface implementation space as possible. If two UTs are consecutive, then they can be merged in a single sequence of acts, expressed by a single UT, leading to is completion in the same way.

The relations between UTs are what designs a BP. The consecutive relation is the most common, as it supports the most usual BP flow. Yet, it is not sufficient to represent more complex services that must be available in different interaction points (also called as touchpoints) which usually have back-end support, and may be visited by the customer, but not necessarily in pre-defined order. This need for flexibility can be attained by the definition of conditional relations between UTs. Hence, we further define the conditional relation, meaning that the execution of a specific path of the BP is conditioned to the will of the responding Actor to carry on his task. This reflects the case when an enterprise suggests its customers the execution of a given action as a sequence of any other interaction, but will never be sure that they will follow the suggestion, and yet, continues to provide that customer the remaining service. The representation of services as a consecutive or conditioned sequence of UTs allows the representation of the service as a BP, and the possibility of well-defining a software architecture that paternally supports the service in a same way it supports the BP.

Figure 3 presents the meta-model of the UT, in which it can be read that: one Actor can carry on many UTs (and vice-versa); one BP can have one or more UTs (and vice-versa); and that one UT can consecutively or conditionally trigger one or more UTs. The example shows the initial UT being triggered by Actor "Customer" and consecutive UTs "Promise" and "Approve" being carried out by Actors "Collaborator" and "Director", and as the response tasks, "State" and "Acknowledge" being carried

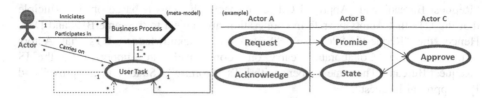

**Fig. 3.** User Task meta-model and example.

out by Actors "Collaborator" and "Customer" respectively. The relation between UT "State" and "Acknowledge" is conditioned to Actor "Customer" will to carry it on.

### 3.3    Step 3–Interaction Space Identification

The Interaction Space (IS) definition is derived from *Wisdom* original concept of Interaction Space, as a space (a User Interface) where the "user interacts with functions, containers and information in order to carry on a task". We adapt this concept to the enterprise context by means of its generalization in order to consider the same purpose for the support of the UTs interaction in person, as in any of the cases, the same BRs and DEs also apply. *Goals* (re)defines the IS as *"The Space that supports a UT (with the same BRs and DEs)"*. Hence, one IS supports the interaction between two users in person or remotely while each one carries on his own UT. Even if many UTs are carried out by many Actors in a cooperative way, the UTs will still be different, since at least one UT has initiated the other(s). If two Actors carry on the same UT remotely, then they are necessarily performing cooperative work [14].

The identification of ISs is derived from the interaction between the sequenced UTs of the BP, in order to support one Actor request and other Actor response, as in any case the same BRs and DEs apply.

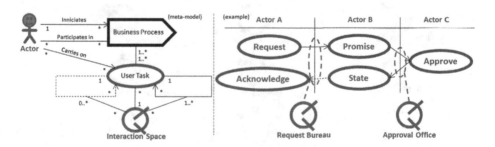

**Fig. 4.** Interaction Space meta-model and example.

Figure 4 presents the meta-model that specifies that an IS supports many UTs, having at least a consecutive relation and at most one conditional relation. The example shows the derivation of ISs that supports the interaction between Actors "Customer" and "Collaborator", and Actors "Collaborator" and "Director", by means of ISs

"Request Bureau" and "Approval Office" respectively. This is based on the principle that the UTs that Actors operate in cooperation are subject to the same BRs and DEs. Hence, the "Request", "Promise", "State" and "Acknowledge" UTs that Actors "Customer" and "Collaborator" carry on cooperatively are supported by the IS "Request Bureau". The same happens with UTs "Promise", "State" and "Approve" and IS "Approval Request".

### 3.4    Step 4–Business Rule Identification

The Business Rule (BR) definition is provided by DEMO notion of Action Rule, which defines a structure of decision (using pseudo-code) that applies restrictions to the identified Object Classes concerning the execution of business Transactions. These restrictions are paradigmatic relations (considering a semiotic association [16]) which are applied to the syntactic relations (also considering a semiotic definition) that exist between Data Entities (DEs), producing a new valuable business concept that cannot be expressed by the simpler relations between DEs. Hence, we define the BR as "*A Restriction over DEs Structural Relations*".

BRs represent regulations or explicitly defined requirements that should be elicited during the Analysis Phase in order to understand the constraints which the user is subject to when carrying on a UT. One important clarification is that BRs do not represent collaboration impositions between Actors, since these rules are already expressed by the BP design. BRs are the grounding foundation of the Information System Business Logic (given an MVC pattern), as they are the more business-specific programmed class concerning the structuring of this layer. The Business Logic will also be complemented with programmed parts that are responsible for the IS (User Interface) presentation and for the DEs (database) management, as will be presented in Step 8–Business Logic Structuring.

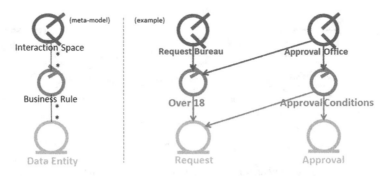

**Fig. 5.** Business Rules meta-model and example.

Figure 5 presents the meta-model concerning the relation between BRs, IS and DEs, in relations of many to many. The example shows that IS "Request Bureau" uses BR "Over 18", and that IS "Approval Office" uses BR "Approval Conditions". It also defines that BR "Over 18" uses DE "Request", and that BR "Approval Conditions" uses DEs "Request" and "Approval".

### 3.5  Step 5–Data Entity Identification

The Data Entities (DE) definition is provided by *Wisdom* as a "class of perdurable information about a business concept". This means that persistency will be maintained by the Information System, and that it will enclose meaningful concepts which are recognized within the enterprise by those who have knowledge about it. The enclosed meanings (the concepts) can also be related between each other, allowing a representation of reality by means of a computerized system which is made available for usage by means of a database application. These "meanings" are represented by Data Entities in *Goals*, and enclose attributes. In terms of common database objects, DEs are implemented by tables, and attributes are implemented by fields.

DEs are related between each other by means of the semiotic association of syntactic relations, which are expressed in *Goals* using an Unified Modeling Language (UML) [17] association, which also implies the definition of the multiplicity between the related DEs. The association multiplicity will typically be of one to many, or many to many. The definition of a specific multiplicity (e.g. 1 to 5) is uncommon, and should be expressed by a BR, as it is usually volatile (it will eventually change). The definition of relations of one to one is also uncommon, as in those cases the DEs meaning can usually be conciliated in a single DE.

As mentioned in Step 1–Business Process Identification, the identification of DEs should be carried along the BP identification and the consequential Steps, so that the analyst at this stage already has a well-defined notion of the concepts involved in the BPI under analysis (and also how they relate between each other). In the current Step, the DEs only need to be identified and related to the BRs in order to compose the Enterprise Structure, the final artefact of the Analysis Phase, as depicted in Fig. 6 with the DEs as a support of the Enterprise Structure.

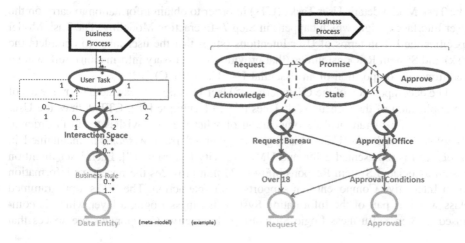

**Fig. 6.** Enterprise Structure meta-model and example.

The Enterprise Structure presented in Fig. 6 is composed by every identified component until this moment and also by their relation to other components. It represents a relation which is representative of the enterprise in terms of a logic that relates BPs, UTs, ISs, BRs and DEs in terms of dependency and functional specification. It can be used in order to identify the implications of changing the enterprise in terms of its impact in the software structure, since, changing BPs, UTs or BRs, which is common in the business management domain, will inevitably change the underlying Information System to which the three lower levels layers (IS, BR and DE) are an inherent part.

The SDP continues with the elaboration of the Design Phase.

# 4    Design Phase

The Design Phase details the Enterprise Structure by means of the application of specific techniques that further specify and complement each component (Business Process (BP), User Task (UT), Interaction Space (IS), Business Rule (BR) or Data Entity (DE)) with new software specific components that structure the Software Architecture. The final Software Architecture is composed by the User Interface (View), Business Logic (Controller) and Database (Model) layers, which are related to the IS, BR and DE concepts respectively, given an MVC architectural pattern [6].

Each Software Architecture component is conceived in a top-down methodological process that details and completes the User Interaction (Step 6–Task Model), the User Interface (Step 7–Interaction Modeling), the Business Logic (Step 8–Business Logic Structuring) and the DE layer (Step 9–Database Structuring), and finishes with the composition and analysis of the Software Architecture (Step 10–Software Architecture Composition).

## 4.1    Step 6–Task Model

The Task Model details User Tasks (UTs) in order to obtain information to carry on the User Interface design, which happens in Step 7–Interaction Modeling. The Task Model specifies the UT in terms of User Intentions (steps that the user takes to complete the task) and System Responsibilities (that provide the necessary information), following a traditional decomposition of an Essential Use Case (EUC) [10].

The decomposition of the UT in terms of User Intentions is carried out my means of the application of the Concur Task Trees (CTT) technique [18]. CTT defines the User Intentions as a hierarchical decomposition of what the user wishes to do in order to complete his task (the UT). This logic, is inherited from *Wisdom*, is maintained in *Goals*, and is represented using and UML Activity Diagram [17]. Each User Intention has an associated System Responsibility (SR) that provides the necessary information to an Interactive Component that supports User Interaction. The SR is a programmed class which is part of the Information System Business Logic, a layer which is composed in Step 8–Business Logic Structuring. Interactive Components are spaces that provide the adequate implementation to allow data management, and are implemented by means of a User Interface programming language e.g. PHP.

The Task Model presents the flow of User Intentions that lead to the accomplishment of the UT. Each User Intention uses an Interaction Component by means of one or more User Interaction that in its turn also use System Responsibilities (SR) that supplies it with the necessary information. This relation is defined as the *Wisdom* architectural specification pattern i.e. the human-computer interaction happens in a User Interface part (the Interaction Component) and is supported by a programmed class (the SR). This type of SR is called as User Interface SRs. The last User Intentions of the Activity Diagram always lead to SRs that manages information, which in this case are called as Database SRs. If new Data Entities (DE) are identified by means of the Task Model elaboration, then they must also be represented in the DEs structure, which occurs in Step 9–Database Structuring.

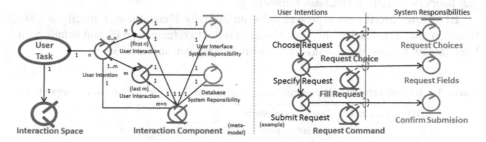

**Fig. 7.** Task Model meta-model and example.

Figure 7 presents the meta-model of the Task Model, where it can be read that a UT has up to $n$ initial User Intentions, and up to $m$ last User Intentions that use $m + n$ Interaction Components (which compose the IS that supports the UT). Each Interaction Component supports one User Intention, and uses one User Interface System Responsibility (SR) or one Database SR. The example shows the decomposition of UT "Request", which has two initial User Intentions ("Choose Request" and "Fill Request") and one final ("Submit Request"). The first two relate to User Interface SRs "Request Choice" and "Fill Request", and the last relates to Database SR "Confirm Submission", meaning that the UT can be carried out by means of 3 interactions, which are supported by 3 System Responsibilities and 3 Interaction Components.

### 4.2   Step 7–Interaction Modeling

The Interaction Modeling is carried out by means of the application of the Behavior Driven Development (BDD) method [13] that further specifies each User Intention as User Interactions, and also frames it in terms of used Interactions Spaces (ISs), specifying the navigation between the User Tasks (UT) of the Business Processes (BP). BDD is an agile software development method that describes the system behavior based on a User-Centered Design (UCD) perspective, producing pseudo-code for User

Interface specification. BDD specifies User Stories that state that a system feature (a UT) which is used within a certain scenario (the IS), will result in specific system behavior which is expressed in the User Interface. The pseudo-code has the following syntax.

`Given [State] When [Interaction] Then [System Behavior]`

Where [State] represents the actual state of the system in the current scenario, the Aggregation Space [19], which is (are) the IS(s) where the UT occurs; [Interaction] is a flow of User Interactions that matches the User Intentions of the Task Model, specifying how the UT can be completed; and, [System Behavior] is the expected outcome that triggers User Interface and Database System Responsibilities. BDD interactions also specify the Data Entities (DEs) fields used in each User Interaction. This specification facilitates the mapping between Systems Responsibilities and DEs that occurs in Step 8–Business Logic Structuring, and the completion of the Database specification that happens in Step 9–Database Structuring.

BDD User Stories are represented by an Activity Diagram, and specify a User Intention that occurs before the Task Model in order to reference an IS, and details each User Intention using the pseudo-code which is presented in Table 3.

**Table 3.** Relation between BDD pseudo code syntax and Software Architecture components.

| BDD pseudo-code | Goals Component |
|---|---|
| Given | (*provides Aggregation Space identification*) |
| Feature 'Feature' | User Task 'Feature' |
| Scenario 'Scenario' | User Intention 'Scenario' |
| Click, Choose, Set | User Intentions 'Click', 'Choose' or 'Set' |
| Display 'Page' or Go to 'Page' | User Interface System Responsibility 'Display Page' + Interaction Space 'Page' |
| Field | Data Entity Field |
| Then | (*last*) System Responsibilities |

Figure 8 presents the User Stories User Interaction meta-model and an example that specifies the Task Model User Intentions using the pseudo-code presented in Table 3.

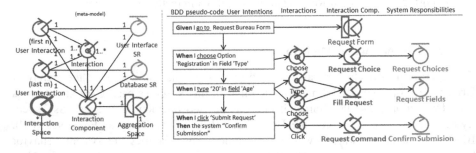

**Fig. 8.** User Interaction meta-model and example.

Now it is possible to design the User Interface by composing the generated components in each Interaction Component. Figure 9 shows a representation of the User Interface which identifies the Aggregation Space "Request Form", that uses the Interaction Space "Request Bureau", and the Interaction Components "Request Choice" that is composed of Field "Type", "Fill Request" which is composed of Field "Age", and the "Request Command" as the button "Submit Request", which trigger the User Interface SRs "Request Choices" and "Request Fields", and Database SR "Confirm Submission", respectively.

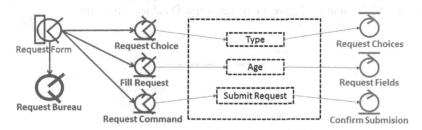

**Fig. 9.** User Interface Design example.

### 4.3 Step 8–Business Logic Structuring

The Business Logic Structuring is carried out by defining the relations that each System Responsibility (SR) has to Data Entities (DEs), since the relation with the Interaction Spaces and Interaction Components is already established. The specification of each relation is dependent on the definition of to which DE the Fields identified in Step 7–Interaction Modeling, belong to, which will also have an impact in the elaboration of Step 9–Database Structuring.

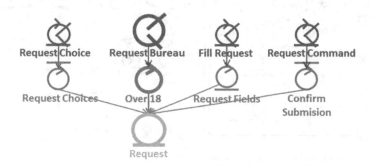

**Fig. 10.** Business Logic Structure example.

Figure 10 shows the manual mapping that was done between SRs and DEs. Business Rule "Over 18" is inherited from the Enterprise Architecture. User Interface SR "Request Choices" has been mapped to DE "Request", and it is assumed that

Fields "Type" and "Age", belongs to DE "Request". By means of the analysis of the semantic of the Database SR "Confirm Submission" manages DE "Request".

## 4.4   Step 9–Database Structuring

The Database Structuring is now possible since all the DEs are identified. Since two DEs (a and B) have been identified, and DE "Request" provides information for a given Field, it is possible to assume that DE "Request" only related to a single record in DE "Approval", yet, on the contrary, any record in DE "Approval" can be related to many records in DE "Request". Figure 11 presents the Database Structure.

**Fig. 11.**  Database Structure example.

## 4.5   Step 10–Software Architecture Composition

The Software Architecture is the model that relates all the previously identified components in a single structure. It can be used to specify implementation responsibilities, and priority (within a software development team).

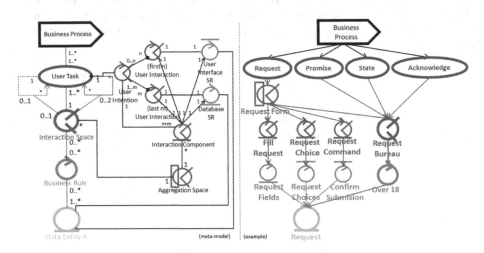

**Fig. 12.**  Software Architecture meta-model and example.

The meta-model of the approach is presented in Fig. 12, where it is possible to identify that the relation between BP and DE is now supported by means of the Software Architecture structure.

The implementation priority applied to the Software Architecture example, would be: DE "A" (since it will be used in) Business Rule "Over 18"; Database SR "Request Choices"; User Interface SR "Request Fields"; and only then User Interface SR "Confirm Submission". Interaction Components "Request Choice", "Fill Request" and "Request Command" can follow any order, and once developed, the IS "Request Bureau" and the Aggregation Space "Request Form" can be implemented and tested. For purposes of implementation, each IS will need a specific template per Actor in order to define its perspective according to "his" Task Model. The SRs will usually imply the definition of complex algorithms, and the Database will usually need the development of interfacing objects that facilitate data retrieval and update.

The architecture provides the advantage that the separation of implementation concerns is already defined at this stage, reducing significantly management efforts.

## 5  Related Work

Our approach can be compared to ArchiMate [20] and BPMN [21] in the perspective that it provides an enterprise and software structuring language. It is different in the perspective that it applies a methodology that derives software implementation specifications from business business models, in a business Model-Driven Architecture (MDA) process.

Concerning existing MDA approaches, and regarding the specific HCI perspective, the closest solutions are methods that design the user interface based on user task and domain models, as Sukaviriya's [22], Sousa's [23] and Cedar [24]. Our approach is different as it complementarily conceives the business logic layer based on enterprise business rules and coordination structures.

The I-Star framework [25] is a requirements engineering method that has a similar approach to *Goals* concerning the user perspective, as it considers the complete task (a UT) as a Goal that is decomposed in Tasks (which are User Intentions), that can be further decomposed in the same way that *Goals* further identifies User Interaction. The main difference between the approaches is that *Goals* further defines the supporting Information System.

There are more holistic MDA approaches to software architecting, like the Living Models [26], the Formal Design Analysis Framework [27], Zikra's [28], which also structure the business logic based on business process models, that yet, do not design the user interface.

Considering the enterprise-driven development, the Generic Software Development Process (GSDP) [29] is based on DEMO models, from which it derives the business rules, data structure, and business process design. And uses this information to conceive an enterprise operating system, which however, does not apply a structured user interface conception [30]. The Inter-enterprise Service Engineering (ISE) [31] uses BPMN business process models to automate the design of the user interface in detail, but, however, does not structure the remaining parts of the Information System.

# 6 Conclusions

Our approach inherently aims at facilitating requirements elicitation, focuses on user needs, and simplifies traceability between business requirements and software implementation, which matches project management needs and user involvement in the SDP, in what we believe to be the more important contribution of our work.

The validation of results, at this moment is mostly empirical, yet since the method as been developed by means of its application for over a decade, the techniques applied, including the notation, have been thoroughly revised. Five projects elaborated using this method were previously statistically analyzed for purposes of software effort estimation, from which it was possible to derive enhanced patterns of effort, which gives some guarantees about the stability of the development process [32].

Despite the existence of 10 Steps, the choice to maintain compatibility of concepts with Enterprise Engineering, Human-Computer Interaction and Software Engineering concepts, facilitates the understanding of the methodology by the specific domain professional experts. Yet, understanding it as a whole is more difficult as it crosses the enterprise and software domains, and for that reason it needs further application in order to be possible to inspect its usage in terms of effectiveness.

The introduced concept of Interaction Space (IS), as a framework of support for enterprise business-driven cooperative work is an extension of the traditional HCI interaction space that aims the simplification of the conception of the user interface. This simplification results in the specification of less implementation components and more manageable software architectures for a single BPI, resulting in more feasible and probably more successful software projects. This forecasts small BPI as a good strategy, since based on The Standish Group reports, projects under 1 M$ (one million dollars) cost are believed to be up to 10 times more successful than 10 M$ projects [1].

A controllable set of architectural components will usually be implemented with great efficiency (concerning work-hours) by programmers with knowledge of the domain. These circumstances induce iterative enterprise and information system development, matching the continuous software development proclaimed by the Agile Manifesto [7].

# 7 Future Work

Future work mostly concerns the continuation of the development of the approach concerning cooperative work, more specifically: a social perspective for the patterned conception of the user interface in terms of information visualization and tool execution permissions; a contextual perspective that facilitates user interface design decisions in terms of usability objectives; the User Interface design and prototype procedure specification; the elaboration of a business process model that supports the specification of cooperative work beyond the 2-actor swinlanes; the development of a Platform Specific Model for software generation; and the application of the approach by other software development teams as a strategy to further validate the presented techniques.

**Ackownledgments.** First author would like the acknowledge the scientific and finantial support from the afilliated institutions.

# References

1. The Standish Group. Chaos Report (2014)
2. Valente, P., Aveiro, D., Nunes, N.: Improving software design decisions towards enhanced return of investment. In: Proceedings ICEIS 2015, pp. 388–394 (2015)
3. Morgenshtern, O., Raz, T., Dvir, D.: Factors affecting duration and effort estimation errors in software development projects. IST **49**, 827–837 (2007)
4. The Standish Group. Chaos Report (2013)
5. Gerogiannis, V., Kakarontzas, G., Anthopoulos, L., Bibi, S., Stamelos, I.: The SPRINT-SMEs approach for software process improvement in small-medium sized software development enterprises. In: Proceedings of ARCHIMEDES III (2013)
6. Zukowski, J.: The model-view-controller architecture. In: John Zukowski's Definitive Guide to Swing for Java 2 (1999). ISBN 978-1430252511
7. Agile Manifesto. http://agilemanifesto.org/iso/en/ Accessed 02 May 2016:
8. Nunes, N.: object modeling for user-centered development and user interface design: the wisdom approach. Phd Thesis. Universidade da Madeira (2001)
9. Valente, P., Sampaio, P.: Process use cases: use cases identification. In: Proceedings of ICEIS 2007, Vol. Information Systems Analysis and Specification, pp. 301–307 (2007)
10. Constantine, L.: Human activity modeling - toward a pragmatic integration of activity theory and usage-centered design. In: Seffah, A., Vanderdonckt, J., Desmarais, M.C. (eds.) Human-Centered Software Engineering. HCI, pp. 27-51. Springer, London (2009)
11. Valente, P.: Goals software construction process: goal-oriented software development. VDM Verlag Dr. Müller (2009). ISBN 978-3639212426
12. Dietz, J.: Enterprise Ontology - Theory and Methodology. Springer, Heidelberg (2006). ISBN 978-3540331490
13. Chelimsky, D., Astels, D., Helmkamp, B., North, D., Dennis, Z., Hellesoy, A.: The RSpec Book (2010). ISBN 1934356379
14. Grudin, J.: Computer-supported cooperative work: history and focus. IEEE Comput. **27**(5), 19–26 (1994)
15. Winckler, M., Cava, R., Barboni, E., Palanque, P., Freitas, C.: Usability aspects of the inside-in approach for ancillary search tasks on the web. In: Abascal, J., Barbosa, S., Fetter, M., Gross, T., Palanque, P., Winckler, M. (eds.) INTERACT 2015. LNCS, vol. 9297, pp. 211–230. Springer, Heidelberg (2015)
16. Damjanovic, V., Gasevic, D., Devedzic, V.: Semiotics for ontologies and knowledge representation. In: Proceedings of Wissens Management, pp. 571–574 (2005)
17. Booch, G., Jacobson, I., Rumbaugh, J.: The Unified Modeling Language Users Guide. Addison-Wesley, Menlo Park (1998)
18. Paternò, F.: Model-Based Design and Evaluation of Interactive Applications. Springer, London (1999)
19. Costa, D., Nóbrega, L., Jardim Nunes, N.: An MDA Approach for Generating Web Interfaces with UML ConcurTaskTrees and Canonical Abstract Prototypes. In: Coninx, K., Luyten, K., Schneider, K.A. (eds.) TAMODIA 2006. LNCS, vol. 4385, pp. 137–152. Springer, Heidelberg (2007)
20. Archimate Foundation: Archimate Made Practical (2008)

21. Völzer, H.: An overview of BPMN 2.0 and its potential use. In: Mendling, J., Weidlich, M., Weske, M. (eds.) BPMN 2010. LNBIP, vol. 67, pp. 14–15. Springer, Heidelberg (2010)

22. Sukaviriya, N., Sinha, V., Ramachandra, T., Mani, S., Stolze, M.: User-centered design and business process modeling: cross road in rapid prototyping tools. In: Baranauskas, C., Abascal, J., Barbosa, S.D.J. (eds.) INTERACT 2007. LNCS, vol. 4662, pp. 165–178. Springer, Heidelberg (2007)

23. Sousa, K., Mendonça, H., Vanderdonckt, J., Rogier, E., Vandermeulen, J.: User interface derivation from business processes: a model-driven approach for organizational engineering. In: Proceedings of 2008 ACM SAC, pp. 553–560 (2008)

24. Akiki, P.: Engineering adaptive model-driven user interfaces. The Open University. PhD Thesis (2014)

25. Aguilar, J., Zaldívar, A., Tripp, C., Misra, S., Sánchez, S., Martínez, M., García, O.: A solution proposal for complex web application modeling with the I-star framework. In: Proceeding International Workshop on Software Engineering Process and Applications, pp. 135–145 (2014)

26. Breu, R., Agreiter, B., Farwick, M., Felderer, M., Hafner, M., Innerhofer–Oberperfler, F.: Living models – ten principles for change–driven software engineering. Int. J. Softw. Inform. (2010)

27. Dai, L., Cooper, K.: Using FDAF to bridge the gap between enterprise and software architectures for security. Sci. Comput. Program. **66**, 87–102 (2007)

28. Zikra, I.: Integration of enterprise modeling and model driven development. Stockholm University. PhD Thesis (2014)

29. Kervel, S., Dietz, J, Hintzen, J., Meeuwen, T., Zijlstra, B.: enterprise ontology driven software engineering. In: Proceedings of ICSoft 2012 (2012)

30. Hintzen, J., Kervel, S., Meeuwen, T., Vermolen, J., Zijlstra, B.: A professional case management system in production, modeled and implemented using DEMO. In: Proceedings of 16th IEEE Conference on Business Informatics (2014)

31. Dividino, R., Bicer, V., Voigt, K., Cardoso, J.: Integrating business process and user interface models using a model-driven approach. Proc. ISCIS **2009**, 492–497 (2009)

32. Alves, R., Valente, P., Nunes, N.: Improving software effort estimation with human-centric models: a comparison of UCP and iUCP accuracy. In: Proceeding of EICS 2013, pp. 287–296 (2013)

# Engineering Context-Adaptive UIs for Task-Continuous Cross-Channel Applications

Enes Yigitbas$^{(\boxtimes)}$ and Stefan Sauer

s-lab - Software Quality Lab, Paderborn University, Zukunftsmeile 1,
33102 Paderborn, Germany
{eyigitbas,sauer}@s-lab.upb.de

**Abstract.** The user interfaces (UIs) of interactive systems become increasingly complex since many heterogeneous and dynamically changing contexts of use (platform, user, and environment) have to be supported. Developing UIs for such interactive systems often requires features like UI adaptivity and seamless task-continuity across devices, demanding for sophisticated UI development processes and methods. While existing engineering methods like human-centered design process and model-based UI development approaches serve as a good starting point, an integrated engineering process addressing specific requirements of adaptive UIs supporting task-continuity across different devices is not fully covered. Therefore, we present a model-based engineering approach for building context-adaptive UIs that enable a personalized, flexible and task-continuous usage of cross-channel applications. Our engineering approach supports modeling, transformation and execution of context-adaptive UIs. To show the feasibility of our approach, we present an industrial case study, where we implement context-adaptive UIs for a cross-channel banking application.

**Keywords:** Model-based development · UI adaptation · Multi-device UI development · Cross-channel applications · Task-continuity

## 1 Introduction

Today users are surrounded by a broad range of networked interaction devices (e.g. smartphones, smartwatches, tablets, terminals etc.) for carrying out their everyday activities. Due to the growing number of such interaction devices, new possible interaction techniques (e.g. multi-touch or tangible interaction) and distributed user interfaces transcending the boundaries of a single device, software developers and user interface designers are facing new challenges. As the user interfaces of interactive systems become increasingly complex since many heterogeneous contexts of use (platform, user, and environment) have to be supported,

This work is based on "KoMoS", a project of the "it's OWL" Leading-Edge Cluster, partially funded by the German Federal Ministry of Education and Research (BMBF).

© IFIP International Federation for Information Processing 2016
Published by Springer International Publishing Switzerland 2016. All Rights Reserved
C. Bogdan et al. (Eds.): HCSE 2016/HESSD 2016, LNCS 9856, pp. 281–300, 2016.
DOI: 10.1007/978-3-319-44902-9_18

it is no longer sufficient to provide a single "one-size-fits-all" user interface. The problem increases even more if we consider dynamic changes in the context of use. In this case, allowing flexible and natural interaction with such devices requires additional features like UI adaptivity to automatically react to the changing context of use parameters at runtime and task-continuity for supporting a seamless handover between different devices. For illustrating the problem, we introduce a real world example scenario which is derived from the banking domain.

While customers accessed banking services solely via isolated channels (through banking personnel or ATM) in the past, using different channels during a transaction is nowadays increasingly gaining popularity. Depending on the situation, customers are able to access their banking services where, when and how it suits them best. In the world of Omni-Channel-Banking, customers are in control of the channels they wish to use, experiencing a self-determined "Omni-Channel-Journey". For example, if the customers pursue an "Omni-Channel-Journey" for a payment cashout process, they can begin an interaction using one channel (prepare cashout at desktop at home), modify the transaction on their way on a mobile channel, and finalize it at the automatic teller machine (ATM) (see Fig. 1). It is important to notice, that each channel has its own special context of use and eventually the contextual parameters (user (U), platform (P), and environment (E)) can change if there is a channel switch. Thus, Omni-Channel-Banking brings the industry closer to the promise of true contextual banking in which financial services become seamlessly embedded into the lives of individual and business customers.

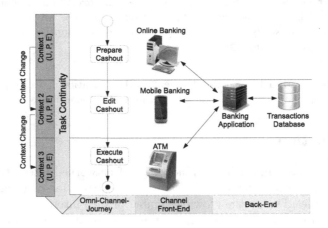

**Fig. 1.** Example scenario: Omni-Channel-Journey with task-continuity

However, the advancement from Multi-Channel- to Omni-Channel-Banking (compare Table 1) is a difficult task for developers of such systems. Developers are facing the following challenges:

- **C1:** Support for modeling and adaptation of heterogeneous user interfaces (UIs) satisfying different contexts of use (user, platform, environment).

**Table 1.** Multi-Channel-Banking vs. Omni-Channel-Banking

| Multi-Channel-Banking | Omni-Channel-Banking |
| --- | --- |
| Fixed channel usage | Flexible channel usage |
| Separation of channels | Integration of channels |
| Data redundancy in channels | Data synchronization between channels |
| Little or no channel switch | Continuous channel switch |

- **C2:** Support for a flexible channel usage depending on the context.
- **C3:** Support for a seamless handover between channels allowing task-continuity. When the user moves from one device to another, the user is able to seamlessly continue her task.

According to Petrasch [1], the effort of implementing an application's user interface constitutes at least 50 percent of the total implementation effort. Developing separate applications for each potential device and operating system is neither a practical nor a cost effective solution, especially if we consider heterogeneous contexts of use as they were described in the example scenario above. Model-based User Interface Development (MBUID) is a promising candidate for mastering the complex development task in a systematic, precise and appropriately formal way. For tackling the above mentioned challenges we present a model-based engineering process for context-adaptive UIs which integrates human-centered design aspects into the development process. Our engineering approach provides specific support especially for modeling, transformation, and execution of context-adaptive UIs enabling task-continuous usage of cross-channel applications.

The paper is structured as follows: First, we describe some background information and related work in the area of engineering methods for UIs, covering multi-device and cross-channel UI development as well as UI adaptation. Then, we present our model-based engineering approach for the development of context-adaptive UIs supporting task-continuity. After that, we present the instantiation of our engineering approach based on a case study from the banking domain. Finally, we conclude with a summary and an outlook for future research work.

## 2 Background and Related Work

In recent years, a number of approaches have addressed the problem of engineering user interfaces for different contexts of use. Our work is inspired by and based on existing approaches from the area of model-based UI development, adaptive UIs and distributed user interfaces (DUIs). In this section, we especially review prior work that explores the development of multi-device, cross-channel and adaptive user interfaces (UIs) supporting task-continuity.

## 2.1 Multi-device UI Development

The development of multi-device UIs has been subject of extensive research [2], where different approaches were proposed to support efficient development of UIs for different target platforms. On the one hand, model-based UI development approaches were proposed which aim to create multi-device UIs based on the transformation of abstract user interface models to final user interfaces. Widely studied approaches are UsiXML [25], MARIA [3] and IFML[1] that support the abstract modeling of user interfaces and their transformation to multi-device UIs including web interfaces. In [4], we present a specialized approach for model-based development of heterogeneous UIs for different target platforms including self-service systems like ATMs. On the other hand, there are also existing approaches like Damask [5] and Gummy [6] following the WYSIWYG paradigm. While Damask is a prototyping tool for creating sketches of multi-device web interfaces, Gummy is a design environment for graphical UIs that allows designers to create interfaces for multiple devices using visual tools to automatically generate and maintain a platform-independent description of the UI. While above mentioned approaches support the development of multi-device UIs regarding specification and generation of UIs for different target platforms, they do not cover mechanisms to support channel switches and data synchronization between different target platforms at runtime.

## 2.2 Cross-Channel UI Development

Previous work by the research community has covered concepts and techniques to dynamically support the distribution of UIs by supporting task-continuity for the end-users. One of the concepts is called *UI migration*, which follows the idea of transferring a UI or parts of it from a source to a target device, while enabling task-continuity through carrying the UI's state across devices. In [9], we present a model-based framework for the migration and adaptation of user interfaces across different devices. In [7] and similarly in [24], the authors present a solution to support migration of interactive applications among various devices, including digital TVs and mobile devices, allowing users to freely move around at home and outdoor. The aim is to provide users with a seamless and supportive environment for ubiquitous access in multi-device contexts of use. In the case of web applications, most solutions rely on HTML proxy-based techniques to dynamically push and pull UIs [8]. An extension of this concept is presented in [10], where the authors propose XDStudio to support interactive development of cross-device UIs. In addition, there is also existing work on the specification support for cross-device applications. In [11] for example, the authors present their framework Panelrama which is a web-based framework for the construction of applications using DUIs. In a similar work [12], the authors present Conductor, which is a prototype framework serving as an example for the construction of cross-device applications. While above mentioned approaches support the

---

[1] http://www.ifml.org.

specification and development of cross-channel UIs for different target platforms, they do not address combining the aspect of UI adaptation for different contexts of use with task-continuity.

## 2.3  Adaptive UIs

In recent research works, adaptive UIs have been promoted as a solution for context variability due to their ability to automatically adapt to the context of use at runtime. A key goal behind adaptive UIs is plasticity, denoting a UI's ability to preserve its usability across multiple contexts of use [13]. Norcio and Stanley [14] consider that the idea of an adaptive UI is straightforward since it simply means: "The interface should adapt to the user; rather than the user must adapt to the system." Based on [15] we can generally differentiate between the following types of adaptive UIs:

*Adaptable user interfaces* allow interested stakeholders to manually adapt the desired characteristics; example: a software application that supports the manual customization of its toolbars by adding and removing buttons. *Semi-automated adaptive user interfaces* automatically react to a change in the context-of-use by changing one or more of their characteristics using a predefined set of adaptation rules. For example: an application can use a sensor to measure the distance between the end-user and a display device, and then trigger predefined adaptation rules to adjust the font-size. *Fully-automated adaptive user interfaces* can automatically react to a change in the context-of-use. However, the adaptation has to employ a learning mechanism, which makes use of data that is logged over time. One simple example is a software application, which logs the number of times each end-user clicks on its toolbar buttons and automatically reorders these buttons differently for each end-user according to the usage frequency.

A classification of different adaptation techniques was introduced by Oppermann [18] and refined by Brusilovsky [17]. UIs with adaptation capabilities have been proposed in the context of various domains (e.g. [19, 20, 26] or [27]) and there are also proposals for integrating adaptive UI capabilities in enterprise applications (e.g. [16]). Although above mentioned approaches already present technical solutions for supporting UI adaptivity and model-based development approaches were proposed in the past (e.g. [23]), an engineering process for the development of context-adaptive UIs enabling task-continuity is not fully covered. Leaning on existing concepts of adaptive/cross-channel UIs and our previous work [21], where we propose a meta-method for engineering advanced user interfaces, we present a model-based engineering approach for developing context-adaptive UIs enbaling task-continuous usage of cross-channel applications.

## 3  Engineering Process

In this section, we present a model-based engineering process for development of context-adaptive UIs in order to tackle the motivated challenges C1, C2 and C3. Figure 2 gives a general overview of our engineering process which is

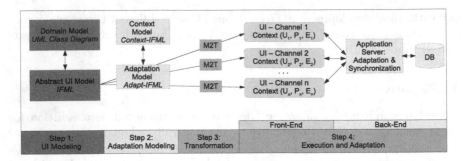

**Fig. 2.** Model-based engineering approach for developing context-adaptive UIs supporting task-continuity

divided into four main steps:: *UI Modeling, Adaptation Modeling, Transformation,* and *Execution and Adaptation.*

In the following subsections each engineering step is explained in more detail by describing the used artifacts and activities.

### 3.1   UI Modeling

For supporting the development of various UIs allowing access for different channels and minimizing recurrent development efforts in establishing the needed Front-ends, our engineering process begins with the *UI Modeling* step. The goal of this step is specification of an abstract UI representation that serves as a basis for the transformation and generation of heterogeneous UI variants for different channels. For accomplishing this step, we decided to use existing modeling languages standardized by the Object Management Group (OMG). As a consequence, in the *UI Modeling* step we make use of *UML Class Diagrams* and the *Interaction Flow Modeling Language (IFML).* In the beginning of the engineering process, the developers use *UML Class Diagrams* for specifying a *Domain Model* describing the data entities of the user interface. After that, they make use of the *Interaction Flow Modeling language (IFML)* that supports the modeling of the structure, content and navigation needed to characterize the UI Front-End in an abstract manner. For performing the *UI Modeling* step, the developers are able to use the open source IFML Editor Eclipse plugin[2] that enables a complete specification of the *abstract UI model* referencing the *Domain Model* entities.

### 3.2   Adaptation Modeling

After modeling the core UI characteristics using a *Domain* and *Abstract UI* model, the developers need to specify adaptation rules that decide how the user interface is adapted to specific contextual parameters (e.g. user, platform and environment) at runtime. Therefore, our engineering approach provides an *Adaptation Modeling* step, which allows explicit modeling of UI adaptation rules.

---

[2] http://ifml.github.io.

For defining the adaptation rules, we first introduce a metamodel for context modeling (*Context-IFML*) that serves as a basis for describing the contextual parameters in a fine grained and extensible manner. After that, we introduce an adaptation metamodel (*Adapt-IFML*) for specifying complete adaptation rules.

Figure 3 gives an overview of our metamodel for context modeling. The metamodel *ContextModel* (*Context-IFML*) consists of the three main classes *User*, *Platform*, and *Environment* that characterize the specific contextual parameters. The class *User* for example, is subclassified in *PersonalInformation*, *Preferences* and *Knowledge*, while the classes provide different attributes to specify varying peculiarities of a user. Similarly different forms of the platform and characteristics of the environment can be specified with the help of *Context-IFML*. This way, the developers are able to specify heterogeneous context of use scenarios and to explicitly define the events and conditions for adapting the UI. For the complete definition of an adaptation rule we introduce the metamodel for adaptation modeling (*Adapt-IFML*) that is depicted in Fig. 4. Regarding our metamodel an adaptation model consists of different adaptation rules that are structured according to the Event-Condition-Action (ECA) paradigm. While the preconditions of an adaptation rule (event and condition) are specified based on the context model, the *Action* class provides different mechanisms to adapt the UI at runtime. Basically three different UI adaptation operations are supported, namely *Task-*, *Navigation-* and *Layout-ChangeOperation*, while each of them can be aggregated to more complex UI adaptation operations called *ComposedAction*. *Task-ChangeOperations* support adaptation by flexibly showing and hiding interaction elements of the UI. By using the operations *AddViewComponent* or *DeleteViewComponent* specific UI interaction elements like tables, textfields etc. can be shown or hidden depending on the specified adaptation rule. In a similar way, the *Navigation-ChangeOperation* can be used for adding, deleting and redirecting links between user interface flows. This way, the navigation flow of the UI can be flexibly adapted based on the contextual parameters that are defined in the preconditions. Our metamodel for adaptation modeling also supports the definiton of *Layout-ChangeOperations* like *ChangeFont* or *SplitViewContainer* for dividing a complex UI view container into multiple view containers, so that small screen sizes for example are satisfied. For supporting the *Adaptation Modeling* step, we extended the standard IFML metamodel with *Context-IFML* and *Adapt-IFML* according to the previous description. Based on this extensions the developers are able to specify different UI adaptation rules that are evaluated at runtime.

## 3.3 Transformation

After finishing the modeling steps, the developers are facing the task to define transformations to generate numerous UI Front-Ends for different channels. Therefore, in the transformation step several model-to-text transformation (M2T) templates are defined that transfer the abstract UI models into final UIs that are running on different target platforms in order to support access to

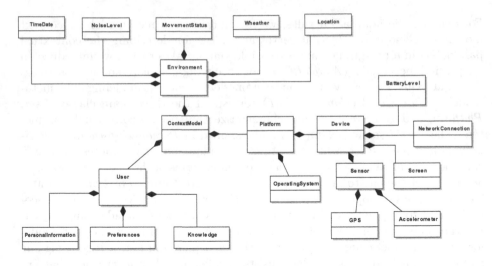

**Fig. 3.** Metamodel for context modeling (Context-IFML)

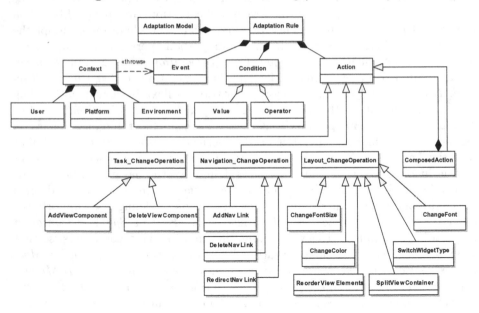

**Fig. 4.** Metamodel for adaptation modeling (Adapt-IFML)

different channels (Front-End). By generating different UI views and supporting different UI - Channels, users are able to flexibly select the channel of their choice depending on the context. For supporting the transformation step, we implemented an Xtend[3] plugin that maps the abstract UI model elements to specific elements of a target language/technology. The implemented Xtend

---

[3] http://www.eclipse.org/xtend.

plugin includes different Xtend templates to transfer the IFML source model into final user interfaces that support different context of use parameters. During the transformation process, not only the mapping between the source abstract UI model and the target final user interface (FUI) is established, but also the specified adaptation rules are transformed into the target language of the FUI, so that the generated UI can adapt itself at runtime according to the predefined rules.

### 3.4   Execution and Adaptation

For practical usage of the resulting final user interfaces that were reached after the modeling and transformation steps, the developers need an execution environment that executes and adapts the UIs according to the specified adaptation rules. For supporting this task, we present a solution architecture enabling automatic UI adaptation and synchronization. Figure 5 gives an architectural overview of the execution environment for context-adaptive UIs. The solution architecture is based on IBM's MAPE-K [22] loop, where an *Adaptation Manager* monitors and adapts the *Context-Adaptive UI* that can run on different platforms. The *Adaptation Manager* consists of five main components that work according the adaptation rules that were specified in the *Adaptation Model*: The *Monitor* component is responsible for observing context information that are provided by the *Context Manager*. All contextual parameters that were defined based on the *Context Model* are observed, so that the *Analyze* component is able to decide whether adaptation is needed. Therefore, the conditions for triggering an adaptation rule are analyzed and if adaptations are required, an adaptation schedule is done by the *Plan* component. Finally, the adaptation operations are performed by the *Execute* component, so that an adapted UI can be presented. The *Knowledge* base is responsible for storing data that is logged over time and can be used for inferring future adaptation operations. In addition to UI adaptation, for supporting a seamless handover between channels and allowing task-continuity for the user, our solution architecture includes a dedicated *Synchronization Server* which is responsible for storing and sharing of data (e.g. UI

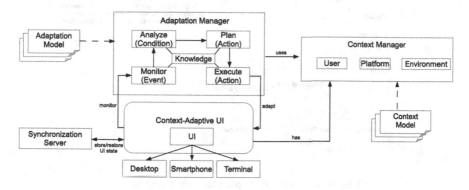

**Fig. 5.** Architectural overview of context-adaptive UIs

state or user preferences). The UI state including entered input data by the users is stored and restored so that when the user moves from one channel to another, the user is able to seamlessly continue her task on the new UI-Channel.

# 4 Instantiation of Engineering Process

In this section, the instantiation of the development process according to the previously described engineering process is presented in more detail. To show the feasibility of our approach, we first present the setting of an industrial case-study dealing with the implementation of context-adaptive UIs for a cross-channel banking application employing web-based technologies. After that, we present the instantiation of the engineering process by describing the implementation of the different steps.

## 4.1 Setting of the Case Study

Our "Omni-Channel-Banking" case-study supports a variety of different channels to access banking services. Figure 6 shows its overall architecture.

On each device - *PC, Mobile, ATM* - the client application is running as a single-page web application inside a browser. Each device has an underlying *Context Manager* that observes and delivers context information to the *Back-End Server*, which is responsible for

- serving an application to the browser, adapted to a particular context of use,
- serving application specific data to the client via HTTP/REST,
- managing application state and UI adaptation,
- requesting information from a *Transaction Processing Back-End* and serving it to the client,
- sending financial transactions to the *Transaction Processing Back-End* for execution.

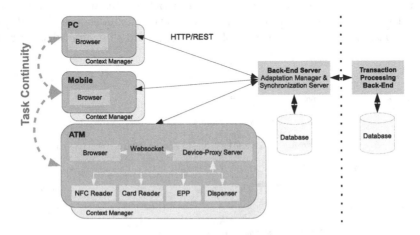

**Fig. 6.** Case-Study application architecture

The data format for all data exchanged through HTTP/REST requests is *JavaScript Object Notation* (JSON).

The *Transaction Processing Back-End* is not part of our application, but represents an existing infrastructure for processing financial transactions. The *Back-End Server* communicates with this transaction processing system. The communication protocol between the *Transaction Processing Back-End* and our sample application's *Back-End Server* depends on an existing infrastructure. Thus, the *Back-End Server* needs to provide a custom adapter for interfacing with this system.

In our case study, PC and mobile applications are identical concerning their functionality. The main difference comes from adaptation to different context of use scenarios (e.g. screen sizes, operation through keypad/touch screen etc.). This also includes spreading of functiontionality on the mobile device over multiple dialogs, compared to the PC application. In contrast to PC and mobile clients, the application architecture of the ATM client is significantly different. This is due to the need for supporting a whole variety of ATM specific hardware devices, like *NFC Reader, Card Reader, Encrypting Pin Pad (EPP), Cash Dispenser*, etc. For interoperability reasons, ATM vendors are using a common software stack called XFS, which is layered on top of device specific drivers. XFS stands for *Extensions for Financial Services* and is standardized by CEN, the *European Commitee for Standardization.* Since a browser itself can not directly access the XFS-API, we delegate device control to a *Device-Proxy Server* running directly on the ATM.

## 4.2   UI/Adaptation Modeling and Transformation

For realizing the modeling (UI and adaptation) and transformation step of the engineering approach, we have implemented a model-based UI development (MBUID) process which is depicted in Fig. 7. This MBUID process supports the modeling of UIs and adaptation rules as well as their transformation to final user interfaces, which are the view parts of the single-page application rendered as HTML5 by the browser. Based on the open source IFML Editor Eclipse plugin developers are able to specify the domain and abstract UI model. In Fig. 8 the domain model and an excerpt of the abstract UI model showing the login view are depicted for the example scenario of our case study. As a complementary modeling step, the IFML extensions *Context-IFML* and *Adapt-IFML* allow the specification of adaptation rules for UI adaptation at runtime. For showing the structure of such adaptation rules, Fig. 9 shows two exemplary adaptation rules represented as a table. For transforming these models into final web UI views, we implemented an Xtend plugin that maps the IFML model elements to specific HTML5 elements. The Xtend plugin includes different Xtend templates to transfer the IFML source model into web UIs supporting different context of use parameters.

During the transformation process, the application's view is built upon basic components with a custom look &feel, like buttons, text input fields, dropdown lists, tables, etc. As a basis for these components, we did not use AngularJS

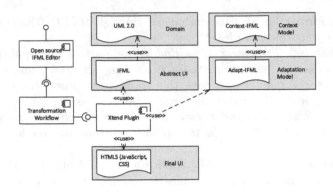

**Fig. 7.** Implemented model-based UI development process

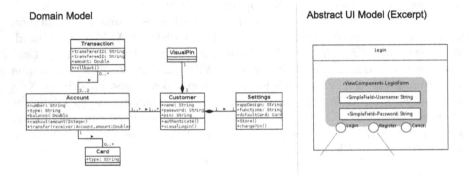

**Fig. 8.** Exemplary domain model and excerpt of the abstract UI model

directives, but implemented components based on the *HTML5 Web Components*[4] specification promoted by Google as W3C standard.

Our custom components are sensitive to the context of use they are being used in and adapt themselves accordingly. On mobile devices and on the ATM, for example, buttons are larger and more suitable for touch operation than on desktop devices.

Figure 10 shows buttons and text input fields. Their desktop representation is depicted on the left side, their mobile appearance on the right side of the picture.

During the transformation process for all device classes, a button is created the same way:

```
<komos-button colorscheme="cs1" ng-click="confirm()">
   Confirm
<komos-button>
```

---

[4] https://www.w3.org/TR/components-intro.

| Adapation Rule - Example 1 | |
|---|---|
| Event | User.Preferences.FontSize = 18 |
| Condition | Value.DefaultFontSize < 18 ? |
| Action | Layout_ChangeOperation.ChangeFontSize() |

| Adapation Rule - Example 2 | |
|---|---|
| Event | Platform.Device = Mobile<br>Platform.Device.Screen = small |
| Condition | Operator.Compare(DefaultScreenSize, TargetScreenSize) |
| Action | Layout_ChangeOperation.SplitViewContainer() |

**Fig. 9.** Examples for adaptation rules

**Fig. 10.** Buttons and text fields for desktop and mobile

The following example shows how to create a text input field with a label by mapping an IFML simple field element to the following code snippet:

```
<komos−textfield label="Current _PIN" ng−model="model.currentPin">
  </komos−textfield>
```

In order to provide a unified layout management for our application, our model-to-text (M2T) transformation process implements a custom layout manager. It provides an easy to use grid layout system, based on row and column elements realized as AngularJS directives. Under the hood, it uses HTML5 Flexbox. Figure 11 shows the generated code snippet to create the login dialog that is depicted below.

Beside the mapping from abstract UI models to HTML5 views, we have established a transformation process for translating the adaptation rules into the target language of the final user interface, so that runtime adaption of the UI can be supported. As we have decided to use the Nools[5] engine as a rule-based execution environment for executing context-adaptive UIs (see Subsect. 4.4 for details), we implemented particular Xtend templates to transform the *Adapt-IFML* adaptation rules to rules specified with the Nools DSL. The result of such a generated adaptation rule is shown in Fig. 12.

## 4.3 Execution and Adaptation (Front-End)

While the previous subsection presented our MBUID process to support the modeling and generation of view aspects of the *Front-End*, this subsection deals with the execution of the resulting UIs. In this context, we especially present the controller part of the *Front-End*, which is responsible for application logic and communication with the *Back End Server*. In conjunction with this topic,

---

[5] https://github.com/C2FO/nools.

```
<komos-container>
  <komos-row>
    <komos-column span-3>
      <komos-label>Username</komos-label>
    </komos-column>
    <komos-column span-8>
      <komos-textfield name="username" ng-model="model.username">
        </komos-textfield>
    </komos-column>
  </komos-row>

  <komos-row>
    <komos-column span-3>
      <komos-label>Password</komos-label>
    </komos-column>
    <komos-column span-8>
      <komos-textfield name="password" ng-model="model.password">
        </komos-textfield>
    </komos-column>
  </komos-row>

  <komos-row>
    <komos-column offset -3 span-8>
      <komos-button colorscheme="cs1" ng-click="login(form)">
        Login
      </komos-button>
      <komos-button colorscheme="cs5" ui-sref="public.signup">
        Register
      </komos-button>
      <komos-button colorscheme="cs3" ng-click="reset(form)">
        Cancel
      </komos-button>
    </komos-column>
  </komos-row>
</komos-container>
```

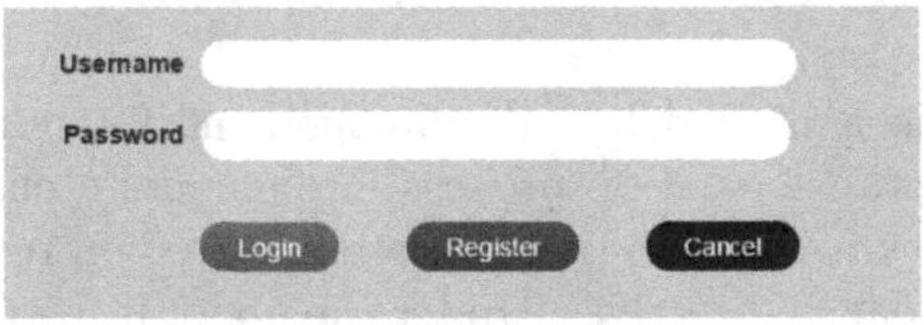


**Fig. 11.** Desktop UI: generated code snippet and corresponding login dialog

```
rule AtmProfile {
    when {
        p : Platform p.type == "atm";
    }
    then {
        displayProperties.type = p.type;
        displayProperties.controlActionType = "atm-action-button";
        displayProperties.singleChoiceType = "single-choice-list";
    }
}
```

**Fig. 12.** Example of a generated adaptation rule that is represented in the Nools DSL

we also present the aspect of channel handover and task-continuity. The aspect of UI adaptation at runtime will be explained in the next subsection.

As shown in Fig. 13, the *Front-End* consists of a HTML5/JavaScript single-page application running in a web browser. It exchanges JSON messages with the *Back-End Server* through HTTP/REST.

The browser application's main building blocks are:

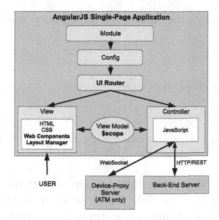

**Fig. 13.** Front-End Architecture

- AngularJS[6]: Google's open-source web application framework for developing single-page applications in JavaScript
- UI Router[7]: flexible client-side routing with nested views in AngularJS
- Web Components: UI components with custom look & feel
- Layout Manager: custom layout manager

AngularJS supports the model-view-controller (MVC) design pattern by decoupling the application's presentation layer, which is defined through HTML5 (see previous subsection), from the model and application logic by two-way data-binding through a `$scope` object. In addition, AngularJS provides a variety of other services, including modularization and definition of custom directives.

UI Router is the client-side routing component of AngularJS and the central key component to implement task continuity. The developer assigns a particular application state, identified by a name (`protected.main`), with a view (`main.html`) and a controller (`MainCtrl`):

```
angular.module('komosApp').config(function ($stateProvider) {
  $stateProvider
    .state('protected.main', {
      url: '/',
      templateUrl: 'protected/main/main.html',
      controller: 'MainCtrl',
      authenticate: true
    });
});
```

In order to support task continuity and transfer application state between devices, the current state name and its associated context are saved to the *Back-End Server*.

Inside a view controller and prior to saving a state, all context information necessary for recovery is added to a state-context object. This includes the UI's

---

[6] https://angularjs.org.
[7] https://github.com/angular-ui/ui-router/wiki.

view-model, as well as any other necessary information associated with the current state.

```
var context = {
  // the view model:
  viewModel: $scope.model,
  // state specific arbitrary properties:
  param1: someValue,
  data: someData
};

PersistStateService.save('protected.main', context, function (err, data) {
  if (err) model.errors.message = err.data.message;
});
```

We implemented an AngularJS service named `PersistStateService`, which converts the object `context` to JSON and sends it to the *Back-End Server*, where it is stored under the name of the state, e.g. `protected.main`. To invoke a previously saved state, the application just needs to retrieve the current state name and invoke it:

```
$rootScope.$state.go('protected.main');
```

On instantiation of the AngularJS controller associated with this state, the controller calls the service's restore method to retrieve the previously stored information:

```
PersistStateService.restore('protected.main', function (err, context) {
  if (err) {
    model.errors.message = err.data.message;
  } else {
    // context now contains the previously saved information
    $scope.model = context.viewModel; // this updates the UI!!
    someValue = context.param1;
    someData = context.data;
  }
});
```

Both, saving and retrieving context data for a state happens within the same controller. Each controller knows exactly which data needs to be saved in order to be able to restore itself. This information is hidden from other parts of the application. The only knowledge necessary from the outside is the name of the state, `protected.main` in our example.

Because of AngularJS' two-way data-binding, assigning the view-model to `$scope.model` immediately updates the view.

### 4.4   Execution and Adaptation (Back-End)

The application's *Back-End* is implemented in JavaScript (see Fig. 14) and uses Node.js[8] as its runtime environment. It is built upon Google's V8 JavaScript engine also used by Google Chrome and provides a high-performance runtime environment for non-blocking and event-driven programming.

ExpressJS[9], which is a middleware for Node.js, provides components for processing of requests and routing. An application sets up request handlers,

---

[8] https://nodejs.org.
[9] https://expressjs.com.

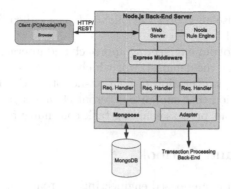

**Fig. 14.** Back-End architecture

**Fig. 15.** Context-Adaptive UIs for a cross-channel banking web application supporting task-continuity

which are automatically invoked when a client request arrives. Within a request handler, the request is processed, a response is prepared and returned. Request handlers communicate with the database or *Transaction Processing Back-End*.

For execution and adaptation of the final UIs at runtime, our Back-End Server integrates *Nools* as a rule-based execution environment for representing the *Adaptation Manager*. *Nools* is an efficient RETE-based rule engine for Node.js written in JavaScript and provides an API and rule language (DSL) for specifying fact and rules. By transforming context information to facts and translating the specified adaptation rules to *Nools* rules, the *Nools* engine supports the automatic adaptation of UIs at runtime as reaction to dynamically changing context of use parameters.

The document database *MongoDB*[10] belongs into the category of NoSQL ("Not Only SQL") databases. In this context, a "document" consists of a user-defined data structure of key-value pairs, which is associated with a key. Documents can also contain other documents. The schema of a database is dynamic and can be modified at runtime. To access the database in an object-

---

[10] https://www.mongodb.org.

oriented fashion, we use an *Object Document Mapper* called *Mongoose* on top of MongoDB's Node.js driver.

The instantiation of our engineering approach and interaction of all described technologies resulted in the demonstrator which is shown in Fig. 15. Our demonstrator shows the implementation of context-adaptive UIs for a cross-channel banking web-application that supports different channels (Desktop, Tablet, and ATM) for a cash payout process enabling task-continuity for the customers.

## 5   Conclusion and Outlook

This paper presents a model-based engineering approach that supports systematic and efficient development of context-adaptive UIs for heterogeneous and dynamically changing contexts of use (user, platform, environment). The proposed engineering approach supports modeling, transformation and execution of context-adaptive UIs that enable a personalized, flexible and task-continuous usage of cross-channel applications. The feasibility of the approach was shown based on an industrial case study, where the implementation of context-adaptive UIs for a cross-channel banking web application is presented. Furthermore, industrial experiences resulted in positive feedback regarding the applicability and efficiency of the approach. However, we plan to evaluate the efficiency and effectiveness of the approach in more complex development scenarios. Future work will also cover the evaluation of usability aspects for end-users of the generated and adapted UIs as well as for the developers using the tools and languages proposed in our approach.

## References

1. Petrasch, R.: Model based user interface design: model driven architecture und HCI patterns. In: GI Software-technik-Trends, Band 27, Heft 3, pp. 5–10 (2007)
2. Paternò, F., Santoro, C.: A logical framework for multi-device user interfaces. In: Proceedings of the 4th ACM SIGCHI Symposium on Engineering Interactive Computing Systems (EICS 2012), pp. 45–50. ACM, New York (2012)
3. Paternò, F., Santoro, C., Spano, L.D.: MARIA: a universal, declarative, multiple abstraction-level language for service-oriented applications in ubiquitous environments. ACM Trans. Comput.-Hum. Interact. **16**(4), 19 (2009)
4. Yigitbas, E., Fischer, H., Kern, T., Paelke, V.: Model-based development of adaptive UIs for multi-channel self-service systems. In: Sauer, S., Bogdan, C., Forbrig, P., Bernhaupt, R., Winckler, M. (eds.) HCSE 2014. LNCS, vol. 8742, pp. 267–274. Springer, Heidelberg (2014)
5. Lin, J., Landay, J.A.: Employing patterns and layers for early-stage design and prototyping of cross-device user interfaces. In: Proceedings of the SIGCHI Conference on Human Factors in Computing Systems (CHI 2008), pp. 1313–1322. ACM, New York (2008)
6. Meskens, J., Vermeulen, J., Luyten, K., Coninx, K.: Gummy for multi-platform user interface designs: shape me, multiply me, fix me, use me. In: Proceedings of the working conference on Advanced Visual Interfaces (AVI 2008), pp. 233–240. ACM, New York (2008)

7. Paternò, F., Santoro, C., Scorcia, A.: Ambient intelligence for supporting task continuity across multiple devices and implementation languages. Comput. J. **53**(8), 1210–1228 (2010)
8. Ghiani, G., Paternò, F., Santoro, C.: Push and pull of web user interfaces in multi-device environments. In: Proceedings of the International Working Conference on Advanced Visual Interfaces (AVI 2012), pp. 10–17. ACM, New York (2012)
9. Yigitbas, E., Sauer, S., Engels, G.: A model-based framework for multi-adaptive migratory user interfaces. In: Kurosu, M. (ed.) HCI 2015. LNCS, vol. 9170, pp. 563–572. Springer, Heidelberg (2015)
10. Nebeling, M., Mintsi, T., Husmann, M., Norrie, M.: Interactive development of cross-device user interfaces. In: Proceedings of the SIGCHI Conference on Human Factors in Computing Systems (CHI 2014) (2014)
11. Yang, J., Wigdor, D.: Panelrama: enabling easy specification of cross-device web applications. In: Proceedings of the SIGCHI Conference on Human Factors in Computing Systems (CHI 2014), pp. 2783–2792. ACM, New York (2014)
12. Hamilton, P., Wigdor, D.J.: Conductor: enabling and understanding cross-device interaction. In: Proceedings of the SIGCHI Conference on Human Factors in Computing Systems (CHI 2014), pp. 2773–2782. ACM, New York (2014)
13. Coutaz, J.: User interface plasticity: model driven engineering to the limit! In: Proceedings of the 2nd ACM SIGCHI Symposium on Engineering Interactive Computing Systems, p. 18. ACM (2010)
14. Norcio, A.F., Stanley, J.: Adaptive human-computer interfaces: a literature survey and perspective. IEEE Trans. Syst. Man Cybern. **19**, 399–408 (1989)
15. Akiki, P.A., Bandara, A.K., Yijun, Y.: Adaptive model-driven user interface development systems. ACM Comput. Surv. **47**(1), 33 (2014). Article 9
16. Akiki, P.A., Bandara, A.K., Yijun, Y.: Integrating adaptive user interface capabilities in enterprise applications. In: Proceedings of the 36th International Conference on Software Engineering (ICSE 2014), pp. 712–723. ACM, New York (2014)
17. Brusilovsky, P.: Adaptive hypermedia. User Model. User-Adap. Inter. **11**(1–2), 87–110 (2001)
18. Oppermann, R.: Individualisierte Systemnutzung. In: Paul, M. (ed.) GI - 19. Jahrestagung I. Informatik-Fachberichte, vol. 222, pp. 131–145. Springer, London (1989)
19. Gajos, K.Z., Weld, D.S., Wobbrock, J.O.: Automatically generating personalized user interfaces with Supple. Artif. Intell. **174**(12–13), 910–950 (2010)
20. Jovanovic, M., Starcevic, D., Jovanovic, Z.: Bridging user context and design models to build adaptive user interfaces. In: Sauer, S., Bogdan, C., Forbrig, P., Bernhaupt, R., Winckler, M. (eds.) HCSE 2014. LNCS, vol. 8742, pp. 36–56. Springer, Heidelberg (2014)
21. Sauer, S.: Applying meta-modeling for the definition of model-driven development methods of advanced user interfaces. In: Hussmann, H., Meixner, G., Zuehlke, D. (eds.) MDD of Advanced User Interfaces. SCI, vol. 340, pp. 67–86. Springer, Heidelberg (2011)
22. Kephart, J.O., Chess, D.M.: The vision of autonomic computing. Computer **36**(1), 41–50 (2003)
23. Clerckx, T., Luyten, K., Coninx, K.: DynaMo-AID: a design process and a runtime architecture for dynamic model-based user interface development. In: Feige, U., Roth, J. (eds.) DSV-IS 2004 and EHCI 2004. LNCS, vol. 3425, pp. 77–95. Springer, Heidelberg (2005)

24. Luyten, K., Van den Bergh, J., Vandervelpen, C., Coninx, K.: Designing distributed user interfaces for ambient intelligent environments using models and simulations. Comput. Graph. **30**(5), 702–713 (2006)
25. Limbourg, Q., Vanderdonckt, J., Michotte, B., Bouillon, L., López-Jaquero, V.: USIXML: a language supporting multi-path development of user interfaces. In: Feige, U., Roth, J. (eds.) DSV-IS 2004 and EHCI 2004. LNCS, vol. 3425, pp. 200–220. Springer, Heidelberg (2005)
26. Demeure, A., Calvary, G., Coninx, K.: COMET(s), A software architecture style and an interactors toolkit for plastic user interfaces. In: Graham, T.C.N. (ed.) DSV-IS 2008. LNCS, vol. 5136, pp. 225–237. Springer, Heidelberg (2008)
27. Ghiani, G., Manca, M., Paternò, F., Porta, C.: Beyond Responsive Design: context-dependent multimodal augmentation of web applications. In: Awan, I., Younas, M., Franch, X., Quer, C. (eds.) MobiWIS 2014. LNCS, vol. 8640, pp. 71–85. Springer, Heidelberg (2014)

# UCProMo—Towards a User-Centred Process Model

Tom Gross[✉]

Human-Computer Interaction Group,
University of Bamberg, Bamberg, Germany
tom.gross@uni-bamberg.de

**Abstract.** The field of Software Engineering has a long tradition of developing sophisticated process models and methods and tools for its support. At the same time in the field of Human-Computer Interaction process models, methods, and tools have been developed and standardised internationally. Approaches from both fields have a lot to offer. However, despite great approaches for joining strengths and advantages of both fields, synergies are not yet fully used. In this paper I present the *UCProMo* User-Centred Process Model that provides an integrated approach by leveraging on existing process models, methods, and tools from both fields. *UCProMo* capitalises on clear phases, iteration, and strong involvement and participation of users throughout the whole process, which leads to integrated results and models of technology (esp. software) and ultimately to smooth user journeys through the whole system.

**Keywords:** Software engineering · Human-Computer Interaction · Process model · Methods and tools

## 1 Introduction

In any kind of endeavour to design and develop systems, a structured approach is indispensable. This particularly applies to Software Engineering (SE) and Human-Computer Interaction (HCI). Process models support a structured approach by suggesting process phases and the order in which those phases should be gone through.

In SE over the last decades many great process models have been presented. The traditional waterfall model already provided a list of steps [18]. Later, Boehm published the famous 'Spiral Model of Software Development and Enhancement' in [3]. It suggests to go through the steps in a spiral from inside out and to continually expand the results of each phase in each circle. The Unified Process [14] has been a big leap and seen many variations and refinements. Many other process models contributed to a heterogeneous landscape of process models.

In HCI a parallel emergence and evolution of process models could be witnessed. These models have many similarities with those in SE. Yet, two distinctions are that in general in HCI the involvement of users throughout the whole process played a central role, and the evaluation of the results with users had a high priority. For instance, the 'Star Life Cycle' of Hartson & Dix [10] suggested that from any phase there should be a connection to an evaluation phase that is in the heart of the process model. The diversity

© IFIP International Federation for Information Processing 2016

Published by Springer International Publishing Switzerland 2016. All Rights Reserved
C. Bogdan et al. (Eds.): HCSE 2016/HESSD 2016, LNCS 9856, pp. 301–313, 2016.
DOI: 10.1007/978-3-319-44902-9_19

of process models within HCI, eventually led to a standard process model for the 'Human-Centred Design of Interactive Systems' recommended by the International Standardisation Organisation (ISO) in the ISO 9241-210 [13].

Great contributions have been made towards combining approaches from SE and HCI. Most prominently, Usage-Centred Design is based on the idea to use 'abstract models to solve concrete problems' [8, p. 26]. It combines the HCI perspective of an early focus on users, their tasks, and their contexts with the SE paradigm of a strong focus on clear abstract models for analysis and design. Later, Activity Theory was integrated into the Usage-Centred Design model to become the Human Activity Modelling approach with better representations of human use of tools and artefacts [6]. Nunes picked up the strong orientation of actual usage or use and suggested a use-case-driven software development approach to combine SE and HCI [17].

Despite such great approaches for joining strengths and advantages of both fields, the potential for synergies is not yet fully used. Clearly both communities—the SE and the HCI—have reached out mutually. For instance, agile approaches put a strong focus on users and early on put a priority to user stories and user interfaces, etc. [1]. Yet, a challenge that remains is that some basic paradigms in SE and HCI are not commensurable. For instance, by and large in SE the perspective is abstract that leads to a great overview by focusing on the fundamental structure and behaviour of the overall system, and in HCI it is concrete that gives a detailed impression of the user interface by early focusing on the user experience. These perspectives shine through—even in combinations such as Usage-Centred Design there is a clear priority for models over interfaces; the authors call it a 'model-driven approach' [8, p. 42]. Other approaches such as the Human Activity Modelling offer a compromise of perspectives, but at the price of losing the original expressive power of both sides (i.e., high abstraction in SE; high concreteness in HCI).

In this paper I present the *UCProMo* User-Centred Process Model that provides an integrated approach by leveraging on existing process models from SE and HCI. Using the *UCProMo* model is easy and straightforward—designers and developers individually or in teams just need basic knowledge and experience in either field. Overall the approach follows the requirements for light, agile, and lean development published very recently in [15]. In the next section I discuss the background and related work of process models in SE, HCI, and beyond. Then I present the *UCProMo* User-Centred Process Model with its generic method-agnostic processes. A discussion and conclusions summarise the contributions and glance at future work.

## 2  Background and Related Work

Three categories of process models are relevant to our approach—process models from SE, from HCI, and combinations.

## 2.1 Process Models in SE

The field of SE has a long tradition of sophisticated process models and methods and tools for its support. Sommerville explains: 'the systematic approach that is used in software engineering is sometimes called a software process. A software process is a sequence of activities that leads to the production of a software product.' [19, p. 9]. And he continues: 'a software process model is a simplified representation of a software process. [...] These generic models ... are abstractions of the process that can be used to explain different approaches to software development.' [19, p. 28].

The waterfall model and the spiral modal are important early predecessors. The waterfall provided a detailed list of steps everybody should follow: system requirements; software requirements; analysis; program design; coding; testing; operation. It foresaw small iterations [18]. Its fundamental contribution was to lay out basic steps that are still relevant today. Later, Boehm published the 'Spiral Model of Software Development and Enhancement' [3]. It suggests to go through the steps in a spiral—inside out—and to continually expand the results of each phase in each cycle. The very important take away message—that is still important today—is to iterate and especially to continually re-evaluate the results.

More recently, the Unified Process was suggested as a 'set of activities needed to transform a user's requirements into a software system' [14, p. 4]. It is use-case driven (i.e., it departs from users and functionality for them); architecture-centric (i.e., all static and dynamic aspects of the system to be built); and iterative-incremental (i.e., it 'divides the work into smaller slices or mini-projects.' [14, p. 7]). Each cycle has four phases: inception (i.e., development of ideas), elaboration (i.e., specification of use cases and design of system architecture, construction (i.e., development of the system), and transition (i.e., movement from development via first beta-tests towards deployment). Orthogonal to the phases the Unified Process defines five core workflows. Requirements mainly fall into inception and elaboration; analysis mainly into elaboration; design between elaboration and construction; implementation into construction; and test between construction and transition [14]. The Unified Process was probably the biggest leap towards systematically including users and users' needs and requirements. Since then many variations and refinements were suggested—a very wide-spread being the Rational Unified Process by Kruchten [16].

## 2.2 Process Models in HCI

In HCI many process models have been suggested. Despite the fact that the basic goal and also some basic steps are the same as in SE there are quite some differences.

For many years the HCI community has been using a standard process model with the title 'Human-Centred Design of Interactive Systems'. It is now part of the ISO 9241 on Ergonomics of Human-System Interaction in the part ISO 9241-210 Human-Centred Design Processes for Interactive Systems [13] (formerly it was published in ISO 13407:1999 [12]). Its processes are: identification of the need for human-centred design; understanding and specification of the context of use; specification of the user and organisational requirements; production of the design solutions; and evaluation of the design against the requirements.

Also Unified Reference Frameworks have been developed to facilitate the process of developing user-centred systems by abstracting from hardware properties in abstract user interfaces [4]. And, Contextual Design offers a process model that has a strong focus on understanding users activities and requirements in the context where the users are using the system [11].

## 2.3    Process Models that Combine SE and HCI

Out of the approaches that combine process models from SE and HCI the Usage-Centred Design and the Human Activity Design have been most influential to our approach.

The Usage-Centred Design (UCD) draws from the Unified Process and combines it with principles from HCI. Like the Unified Process it is based on models; it uses 'abstract models to solve concrete problems' [8, p. 26]. Whereas the Unified Process suggests models that roughly correspond to its core workflows (i.e., a use-case model; an analysis model; a design model; a deployment model; an implementation model; and a test model), the UCD has three simple models at its core: the role model representing the relationships between users and the system; the task model showing the structure of the tasks that users need to perform; and the content model laying out the functionality of the user interface. Through the focus on these three principal models UCD aims to move away from an early focus on concrete users and concrete user interface designs that often prevail in HCI.

In the later Human Activity Modelling (HAM) [6] Constantine extended his UCD with Activity Theory. The cornerstones are activities, which are basically seen as a collective endeavour in which a community of participants transforms a material into an object. This community of participants uses tools and applies rules and division of labour to organise itself. HAM has three principal models: the activity context model that did not exist in UCD represents human activities; the participation model is an adaptation of the role model and describes user roles, yet now including the context of the activities in which they occur; and the performance model is based on the previous task model and contains user actions targeted at either other users or artefacts.

## 2.4    Summary of Background and Related Work

Overall the gap between both fields has not been fully bridged. As we have seen—despite the great progress in process models in SE and in HCI as well as stimulating combinations of SE and HCI approaches in the UCD and HAM—an integrated approach that leverages on the expressive power of both SE and HCI and can be flexibly applied by designers and developers of software with any knowledge and experience is still missing.

The related work also shows that some terms are not used consistently, which can be misleading—especially with respect to clearly distinguishing users and developers. For instance, as we have seen in the quotes above, the term *activity* has been used in the literature to refer to both, the things that developers are doing to develop concepts and systems and the things that users are doing with the system. In order to disambiguate terms this paper uses the following: a process refers to the whole endeavour of developing a system from the beginning to the end and independently of the path that is taken. A phase refers to a distinct and significant part of the process. Iteration refers to one cycle of steps that can be repeated eventually. The terms task, activity, and action are only used for user interaction with the system.

# 3 The *UCProMo* User-Centred Process Model

In the this section I present the *UCProMo* User-Centred Process Model with its generic method-agnostic phases. The related work above provides great stimuli for our process model. It leads to the following requirements for our process model that can be seen as an aggregated summary of the different advantages and strengths:

- *Phases* should be clearly defined and have definite beginnings and endings while at the same time allow flexible coupling, feedback and feedforward to other phases for an iterative as well as incremental process.
- *Abstract* modelling that allows keeping the complete system in focus should be combined with *concrete* users, user requirements and needs, and designs.
- *Heterogeneous* approaches and results throughout analysis and exploration, specification, design and development, and testing should be supported.
- There should be a clear paradigm of *analysis* (i.e., modelling the status quo) on the one hand and *design* (i.e., modelling the future system) on the other. At the same time analysis and design should go hand in hand; and appropriate redesign should always be possible (i.e., this is in contrast to UCD and HAM where tasks are primarily analysed and modelled rather than (re-)designed).

Subsequently I introduce the core phases of the *UCProMo* User-Centred Process Model.

## 3.1 Plan the Human-Centred Design Process

Before the actual phases of the human-centred design process (HCD) can start, all parts of the project need to be planned and time and resources need to be allocated. This can be seen as phase zero of the process. At the beginning it should be clarified how usability is addressed throughout the whole process. The ISO 9241-210 recommends: to analyse 'how usability relates to the purpose and use of the product, system or service (e.g., size, number of users, relationship with other systems, safety or health issues, accessibility, specialist application, extreme environments); and to estimate how bad usability might negatively influence the project by analysing 'the levels of the various types of risk that might result from poor usability (e.g., financial, poor product differentiation, safety, required level of usability, acceptance)'; and finally, to be clear about the general conditions of the project in the sense of the 'nature of the development environment (e.g., size of project, time to market, range of technologies, internal or external project, type of contract)' [13, p. 8].

## 3.2    Understand and Define Users, Tasks, and Contexts

After the project planning the first real phase aims at understanding and specifying users, tasks, and contexts. The best way to do that is to go through the following steps: produce an inventory of all items; describe a profile of the most central characteristics for each item; and chart a map of the structure and relationships among all items.

The *user model* consists of the user inventory; user profiles; and a user map.

The *user inventory* contains the essential roles (e.g., author of a book), and role characteristics (e.g., expectations, responsibilities), as well as the essential user characteristics that have an influence on how they play their role (e.g., knowledge, skills, experience). For the *user profiles* it is advisable to identify permutations of common essential user roles and user characteristics and generate profile descriptions for them (e.g., author of a book with limited technical knowledge). The *user map* is a chart consisting of a node as a stan-

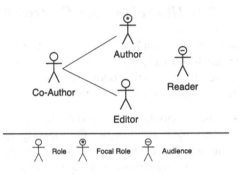

**Fig. 1.** *UCProMo* User Map example.

dardised labelled icon for each individual user profile and links as lines representing connections between them. In the basic form simple links are used, if needed, links can have types and directions to represent specific relationships among users (e.g., a hierarchy). If more semantics are preferable, further details can be added to the nodes representing central characteristics visually (i.e., an active role which actively participates vs. a focal role which is mandatory vs. a passive role of audience who passively participates). Figure 1 shows a simple example of a user map.

The *task model* consists of a task inventory; task profiles; and a task map. The *task inventory* is a collection of all essential tasks, where each task consists of events and processes that are clustered together and have a logical sequence (e.g., invite co-author for writing book together). Very often tasks are nested and a hierarchical decomposition helps for gaining a better understanding. Tasks are comparable to use-cases in SE, and to scenarios in HCI in that they also represent and structure the users' activities. Each *task profile* contains a structured description of a sequence of user activities that is free of technical details. The *task map* is—like the user map—a chart that puts the essential individual tasks into perspective and in relation to each other. Since for large systems task maps can get quite complex, it is very important from the beginning to focus on essential tasks that are of vital interest to the users as well as the project team. In analogy to user maps, in the simplest form, the task map provides a simple, yet informative, overview containing a node as a standardised labelled box for each task and links as lines showing connections between them. To add more semantics links can be typed (e.g., showing temporality, specialisation, extension, or composition). Figure 2 shows a simple task map.

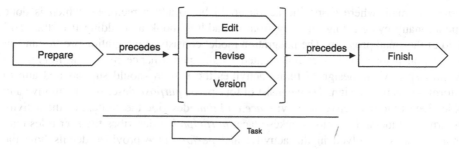

**Fig. 2.** *UCProMo* Task Map example.

The *context model* consists of a context inventory; context profiles; and a context map. Here a context is defined as: 'the interrelated (i.e. some kind of continuity in the broadest sense) conditions (i.e. circumstances such as time and location) in which something (e.g. a user, a group, an artefact) exists (e.g. presence of a user) or occurs (e.g. an action performed by a human or machine)' [9, p. 286]. The *context inventory* brings together all contexts in which users perform their tasks. Furthermore, mobile use needs to be considered when analysing the context. The *context profiles* should for each context or trajectory identify all information relevant to the user performing the respective task. A profile should include the technical (e.g., hardware, software, network connectivity), the physical (e.g., noise, thermal conditions, vibration, space and furniture), the organisational (e.g., work practices, assistance, interruptions), and the social environment (e.g., other persons in the same room). The *context map*—analogous to the user map and the task map—provides a visual overview of all contexts and their relations. It shows individual contexts as nodes in labelled boxes and links between contexts as simple lines. Again, in the basic form the context map includes all contexts and their connections; in more detailed versions the links represent the relationships between contexts—contexts can have temporal relations (e.g., followed-by) and can be nested (e.g., contains vs. part-of).

### 3.3 Specify System Requirements

This phase also defines a core model—the integration model. Despite the similarities and overlaps with the models that define users, tasks, and contexts there is one essential difference regarding the attitude with which the model is created in this phase: whereas in the previous phase the models have pure analytical purposes and document the state-of-the art, the model of this phase is design-oriented and anticipates, specifies, and defines future aspects of the system and related issues.

The *integration model* provides a hierarchical description of the task that users can perform with the future system, where activities are interactions with the system towards solving specific problems and with a purpose. Activities are composed of actions, and actions are composed of operations. For instance, an activity could be to write an email, where a specific action could be to add a recipient, which is done operationally by selecting an entry from the address-book and adding it to the 'To:' field of the email program. The integration model consists of integration profiles and an integration map; and it is complemented by the performance map. The *integration profiles* specify the design of future activities the system should support and aim to inform interaction design. They consist of four parts: *purpose* describes the motive and objective of the respective activity; *place and time* describe the context of the activity in terms of time and location it takes place; *participation* describes the user roles (and characteristics) involved in the activity; and *performance* provides details how the activity is performed. The *integration map* is a complex chart that not only builds on and integrates the user map, task map, and context map from the previous phase, but also moves from a presentation of the state-of-the-art to an anticipation and specification of the future system. It consists of different categories of nodes representing users with activity levels, roles, centrality; and tasks that are clustered into contexts. Figure 3 shows an example of an integration map (please note that the symbols for boundary, control, and entity class resemble to the extensions of the graphical notation of UML by [14, p. 439]).

The *performance map* goes beyond the task map and is also design-oriented rather than analysis-oriented. In the simple version the performance map includes nodes as standardised labelled boxes representing activities and links as untyped connections between the nodes. The basic model can be extended by tasks—so for each decomposable activity all contained tasks are drawn into the model. This provides more information on the users' interaction with the system. Figure 4 shows a generic example of a performance map.

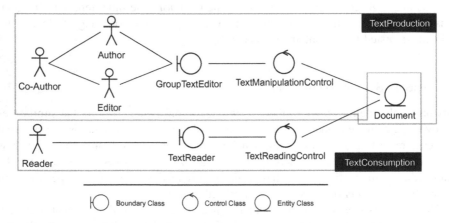

**Fig. 3.** *UCProMo* Integration Map example with a text production context (top) and a text consumption context (bottom).

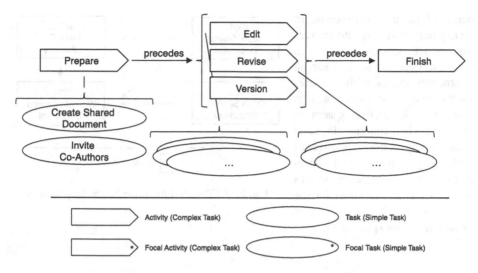

**Fig. 4.** *UCProMo* Performance Map example.

## 3.4   Design User Tasks, and User Interactions

The tasks designs and interactions designs should—given they were carefully specified —logically follow from the previous models. Theoretically task designs describe how the users will accomplish their tasks with the system, whereas interaction designs illustrate how the tasks will exactly be performed with the future system. With the aim of remaining generic in the *UCProMo* process model (i.e., not diving into concrete screen designs, etc.) the two perspectives are combined into one unified *interaction space model*. This model describes the interaction between the users and the system in the form of summaries of the abstract path the users can take through the system. It consists of interaction space profiles, and an interaction space map.

The *interaction space profiles* contain abstract, yet detailed, information on individual interfaces in terms of its information contents and interaction components for user input. It is important to note that the interaction space profiles initially do not need to have any visual representation (e.g., showing the proportions of the different parts of the user interface). Interaction space profiles resemble essential use cases of Usage-Centred Design [7]. However, approaches such as Usage-Centred Design [7] and Contextual Design [11] often proceed in a bottom-up manner—that is, depart from individual cases and aggregate them. The *UCProMo* suggests a hybrid approach, where the interaction space profiles and map are developed in sync having the user journey or customer journey in mind. This is important for many reasons—such as for consistency in similar interaction types among individual profiles.

The *interaction space map* has nodes as standardised labelled boxes for each interaction space as well as links as lines representing connections of interaction spaces. The connections between the interaction spaces are navigation paths that the users can follow when using the system. This map provides a general overview of the interaction space landscape, and additionally serves as a tool to judge and optimise the breadth and depth of the user interaction. In fact, when designing the interaction space model there is a trade-off between having simple interaction spaces with few elements (and consequently a high number of interaction spaces to cover the whole functionality) and having complex interaction spaces with many elements (and consequently fewer interaction spaces and less navigation effort for the users). Figure 5 shows an excerpt of an interaction space map.

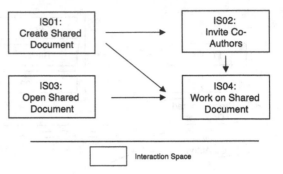

**Fig. 5.** *UCProMo* Interaction Space Map excerpt.

## 3.5  Develop the System

The actual implementation and test of the system are core activities in each process model—both in terms of their importance for the overall success of the project, and in terms of the money, time, and other resources spent in this phase in comparison to the other phases.

Still, the actual implementation is in many process models only briefly covered. This probably has several reasons, one of which being that it is a rather practical endeavour and a completely different terrain. As Jacobson et al. write in their book on 'The Unified Software Development Process' in the introduction to their chapter on 'Implementation': 'Fortunately, most of the system's architecture is captured during design. The primary purpose of implementation is to flesh out the architecture and the system as a whole.' [14, p. 267].

## 3.6  Evaluate the System

The evaluation of the system from a HCD perspective in general (besides expert evaluations and simulations) involves direct contact with users—typically presenting them some results and getting feedback. These results do not only refer to the final product, but also to any result that is generated throughout the process—particularly including the different models that can and should be verified with users.

ISO has clear recommendations on how evaluations should be done. They should include adequate allocation of resources to evaluation; early planning of evaluation; enough testing and analysing of the results and eventually prioritising the reactions triggered by the results; and appropriate communication with all stakeholders involved [13].

As a matter of fact user evaluation is also a vital part of the overall software testing that is very important for any kind of software (and hardware) project. From this perspective the software test has two goals [19]: to show that the software successfully fulfils all requirements; and to eventually find problems which can then be solved. It is important to note what Sommerville—quoting Dykstra—points out: 'Testing can only show the presence of errors, not their absence' [19, p. 206]. Likewise user evaluation can only proof the effectiveness (degree to which the users reach their goal), efficiency (effort that is required to reach the goal), and satisfaction (comfort and pleasure when using the system) of the current users, and only assume that the same holds true for future user populations.

### 3.7 Deploy the System

The final phase after a successful evaluation is Deploy the System. A successful evaluation can happen already in the first iteration, or in later iterations, and at least theoretically it could also be possible that it never happens but that the system is still rolled out. This phase is beyond the scope of this paper.

## 4 Discussion and Conclusions

In this paper I motivated the need for an integrated process model leveraging on both SE and HCI processes. I introduced the generic *UCProMo* User-Centred Process Model with its phases and models that can be easily followed and produced by designers and developers without an SE or HCI background.

*UCProMo* supports clearly defined phases and iterative and incremental feedforward and feedback cycles. It combines abstract modelling from SE with concrete user experience design from HCI. And it supports the whole range of activities from analysis and exploration to specification to design and development and testing. Finally, it is lean and lightweight but at the same time has built-in redundancy between analysis and design—that is, it documents the state-of-the-art in user, task, and context models for analysis; and it generates an integration model (i.e., integration map and performance map) as abstract representation of the statics and dynamics of the future system and the interaction space map as concrete design of the interaction with the future system.

It is on purpose that the interaction spaces and the interaction space map in the design phase resemble use-cases that are in many process models very early in the analysis phase. Indeed, human-centred analysis and design should not take for granted and analyse the activities as they are and build a system around them, but rather it should creatively reflect current practice and—together with the users—eventually redesign activities where appropriate. An example of theory-based creative modelling is [2], where the authors depart from a framework of social interaction from social science as input for their models.

The fact that *UCProMo* aims at rapid modelling should not be confused with other approaches with similar goals. For instance, agile modelling by Ambler has great suggestions on how to apply existing UML models and notations in a lean way [1]. The *UCProMo*, however, suggests generic models that complement existing UML models and notations.

Finally, I did not have the space to address basic principles that apply to many areas of design likewise. For instance, Cockton has suggested 'meta-principles for any design process: receptiveness, expressivity, committedness, credibility, inclusiveness, and improvability' [5, p. 2223].

While the process model leverages on fantastic input from great existing work in HCI and SE, it still would benefit from a proper validation. In the future it should be applied to human-centred software engineering projects to get feedback of designers and developers.

**Acknowledgements.** I would like to thank all members of the Cooperative Media Lab in Bamberg as well as the colleagues from the Madeira Interactive Technologies Institute for inspiring discussions. Thanks to the anonymous reviewers for great feedback.

# References

1. Ambler, S.: Agile Modelling: Effective Practices for eXtreme Programming and the Unified Process. Wiley, New York (2002)
2. Beckmann, C., Gross, T.: Social computing–bridging the gap between the social and the technical. In: Meiselwitz, G. (ed.) SCSM 2014. LNCS, vol. 8531, pp. 25–36. Springer, Heidelberg (2014)
3. Boehm, B.W.: A spiral model of software development and enhancement. IEEE Comput. **21**(5), 61–72 (1988)
4. Calvary, G., Coutaz, J., Thevenin, D., Limbourg, Q., Bouillon, L., Vanderdonckt, J.: A unifying reference framework for multi-target user interfaces. Interact. Comput. **15**(3), 291–315 (2003)
5. Cockton, G.: Getting there: six meta-principles and interaction design. In: Proceedings of the Conference on Human Factors in Computing Systems - CHI 2009, pp. 2223–2232. ACM, New York (2009)
6. Constantine, L.L.: Human activity modelling: towards a pragmatic integration of activity theory and usage-centred design. In: Seffah, A., Vanderdonckt, J., Desmarais, M.C. (eds.) Human-Centred Software Engineering: Software Engineering Models, Patterns, and Architectures for HCI, pp. 27–51. Springer, Heidelberg (2009)
7. Constantine, L.L., Lockwood, L.A.D.: Software For Use: A Practical Guide to the Models and Methods of Usage-Centred Design. Addison-Wesley, Reading (1999)
8. Constantine, L.L., Lockwood, L.A.D.: Usage-centred engineering for web applications. IEEE Softw. **19**(2), 42–50 (2002)
9. Gross, T., Prinz, W.: Modelling shared contexts in cooperative environments: concept, implementation, and evaluation. Comput. Support. Coop. Work: J. Collaborative Comput. **13**(3–4), 283–303 (2004)
10. Hartson, H.R., Hix, D.: Human-computer interaction development: concepts and systems for its management. ACM Comput. Surv. **21**(1), 5–92 (1989)
11. Holtzblatt, K., Beyer, H.R.: Contextual design. In: Soegaard, M., Dam, R.F. (eds.) The Encyclopedia of Human-Computer Interaction, 2nd edn. The Interaction Design Foundation, Aarhus (2016)
12. ISO. ISO 13407: 1999 - Human-Centred Design Processes for Interactive Systems. ISO - International Organisation for Standardisation

13. ISO/IEC. ISO 9241-210:2010: Ergonomics of Human-System Interaction - Part 210: Human-Centred Design for Interactive Systems. International Organization for Standardization
14. Jacobson, I., Booch, G., Rumbaugh, J.: The Unified Software Development Process. Addison-Wesley, Reading (1998)
15. Jacobson, I., Spence, I., Kerr, B.: Use-case 2.0. Commun. ACM **59**(5), 61–69 (2016)
16. Kruchten, P.B.: The Rational Unified Process: An Introduction. Addison-Wesley, New York (2003)
17. Nunes, N.J.: What drives software development: bridging the gap between software and usability engineering. In: Seffah, A., Vanderdonckt, J., Desmarais, M.C. (eds.) Human-Centred Software Engineering: Software Engineering Models, Patterns, and Architectures for HCI, pp. 9–25. Springer, Heidelberg (2009)
18. Royce, W.W.: Managing the development of large software systems. In: Proceedings of the Ninth International Conference on Software Engineering – ICSE 1987, pp. 328–338. IEEE Computer Society Press, Los Alamitos (1987). Reprint from 1970
19. Sommerville, I.: Software Engineering 9. Pearson Education Limited, Harlow (2011)

# Using and Adopting Tools

# Collaborative Task Modelling on the Web

Marco Manca[✉], Fabio Paternò, and Carmen Santoro

CNR-ISTI, HIIS Laboratory, Via Moruzzi 1, 56124 Pisa, Italy
{marco.manca,fabio.paterno,carmen.santoro}@isti.cnr.it

**Abstract.** Task modelling is a widely recognized activity when designing interactive applications. In this perspective, it is the meeting point between various
stakeholders. However, most of the automatic environments that currently allow
task modelling only support single users, thus limiting the possible interactions
and discussions amongst them. In this paper we present Collaborative CTT, a new
Web-based multi-user tool for specifying task models. The tool allows several
users, who may even be physically separated, to work on the same model at the
same or different time. Among its features, the tool includes mechanisms specific
for this type of HCI modelling in order to support coordination, communication
and mutual awareness among participants. We discuss the aspects we have
addressed in designing the task modelling tool, its main collaborative features,
and also report on user feedback gathered through formative tests.

**Keywords:** Task models · Collaborative modelling · Responsive Web

## 1 Introduction

Task modelling is a useful method for various activities in the user interface design and
development process. It helps to better understand the application domain, record the
results of interdisciplinary discussions, support user interface design, usability evaluation, and documentation. The nature of task modelling as a multi-disciplinary process
is widely accepted: in order to properly carry out task modelling it is important to involve
various experts, stakeholders, designers and users. In addition, with the increasing need
for collaboration among stakeholders, and also the need to reduce costs, which often
forces teams to collaborate also from different locations, it is becoming increasingly
important to create a shared understanding and joint representations of the interactive
systems being designed. As a consequence, enabling interactive collaborative modelling
in this area can prove to be valuable as it could make collaborations more effective and
productive. For instance, in some situations it might be interesting for UI designers to
carry out the modelling work together with users at the same time but from different
locations, or it would be interesting for the members of the same design team to be able
to carry out the modelling activity in a collaborative manner. Unfortunately, most of the
tools that support task modelling only allow for single users, and they do not enable
various users to share the task models and collaboratively edit them. Thus, we judged
it interesting to investigate the opportunities offered by a multi-user, collaborative, Web-
based task modelling tool.

© IFIP International Federation for Information Processing 2016
Published by Springer International Publishing Switzerland 2016. All Rights Reserved
C. Bogdan et al. (Eds.): HCSE 2016/HESSD 2016, LNCS 9856, pp. 317–334, 2016.
DOI: 10.1007/978-3-319-44902-9_20

In particular, the main goals of this work are to design a tool able to:

- Support a shared view of task models across various devices and associated users;
- Support concurrent editing of task models by multiple users;
- Provide mechanisms to synchronize editing of some parts of the task models;
- Provide mechanisms to create mutual awareness of the concurrent activities in the modelling process.

To these ends, we have opted for a responsive Web-based implementation because this would facilitate its adoption given its wide interoperability across various devices, and we have adopted the ConcurTaskTrees (CTT) notation [19] since it is widely known in the task modelling community.

In the paper after reviewing the state of the art, we introduce some scenarios that have motivated our work; next we discuss how we have designed the features that support the collaboration in editing the task model, describe how it has been implemented, and report on two user tests. Lastly, we draw some conclusions and provide indications about future work.

## 2   State of the Art

Collaborative modelling has received some attention in some domains. For example, Collaborative Protégé and WebProtégé [12] are extensions of the existing Protégé (http://protege.stanford.edu), also enabling collaborative ontology editing. Support in this direction is also provided by some commercial tools. For example, VPository (from Visual Paradigm, http://www.vpository.com/) offers a central repository for storing user's software design projects with version control capabilities and, in this regard, it is far from providing the support offered by a truly collaborative environment. In [18] a review of tools that support collaborative processes for creation of various forms of structured knowledge was presented. However, we note that little attention has been paid to collaborative modelling support in HCI so far.

Before analysing this aspect more closely, it can be useful to highlight the difference between tools for collaborative task modelling, and tools supporting task modelling of collaborative applications. The first case is the one which we address in this paper, i.e. we analyse tools enabling users to jointly create a model in remote or co-located places (e.g. collocated groups of designers in a room, team members in distant places), in a synchronous or asynchronous manner. In the second case, the focus is on tools allowing designers to model systems where multiple users act in a collaborative manner. So, in the first case the multi-user dimension concerns the users of the modelling tool, in the second case it regards the users of the application to design.

On the one hand, the latter case (tools supporting task modelling of collaborative applications) has been the subject of several contributions. Indeed, proposed notations for modelling multi-user applications include: the COMM (COlaborative and Multi-Modal) notation and its on-line editor for specifying multi-user multimodal interactive systems [13]; CTML [3, 26], a task-based specification framework for collaborative environments, consisting of a language and a tool for editing/animating CTML models;

CUA (Collaboration Usability Analysis) [22], a modelling technique allowing designers to model the main features of a group work situation that will affect groupware usability. Other proposals along the same lines have been put forward by Penichet et al. [21], van der Veer et al. [25], Guerrero-Garcia et al. [8], Giraldo et al. [9], Molina et al. [15, 16]. On the other hand, little has been proposed for collaborative task modelling tools. Even recent proposals [1] have addressed the issue of adapting to various device types but not collaborative aspects. Some basic support for collaboration during task modelling has been provided in tools such as HAMSTERS [14] and CTTE [17], which enable users to re-use fragments of task models (even created by other users) within their own task model specifications. However, our goal is to provide a truly collaborative tool in which users actually share the same model, which they can collaboratively modify even at the same time.

A literature review of approaches in the area of collaborative modelling, although not specifically focused on task modelling is in [23], other proposals still in the same area are [10, 24]. Some degree of collaborative support is provided by FlexiLab [11], a UI multi-model editor for HCI implemented as a Web-based application. It mainly supports the possibility of interactively sending fragments of the model from one user to another. This allows several designers to work on separate fragments of the same model, which is especially useful when dealing with large models. While FlexiLab provides some level of collaboration and communication support, our proposal addresses the concurrent editing of the same model by multiple users with multiple devices, which implies additional features also for mutual awareness and coordination (e.g. sharing focus, locking a task for editing).

In this area, one relevant experience to mention is SPACE-DESIGN [2, 5], which is a synchronous, generic (i.e. domain independent) collaborative modelling tool, which is extensible and also reconfigurable for a specific domain. SPACE-DESIGN has been used for task modelling through the CTT notation [4]: starting with a CTT specification, the tool adapts its UI to provide some collaborative support for modelling with this notation by including widgets for awareness, communication and coordination. Such paper also reports on a user test that indicates that a generic collaborative modelling tool has advantages in comparison to the use of a single-user tool (such as CTTE) combined with a shared window system such as NetMeeting, especially in regards to the awareness mechanisms offered. The test indicated that when using SPACE-DESIGN, fewer situations of conflict occurred with respect to the alternative setting (CTTE + NetMeeting). While we agree on the fact that the collaborative modelling approach is a more suitable solution, we note that SPACE-DESIGN was able to support only a limited number of basic modelling functionalities (e.g. create, read, update and delete models).

Another relevant experience has been Quill [6, 7], a Web-based development environment that aimed to enable various stakeholders of a Web application to collaboratively adopt a model-based UI design. Quill attempted to support several users to concurrently participate in a common work project in a distributed fashion with live updates. In Quill each user has a specific role (junior or senior), which provides access to specific features of the application. Quill also has a revision control mechanism by which the changes suggested by juniors are passed for review to the senior who has the responsibility for committing them. Similarly to Quill, the results of Collaborative CTT can be included in a comprehensive MBUI-development framework (such as MARIAE [20]). However, in our case the mechanism for deciding the changes is more flexible since rights can be assigned dynamically and not statically to the users. Overall, we can conclude that our proposal addresses an area still underexplored concerning the possibility of supporting collaboration in task modelling.

## 3   Target Scenarios

The design of the tool has been driven by some scenarios that we briefly describe in this section and are based on our experience in teaching task modelling and in research projects in which task modelling has been used.

*Educational use in the classroom.* In our experience teaching how to create and modify a task model may not be trivial. Once the conceptual aspects have been introduced and studied there is a strong need to do some concrete exercise to better understand how to apply in practise the concepts. An effective exercise is to develop the task model together (teacher and students) in a laboratory in which all students have their own computer (it can be a PC or a tablet or a smartphone). The teacher can start the modelling to show how to approach the associated issues and the students can see the results directly in their devices, while at the same time they can browse the model in order to analyse its features without immediately make any change. At some point the teacher may want to highlight some parts of the model and so impose his/her view on all the devices, centred on the selected part. Once students start to be familiar with the modelling activity it can be useful to gradually allow them to directly carry it out. A good exercise is to make some extension or some modification to the model in the class exercise given that creating a task model from scratch may still be premature. Thus, the teacher may want to ask specific student(s) to detail how a high level task should be carried out or perform some modification on a part of the model developed. This implies the need to assign the possibility of editing the shared model to a specific student and make it possible that her modifications are updated in the teacher and other students views.

*A workgroup aiming at designing an application.* An example of sector in which CTT has been often applied is the air traffic control domain[1] in which the design decisions need to be carefully analysed in order to prevent human errors that can even threaten human life. In designing such applications it is important to involve all the relevant stakeholders, such as the air traffic controllers, the application developers, the experts in the relevant regulations. When such groups are in the same room (same place/same time) their discussion could be more effective with a collaborative modelling tool. Thus, they could start the discussion with the task model developed by one of them, and the others can point issues associated with some design decisions using a shared focus, and more clearly indicate alternative ways to accomplish some tasks by directly editing the shared model.

---

[1]   https://www.eurocontrol.int/ehp/?q=node/1617.

*Distributed synchronous workgroup (different places/same time).* For various reasons the meetings amongst the various stakeholders in the same room are not always possible. Thus, it is useful to support the possibility of collaboratively editing the task model remotely. In this case there is a need for additional tools that support the communication among the participants (e.g. a chat), to have a precise indications of what editing has been made by each involved participant (e.g. a shared log) and to have dynamic feedback on what the other users are doing.

*Distributed asynchronous workgroup (different place/different time).* In some cases it is not even possible to arrange a remote meeting because of work constraints. Thus, it is still useful to have the possibility of sharing a model, which can be eased by some cloud support, and facilitate its collaborative editing. In this way when one participant accesses the shared model s/he can work on the modifications carried out by the others. There can be some different opinions regarding how to design some parts, thus it is still important on the one hand to give all participants the possibility of proposing and discussing their solutions, and on the other hand to make a final decision, which can be taken by the moderator or through a vote.

## 4 The Design of the Collaborative Features

In this section we describe how we addressed the requirements raised by the target scenarios in the proposed tool.

### 4.1 Roles and Access Rights in Handling Task Models

In terms of roles we have adopted a solution in which there is a 'Moderator' who is the user who starts the collaborative session and invites the other participants ('Collaborative Users'). The latter can have various ways to participate, which are defined by their assigned access rights.

Such rights/authorizations are related to the ability to modify the model, invite further participants, and/or the possibility to assign the shared focus to other members.

Thus, all users can read the models (e.g. visualise, navigate, etc.), but only those who have received the corresponding rights can modify them (a locking mechanism is provided in order to avoid that the models get inconsistent states due to e.g. simultaneous changes).

The environment supports dynamic groups, thus users can be added or leave the collaborative session at any time.

### 4.2 Enhancing Mutual Awareness Among Users

Users can independently browse the task model. When they set the focus on one task then their personal view is adapted in such a way to centre the entire model around that task. Figure 1 shows an example in which two users have different focuses on the same model at the same time, and thus receive different views of it. One user has the focus on the *EnableAccess* task while the other on *WithDrawCash*. The red circles in Fig. 1 indicate the number of task that are not visualized because they are out of the screen area.

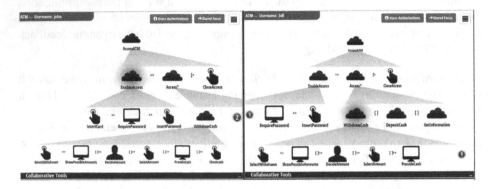

**Fig. 1.** Example of multiple views of the same task model (Color figure online)

Figure 1 refers to the initial version of the application. In the second version, we added some cues **for enabling users be aware of which task the other users are currently focusing on**. The various local focus of the other users are represented through small circles shown near the correspondent tasks, to highlight the part of the model that is being considered at that time by the other users. The circles have different colors (each colour is associated to a different user) and contain the initial letters of the name of the corresponding user (see Fig. 2).

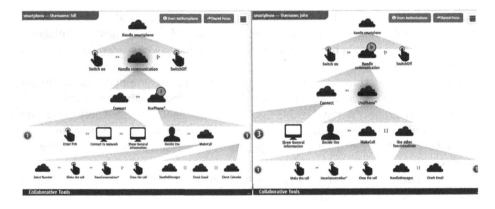

**Fig. 2.** Task models annotated with representations of the local focus of the other users

In addition, each user has an **event logger** panel (see Fig. 3 bottom-left part), listing in temporal order all the actions carried out by each user while collaboratively working on a task model. For each action it indicates a timestamp, the user who carried it out, the type of action (e.g. lock, unlock, edit, set shared focus, update temporal operator), and the task(s) involved. The logger considers actions carried out even at different times by different groups of users on the model. It is worth noting that, in the second version of the tool, we decided not visualising anymore the lock/unlock events generated when an authorised user performs a model modification, in order to avoid too long lists of events. Indeed, the lock/unlock events are very frequent and in any case a graphical feedback is provided to users in the main area of the application to highlight the occurrence of such events.

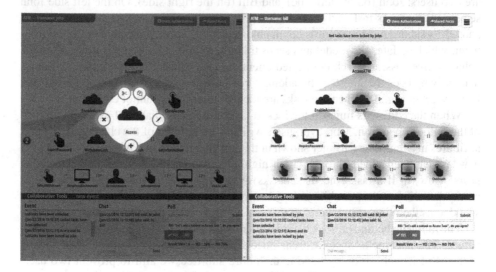

**Fig. 3.** Example of task modification in Collaborative CTT.

### 4.3   Coordination Between Users Collaboratively Handling a Task Model

One further issue addressed in this work has been how to design flexible collaborative editing while supporting an efficient and coordinated way to work. This has been addressed by considering the typical hierarchical structure of task models. In order to support flexibility, users are for example allowed to change at the same time parts of the tree-like task model structure that are independent each other, which means that there is no intersection between the subtrees currently modified by the users. Indeed, modifying a task can involve different types of possible changes, e.g. the user can delete the task and some/all of its children, change name, type, category, associated platforms, specify whether the task is iterative or optional, modify its description, associated objects and pre/post-conditions, if any. In order to coordinate the editing work, when a user is modifying a task, that task and its subtasks (in practise the subtree having as its root the task currently edited) are 'locked' to avoid concurrent changes on that part of the task model by other users at the same time. When this **locking mechanism** occurs, all the other users participating in the collaborative session receive a notification of the lock, and the locked task will be highlighted in red in their view of the task model so that they are aware that it will not be possible to edit it (see Fig. 3) anymore until the other user unlocks it. When a user locks a task, a timeout is set so that if the lock is not released within the defined time interval then the system performs an automatic procedure to release all the locked tasks.

In particular, Fig. 3 shows the user interface of Collaborative CTT (initial version) while modelling an ATM (Automated Teller Machine) system. As you can see, the logger panel, the voting system and the chat are located in the bottom part of the user interface and can be hidden when more screen area is necessary to edit the model. There are two users: John (on the left side), and Bill (on the right side). On the left side John selected the Access task and started editing it: in this way he locked the selected task and all its subtasks. This event is communicated to the server-side part of the environment, which updates the model and sends this information to all clients involved in the collaborative session. Each connected client receives the lock information and automatically updates the interface by adding a red background to the sub-tree locked (see Bill's view in Fig. 3). When the tasks are locked other users cannot edit them.

When the editing is finished the locked tasks are released and all users are notified of the unlock operation. Moreover, users will also be notified of the changes in the task attributes in a temporary banner shown in the top area and in the event console log, if a new task has been added (the new task is highlighted with a blue background in the other users' view) or if a task (and its subtasks) is deleted. The user who plays the role of moderator also has the possibility to reject modifications carried out by other users when s/he deems them inappropriate.

The rationale behind how we have designed the locking was rooted in the hierarchical nature of the task model specification. Since a high-level task is described hierarchically in terms of its sub-tasks, by locking the entire sub-tree we aim to prevent two users editing parts that are semantically tightly connected simultaneously.

In the initial version of the application the locking mechanism was activated as soon as the user opened the panel for editing the task (see an example in Fig. 3, left side). However, sometimes users just open this panel to see additional information about the task and not necessarily to edit it, so these cases do not really require the use of a locking mechanism. Thus, in the second version we decided postponing the time when the locking mechanism is actually activated: it is carried out only when the user actually selects the operation to do (e.g. add/edit/delete task).

By considering in particular the target scenario of educational use in the classroom, and our experiences in the discussions carried out during task modelling activities, we noticed that often there is a need for sharing the same focus on the task model. During a collaborative session, it can happen that different users select different tasks and have different model layouts in front of them at the same time, depending on the task currently having the focus. This supports a flexible way to work but at some point there could be the need to discuss some specific parts of the model, and thus it is important that all users have the same model layout in front of them with the part under discussion shown in the central part of the working area. In Collaborative CTT this is achieved through the possibility to **set a shared focus**. This operation allows all users participating in the collaborative session to coordinate their focus on a particular task (only if they have the corresponding authorization). The selected task will be placed in the centre of their working areas, it will be highlighted in green and the icons associated to this task and its immediate siblings will be enlarged, while the presentation of the neighbouring tasks gradually decrease in size when progressively moving further away from the task that currently has the focus.

### 4.4  Supporting Communication Between Users

In the collaborative application we provided support for communication between the participating users by means of a **chat**, which is especially useful when the involved users are not in the same place. Figure 3 shows the chat (in the first version of the tool). In the second version we provided users with the possibility to interactively select tasks within the chat. By means of typing the *[task]* keyword within the chat, the tool shows a list of the tasks included in the currently task model, from where they can interactively select the task to refer within a conversation. In addition, if the user types some letters of the task name the list of the task names is automatically filtered accordingly. After the message is sent by a user, it is added to the chat area of all users. If a chat message contains a task identifier this is shown as a link, which can be selected in order to place the corresponding task in the centre of the working area.

Within the application we also provided users with a **voting system**, which can be useful to make a decision when there are different views on how to address a specific aspect of a task model. It allows a user to propose a topic for the vote, which is shown to all users who can express their agreement or not, and finally shows the result. If the topic concerns a task, selecting the task name in the topic description makes it possible to centre the model in the personal view around such task. It is worth noting that in the evaluations reported in this article the voting system was not used because just two users were considered for each test session.

### 4.5  Cloud Support for Sharing Task Models

Users who collaboratively edit a task model may be located in various places and using different devices, thus we decided making the models shared in a collaborative session available in the cloud. In particular, all the users have a private repository and also have access to a shared repository in which the models collaboratively shared by users are saved. It is worth noting that, since the task models created through Collaborative CTT and those created through Desktop CTTE share the same XSD schema describing the underlying language, users can indifferently use Collaborative CTT and desktop CTTE for accessing the models contained in their spaces.

### 4.6  Implementation

From the implementation point of view Collaborative CTT has been obtained by applying the Model View Controller (MVC) pattern. The model is the task model description stored in the server-side. Each user request that implies some modification in the task model is sent to the controller (server-side), which manipulates the model and sends back the response to all involved clients that update their view accordingly. All the communication involving the collaborative functions exploits Web socket mechanisms that allow pushing information from server to clients avoiding polling. When a user accesses Collaborative CTT, a Web socket connection to the server is opened and the client subscribes to receiving updates about collaborative functions (such as shared focus, current users focus, temporal operator update, add/edit/delete a task, chat messages, propose or vote a topic) specifying the corresponding callback function that will handle the received information.

## 5   User Feedback

Two formative tests were conducted to collect user feedback on the usability and useful-ness of the features provided in the tool, and receive suggestions for improvements. In both cases the tests were carried out in pairs.

In the initial test the two users were in the same room, while in the second the two users were in different rooms. Thus, the first evaluation addressed the same time/same place setting, and represents the first (but also the second) scenario, whereas the second evaluation covered the same time/different place setting (distributed synchronous work-group scenario). For the initial assessment we deemed it more useful to deal with users in the same room to better control the experiment and more easily monitor the users' behaviour.

The second test was carried out with a version of the tool which had undergone some small refinements as a result of the first formative test in order to improve its usability. In particular, in the second version we reduced the time when a task is actually locked in order to increase the possibility for users to work in parallel, we refined the chat (which was not used much during the first exercise), and we improved the mutual awareness between users by also showing where the local focus of each user was positioned. The purpose was not to provide a formal comparison between the two tests because various conditions changed, but to obtain progressive feedback that has been useful to orient the evolution of the tool.

### 5.1   Participants and Tasks

**Initial Test.**   Fourteen people (2 females) aged 25 to 47 (M = 32.2, SD = 6) participated. All had good experience/familiarity with CTT. They were selected by using the profes-sional network of authors, choosing people having familiarity with CTT notation and potentially interested in the tool. In the end, a pool including experts in HCI (e.g. academic researchers) and Computer Science students (with familiarity with CTT) participated in the evaluation exercise. For the test, users were asked to edit a previously created task model, which describes an ATM system in its "current" design. By using the tool, they had to edit this task model in a collaborative manner so that the new model would describe a possible, envisaged, "new" ATM system. The description of the features that the new system should support (and which they had to include in the model), were provided to them through four tasks to carry out.

In particular, users were required to include the specification of the following tasks in the model: (i) add the possibility to access the ATM system using additional modalities apart from the current one (which is typically done through inserting a card and then typing in the code), namely: using either fingerprints, a smartphone or a smartwatch; (ii) once a user has logged in to the system, the presentation should adapt by means of e.g. enlarging the fonts, improving the contrast, removing elements in the UI; (iii) once the user has selected withdrawal, the system should calculate the amount that the user typically gets and then suggests it to the user, who can accept it or not; (iv) the possibility to visualise the current user balance and see the transactions made during a certain interval of time (the user would have to choose a timeframe from: today/1 week/15 days/ 1 month). After jointly accomplishing such tasks, users had to independently fill in an online questionnaire.

**Second Test.** We were not able to involve four of the 14 people who participated to the first user test, so in the end only 10 users (2 females), aged 25 to 47 participated in the second test (M = 33.4, SD = 6.2), all having quite a good experience/familiarity with CTT.

For the test we asked the users to edit a task model containing a *partial specification* of the features typically supported by a smartphone (e.g. enter a pin to access, make a call, handle messages). In the test, users were requested to edit the task model so that it will also include additional possibilities according to the following tasks. *Task1*: refine a task named "*Show General Information*" by further showing the time, the battery level and the network connectivity level. *Task2*: edit the "*HandleMessages*" task by modelling the tasks supporting users while they *create a message to send to a contact*. In our case, only two types of messages were considered: SMS and Whatsapp messages. Users had to model the fact that, in both cases the user can use text to create the content of the message. However, in the case of SMS messages, the user can also send, attached to the textual message, *memos, contacts, calendar events*, and *notes*. In the case of Whatsapp messages, the user can send additional types of files: images, videos, and audio files (in addition to memos, contacts, calendar events, and notes). *Task3:* add the possibility that a telephone call can occur *any time* during the use of the phone and then interrupt any task the user was currently doing with the smartphone. At the end of the telephone call, the user should be able to continue the interaction suspended previously.

As in the previous test, after jointly accomplishing such tasks, users had to independently fill in an online questionnaire.

## 5.2   Procedure and Design

Before the tests, the users were provided with instructions about how to access the tool, a general textual introduction, and a video showing its main features. In both tests users performed the test in pairs. For the first test they were in the same room, each using a PC, and they were placed in such a way that they could easily talk to each other, but could not see the screen of the other participant. They were allowed to talk and chat freely during the test. For the second test, the two users were in different rooms, still using the same equipment as in the first test (PCs). In both cases, two researchers observed the interactions occurring during the experiment.

One of the users initially acted as the moderator, inviting the other user to join the collaborative session: in this condition the two users completed the first two tasks, and then they swapped their roles. This was done in order to have both users act in both roles and test the corresponding functionalities.

After the test, the users filled in a questionnaire, which included first a demographic section (about e.g. education, experience/familiarity with task modelling), and then a section with questions specifically related to the tool.

## 5.3   Results

In the questionnaire, a 5-point scale was used to provide ratings on the tool features: [1 to 5; 1 = not usable at all/not useful at all, 2 = not very usable/not very useful, 3 = neutral, 4 = usable/useful, 5 = very usable/very useful]. We report the median and Interquartile Range (IQR) values.

**Setting Shared Focus.** *First test.* Usability [Median = 4; IQR = 5-3.25 = 1.75] Usefulness [Median = 4.5; IQR = 5-4 = 1].

Many users found this mechanism useful (one user even suggested extending it to temporal operators) for better turning/pointing the team's attention toward a specific task-related issue/discussion, and especially useful to quickly focus on a task when dealing with large model specifications. However, from the usability point of view, one user found the provided mechanism difficult to understand since it requires two actions (clicking on the task and then select the button for setting a shared focus). Another user suggested making the visualisation of the shared focus different from the user's own focus (although each user has only one focus at any given time), to better distinguish them. There was only one user who explicitly criticised having his current focus changed by others: instead, he would have preferred to see where the other users currently had the focus and then decide to change his own focus accordingly. The second version of the tool addressed this issue to some extent by providing the possibility to show also the local focus of the other users.

*Second test.* Usability [Median = 4; IQR = 4.75-4 = 0.75] Usefulness [Median = 4.5; IQR = 5-4 = 1].

A user said "*sometimes I forgot that the other user had set the shared focus, thus I made modifications to a wrong subtree.*" Another user said that he would have liked to use the mouse right click to access the button to activate the shared focus instead of using the menu in the top-right part of the application. Regarding the usefulness of this functionality, one user suggested further testing this functionality with more than two users. Another user had qualms about the fact that when using this functionality the overall interaction would slow down a bit.

**User Authorisations.** *First test.* Usability [Median = 4; IQR = 5-4 = 1] Usefulness [Median = 4.5; IQR = 5-4 = 1].

Two users would have preferred a different, more compact layout for their settings (e.g. one row per user, using checkboxes or toggle switches).

*Second test.* Usability [Median = 4; IQR = 4-4 = 0] Usefulness [Median = 4.5; IQR = 5-4 = 1].

Nothing was particularly noted apart the fact that, in line with what had already been highlighted in the previous test, a user suggested having a more compact layout for visualising users' access rights (he suggested using accordion menus).

**Mutual Awareness Mechanisms.** *First test.* Usability [Median = 4; IQR = 5-4 = 1] Usefulness [Median = 4; IQR = 5-4 = 1].

Users were asked whether it was easy for them to be aware of other people participating in the same session and their current activities (e.g. understand when another user joins a collaborative session, or be informed of the actions that other users are doing/ have done on the shared model). Overall, users expressed high appreciation of the usefulness of the support provided by the tool allowing them to be aware of other users' activities. Nonetheless, three users recommended some further improvements to its usability, with different suggestions: one proposal was to associate a colour to each participant to more easily identify users in the same session (and also the user who currently acts as the moderator), and/or to identify the current users by changing different portions of the task model; another user suggested using a short sound to signal when a new user joins a session; another user suggested using a small square around the graphical task representation and then identify the users who are currently focusing on that task by displaying their names (or initials) beside the square. Some of these aspects were addressed in the second version.

*Second test.* Usability [Median = 4.5; IQR = 5-4 = 1] Usefulness [Median = 5; IQR = 5-5 = 0].

In the second test one user expressed concerns over the possibility that using the users' initials could cause conflicts, and so suggested using icons rather than initials. Another user raised the issue that it is difficult to know who the users currently connected in the session at any given time are. Another user said: "*As 'Owner' of the task, I received an overwhelming amount of notifications of task modifications, which interrupted my work several times. I suggest collecting all the notifications into a side box, in order to not block the owner's work.*"

**Chat.** *First test.* Not evaluated in the first test because users were in the same room.

*Second test.* Usability [Median = 4.5; IQR = 5-4 = 1] Usefulness [Median = 5; IQR = 5-5 = 0]. One user raised an issue connected with the fact that it was difficult for the moderator to discuss a modification to the model suggested by another user before accepting/rejecting it. In addition, the same user said "*When the chat window is minimized, every time I receive a new message/information about a new event, I must maximize it in order to read the message/event notification. I suggest that you write (the first part of) the event notification/text message in the window header. In this way, while the chat window is minimized, I can get an idea of the event notification/message*" Other two users also highlighted the importance of better drawing the user's attention to the most recent message (e.g. by blinking for a few seconds). A user suggested having the possibility to have a voice chat for more easily communicating with the other users.

**Visualisation of Logged Events.** *First test.* [Median = 4; IQR = 5-4 = 1] Usefulness [Median = 4; IQR = 4-4 = 0]. This feature received quite mixed comments. On the one hand, one user found it very useful and reported looking more often at the area dedicated to event logging than the one showing the model. Nevertheless, the user suggested better structuring the visualization of the logs, by indicating, for example, first the type of event and the author, in order to speed up the extraction of relevant information. On the other hand, a pair of users said that they did not look much at this panel, while one highlighted the usefulness of this feature especially for remote users. Indeed, users often talked to each other, not only to identify a shared strategy for editing the task model, but also to request confirmation of actions made through the tool (instead of just checking the event log). Another user suggested rendering just the editing events in the panel (e.g. not providing information on the locking events), since they are the really meaningful ones from the user's perspective. Another user suggested adding the possibility to go through past events and even 're-play' them.

*Second test.* Usability [Median = 4; IQR = 4-3 = 1] Usefulness [Median = 4; IQR = 4.75-3 = 1.75].

Two users suggested hiding it by default and having the possibility to show it on request. Another user said that he noticed some changes sometimes but then he preferred looking at the model to understand what happened. Another user suggested classifying the events, by distinguishing between events occurring on the task model and other types of events (e.g. chat modifications, notifications about user joining the session, etc.)

**Coordination (Lock Mechanism).** *First test.* Usability [Median = 4.5; IQR = 5-3 = 2] Usefulness [Median = 5; IQR = 5-5 = 0]. Users really appreciated the availability of the locking mechanism to avoid including inconsistencies in the model due to concurrent and uncontrolled modifications. However, some users highlighted that the lock mechanism can slow down the collaborative process excessively, suggesting keeping it only for the time that it is strictly necessary (e.g. when the user actually starts modifying some property of the model, and releasing it just afterwards).

*Second test.* Usability [Median = 4; IQR = 5-4 = 1] Usefulness [Median = 5; IQR = 5-4 = 1].

A user complained that, as the moderator of the session, he received many notifications about task changes, which made it difficult to work on the model properly: "*As owner of the task, I received many notifications of task modifications, which interrupted my work several times. I suggest collecting all the notifications into a side box, in order to not block the owner's work.*" Another user said that the locking mechanism could be difficult to handle, he suggested better using the chat for coordinating the work.

**Rejection/Acceptance.** *First test.* Usefulness [Median = 4; IQR = 4.75-4 = 0.75].

On the one hand, users acknowledged the need and the importance of providing the moderator with the possibility to act as "super-user" to decide on the modifications to actually apply to the model (among the ones proposed by other users), and then maintaining the control of it. Nonetheless, two participants suggested providing the moderator with some means for justifying rejection of a proposal made by another user (e.g.

by means of adding a text field where the moderator can explain the reasons for rejecting a change), so that all members can develop and keep a shared mutual knowledge/view of the correctness of the specification (documented in the model) and its rationale and evolution. On the other hand, confirming every step done by the other partners was judged a bit tiring from the moderator's point of view (a user admitted sometimes having lost his own focus to check requests of change from the other user).

*Second test.* Usefulness [Median = 4; IQR = 4.75-4 = 0.75].

Two users acknowledged its usefulness but at the same time they highlighted that the moderator frequently had to interrupt his work to deal with accept/reject requests. Another user pointed out the fact that when a request arrives, the user cannot discuss it with the partner but just accept/reject it.

**Most Usable Functionality and Least Usable Functionality.** *First test.* The functionalities that were most appreciated from a usability point of view were the shared focus (seen as a way to have a better "organised" collaborative session), and the possibility to concurrently modify a model. Among the least usable functionalities, users reported the locking mechanism (which could slow down the collaborative editing), and the event log list (not particularly structured and currently including events not very meaningful from the user's perspective).

*Second test.* Four users particularly appreciated the chat (which was improved), one user most liked the fact that the task model portions been edited by other users are highlighted graphically. Regarding the least useful functionalities, one user mentioned the logger, and two mentioned the locking mechanism.

**Most Useful Scenario(s) of Use.** *First test.* For assessing this aspect we envisioned four basic scenarios of use (corresponding to those introduced in Sect. 3) and we asked users to select the scenario(s) (one or more than one) they found most suitable for exploiting the features of Collaborative CTT. The usage scenarios which received the highest approval were: distributed workgroup (selected 10 times) and workgroups aiming at designing an application (10 times as well). The educational scenario was also rated highly (9 times). The scenario that was judged the least useful was the different places/different times scenario (2 times). In any case, the tool was judged by users as highly flexible in supporting rather different scenarios. From users' comments it seems to offer the best opportunities when synchronous (same time) scenarios are to be supported. An advantage highlighted by users is the fact that, by using the tool, users do not need to exchange task model specifications. The educational setting was also judged appropriate for using the tool because in such settings the tool is able to support a good interaction between the teacher and the students while facilitating the work of both. In other words, Collaborative CTT facilitates teachers explaining task models (by using e.g. shared focus functionality and being a Web-based tool) and at the same time it makes possible an active and collaborative participation of students in building task models, giving them the opportunity to put in practice and apply the theoretical knowledge gained in concrete examples.

*Second test.* One user said that the tool can be fruitfully used in all the four mentioned settings. However, for a future version of the tool he suggested improving that the mechanism used by the moderator to accept/reject the suggested modifications because it is time consuming (and thus he has less time available for working on the model). One user declared that the application should fit all the target scenarios, especially the "same time/different places" one. Another user declared that the Educational use fits particularly well. However, also other settings are suitable, but in these cases there should not be anyone needed to confirm/reject the changes of other members.

**Further Suggestions.** *First test.* One user suggested adding a non-transparent background when the circular menu for task editing appears, in order to avoid visualisation problems between the circular menu and the task model visualised underneath. Additional suggestions included adding a voice chat in the system and using sounds for notifying important events.

*Second test.* A user suggested removing the locking mechanism and increasing mutual awareness through user icons; another user suggested adding the possibility to edit tasks with drag-and-drop; another user suggested enabling right-click when possible.

## 5.4   Discussion

*First test.* Overall, the results of the test show that Collaborative CTT was appreciated although some aspects (e.g. the lock mechanism and the limited level of mutual awareness) should be subjected to further refinement. Participants especially liked the flexibility provided by the tool in supporting different types of scenarios of use, the most promising ones being when users exploit the tool in a synchronous manner. Another aspect that users particularly liked was the possibility to work (through a Web-based tool) on the same shared model in a concurrent yet organised/controlled manner. In this way the possibility of reworking and duplication as well as the need of exchanging models between members should be reduced, thereby leading to faster and more productive task modelling sessions. As evaluators, we noticed low parallelism between users (i.e. when one user started to edit one task the other rarely started editing another task). However, this can be explained by the users' low familiarity with the tool, and the fact that they tended to follow the sequence of test tasks strictly. Participants verbally discussed the strategy to follow to build the task model for satisfying the test requirements and, being in the same room, they did not use the chat much. Nonetheless, they fruitfully used other tool features (e.g. shared focus) to coordinate their activities during actual editing.

*Second test.* The researchers noticed increased parallelism among participants: in all the tests users started to work on different tasks from the beginning and then they used the tool features to coordinate/verify their work for finally satisfying the test requirements. This enabled us to test the appropriateness of the tool in situations where users actually edit different parts of the model in parallel. This improved parallelism was probably due to two factors. The first one could be greater users' familiarity with the tool: users felt more confident controlling the tool and its features, and therefore exploited it in a more flexible manner. Another possible explanation could be that the remote chat-based communication used in the second experiment was slower than the direct communication used in the first test, therefore users were further stimulated to more efficiently and concurrently edit the model to save time. Nonetheless, the comments received suggest further refining the mechanism supporting the modifications made to the shared task models, which currently may overload the work of the moderator, especially when many requests for modifications have to be analysed in a short time.

## 6  Conclusions

Currently, most of the automatic environments enabling task modelling only support single users, thus limiting the possible interactions and discussions amongst them. In this paper we present a new Web-based multi-user tool for specifying task models. Among its features, the tool includes relevant mechanisms supporting coordination, communication and mutual awareness between participants. In the paper we discuss the aspects we have addressed in designing the collaborative features in a task modelling tool, what type of mechanisms have been developed for their support, and also report on two formative user tests which provided promising feedback, also identifying aspects that could be subject to further refinement. A video showing the tool is available at https://www.youtube.com/watch?v=AapwdNIz5V8&feature=em-share_video_user. The tool is publicly available at http://coll-ctt.isti.cnr.it.

Future work will be dedicated to further empirical testing in both educational and industrial projects.

## References

1. Anzalone, D., Manca, M., Paternò, F., Santoro, C.: Responsive task modelling. In: Proceedings of EICS 2015, pp. 126–131. ACM Press (2015)
2. Duque, R., Gallardo, J., Bravo, C., Mendes, A.J.: Defining tasks, domains and conversational acts in CSCW systems: the SPACE-DESIGN case study. J. UCS **14**(9), 1463–1479 (2008)
3. Forbrig, P., Dittmar, A., Brüning, J., Wurdel, M.: Making task modeling suitable for stakeholder-driven workflow specifications. In: Stephanidis, C. (ed.) Universal Access in HCI, Part I, HCII 2011. LNCS, vol. 6765, pp. 51–60. Springer, Heidelberg (2011)
4. Gallardo, J., Molina, A.I., Bravo, C., Redondo, M.A.: Collaborative modelling of tasks with CTT: tools and a study. In: CADUI 2008, pp. 245–250 (2008)
5. Gallardo, J., Molina, A., Bravo, C., Gallego, F.: A system for collaborative building of use case models: communication analysis and experiences - experiences of use and lessons learned from the use of the SPACE-DESIGN tool in the domain of use case diagrams. In: Proceedings of the 9th International Conference on Evaluation of Novel Approaches to Software Engineering (ENASE 2014), pp. 59–68 (2014)
6. Genaro Motti, V., Raggett, D., Van Cauwelaert, S., Vanderdonckt, J.: Simplifying the development of cross-platform web user interfaces by collaborative model-based design. In: SIGDOC 2013, pp. 55–64 (2013)
7. Genaro Motti, V., Raggett, D.: Quill: a collaborative design assistant for cross platform web application user interfaces. In: WWW (Companion Volume) 2013, pp. 3–6 (2013)

8. Guerrero-Garcia, J., Gonzalez-Calleros, J., Vanderdonckt, J.: Comparative analysis of task model notations, vol. 22 (NE-1), pp. 90–97. ENC, March 2012

9. Giraldo, W.J., Molina, A.I., Ortega, M., Collazos, C.A.: Integrating groupware notations with UML. In: Forbrig, P., Paternò, F. (eds.) HCSE/TAMODIA 2008. LNCS, vol. 5247, pp. 142–149. Springer, Heidelberg (2008)

10. Gutwin, C., Penner, R., Schneider, K.A.: Group awareness in distributed software development. In: CSCW 2004, pp. 72–81 (2004)

11. Hili, N., Laurillau, Y., Dupuy-Chessa, S., Calvary, G.: Innovative key features for mastering model complexity: flexilab, a multimodel editor illustrated on task modeling. In: EICS 2015, pp. 234–237 (2015)

12. Horridge, M., Tudorache, T., Nyulas, C., Vendetti, J., Fridman Noy, N., Musen, M.A.: WebProtégé: a collaborative Web-based platform for editing biomedical ontologies. Bioinformatics 30(16), 2384–2385 (2014)

13. Jourde, F., Laurillau, Y., Nigay, L.: COMM notation for specifying collaborative and multimodal interactive systems. In: EICS 2010. ACM (2010)

14. Martinie, C., Barboni, E., Navarre, D., Palanque, P.A., Fahssi, R., Poupart, E., Cubero-Castan, E.: Multi-models-based engineering of collaborative systems: application to collision avoidance operations for spacecraft. In: EICS 2014, pp. 85–94 (2014)

15. Molina, A.J., Redondo, M.A., Ortega, M.: A methodological approach for user interface development of collaborative applications: a case study. Sci. Comput. Program. 74(9), 754–776 (2009)

16. Molina, A.I., Redondo, M.A., Ortega, M.: A conceptual and methodological framework for modeling interactive groupware applications. In: Dimitriadis, Y.A., Zigurs, I., Gómez-Sánchez, E. (eds.) CRIWG 2006. LNCS, vol. 4154, pp. 413–420. Springer, Heidelberg (2006)

17. Mori, G., Paternò, F., Santoro, C.: Design and development of multi-device user interfaces through multiple logical descriptions. IEEE Trans. Softw. Eng. 30(8), 507–520 (2004). IEEE Press

18. Noy, N.F., Chugh, A., Alani, H.: The CKC challenge: exploring tools for collaborative knowledge construction. IEEE Intell. Syst. 23(1), 64–68 (2008)

19. Paternò, F.: Model-based Design and Evaluation of Interactive Applications. Springer, New York (1999). ISBN 1-85233-155-0

20. Paternò, F., Santoro, C., Spano, L.D.: Engineering the authoring of usable service front ends. J. Syst. Softw. 84(10), 1806–1822 (2011). Elsevier

21. Penichet, V.M., Lozano, M.D., Gallud, J.A., Tesoriero, R.: Task modelling for collaborative systems. In: Winckler, M., Johnson, H. (eds.) TAMODIA 2007. LNCS, vol. 4849, pp. 287–292. Springer, Heidelberg (2007)

22. Pinelle, D., Gutwin, C., Greenberg, S.: Task analysis for groupware usability evaluation: modeling shared-workspace tasks with the mechanics of collaboration. ACM Trans. Comput.-Hum. Interact. 10(4), 281–311 (2003)

23. Renger, M., Kolfschoten, G.L., de Vreede, G.-J.: Challenges in collaborative modeling: a literature review. In: Dietz, J.L.G., Albani, A., Barjis, J. (eds.) CIAO! 2008 and EOMAS 2008. LNBIP, vol. 10, pp. 61–77. Springer, Heidelberg (2008)

24. Rittgen, P.: Group consensus in business process modeling: a measure and its application. IJeC 9(4), 17–31 (2013)

25. Van der Veer, G., Kulyk, O., Vyas, D., Kubbe, O., Ebert, A.: Task modeling for collaborative authoring. In: ECCE 2011, pp. 171–178 (2011)

26. Wurdel, M., Sinnig, D., Forbrig, P.: Toward a formal task-based specification framework for collaborative environments. In: López-Jaquero, V., et al. (eds.) Computer-Aided Design of User Interfaces VI, Chap. 20, pp. 221–232. Springer, London (2009)

# Ceiling and Threshold of PaaS Tools:
# The Role of Learnability in Tool Adoption

Rui Alves[1(✉)] and Nuno Jardim Nunes[1,2]

[1] Madeira Interactive Technologies Institute,
Polo Científico e Tecnológico da Madeira,
2nd Floor Caminho da Penteada, 9020-105 Funchal, Madeira, Portugal
`rui.alves@m-iti.org`, `njn@uma.pt`
[2] Universidade da Madeira, Campus Universitário da Penteada,
9020-105 Funchal, Madeira, Portugal

**Abstract.** Cloud services are changing the software development context and are expected to increase dramatically in the forthcoming years. Within the cloud context, platform-as-a-service tools emerge as an important segment with an expected yearly growth between 25 to 50 % in the next decade. These tools enable businesses to design and deploy new applications easily, thereby reducing operational expenses and time to market. This is increasingly important due to the lack of professional developers and it also raises a long standing issue in computer-aided software engineering: the need for easy to learn (low-threshold), functional (high-ceiling) tools enabling non-experts to create and adapt new cloud services. Despite their importance and impact, no research to date addressed the measurement of tools' ceiling and threshold. In this paper we describe a first attempt to advance the state of the art in this area through an in-depth usability study of platform-as-a-service tools in terms of their threshold (learnability) and ceiling (functionality). The measured learnability issues evidenced a strong positive correlation with usability defects and a weaker correlation with performance. Remarkably, the fastest and easiest to use and learn tool falls into the low-threshold/low-ceiling pattern.

**Keywords:** PaaS · Threshold · Ceiling · Learnability

## 1 Introduction

Within the next 30 years the demand for software applications will grow exponentially[1]. Yet, our capability to increase the number of professional software developers and/or their productivity will at best stabilize or grow linearly. Bezivin call it the impossible equation (see Fig. 1) stating that "How, with the same amount of people (code producer and managers, about 1 % of the total population), to produce an order of magnitude more of software applications than now?"[2].

---

[1] http://semat.org.
[2] https://modelseverywhere.wordpress.com/2013/02/15/one-percent-software-professionals-in-advanced-countries/.

© IFIP International Federation for Information Processing 2016
Published by Springer International Publishing Switzerland 2016. All Rights Reserved
C. Bogdan et al. (Eds.): HCSE 2016/HESSD 2016, LNCS 9856, pp. 335–347, 2016.
DOI: 10.1007/978-3-319-44902-9_21

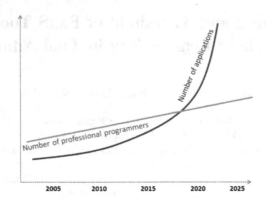

**Fig. 1.** The impossible equation (from http://modelseverywhere.wordpress.com)

This equation seems impossible to solve because, on one hand it is not practical to educate a larger percentage of the world population to develop professional software. On the other hand, lessons from the past show that whatever progress we may achieve in software tools, the productivity of software professionals will not improve by a major factor. As stressed by Bezivin, the key to solving these problems probably lies in the collaboration between professional developers and end-users.

This is a long-standing challenge in engineering interactive systems. In order to enable end-users to contribute to software development, we need to provide new languages and development environments that effectively suite their needs and are easy to learn and operate. These tools are known after the seminal paper about "the past, present and future of user interface software tools" [1] as low-threshold and high ceiling tools. In fact, a major trait in tools' acceptance is the role of threshold and ceiling (the threshold is how difficult it is to learn how to use a tool and the ceiling is how much can be done using the tool). Successful tools in the past 25 years are claimed to either be low-threshold/low-ceiling, or high-threshold/high-ceiling [1]. Despite all efforts we struggle to find tools that enable low-threshold and high-ceiling.

Currently, one major trend lies in what is usually known as cloud infrastructure, involving platforms and solution stacks as a service model of computing. These involve software-as-a-service (SaaS), infrastructure-as-a-service (IaaS) and platform-as-a-service (PaaS). The focus of this paper is the PaaS model in which the end-user controls software deployment and configuration settings, while the vendor provides everything required to host the application [2]. PaaS are characterized by providing low initial cost, incremental growing, self-service, resource sharing, automated deployment, management services, lifecycle management and reuse [3].

In this paper we attempt to advance the state of the art by increasing our under-standing about what these concepts mean and how they can be effectively measured. We do this through: (1) a methodological approach to assess the usability and functionality of PaaS tools, (2) the results from a comparative study of three PaaS tools with 22 subjects and (3) statistical analysis looking for correlations between dimensions such as learnability issues, usability defects and performance. Lastly, in the discussion section, we contrast our findings with the prevailing literature and then present our conclusions.

## 1.1 State of the Art

Both software engineers and designers often complain that their tools are unsupportive and unusable [1]. While many studies have analyzed and tried to better support general software development practices [4, 5], qualitative studies on user interface related practices, in software development, are relatively rare. Furthermore, the work of Seffah and Kline, showed a gap between how tools represent and manipulate programs and the actual experience of the developer [5]. However, ceiling and threshold related issues were not specifically addressed.

Among the distinct sets of existing development tools, there is a group of literature on computer-aided software engineering (CASE) tools [1, 4, 6, 7], which we think worth assessing if the findings related to these tools prevail in the scope of this work. This prior research suggests that: (1) few organizations use CASE tools; (2) many organizations abandon the use of the tools; and (3) countless developers, working for organizations that own CASE tools, do not actually use them. Moreover, Jarzabek and Huang argued that CASE tools should be more user-oriented and use rigorous modeling, in order to better blend into the software development practice [7]. Yet, figures on the adoption of these tools seem to contradict the goals driving their development. Though, a new breed of tools has emerged, in particular Platform-as-a-Service (PaaS), which claim to bridge previous gaps and promise easier and faster development, even for non-experts. Intrigued by these apparently conflicting forces, we found room to contribute by researching the role of learnability in tools adoption.

# 2 Research Question

Since practitioners often complain about the suitability of tools for their work, we realized that threshold and ceiling are claimed as attributes that play a major role in tools adoption. Moreover, successful tools are said to either be low-threshold/low-ceiling or high-threshold/high-ceiling. The issue is that we lack knowledge on how to measure these concepts. Thus, we hypothesized that the threshold is associated with tool's adoption. So, if a tool is hard to learn then it's adoption is more likely to be low, since people will seek out easier solutions. The work presented here is part of a major project, which in the future will help us shed some light on tools adoption and we focus on how to define and measure the core concepts of the framework for tools' threshold and ceiling measurement.

In this paper we measure the initial learnability of tools and assess the relationships between the learnability issues and the usability defects, as well as eventual impacts on subjects' performance. Additionally, recognizing that the terminology is not consistent and before jumping into the details, we would like to clarify the core concepts used in this paper. For instance, learnability is the attribute of a system, which allows users to rapidly begin working with it [8]. In this paper a learnability issue is any problem preventing users from quickly understand how to use the system to do a task. A defect is a breakdown in usability, an obstacle to perform a desired task or a problem in the smooth functioning of the system. A usability defect is generally a mismatch between what the user wants, needs or expects and what the system provides. Finally, performance is the time a participant took to do a task.

# 3  Study

The research study described here was conducted over a period of six months (September 2013–February 2014) and expands the sample of the study described in a previous publication [9]. Participants were asked to play the role of a small shop owner willing to replace his spreadsheet to manage products with a web application. For that purpose, this owner is giving a try to PaaS tools and will try three tools (Knack [10], Mendix Business Modeler 4.7.0 [11] and OutSystems Studio 8.0 [12]).

PaaS is a growing and highly competitive sector with more than 70 vendors, making it hard to select which PaaS tools to test. We surveyed the web for comparisons and picked two tools that are popular and comparable to the tool proposed by the vendor that asked us to evaluate their tool. Additionally, prior to deployment, we performed three pilots to improve the test instructions, assess the duration, completeness and suitability of proposed tasks. Furthermore, we faced two major challenges to run this study: (1) how to record subjects' actions so that they did not felt observed and (2) the test duration. To address both, upon subjects' informed consent, we recorded video and audio and captured screen actions using 15" laptop built-in features. Having no extra hardware helped subjects perceive it naturally. Additionally, the amount of tools tested was constrained by the fact that subjects will do the same set of tasks on each tool. As such, it proved unfeasible to add more tools (due to subjects' engagement and motivation) since the test duration roughly spanned from 2.5 h to 3 h per subject. Because of this plus the fact that we required participants to be completely new (initial learnability) to all tested tools, volunteers were scarce.

## 3.1  Sample

We used a sample of 22 subjects from both genders, divided into two even groups: (G1) comprised people who run small businesses and (G2) IT experts. The rationale for choosing these groups was to contrast their results and assess if PaaS is ready for non-IT experts, as claimed by some vendors. On average, subjects were 30 years old (minimum 22 and maximum 43). Circa 30 % had worked for less than one year and 40 % had between four and nine years of experience, while 20 % had already worked for more than ten years. The vast majority (60 %) holds a bachelor degree and 35 % hold a master's degree. Additionally, none of the G1 subjects had any experience building web applications or had ever used the tools of the trade, whereas all, but one, G2 subjects were experienced in building web apps. Among the G2 subjects, IDEs were popular tools used to create web apps (50 % uses Netbeans, 40 % Dreamweaver) but no one had used or even knew of PaaS tools.

## 3.2  Methodology

As previously stated, this paper expands (from ten to 22 subjects) and builds on top of a previous publication [9]. A detailed explanation of the methodology used was already provided in the methodology section of [9], please refer to this reference for further detail on the methodology used. Here we focus on the results and provide a statistical analysis of the results to complement the claims and findings stated in [9].

## 4   Results

Three dependent variables were measured in this study, specifically (i) learnability issues, (ii) usability defects, and (iii) performance. Additionally, based on subjects' level of success to complete each task, learnability scores were computed also.

### 4.1   Learnability Issues

Grossman's et al. classified learnability issues into five categories: (i) awareness, (ii) locating, (iii) transition, (iv) task-flow and (v) understanding. For detailed explanation on each category please refer to [16]. Table 1 summarizes each category measured weight. The most frequent categories are highlighted in bold and account for 50 % + of issues per group/tool. The transition category is the less frequent, except for G1 in Knack. We used the transition category to compute a ratio between all categories and transition, to learn what categories hinders users the most. Table 2 stresses the proportionality among categories and we found evidence that understanding and task-flow issues hinder users the most, being three times more prevalent than transition issues. In brief, these figures provide empirical evidence that Knack was easier to learn than Mendix and Outsystems. Moreover, all tested tools seem to have a lot of technicalities since all fail to make it easier for non-technical users to quickly learn how to use the tool, risking their putative success in this niche.

**Table 1.** Learnability issues weight per tool.

| Category | Knack | | | | Mendix | | | | Outsystems | | | |
|---|---|---|---|---|---|---|---|---|---|---|---|---|
| | G1 | | G2 | | G1 | | G2 | | G1 | | G2 | |
| | Σ | % | Σ | % | Σ | % | Σ | % | Σ | % | Σ | % |
| Awareness | 5 | 8 | 11 | 26 | 16 | 17 | 9 | 15 | 16 | 16 | 8 | 17 |
| Locating | 11 | 18 | 9 | 21 | 26 | 27 | 20 | 33 | 14 | 14 | 7 | 15 |
| Transition | 6 | 10 | 5 | 12 | 9 | 9 | 6 | 10 | 3 | 3 | 6 | 13 |
| Task-flow | 10 | 17 | 5 | 12 | 33 | 35 | 12 | 20 | 25 | 26 | 13 | 27 |
| Understanding | 28 | 47 | 13 | 30 | 11 | 12 | 13 | 22 | 40 | 41 | 14 | 29 |
| Total | 60 | | 43 | | 95 | | 60 | | 98 | | 48 | |

### 4.2   Usability Defects

The usability defects were categorized according to their relation to the interface. The icons/graphics category are related to a graphical design issue (similar icons). The bars/windows category is directly related to using bars or high level commands. When the defect was related to buttons or input fields then it was categorized as menus/commands, whereas defects classified as interaction are, for instance, double clicking creates

**Table 2.** Relative impact of each learnability issue category.

| Category | G1 | G2 | Knack | Mendix | Outsystems | Total |
|---|---|---|---|---|---|---|
| Awareness | 2 | 2 | 1 | 2 | 3 | 2 |
| Locating | 3 | 2 | 2 | 3 | 2 | 2 |
| Task-flow | 4 | 2 | 1 | 3 | 4 | 3 |
| Understanding | 4 | 2 | 4 | 2 | 6 | 3 |
| Transition | 1 | 1 | 1 | 1 | 1 | 1 |

something without questioning the user). Finally, the text/feedback category are issues on the textual terminology and text feedback on the interface.

Table 3 summarizes the weight of each usability defect category, per tool and group. In the same table we have highlighted, in bold, the top two categories per group and tool, which account for more than 50 % of all defects. Similarly to learnability issues, we have also computed a ratio between all categories and bars/windows, to grasp an idea of what categories have a stronger impact on subjects Table 4. In brief, the trend found on learnability issues is also true here and provides empirical evidence that Knack was easier to use than Mendix and Outsystems. Moreover, all tools seem to suffer from usability defects and fail to make it fully usable for non-technical users, which PaaS vendors claim to be their target.

**Table 3.** Usability defects weight per tool.

| Category | Knack | | | | Mendix | | | | Outsystems | | | |
|---|---|---|---|---|---|---|---|---|---|---|---|---|
| | G1 | | G2 | | G1 | | G2 | | G1 | | G2 | |
| | Σ | % | Σ | % | Σ | % | Σ | % | Σ | % | Σ | % |
| Bars/Windows | 6 | 8 | 3 | 5 | 13 | 13 | 8 | 12 | 22 | 16 | 9 | 12 |
| Icons | 3 | 4 | 5 | 8 | 21 | 21 | 9 | 13 | 27 | 20 | 10 | 14 |
| Interaction | 2 | 3 | 22 | 37 | 12 | 12 | 5 | 7 | 27 | 20 | 18 | 24 |
| Menu/Commands | 2 | 2 | 14 | 24 | 32 | 32 | 27 | 40 | 20 | 14 | 10 | 14 |
| Text/Feedback | 0 2 | 6 3 | 15 | 25 | 21 | 21 | 18 | 27 | 25 | 18 | 20 | 27 |
| Total | 7 | | 59 | | 99 | | 67 | | 13 | | 74 | |

**Table 4.** Relative impact of each usability defect category.

| Category | G1 | G2 | Knack | Mendix | Outsystems | Total |
|---|---|---|---|---|---|---|
| Icons | 1 | 1 | 1 | 1 | 1 | 1 |
| Interaction | 2 | 2 | 5 | 1 | 1 | 2 |
| Menus/Commands | 2 | 3 | 4 | 3 | 1 | 2 |
| Text/Feedback | 2 | 3 | 4 | 2 | 1 | 2 |
| Bars/Windows | 1 | 1 | 1 | 1 | 1 | 1 |

## 4.3 Performance

Table 5 shows the performance, in hours, per group/tool. Curiously, the tasks that took longer in each tool, took longer for both groups. Additionally, we found that the amount of time spent in each task ranged a lot per tool, although the tasks were the

**Table 5.** Performance (aggregated time spent) in hours.

| Task | Knack | | | | Mendix | | | | Outsystems | | | |
|---|---|---|---|---|---|---|---|---|---|---|---|---|
| | G1 | | G2 | | G1 | | G2 | | G1 | | G2 | |
| | Σ | % | Σ | % | Σ | % | Σ | % | Σ | % | Σ | % |
| T1 | 0.81 | 17 | 0.55 | 14 | 1.08 | 16 | 0.55 | 12 | 0.67 | 10 | 0.66 | 13 |
| T2 | 1.08 | 23 | 0.85 | 22 | 2.56 | 39 | 2.05 | 43 | 2.49 | 39 | 2.01 | 38 |
| T3 | 0.44 | 9 | 0.39 | 10 | 0.78 | 12 | 0.43 | 9 | 2.18 | 34 | 1.67 | 32 |
| T4 | 1.21 | 26 | 1.00 | 26 | 0.53 | 8 | 0.44 | 9 | 0.69 | 11 | 0.47 | 9 |
| T5 | 1.16 | 25 | 1.08 | 28 | 1.68 | 25 | 1.26 | 27 | 0.40 | 6 | 0.46 | 9 |
| Total | 4.70 | | 3.86 | | 6.64 | | 4.72 | | 6.42 | | 5.27 | |

same for all tools tested. For instance, while in Knack the T4 and T5 were the tasks that took more time to do, in Outsystems these two tasks were the quickest ones. These differences could evidence the intrinsic difficulty to accomplish a task in one tool, which in turn could be associated with high, or low frequency of learnability issues, thus impacting tools' threshold. In brief, our results provide evidence that the longer it takes to finish the task, the harder it is to learn how to do it. Performance figures follow the trend found in Sects. 4.1 and 4.2, providing empirical evidence that Knack is faster to use than Mendix and Outsystems.

### 4.4 Statistical Analysis

The results highlighted a difference between tools where Knack (classified as low-threshold/low-ceiling) was the fastest, easiest to learn and use tool being tested, whereas the other two tools produced similar performance results. In this section we investigated if there is statistical evidence, which could ground the previous claims. The tools used in this study were encoded in one independent variable and we measured the differences for each dependent variable (learnability issues, usability defects and performance). Additionally, we also sought for possible correlations.

**Differences.** We have used a repeated measure analysis of variance (ANOVA) to test if there are differences between conditions (Knack, Mendix and Outsystems), where the same participants are being measured on the same variable (learnability issues, usability defects or performance). The groups are related because they contain the same cases (the subjects) and each group is a repeated measurement on a dependent variable. This led us to the null hypothesis: H0: all related group means are equal. The alternative hypothesis is Ha: at least one related group mean is different, which would provide evidence on statistical differences between tools, if verified. We verified all the assumptions and found no outliers, in learnability issues, by inspecting the boxplots for values greater than 1.5 box-lengths from the edge (dark grey boxplots on Fig. 2). Data is normally distributed in all three conditions, as assessed by Shapiro-Wilk's test ($p > 0.05$) and Mauchly's Test of Sphericity indicated that the sphericity assumption has not been violated, $\chi^2 (2) = 1.048$, $p = 0.592$. Having satisfied all assumptions, we computed the repeated measures ANOVA, which yielded statistically significant changes in the amount of learnability issues found per tool, $F(2, 42) = 8.868$,

$p < 0.001$, partial $\eta2 = 0.297$. Although this result rejects the null hypothesis and retains the alternative hypothesis, we cannot directly determine where exactly the differences between groups lie. To clarify this uncertainty, a post hoc analysis with a Bonferroni adjustment revealed that the amount of learnability issues significantly decreased from Outsystems to Knack (1.68 (95 % CI, 0.25 to 3.12) issues per subject, $p < 0.05$) and from Mendix to Knack (2.64 (95 % CI, 0.97 to 3.76) issues, $p < 0.01$), but not from Mendix to Outsystems (0.68 (95 % CI, −0.98 to 2.34) issues, $p = 0.895$). As such, these results provide statistical evidence that Knack offers less learnability issues for first time users than the other tested tools.

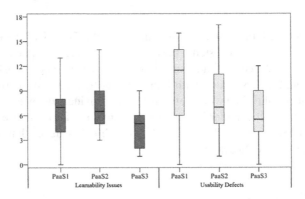

**Fig. 2.** Learnability issues and usability defects

The same procedure was applied to usability defects and we found no outliers (light grey boxplots on Fig. 2). Yet, we realized that Knack data was not normally distributed ($p = 0.041$), although it is normally distributed for Mendix and Outsystems, $p > 0.05$. Nevertheless, we run the test because the repeated measures ANOVA is fairly robust to deviations from normality. Mauchly's Test of Sphericity indicated that the assumption of sphericity was met ($\chi2 (2) = 2.46$, $p = 0.292$) and the repeated measures ANOVA test elicited a statistically significant change in the amount of usability defects per tool, $F(2, 42) = 12.519$, $p < 0.0005$, partial$\eta2 = 0.373$. A post hoc analysis with Bonferroni's adjustment revealed that the amount of usability defects significantly decreased from Mendix to Knack (2.091 (95 % CI, 0.01 to 4.2) defects per subject, $p < 0.05$) and from Outsystems to Knack (3.455 (95 % CI, 1.7 to 5.2) defects per subject, $p < 0.0005$), but not from Mendix to Outsystems (1.364 (95 % CI, 0.2 to 2.93) defects per subject, $p = 0.102$). Given these results, there is statistical evidence that Knack has less usability defects than the other tested tools.

In what concerns performance, the first assumption was violated since there are outliers in Knack and Mendix datasets. Moreover, although the Shapiro-Wilk's test yielded $p > 0.05$ for Knack and Outsystems, the normality test returned a negative result for Mendix ($p = 0.038$). Thus, contrarily to what happened with learnability issues and usability defects, we cannot make any statement about statistical evidence on performance differences between the three tools by using this test.

To sum up, we found statistical evidence that (1) Knack was easier to learn (for first time users) than Mendix and Outsystems, (2) Knack was easier to use than Mendix and Outsystems. These findings are in line with the results section. However, we found no statistical evidence that subjects were faster in Knack than in Mendix or Outsystems, although the figures in the results section point towards that direction.

**Correlations.** There is no statistical test to determine the association between three continuous variables, which is our case and Pearson's correlation was not suitable since there was no linear relationship between variables, as assess by inspecting a scatterplot. As such, we opted for Spearman's correlation. Thus, the null hypothesis is H0: there is no association between the variables and the alternative hypothesis is Ha: there is an association between the variables. Two of the three assumptions of the Spearman's correlation relate to the study design, which we met both (to have two continuous or ordinal variables and the two variables represent paired observations). The third assumption requires to determine whether there is a monotonic relationship between two variables. A monotonic relationship does one of the following: (i) as the value of one variable increases, so does the value of the other variable or (ii) as the value of one variable increases, the other variable value decreases. The Spearman's correlation test unveiled that there was a strong positive correlation between the amount of identified learnability issues and usability defects, $rs(20) = 0.724$, $p < 0.01$. Preliminary analysis showed the relationship to be monotonic, as assessed by visual inspection of a scatterplot. In the other two cases, although the monotonic relationship was not fully clear, there was a remarkably positive correlation between the amount of learnability issues and subjects' performance ($rs(20) = 0.466$, $p < 0.01$) and a moderately positive correlation between the amount of usability defects found and subjects' performance, $rs(20) = 0.352$, $p < 0.01$.

# 5  Threshold and Ceiling

As successful tools are said to either be low-threshold/low-ceiling, or high-threshold/high-ceiling, we plotted the tested tools within this framework [1]. We achieved the threshold by measuring the learnability of tools. As aforementioned, Knack is easy to learn whereas Mendix and Outsystems scored as regular. Yet, the other attribute i.e. ceiling, was missing. Since ceiling shows how much can be done using the system, there are two major approaches one can take to assess it: (1) compare tools usage over time or (2) compare the features each tool offers [1]. The first option, which could yield results based on empirical data and could be grounded on actual tool usage, proved impractical due to time constraints and lack of actual users to whom we could refer. Thus, we selected the second option and measured each tool ceiling by comparing the features offered by the tool. To do this we identified another tool (www.force.com), which is supposedly one of the most complete in the PaaS context, and compared it to the tested tools feature set. This approach yielded that from a total of 31 features, Knack matches with seven, Mendix matches 29 features and Outsystems 31 features. Therefore, the computed ceiling was 23 % for Knack, 94 % for Mendix and 100 % for Outsystems.

Additionally, we ranked it according to this ceiling scale: (i) very low [0 to 19 %], (ii) low [20 to 39 %], (iii) regular [40 to 59 %], (iv) high [60 to 79 %] and (v) very high [80 to 100 %]. This means that according to our measure Knack is low ceiling and Mendix and Outsystems are both very high ceiling. Table 6 summarizes the threshold and ceiling classification based on aggregated data (for initial learnability). Threshold is a measure for how difficult it is to learn a tool and is obtained by inverting the learnability scores. Upon surveying the literature, we found several learnability metrics from which we selected two: (M1) the percentage of users who complete a task without any help and (M2) the percentage of users who complete a task optimally [16]. In M1 users could not ask task-flow related questions. In M2 users must complete the task without help [17]. The aggregated results based on all 330 tasks (22 subjects did five tasks each in three distinct tools) performed, provide empirical evidence that Knack is the easiest tool tested, which reached the easy to learn score with 63 %, followed by Outsystems with a score of regular (53 %) and Mendix ranked last with 46 %. This means that if a tool is easy to learn then the threshold is low or if a tool is very difficult to learn then the threshold is very high. Inversely, the ceiling is determined directly (100 % matching of features is very high ceiling). As such, only one tool (Knack) matches the low-threshold/low-ceiling or high-threshold/high-ceiling pattern identified in [1]. The other tools do not match this pattern. The difference in Outsystems was only 7 %, which made us wonder if a bigger sample would make a difference or if it will make the gap between tools even bigger.

**Table 6.** Overall threshold and ceiling classification.

| Threshold | Ceiling | | | | |
|-----------|---------|-----|---------|------|-----------|
|           | Very    | Low | Regular | High | Very High |
| Very High |         |       |         |      |           |
| High      |         |       |         |      |           |
| Regular   |         |       |         |      | **Mendix/Outsystems** |
| Low       |         | **Knack** |    |      |           |
| Very Low  |         |       |         |      |           |

## 6 Discussion

The work presented here is part of a major project addressing other tools and development environments, here we focused only on the building blocks of the framework for tools' threshold and ceiling measurement, because they were reported as key attributes in tools adoption [1]. As such, we measured the learnability issues and usability defects found per subject and tool, as well as subject performance.

With regard to the learnability issues, the Grossman et al. classification [16] was helpful for clustering issues. The raw data and the statistical analysis provided evidence that Knack was easier to learn than Mendix and Outsystems. This is arguably of little interest for generalization purposes. Yet, the fact that, in general, task-flow and understanding related issues are three times more prevalent than transition issues, presents a clear hint for aspects that vendors need to observe in order to increase their tools learnability. This previous claim is moderately in line with the findings from [9] where understanding and task-flow related issues hinders users the most, although with distinct proportionality. One fact that could justify this difference is the sample size which comprised ten subjects in [9] and 22 here.

Regarding the usability defects, which were reported as a major issue preventing adoption [18], we found statistical evidence that Knack was easier to use than Mendix and Outsystems. Additionally, the differences between categories of defects was not as evident as the learnability issues, yet, defects related to interaction, menus/commands and text/feedback happen twice as often as defects related to bars and windows. Again, tools creators should take this evidence into account so that they can diminish the existing usability barriers and make these tools fully usable for non-technical users, which some PaaS vendors target for. Moreover, the performance data shows that Knack was quicker to use than Mendix and Outsystems, although no statistical evidence was found (not all needed assumptions to run the repeated measures ANOVA test were met).

Remarkably, the correlation tests revealed a strong positive correlation between the number of learnability issues and the usability defects, which stresses the visceral relationship between these two attributes. Noteworthy is also the positive correlation between the number of learnability issues and performance issues (this result hints that the more learnability issues, the longer it takes to do the task) yet, correlation is not an implication. Lastly, a moderately positive correlation between usability defects and performance should also be highlighted.

Additionally, regarding the ceiling/threshold, our findings are in line with Myers et al., who claim that successful tools are either low-threshold/low-ceiling or high-threshold/high-ceiling [1]. The fact is that the fastest, easiest to learn and use tool was the only low-threshold/low-ceiling tool tested (Knack). Yet, the success and adoption of tools is far more complex than simply measuring a tool's threshold and ceiling (social and motivational factors, for instance, are claimed to play a major role). As such, since our sample comprises only three tools we cannot make any claim based on this finding. Having said that, we came to realize that both academia and industry are still failing, to build tools that allow us to create sophisticated systems easily (low-threshold and high ceiling) [19], and that this is a demanding challenge which requires further research to address it.

Jeng claims that learnability is inferred from the amount of time required to achieve user performance standards [20]. Yet, in our study, we had no access to real users' performance figures. To do that we would need to perform an extended test with more tools and users. Nevertheless, our goal in this phase was to measure initial learnability, and was not intended to be a longitudinal study.

A note of caution when interpreting these results should be observed due to the intrinsic subjectivity of these evaluations. The fact that all measures were obtained from analyzing video and audio recordings is prone to subjective interpretation. For instance, when identifying learnability issues, one researcher can consider a fact as an issue whereas another person could skip it. However, if there is no perfect way to do this, it does not mean that we should give up. Instead, to know and understand the underlying facts that impact tool adoption is an objective worth pursuing, and one which could benefit the entire community. As such, we suggest that a pool of analysts should review the recordings and doubtful cases should be pair reviewed to reduce bias. Another hypothetical weakness of this work is the sample size, which is arguably small. However, we cannot ignore how complex this kind of study is. Knowing that (1) subjects should have no experience at all in all three tools, and that (2) each subject spent roughly 2.5 to 3 h using these tools and got no incentives to do so, we can easily understand why did it took us half a year to reach 22 subjects, which heavily limited our efforts to have a bigger sample, with a larger set of tools.

# 7 Conclusion

The cloud infrastructure is pushing the requirements of development tools in the face of the increasing needs of software and the growing importance of cloud infrastructure. PaaS is becoming an important because it facilitates the deployment of applications or services reducing cost and complexity. PaaS are required to handle tasks from editing code to debugging, deployment, runtime, and management. The prevailing literature on development tools hints at several factors contributing to PaaS adoption: (1) software engineers and designers often complain that their tools are unsupportive and unusable [1], (2) there is a demand for tools more user-oriented tools, which better blend into the software development practice [7] and (3) a gap between how tools manipulate programs and the developers' actual experiences [1].

Since tools ceiling and threshold are among the key factors impacting tools adoption [2] and, due to the lack of existing knowledge on how to measure these attributes, we researched how to measure the threshold by assessing tools initial learnability. For that purpose, we have used a hybrid protocol by making use of think-aloud and question-asking. In brief, all tested tools seem to fail to make it easy to learn, use and perform for non-technical users, which some PaaS vendors claim to be their major target market. Additionally, although threshold and ceiling measurement proved to be challenging and the findings must be thoughtfully analyzed (for instance, high learnability may be necessary for a low threshold, but high learnability may not guarantee a low threshold), we think this is an effort worth pursuing, in light of contributing to our understanding on how to design the tools of the future.

The authors would like to thank Claudio Teixeira, Amanda Marinho and Monica Nascimento for their help to conduct the study described in this paper.

# References

1. Myers, B., Hudson, S.E., Pausch, R.: Past, present, and future of user interface software tools. ACM Trans. Comput. Hum. Interact. **7**, 3–28 (2000)
2. Rimal, B.P., Choi, E., Lumb, I.: A taxonomy and survey of cloud computing systems. In: Fifth International Joint Conference on INC, IMS and IDC 2009, NCM 2009, pp. 44–51. IEEE (2009)
3. Lawton, G.: Developing software online with platform-as-a-service technology. Computer **41**, 13–15 (2008)
4. Iivari, J.: Why are CASE tools not used? Commun. ACM **39**, 94–103 (1996)

5. Seffah, A., Metzker, E.: The obstacles and myths of usability and software engineering. Commun. ACM **47**, 71–76 (2004)
6. Campos, P., Nunes, N.J.: Practitioner tools and workstyles for user-interface design. Softw. IEEE **24**, 73–80 (2007)
7. Jarzabek, S., Huang, R.: The case for user-centered CASE tools. Commun. ACM **41**, 93–99 (1998)
8. Holzinger, A.: Usability engineering methods for software developers. Commun. ACM **48**, 71–74 (2005)
9. Alves, R., Teixeira, C., Nascimento, M., Marinho, A., Nunes, N.J.: Towards a measurement framework for tools' ceiling and threshold. In: Proceedings of the 2014 ACM SIGCHI Symposium on Engineering Interactive Computing Systems, pp. 283–288. ACM, Rome (2014)
10. Knack- the easiest online database builder and web app builder. https://www.knackhq.com/?ref=getapp
11. App Platform for The Enterprise | Mendix. http://www.mendix.com/
12. OutSystems Platform - High Productivity Platform as a Service – PaaS. http://www.outsystems.com/platform/
13. Hanington, B., Martin, B.: Universal Methods of Design: 100 Ways to Research Complex Problems, Develop Innovative Ideas, and Design Effective Solutions. Rockport Publishers, Beverly (2012)
14. Lewis, C., Rieman, J.: Task-centered user interface design. A Practical Introduction (1993)
15. Kato, T.: What "question-asking protocols" can say about the user interface. Int. J. Man Mach. Stud. **25**, 659–673 (1986)
16. Grossman, T., Fitzmaurice, G., Attar, R.: A survey of software learnability: metrics, methodologies and guidelines. In: Proceedings of the SIGCHI Conference on Human Factors in Computing Systems, pp. 649–658 (2009)
17. Linja-aho, M.: Evaluating and Improving the Learnability of a Building Modeling System. Helsinki University of Technology (2005)
18. Malavolta, I., Lago, P., Muccini, H., Pelliccione, P., Tang, A.: What industry needs from architectural languages: a survey. IEEE Trans. Softw. Eng. **39**(6), 869–891 (2013)
19. Myers, B.A., Rosson, M.B.: Survey on user interface programming. In: Proceedings of the SIGCHI Conference on Human Factors in Computing Systems, pp. 195–202. ACM, Monterey (1992)
20. Jeng, J.: Usability assessment of academic digital libraries: effectiveness, efficiency, satisfaction, and learnability. Libri **55**, 96–121 (2005)

# Demos and Posters

# User Experience Evaluation Methods: Lessons Learned from an Interactive TV Case-Study

Dimitri Drouet[1] and Regina Bernhaupt[2(✉)]

[1] IRIT, ICS Group, 118, Route de Narbonne, 31062 Toulouse, France
Dimitri.Drouet@irit.fr
[2] Ruwido, Köstendorferstr. 8, 5202 Neumarkt, Austria
Regina.Bernhaupt@ruwido.com

**Abstract.** Evaluating user experience (UX) is a complicated endeavour due to the multitude of existing factors, dimensions and concepts that all contribute to UX. We report lessons learned from conducting a user study that was adapted to not only evaluate usability but also several aspects of the user experience. In this study we evaluated some of the most important factors of user experience including aesthetics, emotions, meaning and value as well as naturalness. Based on these experiences we propose a set of possible improvements to enhance existing user study approaches. These improvements aim at incorporating a variety of methods to support the various aspects of user experience including all experiences before, during and after interaction with a product.

**Keywords:** User experience · Evaluation methods · Aesthetics · Emotion · User-centered development process

## 1 Introduction

User Experience (UX) is defined as "a person's perception and the responses resulting from the use or anticipated use of a product, system, or service." following the ISO standard [6]. McCarthy and Wright [15] argue that UX is a holistic term, as the sum of a set of factors or concepts can be more than just the individual parts. Using a more industry oriented approach, user experience has to be evaluated somehow by enabling some kind of measurement or feedback, to be able to improve the experience. One way is to focus on a set of (well defined) factors or dimensions that are known to be contributing to the overall user experience. In the domain of interactive TV the following UX dimensions have been mentioned to be of importance [5]: aesthetics, emotion, meaning and value, identification/stimulation and (if the interactive TV systems support such functionality) social connectedness. Depending on what the specific interactive TV system offers in terms of interaction technique, functionality or content, these dimensions are complemented by factors like perceived quality of service (smoothness), naturalness of the interaction technique (e.g. naturalness, eyes-free usage) or engagement.

Evaluation of user experience is still a challenging task. There is a summary of methods available at allaboutUX [1], describing methods like experiential contextual

© IFIP International Federation for Information Processing 2016
Published by Springer International Publishing Switzerland 2016. All Rights Reserved
C. Bogdan et al. (Eds.): HCSE 2016/HESSD 2016, LNCS 9856, pp. 351–358, 2016.
DOI: 10.1007/978-3-319-44902-9_22

inquiry [1] that is a variation of contextual inquiry focusing on emotional aspects when performing the method instead of focusing on usability problems. Other methods like UX expert evaluation also have their origin in the evaluation of usability and have been adapted to support user experience evaluation. Other methods including questionnaires, like the AttrakDiff, [2] are applicable once a first prototype or system is available, enabling the user to interact and experience the product. The main problem of all these methods originally developed for usability evaluation is that they have to be adapted. What is important for such and adaptation is the fact that user experience is not just the experience during usage but can be divided in momentary, episodic, cumulative user experience [1]. In our case we are working on the evaluation of user experience in the field of interactive TV. The usage context thus is in people's homes, especially in the living room. Thus different dimensions of user experience are evaluated for this specific context.

Our goal was to identify how standard usability studies can be adapted to include factors or (sub-) dimensions of user experience. We focused on aesthetics, emotions, meaning/value and naturalness of the interaction in this standard laboratory based user study comparing a standard remote control with a remote control providing a kind of haptic feedback with continuous input. Based on the case-study we show if and how our adaptations where helpful for the evaluation of user experience, before, during and after interacting with the interactive system. We conclude with a description of specific challenges we faced and present some lessons learned.

## 2   State of the Art

User experience has been defined in several ways. While the ISO definition focuses on the users perceptions it is as important to take the context into account. As Hassenzahl and Tractinsky [9] defines it, user experience is "A consequence of a user's internal state, the characteristics of the designed system and the context within which the interaction occurs.". What is important for user experience is that an experience is mainly made out of the actual experience of usage, but also includes the encounter with the system (before usage) and experience that are after the usage of the product. Figure 1 shows how UX is changing over time with periods of use and non-use, and describing that a user experience is a combination of the experience before, during and after interacting the product, and that the cumulative UX is formed based on a series of momentary and episodic experiences.

For the evaluation of UX there are various methods available [3]. Using the classification on who is involved, we can distinguish method that are expert-oriented (one expert, group of experts), user-oriented (one person, pairs of users, several users) and automatic methods [2]. Classifying methods by development stage or phase [13] we can distinguish methods for the conceptual and design phase like anticipated experience evaluation [7] or co-discovery [11]. Such methods support to design for specific experiences and enable early insights on people's experiences with such a concept [8]. For the implementation and development phase when partly functional or functional prototypes are available user experience can be evaluated performing user studies that are combined with methods that enable the measurement of the user experience. Most of these user experience evaluation methods have in common that they stem from standard usability evaluation methods and have been adapted to incorporate user experience [10].

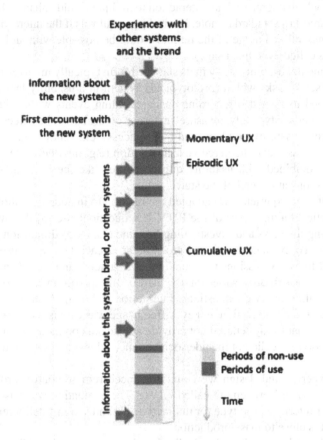

**Fig. 1.** The various types of user experience ranging from the first encounter with the system to long term experiences that form up the overall cumulative user experience from [1] with permission of the authors.

In the area of interactive TV (iTV) the overall user experience has become a distinguishing factor for the choice of the TV system or service [14]. The evaluation of interaction techniques and systems is performed in the majority of studies using combinations of interviews, questionnaires and observation. The development of specific UX evaluation methods for interactive TV systems has been sparse [5].

## 3   Problem Description, Method Selection and Adaptation

Focus of this work was to investigate how to enhance or adapt a standard usability study with UX measurements to be able to evaluate the UX of a newly developed interactive

TV system. This iTV system supports 360° videos with a novel type of remote control with haptic feedback and a kind of continuous input (not a simple button press). Main focus for the set up of the method and the adaptation of the method was the need to understand to which degree such an interaction technique would enhance the user experience, compared to a standard remote. For us important was if the interaction would be perceived as natural and usage of the remote would be possible without looking at the remote (this is called eyes-free usage).

An experimental usability study in its standard form typically involves users that are performing a set of tasks with a (prototypical) system in a usability lab. Activities of users are logged using video recordings and recording events within the interactive system. Such studies typically measure in terms of usability the effectiveness (e.g. number of errors, usability problems and task success), efficiency (e.g. time necessary for performing a task) and the perceived satisfaction (e.g. interview questions). These measures are combined with usability questionnaires like the SUS questionnaire or interview questions at the end of the study.

In terms of user experience we adapted the method to include the following:

For aesthetics: taking a part of the IPTV-UX questionnaire [5] that was filled out after performing the tasks and investigating hedonic quality as dimension provided by the AttrakDiff. To evaluate emotion: Emocards after each task were used and video observation of facial expressions was conducted. To understand identification/stimulation: we used the sub-dimensions of the AttrakDiff questionnaire. To evaluate of meaning and value: interview questions. Interaction technique (naturalness, eyes-free usage): naturalness of interaction and eyes-free usage was evaluated using rating scale question. Given that the system did not provide any social communication features and was just a prototype we did not include social connectedness and service quality as UX dimensions.

For the experimental design we counterbalanced remote control order (standard remote called r 97 vs new remote called r 197). The evaluation was based on a fully functional user interface prototype for interactive TV and a high-fidelity remote control prototype that is close to mass-production.

Figure 2 shows how we have been adjusting the experimental usability study to also cover the various time ranges of the UX. To understand the *first encounter* with the system we video-recorded the user. The video can be used to classify user reaction when first seeing, touching and interacting with the product. During the tasks users are video recorded and eye-gaze is recorded using an eye-tracker. This allows to analyze emotional reactions and to measure objectively the level of eye-gaze towards the remote control). For the *momentary user experience* we asked each study participant after performing a task some rating-questions on the subjective experience (eyes-free perception, naturalness, emotion). The cumulative user experience is measured using the AttrakDiff [2] questionnaire. And the after usage user experience is evaluated using interview questions. With this adaptation not all UX dimensions are explored for all types of user experience (before, during, after, momentary, episodic, cumulative). The decision to incorporate these measurements was informed by several factors: maximal duration of each session should not exceed 1,5 h, availability of validated measures and of course the goal of the evaluation to understand UX of the newly developed interaction technique.

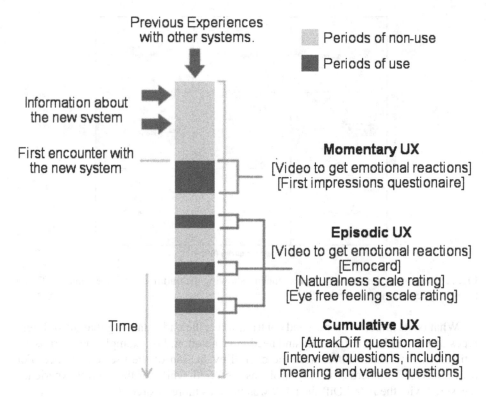

**Fig. 2.** Depiction of the assembly of various methods to investigate user's experiences before, during and after usage

## 4    Procedure and Results

The experimental user study was performed in June 2016 in an office of IRIT that was equipped with a 55″ television screen. The user was seated on a sofa with about 3 m of distance. Each session lasted around 1.5 h. Experimentation involved two different systems, from which we only report the variation of the interaction technique when controlling 360° video. Ten participants (age 19 to 23; mean 21.5, SD 1.27) took part in the study and were awarded 20 € for their participation. The procedure followed closely the steps described in Fig. 2.

For the **momentary UX** the participants description included a wide range of comments that were analyzed qualitative in a word cloud, showing the difference in experience the participants had when interacting with the two different remote controls. The **episodic UX** ranged from surprising to feeling in control. The perception of naturalness was 1.65 (for the r 197) and 1.55 (for the r 97), on a scale from 1 (natural) to 5 (not natural). **Cumulative UX:** Results in terms of user experience showed that the new type of remote control r 197 was in terms of cumulative user experience perceived as desired while the traditional remote r 97 was perceived as task oriented (Fig. 3). Due to limited space we are not able to report all types of data.

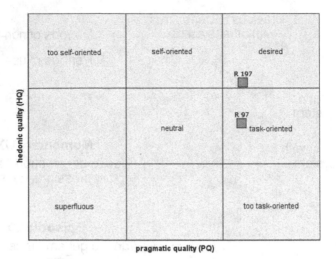

**Fig. 3.** Results for the AttrakDiff questionnaire showing the traditional remote control r 97 and the new type of remote control r 197.

What is the important aspect and contribution is the understanding that the different types of UX can be contradictory and need interpretation. For example the short usage ratings for naturalness differ from the overall evaluation of the user experience. For naturalness the standard remote control was preferred, while for the overall experience measured with the AttrakDiff the r 197 was rated as more desired.

A possible interpretation is that users are facing an unpleasant situation in a user test and thus on a short time evaluation feel more comfortable with a technology there are used to (in this case the r 97). Thus in the short time they got the remote in their hand (7.15 min on average) during the test, it is hard for them to get a real feeling about a new kind of remote control (r 197). This could explain why they are considering the traditional remote control as more natural than the new type of remote despite that they are putting the new type of remote in the desire category and the traditional in the task oriented category. This demonstrates that the combination of various methods can be helpful to understand how the overall user experience develops over time.

## 5    Lessons Learned

To have a general understanding of the overall user experience it is important to combine methods and methodological approaches that enable the measurement before, during and after interacting with the product in a user study. The combination and combined analysis is key to get a more holistic understanding of UX.

Using a user study is a feasible method to get a reasonably fast first understanding on the overall user experience and allows to evaluate user's first impressions and first time or early usages.

Analysis of the multitude of data and their integration into a bigger picture is currently difficult to achieve. There are no standards for how to integrate differing user experience descriptions and how to conclude from them in a quick and easy way. Using textual analysis or grounded theory to interpret text could be a possibility but will be complicated facing the need to also include quantitative data.

One key limitation at the moment is the missing data on later stages of user experience and how user experience is changing over long term use. Figure 1 clearly shows longer term usage experiences, while the user study in Fig. 2 only evaluates very early stages. There is work on these areas [12] on how time affects user experience, but how to integrate longer term evaluation in user studies is currently not solved.

Performing a user study per se incorporates a variety of artifacts due to the methodology [1]. Participants can feel uncomfortable in the testing situation and this might influence the feedback on the UX. Possible counter-steps can be the triangulation of methods and the incorporation of methods that can be applied at later stages (e.g. Field studies or long-term Diaries) to balance limitations of individual methods.

## 6   Conclusion

The inclusion of user experience as a central driver for software development is a difficult endeavor. This paper reports on first results on how to adapt an experimental user study to include user experience measurements for before, during and after usage of a system and discusses briefly lessons learned for such an approach. Our research goal is to start to establish a framework that allows the comparison of adaptations and combinations of UX evaluation methods, e.g. by expanding current work on the notation of UX evaluation results in a task-modeling tool [4].

A special focus of our future work will be on measuring UX after usage e.g. by performing post-usage interviews or using creative forms of reminders to prompt memory of the user to describe these after usage experiences. One possible way would be send a video about the interactive system or product to the user, combined with a set of questions to gather post-usage feedback. We feel that the phase of after usage is currently not reasonably addressed by the HCI research community, but it would be central to the understanding how users form opinions on a product due to the experience they made and how such a post usage experience leads to the establishment of a connection with a product or brand.

## References

1. All about UX: all UX evaluation methods. http://www.allaboutux.org/all-methods
2. AttrakDiff. www.attrakdiff.de
3. Bernhaupt, R. (ed.): Game User Experience Evaluation, p. 285. Springer, London (2015)
4. Bernhaupt, R., Palanque, P., Manciet, F., Martinie, C.: User-test results injection into task-based design process for the assessment and improvement of both usability and user experience. In: Bogdan, C., et al (eds.) HCSE 2016/HESSD 2016. LNCS, vol. 9856, pp. 56–72. Springer, Switzerland (2016)

5. Bernhaupt, R., Pirker, M.: Evaluating user experience for interactive television: towards the development of a domain-specific user experience questionnaire. In: Kotzé, P., Marsden, G., Lindgaard, G., Wesson, J., Winckler, M. (eds.) INTERACT 2013, Part II. LNCS, vol. 8118, pp. 642–659. Springer, Heidelberg (2013)
6. ISO 9241-210 Ergonomics of Human-System Interaction - Part 210: Human-Centred Design for Interactive Systems (2010)
7. Gegner, L., Runonen, M.: For what it is worth: anticipated experience evaluation. In: 8th International Conference on Design and Emotion, London, UK (2012)
8. Hagen, U.: Designing for player experience: how professional game developers communicate design visions. J. Gaming Virtual Worlds 3, 259–275 (2011)
9. Hassenzahl, M., Tractinsky, J.: User experience-a research agenda. Behav. Inf. Technol. 25(2), 91–97 (2006)
10. Hassenzahl, M.: The thing and I: understanding the relationship between user and product. In: Blythe, M.A., Overbeeke, K., Monk, A.F., Wright, P.C. (eds.) Funology, pp. 31–42. Springer, Amsterdam (2003)
11. Jordan, P.: Designing Pleasurable Products. Taylor and Francis, London (2000)
12. Karapanos, E., Zimmerman, J., Forlizzi, J., Martens, J.-B.: Measuring the dynamics of remembered experience over time. Interact. Comput. 22, 328–335 (2010)
13. Lazar, J., Feng, H.J., Hocheiser, H.: Research Methods in Human-Computer Interaction. Wiley, Chichester (2010)
14. Lehtonen, T.K.: The domestication of new technologies as a set of trials. J. Consum. Cult. 3(3), 363–385 (2003)
15. McCarthy, J., Wright, P.: Technology as experience. Interactions 11, 42–43 (2004)

# Endev: Declarative Prototyping with Data

Filip Kis[✉] and Cristian Bogdan

KTH Royal Institute of Technology, Stockholm, Sweden
{fkis,cristi}@kth.se

**Abstract.** The trend of Open Data and Internet-of-Things initiatives contribute to the ever growing amount of data available through web APIs. While building web applications has become easier with recent advancement in web development technologies and proliferation of JavaScript frameworks, the access to data from various APIs and data stores still poses certain challenges. It often requires complex setup and advanced programming skills that hinder the rapid prototyping efforts. Therefore, we propose Endev, a declarative framework for prototyping applications that is built on modern web technologies and supports building modern web applications, that utilize the vast amount of available data, without the need for setup or write complex JavaScript code.

**Keywords:** UI modeling · GUI generation · Interactive prototypes · Discourse model · Query annotations

## 1 Introduction

The Open Data and the Internet-of-Things trends are producing more and more data that users are expected to have access to via GUIs of interactive applications. At the same time building such data-centric applications requires less effort than ever, for skilled developers, thanks to cloud services, popularization of scripting development technologies (e.g. JavaScript, Python) and the omnipresence of web[1]. However, the setup and advanced programming skills required to build interactive prototypes hinders the rapid prototyping efforts.

Prototyping is the key activity in human-centered software engineering process as it allows designers to explore design alternatives and include end-users early on in the process. Various prototyping methods, from sketching to using dedicated prototyping tools, are used in practice, however, the research shows that designers desire better tools that would allow them to prototype the flow of data and advanced interaction [6,9]. Furthermore, a survey of 4000

---

[1] Web is becoming the platform of choice for many applications as it is easier to maintain (no installs or updates) compared to desktop or mobile applications.

© IFIP International Federation for Information Processing 2016
Published by Springer International Publishing Switzerland 2016. All Rights Reserved
C. Bogdan et al. (Eds.): HCSE 2016/HESSD 2016, LNCS 9856, pp. 359–365, 2016.
DOI: 10.1007/978-3-319-44902-9_23

designers [3] shows that HTML is preferred prototyping tool over tools specifically designed for prototyping (e.g. InVisio) or even general design tools (e.g. Photoshop, InDesign).

Building on these research results, and with the aim to support rapid prototyping of data-centric applications, we demonstrate Endev [7] – a declarative prototyping solutions. The declarative HTML annotations allow users to prototype interactions with, and connection to, data. Endev is developed as JavaScript library and utilizes cloud services to support data storage and API access without the need for server setup or dedicate development environments.

## 2   Related Work

Declarative languages have played an important role in UI development and especially in web design where HTML and CSS are dominating as markup technologies for defining UI layout. Modern client-side web development frameworks (e.g. Angular [2], Ember [1]) use declarative data-binding constraints that provide more dynamic features, such as keeping HTML elements automatically in synchronization with the application data values, though they still require significant amount of non-declarative code to access the backend or the API data.

Quilt [4] is a recent solution that provides HTML annotations to connect the interface to a spreadsheet that serves as the datastore. Quilt allows both data read and write and keeps the interface in synchronization with the spreadsheet data. Another solution based on spreadsheets as the datastore is Gneiss [5]. Unlike Quilt, Gneiss is a live programming mashup environment where, instead of using HTML annotations, the users can drag and drop widgets to the page and connect them with spreadsheet values. A key feature of Gneiss is the support for any REST[2] web service returning JSON[3] data which can be interactively combined in the spreadsheet before their data is used in the interface. The main drawback for Gneiss compared to Endev is that the users are limited to working with UI widgets existing in the system, which significantly reduces the design possibilities.

XFormsDB [10] is a declarative data binding solution that binds to server-side data. It is based on the XForms[4], a W3C Recommendation, that was designed to be the next generation of HTML forms. XFormsDB depends on having a complex server setup and supports only XML based databases, thus it is not ideal for quick prototyping. Furthermore, even though XForms are relatively old-standard (first version published in 2007), none of the major browsers currently natively supports it.

---

[2] Representational State Transfer protocol - most widely used protocol for web service APIs.

[3] JavaScript Object Notation - data format often used by exchanging data through web services.

[4] https://www.w3.org/MarkUp/Forms/.

## 3   Setup-Free Prototyping with Endev

During prototyping, it is often important to be able to share the prototype with other stakeholders to solicit feedback. When the prototype is interactive, includes data, or requires a complex setup, it becomes hard to share it beyond screenshots or video recordings that capture only fixed path interaction. However, Endev addresses these challenge by utilizing modern web technologies and cloud services.

With Endev the users can prototype web applications that provide data storage and other features that contemporary users expect (e.g. drag-and-drop interaction, real-time data synchronization) by writing HTML and annotating it with declarative expressions. Such prototypes can be executed in any browser, which makes them easily sharable. In other words, the prototype can be sent by email, shared over Dropbox or put on-line in one of the code playgrounds (e.g. CodePen[5], JsFiddle[6]) for easy access and modification.

We will use an example Wish List app (shown in Fig. 1) to demonstrate how a prototype can be built with Endev. The goal of the Wish List app is to give the users possibility to setup their wish list (e.g. for a birthday or Christmas). Each item on the list can optionally include a picture that the users can retrieve by searching through public pictures on Flickr.

**Fig. 1.** The Wish List prototype showing the items on the list (with name and optionally an image) on the left (Current list) with possibility to add a new item on the right (Add item to the list). At the top right the users can type the name of the new item, while in the bottom right they can search and select a picture that should be associated to the item.

The following sections will describe how the two main challenges (storing the wish list data and getting the pictures from Flickr) are achieved through prototyping

---

[5] http://codepen.io/.
[6] https://jsfiddle.net/.

with Endev. The more comprehensive and interactive tutorial covering the main features of Endev is available on-line[7].

## 4   On-the-fly Creation of Own Data

Storing the data is typically not a concern that is addressed during UI prototyping. The designers normally use dummy data that is either not possible to edit or, at a more advanced stage of the prototyping, the edits are temporary (e.g. refresh of the page or reload of the app reset the data). However, there is a value in working with the data that is stored. For instance, when testing with users they get to experience the flow of the application by experiencing the interaction with the data. Furthermore, if there is a need to quickly modify the design, the user-entered data is still there and thus makes the comparison of alternatives easier to compare.

Listing 1.1 shows the HTML code with Endev annotations needed to list the items from the wish list and add a new item to the list. The code is the same code used for the application shown in Fig. 1 without the additional layout-only HTML code.

```
Current list
<div data-from="firebase:WishList item" data-auto-update="true">
  <input data-value="item.name"/>
  <img src="{{item.image}}"/>
</div>

Add item to list
<input data-value="newItem.name"/>
<img src="{{newItem.image}}"/>
<button data-insert-into="firebase:WishList"
        data-click="insert({name:newItem.name,image:newItem.image})">
  Add
</button>
```

**Listing 1.1.** Endev code of Wish List app (see Fig. 1) for listing the items in the wish list and adding a new item to the list.

In this example `data-from` and `data-insert-into` annotations are used to connect to the data storage for which we use Firebase[8] cloud storage. Firebase is a document-based storage, therefore, there is no need to define the data structure before hand. Instead, data is stored as-is and on-the-fly.

We have seen, in the related work, some solutions use spreadsheets to allow building applications quickly without the need for complex database setup. However, document-based data storage provides more complex data objects compared to spreadsheets thus allowing for more complex use-cases. Furthermore, Firebase is just one of several data providers offered by Endev and others (e.g. spreadsheet storage) can be added easily.

Other annotations like `data-value` and `data-click` serve to bind the values to some UI elements or user actions respectively. Finally, the `data-auto-update` annotation enables automatic updates of the values in the *Current list*, in other

---

[7] http://www.endevjs.org/tutorial.
[8] https://firebase.google.com/.

words, as soon as the users modify any of the items in the list the changes are saved automatically.

## 5  Seamless Integration of API Data

The second challenge of the Wish List app is to integrate with Flickr search API so that an image can be associated with the wish list item. Traditionally such feature would be prototyped with dummy data instead of having a real API integration. However, with more and more web services generating data and applications that work with them it is important that prototyping includes working with real API data. Web service data, compared to proprietary domain-data, comes with certain challenges (e.g. quality, reliability, latency) that are often out of control of application developers. For instance, the end-users or designers might expect the results from API to be the same as when they use the actual service where the data comes from. While, in reality, the service provider might have different algorithms for these two cases. Experiencing the differences early on in the prototyping allows for better management of expectations and thus better design.

Accessing APIs requires certain amount of complex and error-prone code [8] that needlessly increases the prototyping effort. Endev addresses this by providing seamless mechanism for reading web service data that is seen by the users as just another data provider. In other words, the difference between reading their own data (as seen in Listing 1.1) and the data coming from an API is in the string that defines the data source (e.g. **data-from** annotation).

Listing that follows shows how the users can read data from Flickr API based on the inputed search term.

```
Search for an image
<input data-value="searchTerm"/>
<div data-from="yql:flickr.photos.search result"
    data-where="result.text= searchTerm AND
                result.api_key ='_API_KEY_OMITTED_'">
  <div data-from="result.photo photo">
    <img src="http://farm{{photo.farm}}.staticflickr.com/{{photo.server}}/{{
        photo.id}}_{{photo.secret}}.jpg"
        data-insert-into="firebase:PhotoCollection"
        data-click="newItem.image ='_LONG_URL_OMITTED_'">
    <small data-from="yql:flickr.people.info2 people"
          data-where="people.user_id = photo.owner AND
              people.api_key ='_API_KEY_OMITTED_'">
    by {{people.person.username}}
    </small>
  </div>
</div>
```

**Listing 1.2.** Endev code of Wish List app (see Fig. 1) for searching public images on Flickr and, when one image is clicked, adding it to the new item.

The first **data-from** has similar meaning as in Listing 1.1. However, instead of getting data from Firebase, Endev now uses Yahoo Query Language platform[9] to directly access the Flickr search API. Since the data returned by the API is

---

[9] https://developer.yahoo.com/yql/.

hierarchical (i.e. contains an item called `photo` that contains an array of actual photo results) the second `data-from` is used to access each item in the array. The final `data-from` is used to access another Flickr API which returns the information about the owners of the photos based on their ids. Finally, the `data-click` sets the value of the image of the `newItem` which was used in Listing 1.1 when creating the new item for the list.

## 6   Behind the Scenes

Endev is implemented as JavaScript framework with architecture shown in Fig. 2. Endev Core is responsible for caching (on the client-side) and querying the data from one of the Endev Providers which, in turn, access the data and keep it in sync with the data storage. Endev Annotations are built on top of Anuglar, therefore, Endev supports evolutionary prototyping as the prototype can evolve beyond the capabilities provided by Endev. Thus, Endev can be used to either quickly prototype a completely new application or just a new feature in already existing applications. In both cases the prototype can evolve into a more stable system without the need of re-implementing the whole interface from scratch.

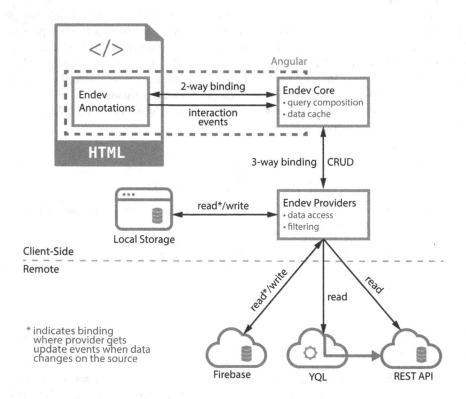

**Fig. 2.** Endev architecture

# 7   Conclusion and Future Work

In this paper we demonstrated Endev, the tool for prototyping interactive applications with data. Endev enables prototyping with real data, created by the users or coming from a web service, through declarative annotations without the need for complex setup or server orchestration. The prototypes are simple HTML files that can easily be shared among all the stakeholders and require only a browser to be executed.

While the declarative annotations employed by Endev provide a uniform way of accessing data, there is a challenge in finding and understanding the growing amount of web service data. Endev currently supports a basic way of exploring the data returned from an API, however, in the future we would like to explore how to better support the discovery and understanding of APIs during prototyping.

# References

1. Ember.js - A framework for creating ambitious web ... (2011). http://emberjs.com/
2. AngularJS - Superheroic JavaScript MVW Framework (2014). https://angularjs.org/
3. The Tools Designers are Using Today (2015). http://tools.subtraction.com/
4. Benson, E., Zhang, A.X., Karger, D.R.: Spreadsheet driven web applications. In: Proceedings of the 27th Annual ACM Symposium on User Interface Software and Technology (UIST), New York, USA, pp. 97–106. ACM, New York (2014)
5. Chang, K.S.P., Myers, B.A.: Creating interactive web data applications with spreadsheets. In: ACM Symposium on User Interface Software and Technology (UIST), pp. 87–96, New York, USA. ACM, New York (2014)
6. Grigoreanu, V., Fernandez, R., Inkpen, K., Robertson, G.: What designers want: needs of interactive application designers. In: IEEE Symposium on Visual Languages and Human-Centric Computing 2009, VL/HCC 2009, pp. 139–146, September 2009
7. Kis, F., Bogdan, C.: Declarative setup-free web application prototyping combining local and cloud datastores. In: 2016 IEEE Symposium on Visual Languages and Human-Centric Computing (VL/HCC). IEEE Computer Society (2016)
8. Myers, B.A.: Separating application code from toolkits. In: Proceedings of the 4th Annual ACM Symposium on User Interface Software and Technology (UIST), New York, USA, pp. 211–220. ACM, New York (1991)
9. Myers, B.A., Park, S.Y., Nakano, Y., Mueller, G., Ko, A.J.: How designers design and program interactive behaviors. In: 2008 IEEE Symposium on Visual Languages and Human-Centric Computing (VL/HCC), pp. 177–184. IEEE Computer Society, Washington, D.C. (2008)
10. Vuorimaa, P., Laine, M., Litvinova, E., Shestakov, D.: Leveraging declarative languages in web application development. World Wide Web 19(4), 519–543 (2016)

# Collaborative Task Modeling: A First Prototype Integrated in HAMSTERS

Marius Koller[1(✉)], Cristian Bogdan[2], and Gerrit Meixner[1]

[1] UniTyLab, Heilbronn University, Heilbronn, Germany
{marius.koller,gerrit.meixner}@hs-heilbronn.de
[2] CSC, MID, KTH Royal Institute of Technology, Stockholm, Sweden
cristi@kth.se

**Abstract.** Task models are introduced in several use-cases in academia. They are usually created in collaboration between different people and disciplines. There exist many notations and associated graphical editors to create the models. However, these editors do not have integrated functions to support collaborative work. In this work, we propose the integration of collaborative functions in the HAMSTERS task modeling tool.

**Keywords:** Task modeling · Collaborative support · HAMSTERS

## 1 Introduction

The creation of task models is a complex undertaking that is usually performed by people from different professions and backgrounds. It is unlikely that just one person is working on task models in a given project. Therefore, task models will often be the result of some kind of collaboration. To support task authors and their daily work, digital support for the collaborative creation of task models is necessary. The needed digital support depends on the nature of task model creation process in each group.

In this demo we propose an integration of collaborative features in the HAMSTERS task modeling tool. We focus on the communication between the collaborators as well as on awareness between them. The proposed and prototyped functions are being implemented and will be evaluated in the future.

## 2 Task Models

Task Models are a well-known concept in research and academia. Task modeling has its foundations in the Hierarchical Task Analysis (HTA) that was defined in 1967 by Annett and Duncan [1]. HTA has the goal to analyze the user's tasks and structure it hierarchically. Many different task modeling notations were defined and are used in different, mostly academic, use cases, for different purposes. For example, the Useware Markup Language (useML) [7] aims to generate user interfaces that are based on the created task models. For this purpose, the in useML defined Usemodel is transformed

© IFIP International Federation for Information Processing 2016
Published by Springer International Publishing Switzerland 2016. All Rights Reserved
C. Bogdan et al. (Eds.): HCSE 2016/HESSD 2016, LNCS 9856, pp. 366–373, 2016.
DOI: 10.1007/978-3-319-44902-9_24

to other models and at the end it is possible to generate the final user interface. The Groupware Task Analysis (GTA) aims to support the task-based development of collaborative applications [14] (we should however distinguish collaboration during task modeling from collaboration of end users modeled by collaboration-aware task models such as GTA). The Méthode Analytique de Description (MAD) is a semi-formal method to record user tasks based on interviews [11] that can be used during the requirements analysis phase. The ConcurTaskTrees (CTT) are and well-known approach [9] which has dominated research approaches lately. CTT aims to analyze and record the user's task and generate models from them. The Human-centered Assessment and Modeling to Support Task Engineering for Resilient Systems (HAMSTERS) [6] uses some concepts from CTT and aims to identify possible human errors and to prevent them.

Most of these notations have graphical representations and editors to create graphical task models. For instance, HAMSTERS (see Fig. 1) and CTT's editors CTTE [10] and Responsive CTT [2] use small icons for the representation of tasks. For the different type of tasks there are specific icons defined and used in the models. UseML's editor Udit [8] represents the items with boxes and differs them using a color-code. CTTE and Udit are stand-alone software whereas Responsive CTT is web-based.

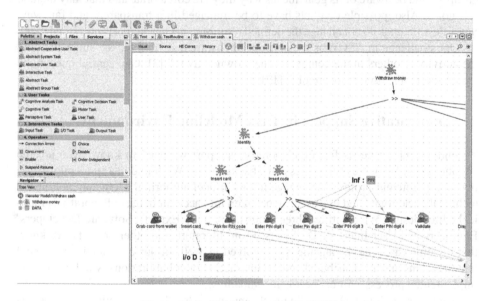

**Fig. 1.** The graphical editor HAMSTERS.

## 3  Computer Supported Cooperative Work

The field of Computer Supported Cooperative Work (CSCW) has been aiming to support technology-mediated collaboration for several decades.

Collaborative editors are an important area of CSCW research, and it is collaborative task model editors that we aim to create a system for collaborative editing. It needs to support the following features, according to [4]:

1. **Distribution**: the clients are not co-located but distributed and connected over the internet or an internal network.
2. **Sharing**: the clients should be able to share documents but be aware with whom they are sharing it.
3. **Autonomy**: a document has an owner that has the right manage it, e.g. grant access.
4. **Reliability**: the stored data has to be robust to connection losses and be accessible when a client crashes.
5. **Reconfiguration**: the clients should easily configure the system and its behavior.
6. **Concurrency**: the system has to allow editing at one time.
7. **Consistency**: the stored data has to be consistent even during the concurrent editing.
8. **Performance**: the responses should have a reasonable delay that allows a fluent working with the system.
9. **High-Quality User Interface**: the provided user interface should support the clients during their work.

Sutcliffe defines requirements for groupware, some of them are similar to the above [13]. He adds for example the "group's collective goal awareness" – that means the group should be aware of its goal, means why they are collaborate and that may include sub-goals. Also, possible conflicts have to be managed in a transparent and fair way. Sutcliffe's findings do not change the defined requirements but support and extend them.

One challenge in CSCW is the concept of "awareness" defined as "understanding the activity of others in the context of one's own activity" [3]. One central question is "what should the user be aware of?" [12].

## 4    Collaborative Support in Task Modeling Environments

To understand the needs for a collaborative support we need to know: who are the collaborators? What are their professions, background? We found in a small pilot-study that many different professions engage in task model authoring. They may not have a technical background and this needs to be taken into account in the collaborative graphical editor design. We identified three groups: Usability Experts, Software Developers/ Engineers and User Interface Designers. From literature and other projects, we know that in some cases the management is involved as well. In our own studies we found that the teams may be distributed and the interaction or collaboration –which means the implemented process - differs between companies.

We looked at four task modeling tools and evaluated their possibilities for cooperation support.

At first we identified features that afford some sort of collaboration. The most basic form for developers is the sharing of file with a Version Control System (VCS) like for example Git or Subversion (SVN). Other ways of sharing files, like simple "saving in the cloud" and sharing with others – at the same or different time. Also an important aspect for collaboration is the communication. There are different communication-channels that could be used: text-based chat, call or video-telephony. For the distributed creation of task models, it is useful if users could comment on tasks, branches of a tree model or on the whole model. Users may want to know how a model evolved during the creation. For that a history feature is useful where the users can see what was changed.

As shown in Table 1, HAMSTERS is the only tool that provides some aspects of collaborative support. HAMSTERS has an integrated version control (VCS) that allows the users to share their project. The history is closely related to the VCS. The view shows the underlying XML-file and shows the differences between the selected version and the current working-copy. There is no possibility to show the differences in the graphical representation.

**Table 1.** Analyzed tools.

| Feature | Udit | CTTE | Responsive CTTE | HAMSTERS |
|---------|------|------|-----------------|----------|
| Sharing | ✕ | ? | ? | ✓ |
| Chat | ✕ | ✕ | ✕ | ✕ |
| Comment | ✕ | ✕ | ✕ | ✕ |
| History | ✕ | ✕ | ✕ | ✓ |

Several incipient collaboration features are supported by other modeling tools as well. In CTTE it is possible to upload the file to a public or private repository at HIIS. Responsive CTTE could be able to share the models. Since it is web-based and the models are saved on servers, it could be possible to share the files. Currently this function is not implemented. Udit has no functionality for collaboration integrated.

Hili et al. [5] introduce with FlexiLab a tool that offers collaborative functions amongst others. They focus in their work on real-time communication and sharing of models. The sharing enables the users to work on different parts of a model and share it.

# 5   Mock-Ups of Collaborative Functions

Since we have some functions that are already integrated in HAMSTERS, we decided to continue working with it adding collaborative support. In order to generate ideas on how a collaborative support could look like, and in order to be able to analyze and judge these design ideas, we developed prototypes for the different collaborative functions. The ideas are being implemented as online prototypes, and prepared for demo. Since HAMSTERS is based on NetBeans™, we intend to stick on the NetBeans tab-based navigation concept.

The first function that we considered is the communication between users. We thus integrated a tab that shows a chat tool We decided to introduce a tab with the same behavior like the other tabs (e.g. tabs could be arranged according to the user's preferences). An important point to keep in mind is that the chat has to be visible for every user, including what was said before he or she joined the talk. The mockup is depicted in Fig. 2.

As a second major function we identified commenting. We believe that for the collaborative creation it is important to tell the other editors how you are thinking while designing a task model. The comments are anchored on specific parts of a task model. Therefore, we intend to introduce comments that can be attached to a specific task or a

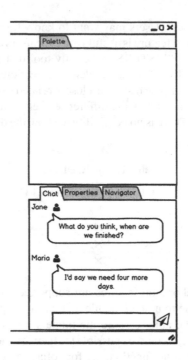

**Fig. 2.** The integrated chat.

branch of the model. The possibility to add a comment will be shown at the object of interest. Depending on the kind of task. e.g. Abstract Task or User Task, the comment will refer to a whole branch or only to this specific task. The first comment in Fig. 3 includes the possibility to comment on the whole branch while the second comment or conversation is regarding this particular task. It will be possible to start discussions within the comments.

The current HAMSTERS implementation of a history is readable only by experts, e.g. Software Engineers, as it is based on version control specific to software. Users from other disciplines that use the application and its models are currently not able to understand the changes without an expert explanation. To support such users, we will introduce a graphical representation of task model history. One design alternative is to display history as grayed-out objects.

The sharing of the model with real-time editing may need changes in the user account structure of HAMSTERS. For example, we need to display the currently active users and which users have access to the model (see Fig. 4). To achieve that, we have to provide a login for the users. Again, to be consistent with the existing UI design of HAMSTERS we will introduce a tab that contains the currently active users and the users that have access to the model.

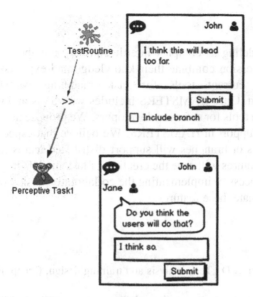

**Fig. 3.** Two comments on tasks.

**Fig. 4.** Sharing the model.

After implementing such basic collaborative support for task editing, we will look into more advanced support, derived from field studies of task modeling that we are conducting. For example, awareness [4, 11] will be initially supported only by our history feature, which is a good beginning is history is shown permanently in a tab, and maybe recent changes are promoted in the tab title. More awareness support can be added to emphasize important task model changes made by collaborators.

## 6  Conclusions

We regard task modeling as complex interdisciplinary collaborative work. Different disciplines and profession combine their knowledge and expertise in these artifacts. However, in the current tools for task modeling we found only little collaborative support. Only HAMSTERS includes with SVN and Git which are well-known collaborative tools for software developers. We propose new features that introduce collaborative support in HAMSTERS. We believe that especially the possibility to comment on tasks or branches will support distributed teams that work asynchronously. The other features will ease the creation of task models in groups, too.

We are in the process of implementing the collaborative task modeling features and we aim to later evaluate these features.

## References

1. Annett, J., Duncan, K.D.: Task analysis and training design. Occup. Psychol. **41**, 211–221 (1967)
2. Anzalone, D., et al.: Responsive task modelling. In: Proceedings of the 7th ACM SIGCHI Symposium on Engineering Interactive Computing Systems, pp. 126–131. ACM, New York (2015)
3. Dourish, P., Bellotti, V.: Awareness and coordination in shared workspaces. In: Proceedings of the 1992 ACM Conference on Computer-supported Cooperative Work, pp. 107–114 ACM, New York (1992)
4. Greif, I., et al.: A case study of CES: a distributed collaborative editing system implemented in Argus. IEEE Trans. Softw. Eng. **18**(9), 827–839 (1992)
5. Hili, N., et al.: Innovative key features for mastering model complexity: flexilab, a multimodel editor illustrated on task modeling. In: Proceedings of the 7th ACM SIGCHI Symposium on Engineering Interactive Computing Systems, pp. 234–237 ACM, New York (2015)
6. Martinie, C., et al.: A generic tool-supported framework for coupling task models and interactive applications. In: Proceedings of the 7th ACM SIGCHI Symposium on Engineering Interactive Computing Systems, pp. 244–253 ACM, New York (2015)
7. Meixner, G., Seissler, M., Breiner, K.: Model-driven useware engineering. In: Hussmann, H., Meixner, G., Zuehlke, D. (eds.) Model-Driven Development of Advanced User Interfaces. SCI, vol. 340, pp. 1–26. Springer, Heidelberg (2011)
8. Meixner, G., et al.: Udit–a graphical editor for task models. In: Proceedings of the 4th International Workshop on Model-Driven Development of Advanced User Interfaces (MDDAUI), Sanibel Island, USA, CEUR Workshop Proceedings. Citeseer (2009)
9. Paternò, F.: ConcurTaskTrees: an engineered notation for task models. In: The Handbook of Task Analysis for HCI, pp. 483–503 (2003)
10. Paternò, F. et al.: CTTE: an environment for analysis and development of task models of cooperative applications. In: CHI 2001 Extended Abstracts on Human Factors in Computing Systems, pp. 21–22 ACM, New York (2001)
11. Rodriguez, F.G., Scapin, D.L.: Editing MAD* task descriptions for specifying user interfaces, at both semantic and presentation levels. In: Harrison, M.D., Torres, J.C. (eds.) Design, Specification and Verification of Interactive Systems 1997, pp. 193–208. Springer, Vienna (1997)

12. Schmidt, K.: The problem with 'awareness': introductory remarks on 'awareness in CSCW'. Comput. Support. Coop. Work CSCW **11**(3–4), 285–298 (2002)
13. Sutcliffe, A.: Applying small group theory to analysis and design of CSCW systems. In: Proceedings of the 2005 Workshop on Human and Social Factors of Software Engineering, pp. 1–6. ACM, New York (2005)
14. Van Der Veer, G.C., et al.: GTA: groupware task analysis—modeling complexity. Acta Psychol. (Amst.) **91**(3), 297–322 (1996)

# Accelerated Development for Accessible Apps – Model Driven Development of Transportation Apps for Visually Impaired People

Elmar Krainz$^{(\boxtimes)}$, Johannes Feiner, and Martin Fruhmann

FH Joanneum, Kapfenberg, Austria
{elmar.krainz,johannes.feiner,martin.fruhmann}@fh-joanneum.at
http://www.fh-joanneum.at

**Abstract.** Implementing usable and accessible user interfaces is a challenge, especially for mobile applications. App developers have to include accessibility in an additional step during the implementation, very often they overlook this extra workload.

There are concepts which combine Model Driven Development (MDD) for apps or semi-automatic support to create accessible software. But helpful tools to support accessibility features for apps during the implementation are hardly discussed in literature.

The aim of this paper is a concept of model-based software development for accessible apps. Within the domain of transportation apps, we provide a model to create an app scaffold with the required elements and accessibility features included from the beginning.

**Keywords:** Model Driven Development · Mobile apps · Accessibility

## 1 Introduction

Mobile applications are one of today's fastest growing software areas[1]. Apps, with simple intuitive user interfaces, are easy to use. The UI is mostly based on graphical representation a touch input.

For visually impaired and blind people this interaction paradigm is a challenge. Accessible web or desktop applications are already widespread, but this know-how cannot always be adopted to mobile apps.

Including accessibility is a challenge for developers and therefore it is handled more like a feature or add-on than a prerequisite. This work shows an approach to use Model-Driven Development (MDD) to create accessible mobile apps.

---

[1] http://www.smartinsights.com/mobile-marketing/mobile-marketing-analytics/mobile-marketing-statistics/.

© IFIP International Federation for Information Processing 2016
Published by Springer International Publishing Switzerland 2016. All Rights Reserved
C. Bogdan et al. (Eds.): HCSE 2016/HESSD 2016, LNCS 9856, pp. 374–381, 2016.
DOI: 10.1007/978-3-319-44902-9_25

## 2 Related Work

The topics *Accessibility, Mobile Applications* and *Model-Driven Development* are part of current research. This is also visualised in Fig. 1, which shows the overlapping domains of Model Driven Development (MDD), Accessibility and Mobile Development. There is already some exiting work which covers the outer intersections. For example, Accessibility *and* Mobile Development or Accessibility *and* Mobile Applications have been covered by previous papers, but seldom all three fields of research are discussed together in the scientific community.

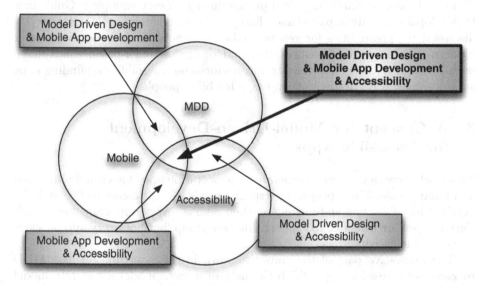

**Fig. 1.** The research focus is in the intersection of Model Driven Development (MDD), Mobile App Development, and Accessibility.

The main contribution of this work lays in the middle of the three circles, namely the intersection of all three domains. Following existing research is related to our approach:

The book Model driven Software Development (MDSD) from Voelter et al. covers the (semi-) automatic generation of software [20], but mentions mobile devices only in one minor example and accessibility is not covered at all. In the fast growing area of mobile applications there is also a need for this agile and effective methods to create software. There are different approaches. Barrnet et al. [4] describes a tool to generate data-driven apps based on a Domain Specific Language (DSL, compare [7]), with $MD^2$ form Heitkoetter et al. [11] even cross-platform apps are created from a model. The latter tool focuses on business apps where common source code is compiled into native iOS and Android apps, sadly neglecting accessibility topics.

MDD also helps to include accessibility in the development process. The *Johar* framework from Andrews and Hussain [1] uses an interface interpreter to create accessible applications for a range of users with different abilities. González-García et al. [8,9] use a model-based graphical editor tool to design an accessible web based media player. The UsiXML presented by Vanderdonckt [19] promotes the integration and use of a User Interface Description Language (UIDL).

For accessibility combined with mobile app development, there are several publication which discuss smartphone-based assistive technologies for the blind. For example, Narasimhan et al. [15] presented in 2009 the mobile phone tool *Trinetra* to assist visually impaired people during grocery shopping. Guidelines to develop for visually impaired and blind people can be found in [17]. Harder [10] discussed the possibilities for general mobility already in 1999, but for several modern approaches of implementation and design of touch-based smartphone interfaces see [4,12–14]. These contributions focus on accessible way-finding apps as well as new ways of touchscreen usage for blind people.

## 3    A Concept for Model-Driven-Development for Accessible Apps

This work shows a concept to generate transportation apps for visually impaired and blind people. These people have special needs when it comes to live an independent life. Traveling and moving on their own is a very important factor [10]. Various apps are available to support this user group, but not every app provides an accessible user interface.

The innovative part of the empirical work in this contribution uses MDD to generate accessible apps. With the help of a meta model a concrete model of an transportation app is designed. Several features and workflows for the domain of transportation apps are included in this model. For example, most transportations apps need the functionality to fetch the current GPS position, which is part of the meta-model. Specifying *getposition* (see Sect. 3.1) in the model adds to appropriate code to the app. With an instance of this model an app scaffold is generated.

Based on best practices for accessible apps (see [4,12–14]) and the adoption of common standards (see [5,18]) required accessibility features are included from the beginning.

App programmers open the generated sources in the development environment (IDE) and can focus on the business logic which is not generated automatically. The resulting app has a simplified workflow and an accessible user interface (see screenshot in Fig. 2).

### 3.1    Model

Concerning the model, we choose a domain specific approach. Which leads to a very specific and a straightforward model. We choose the domain of mobility and

**Fig. 2.** Screenshot of the resulting routing app.

transportation apps. These kinds of apps help visually impaired, and disabled people to be more independent while travelling. For this reason a research on common transportation apps was necessary.

Transportation apps like Google Maps, OSM Routing or apps from different public transport companies have similar features. These are:

- Fetching your actual position
- Entering a target location
- Searching for a location
- Showing a route
- Display a map
- Receiving infos from public transport

These features and workflows within an app are defined in a model. With a defined notation developers are able to build the scaffold of their own transportation app.

### 3.2 Modeling Language

Domain Specific Languages (DSL) help you to describe a model in your domain [7]. In this work an internal DSL is used. The language definition and the dedicated models are written in XML. We choose XML, because there are various tools available to create and process XML-based languages. But in the end it is more the less a personal decision, which language you use [6]. For better usability and non programmers a visual editor to create the model based on this DSL would be helpful.

*Example of an GPS position finder app:*

```
<?xml version="1.0" encoding="UTF-8"?>
<app appname="whereami"
```

```
        package ="at.fhj.modeling">
  <screen name="startscreen"
                  transition="mainscreen">
  </screen>
  <screen name="mainscreen"
                    transition="back" >
    <action function="getposition">
        <input type="button"/>
        <outout type="text"/>
    </action>
  </screen>
</app>
```

## 3.3  App Accessibility

People with special needs are nowadays able to operate standard computers without great difficulties. With the help of, for example, a braille display and build-in features of an operating system a visually restricted person can perform tasks on a PC. Visually impaired and blind people where also used to handle key-based mobile phones with screenreader software as add-on. With the uprise of touch-based smartphones these users had to find new ways of interaction.

On the popular mobile platforms iOS and Android are already some accessibility features included. The VoiceOver[2] system on iPhone allows a blind person to use a smartphone. On the Android platform TalkBack[3] is the integrated accessibility feature to react the user's touch input to voice output. But both systems can only provide an accessible user experience if an app is created properly. Developers have to follow the guidelines for iOS [3] or for Android [2]. Both platforms have some similarities but have also some big differences.

The Web Accessibility Initiative (WAI) of the W3C provides standards to improve accessibility for the Web. The actual standard for web applications is WCAG 2.0 [5] this guideline is based on general principles for accessible development rather then technical solutions. Therefore this standard provides a basis for non web solutions as well. Relevant principles of WCAG 2.0 [5] are:

- Perceivable
- Operable
- Understandable
- Robust

These principles are relevant to modern web applications but can be applied to non-web contents like mobile applications.

Currently a first public draft for a new standard for mobile accessibility [18] is available. This document describes how the principles and guidelines of existing standards like WCAG 2.0 can also be applied to native mobile apps.

---

[2] http://www.apple.com/accessibility/ios/voiceover/.
[3] http://www.google.com/accessibility/on-the-go.html.

In an (semi-) automatic generation process we have to consider platform independent principles and also platform related source code enhancements.

## 3.4    App Generation

With the model specified in Sect. 3.1 we are now able to generate an app scaffold for accessible transportation apps. This step, also known as transformation [20], is handled by a chain of tools. The first one in this chain is JAXB [16], whose task is to read the XML file and transform it into Java objects. Having the information stored in objects allows now to use it in combination with the Android command line tools to create an Android project scaffold. After this we are triggering a templating engine which generates the files, which are needed for the structure specified in the model. The process from XML-based model to a final app is illustrated in Fig. 3. The previous step also includes the mentioned accessibility features which are noticed in the Sect. 3.3.

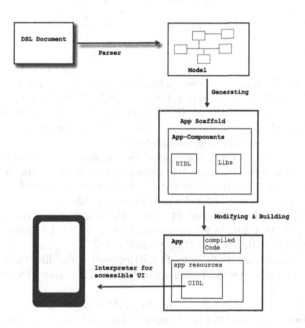

**Fig. 3.** Workflow from Meta-Model to Model to App Scaffold to final App.

The outcome from this transformation process is an app scaffold with accessibility features. All required app components (e.g. start-activity) and libraries (e.g. routing-lib) are available in the app project. Further product flavours can be integrated in the app's source code. Features like content description for integrated screen reader support or active voice output in selected parts of the app are automatically generated.

# 4   Conclusion

In this paper we describe the combination of the topics accessibility, mobile apps and model-driven development. In the Section related work we looked at the intersection of these domains.

In the empirical part of this work we build a meta-model for the domain of transportation apps. With an instance of this model one can create a app-scaffold for accessible transportation apps. In the model-transformation process all main-screens, workflows and platform related accessibility features are produced. Developers can focus on the app features, because accessibility is build in from the beginning.

Further work will be the improvement of this concept concerning the utility and usability of the model generation and transformation.

**Acknowledgments.** This work was funded by the Austrian research funding association (FFG) under the scope of the program *Mobility of the Future* within the research project *PONS*.

# References

1. Andrews, J.H., Hussain, F.: Johar: a framework for developing accessible applications. In: Proceedings of the 11th International ACM SIGACCESS Conference on Computers and Accessibility, ASSETS 2009, pp. 243–244. ACM, October 2009
2. Android: Accessibility - usability - google design guidelines. http://www.google.com/design/spec/usability/accessibility.html
3. Apple: Accessibility on ios. https://developer.apple.com/accessibility/ios/
4. Barnett, S., Vasa, R., Grundy, J.: Bootstrapping mobile app. development. In: Proceedings of the 37th International Conference on Software Engineering, ICSE 2015, vol. 2, pp. 657–660. IEEE Press, Piscataway (2015)
5. Caldwell, B., Reid, L.G., Cooper, M., Vanderheiden, G.: Web content accessibility guidelines (WCAG) 2.0. W3C recommendation, W3C, December 2008. http://www.w3.org/TR/2008/REC-WCAG20-20081211/
6. Fowler, M.: Parserfear (2008). http://martinfowler.com/bliki/ParserFear.html
7. Fowler, M.: Domain-Specific Languages. Pearson Education, Upper Saddle River (2010)
8. González-García, M., Moreno, L., Martínez, P.: A model-based tool to develop an accessible media player. In: Proceedings of the 17th International ACM SIGACCESS Conference on Computers & Accessibility, ASSETS 2015, pp. 415–416. ACM, New York (2015)
9. González-García, M., Moreno, L., Martínez, P., Miñon, R., Abascal, J.: A model-based graphical editor to design accessible media players. J. UCS **19**(18), 2656–2676 (2013)
10. Harder, A., Kasten, E., Sabel, B.A.: Möglichkeiten der mobilität blinder menschen. Aktuelle Augenheilkunde **2**, 8–13 (1999). http://www.med.uni-magdeburg.de/~harder/mob1/mob1.html
11. Heitkötter, H., Majchrzak, T.A., Kuchen, H.: Cross-platform model-driven development of mobile applications with md$^2$. In: Proceedings of the 28th Annual ACM Symposium on Applied Computing, SAC 2013, pp. 526–533. ACM (2013)

12. Krajnc, E., Feiner, J., Schmidt, S.: User centered interaction design for mobile applications focused on visually impaired and blind people. In: Leitner, G., Hitz, M., Holzinger, A. (eds.) USAB 2010. LNCS, vol. 6389, pp. 195–202. Springer, Heidelberg (2010)
13. Krajnc, E., Knoll, M., Feiner, J., Traar, M.: A touch sensitive user interface approach on smartphones for visually impaired and blind persons. In: Holzinger, A., Simonic, K.-M. (eds.) USAB 2011. LNCS, vol. 7058, pp. 585–594. Springer, Heidelberg (2011)
14. Mattheiss, E., Krajnc, E.: Route descriptions in advance and turn-by-turn instructions - usability evaluation of a navigational system for visually impaired and blind people in public transport. In: Holzinger, A., Ziefle, M., Hitz, M., Debevc, M. (eds.) SouthCHI 2013. LNCS, vol. 7946, pp. 284–295. Springer, Heidelberg (2013)
15. Narasimhan, P., Gandhi, R., Rossi, D.: Smartphone-based assistive technologies for the blind. In: Proceedings of International Conference on Compilers, Architecture, and Synthesis for Embedded Systems, CASES 2009, pp. 223–232. ACM, New York (2009)
16. Ort, E., Mehta, B.: Java architecture for xml binding (JAXB). Sun Developer Network, March 2003. http://www.oracle.com/technetwork/articles/javase/index-140168.html
17. Park, K., Goh, T., So, H.J.: Toward accessible mobile application design: developing mobile application accessibility guidelines for people with visual impairment. In: Proceedings of Conference on Human Computer Interaction Korea, HCIK 2015, pp. 31–38. Hanbit Media Inc., South Korea (2014)
18. Patch, K., Spellman, J., Wahlbin, K.: Mobile accessibility: how wcag 2.0 and other w3c/wai guidelines apply to mobile. Technical report, W3C (2015)
19. Vanderdonckt, J., Limbourg, Q., Michotte, B., Bouillon, L., Trevisan, D., Florins, M.: Usixml: a user interface description language for specifying multimodal user interfaces. In: Proceedings of W3C Workshop on Multimodal Interaction WMI, vol. 2004 (2004)
20. Völter, M., Stahl, T., Bettin, J., Haase, A., Helsen, S.: Model-driven Software Development: Technology, Engineering. Management. Wiley, New York (2013)

# Author Index

Printed in the United States
By Bookmasters

Printed in the United States
By Bookmasters